In our increasingly complex world, the teaching of thinking has become imperative. Yet evidence shows that our children are not learning how to think. Matthew Lipman, a leading educational theorist, gets to the heart of our educational problems in *Thinking in Education* and makes profound and workable suggestions for solving those problems.

Thinking in Education describes procedures that must be put in place if students at all levels of education are to become more thoughtful, more reasonable, and more judicious. It recommends that the classroom be converted into a community of inquiry and that the discipline of philosophy be redesigned so as to provide the concepts and values now missing from the curriculum. These recommendations have now been carried out; the community of inquiry is a recognized pedagogical strategy, and traditional academic philosophy has been transformed into a discipline that offers a model of higher-order thinking and an image of what all education can be.

Thinking in education

Thinking in education

MATTHEW LIPMAN
Professor of Philosophy and Director, Institute for the Advancement of
Philosophy for Children, Montclair State College

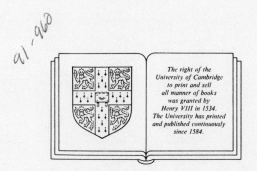

The right of the
University of Cambridge
to print and sell
all manner of books
was granted by
Henry VIII in 1534.
The University has printed
and published continuously
since 1584.

CAMBRIDGE UNIVERSITY PRESS
Cambridge
New York   Port Chester   Melbourne   Sydney

Published by the Press Syndicate of the University of Cambridge
The Pitt Building, Trumpington Street, Cambridge CB2 1RP
40 West 20th Street, New York, NY 10011, USA
10 Stamford Road, Oakleigh, Melbourne 3166, Australia

First published 1991

Printed in the United States of America

Library of Congress Cataloging-in-Publication Data
Lipman, Matthew.
   Thinking in education / Matthew Lipman.
      p.   cm.
   Includes bibliographical references (p.   ) and index.
   ISBN 0-521-40032-5. – ISBN 0-521-40911-X (pbk.)
   1. Thought and thinking – Study and teaching.   2. Critical thinking – Study and
teaching.   3. Creative thinking – Study and teaching.   I. Title.
LB1590.3.L57   1991   91–8542
371.3–dc20   CIP

British Library Cataloguing in Publication Data
Lipman, Matthew
   Thinking in education.
   1. Education. *Role of cognition*
   I. Title
   370.152

   ISBN 0 521 40032 5 hardback
   ISBN 0 521 40911 X paperback

Contents

Introduction   1

Part I Education for thinking

1   The reflective model of educational practice   7
    Rationality as an organizing principle   8
    Schooling without thinking   9
    Normal versus critical academic practice   11
    Restructuring the educational process   13
        Education as inquiry   15
        Community of inquiry   15
        Sensitivity to what is problematic   16
        Reasonableness   16
        Relationship and judgment   16
        Thinking in the disciplines   17
        Conversational apprenticeship   18
        Autonomy   19
        Higher-order thinking   19
        Complex thinking   23

2   Learning the craft of thinking   26
    Reasoning to the rescue   26
    Coming to think in language   30
    Roadblocks to the development of reasoning   31
    How reasoning differs from the basic skills   33
    Orders of cognitive skills   34
    Skills and meanings   36
    Four major varieties of cognitive skills   40
        Inquiry skills   40
        Reasoning skills   40
        Information-organizing skills   41
        Translation skills   45
    Is teaching reasoning worthwhile?   46

v

3   The cornucopia of cognitive performance   49
    Thinking as internalized communication   51
    Some social interpretations of critical thinking   53
    Combating absolutistic thinking: relativism or relationism?   56
    Algorithmic versus heuristic thinking   58
    Relationships: the bearings of judgment   60
    The pedagogy of judgment   62
    Some educational requirements   64

4   Cognition, rationality, and creativity   68
    Resnick's conception of higher-order thinking   69
    Consider the circumstances: Schrag's reply to Resnick   73
    Cognitive operations, moves, and skills   75
    The boundaries of skill   78
    From craft to creativity   80
    Sovereign schemata   85
    Schema theory and creative thinking   87
    Building with and on ideas   89
    Intervention and innovation   90
    Distinctive characteristics of higher-order thinking   92
    Internal texture of higher-order thinking   94
    Higher-order thinking in the schools   96

Part II   Seeking standards for classroom thinking

5   Enter the critical thinking movement   101
    How we got to where we are   102
    Some more recent origins of critical thinking   103
    Dewey and the Deweyans   105
    Analytic skills and cognitive objectives   108
    The emergence of informal logic   110
    Other conversations, other voices   111

6   A functional definition of critical thinking   114
    The outcomes of critical thinking are judgments   115
    Critical thinking relies on criteria   116
    Metacriteria and megacriteria: banisters of the mind   118
    Criteria as bases of comparison   119
    The indispensability of standards   120
    Critical thinking is self-corrective   121
    Critical thinking displays sensitivity to context   121
    Professional education and the cultivation of judgment   122

7   Criteria as governing factors in critical thinking   126
    Criteria as appropriate and decisive reasons   126

More on metacriteria 128
Criteria, relationships, and judgments 130
What can serve as a criterion? 131
  Shared values 132
  Precedent and convention 132
  Common bases of comparison 133
  Requirements 133
  Perspectives 133
  Principles 133
  Rules 134
  Standards 134
  Definitions 134
  Facts 135
  Test results 135
  Purposes 136
The assessment of performance 136
Community experience: the seedbed of criteria 137
Complex thinking: combining the declarative and the procedural 140
Toward complex thinking: enlisting philosophy in the curriculum 141

8   Criteria as the hinges of practice 143
Critical thinking and the inculcation of belief 143
Alternative approaches to teaching practical reasoning 146
  The guidance of practice by reasons 147
  Criterion-based performance 148
  The guidance of practice by hypotheses and consequences 148
Practical reasoning behaviors 150
  Self-correction 150
  Acquiring sensitivity to context 151
  Being guided (and goaded) by criteria 151
  Judgment 152
Teaching for bridging, transfer, and translation 152
What makes higher-order thinking good? 153
The hidden pivots of cognitive excellence 155
Criteria as gauges of value 155
Criteria and experience 158

9   The strengthening of judgment 159
Judgment as critical and judgment as creative 160
The juncture of the universal and the particular 162
Three orders of judgment 164
The balance wheel of judgment in educational settings 171

10   Dichotomies in the application of critical thinking 174
Conceptual obstacles to the strengthening of thinking 175

Disagreements over the nature of thinking   175
Disagreements over the proper psychological approach   177
Disagreements over the role of philosophy   178
Disagreements over preferred educational approaches   179
Practical obstacles to the teaching of thinking   180

11 Faulty assumptions concerning teaching for thinking   183
Teaching for thinking is equivalent to teaching for critical thinking   183
Critical teaching will necessarily result in critical thinking   184
*Teaching about critical thinking is equivalent to teaching for
critical thinking*   185
Teaching for critical thinking involves drill in thinking skills 186
*Teaching for logical thinking is equivalent to teaching for
critical thinking*   188
*Teaching for learning is just as effective as teaching for
critical thinking*   188

Part III   Thinking: the forge of meaning

12 The concept of creative thinking   193
Two axes of creative thinking   195
The discovery–invention axis   197
Generativity   198
Amplification   199
Breaking through   200
Creativity and imagination   201
Creativity and thinking for ourselves   202
Creativity and criteria   204
  How do we identify instances of creativity?   205
  How are criteria employed in creative thinking?   206
Tertiary qualities as contextual values   208
Creativity and dialogue in the community of inquiry   209
Creative thinking and creativity   211

13 Teachers and texts: the springs of inquiry   212
The voice of the text   212
Stories: gateways to understanding   214
Narrative as a portrait of the thinking process   216
Three models of modeling   218
The text as system of concepts and as schema   219
The rational curriculum   222
Cognitive apprenticeship   223
The devising of instructional manuals   224

Part IV The nature and uses of the community of inquiry

14 Thinking in community   229
    Following the argument where it leads   229
    The logic of conversational discourse   232
    The art of conversation   234
    The structure of dialogue   235
    Dialogue and community   236
    Thinking moves and mental acts   237
    The jury as an example of deliberative dialogue   238
    Learning from the experience of others   240
    Toward the formation of classroom communities of inquiry   241

15 The political significance of the inquiring community   244
    The political implications of teaching for inquiry   244
    The mediating role of the classroom community   246
    The political implications of teaching for judgment   248
    Implications for the social studies curriculum   250
    Introducing children to political concepts   252
    Using the community of inquiry to combat prejudice   254
        Sociocultural antidotes   256
        Cognitive antidotes   257
        The community of inquiry as a cognitive/affective strategy   257

Conclusion   261
    The turn to thinking   262
    The case for philosophy   263
    The universities and the schools   264
    Academic freedom   267

Select bibliography   269
Index   273

Introduction

If there is any institution that can legitimately claim to be worldwide, it is probably the school. However different the cultures, the schools resemble one another remarkably. The system of education they provide is founded on the presupposition that children go to school to learn. They learn basic skills, like reading, writing, and arithmetic proficiencies. And they learn content, like geography, history, and literature.

A cynical commentator once observed that human beings invented speech in order to conceal their thoughts. The same observer might have added that they send their children to school to learn in order to keep them from thinking. If so, it is a tactic that has had only limited success. Children are not easily prevented from thinking. Indeed, it is often the case that our most cherished recollections of our school years are of those moments when we thought for ourselves – not, of course, because of the educational system but in spite of it.

Yet there has always been a strand of educational thought that held that the strengthening of the child's thinking should be the chief business of the schools and not just an incidental outcome – if it happened at all. Some have argued in this way because they thought that the schooling of future citizens in a democracy entailed getting them to be reasonable and that this could be done by fostering their reasoning and judgment. Others have argued in this way because they saw the social systems of the world – particularly the economic, bureaucratic, and legal systems – congealing into rationality, and it was by fostering children's rationality that the schools could best prepare children for the world they would face when they grew up. And still others have contended that helping children to think well and think for themselves is required not just for reasons of social utility but because the children themselves have a right to receive nothing less.

Since the mid 1970s, the proponents of thinking in the schools (and colleges) have become distinctly more numerous and more vocal. The banner they have unfurled is emblazoned with the phrase "critical thinking," and although neither they nor those who oppose them are very clear about just what critical thinking entails, the hue and cry continues to mount. In the early 1980s, the textbook industry, after decades of studiously looking the other way, began to make some timid concessions to the advocates of reflective education, adding critical thinking labels to review questions, often regardless of content, and here and there

1

providing a paper-and-pencil drill aimed at strengthening some particular thinking skill. The test industry, uncomfortable with test items that were difficult to assess or grade, long resisted making its tests more reflective on the ground that reasoning cannot be taught. It has now dropped that pretext and is engaged in a broad-scale revision of tests. School administrators are calling for ways of "infusing thinking into the curriculum," apparently on the understanding that thinking can be added to the existing course of studies as easily as we add vitamins to our diet. Thinking-skill programs abound, many of them promising overnight miracles. And schools of education everywhere are offering courses on critical thinking in which prospective teachers dutifully study the results of research in metacognition, divergent thinking, and other areas of educational psychology thought to be connected with critical thinking. Even philosophy departments in colleges and universities have joined the movement, in some cases dropping courses rich with humanities content in order to offer bare-bones critical thinking courses. Nor do state education departments hang back; they even mandate critical thinking courses in state colleges, as California has done. And the press (to whom "thinking in education" seems to be an intriguing paradox) unfailingly treats every local occasion in which a teacher encourages thinking as a moment of great newsworthiness, thereby adding impetus to the groundswell of demands for educational reform.

Further contributing to the hubbub are the voices of those parents who suspect that the existing elementary school curriculum is designed to turn the lively, inquisitive, and thoughtful children who not so long ago entered kindergarten into incurious, uncritical, and thoughtless children by the time they reach fourth or fifth grade. To this the schools, the textbook makers, and the text publishers have been wont to reply in unison that they are only following the recommendations of the most astute of developmental psychologists to the effect that the education of young children should be "concrete" rather than "abstract." Early childhood education should be a period of happy play, sensory and physical but not particularly intellectual – as though the intellect did not offer its own forms of play and its own forms of happiness.

Meanwhile, authoritative opinions drift in from disciplines like cognitive science, artificial intelligence, psycholinguistics, and philosophy of mind that hardly existed a quarter of a century ago. The mind is treated like a computer, like a supercomputer, or like no computer at all. Indeed, there is no agreement on whether or not there even is such a thing as the mind or, if there is such a thing, what it is that the word refers to. So here we are, trying to upgrade our children's education a bit and finding ourselves enmeshed in a mystery as great as any to be found in nature.

What constitutes thinking? To this expert, good thinking is accurate, consistent, and coherent thinking; to that one, it is ampliative, imaginative, creative thinking. This scholar points to examples of good thinking in literature; that one points to instances of it in the history of science or conceives of it as the employment of scientific methodology. One philosopher hails it for its embodying logic and rationality; another, because it embodies deliberation and judgment. One educator acclaims it for helping us decide what to believe; another argues that belief decisions are out of place in a school context and that the teacher should aim at helping students discover only what they have sufficient evidence for asserting.

Amid the confusion, school administrators have to make decisions about how they are going to upgrade the educational offerings in their schools, whether or not teachers are to be retrained, and if so, what approach to critical thinking they are going to employ. To make such decisions, they will need to be guided by definitions that clearly indicate just what critical thinking is and how it can be made operational. They need to determine by what criteria teachers and researchers can decide whether or not such operationalization has been successful.

Thinking in Education is proposed as a step in this direction. It does not claim to be definitive, but it does try to raise many of the questions that need to be raised and to supply some of the answers that can be provided at this very early stage in the development of a thinking-oriented educational process. If John McPeck's *Critical Thinking and Education* was a rather dour assessment of critical thinking (although not therefore a necessarily unsound one), *Thinking in Education* is a positive evaluation of what critical thinking can contribute to the long overdue reconstruction of education. Some chapters stress theory and some reflect on practice; some are philosophical and some pedagogical; some are sociological and some historical.

Thinking in Education makes no claim to being a work of specialized scholarship. Nor does it claim to be impartial and nonjudgmental. It regards the capacity of philosophy, *when properly reconstructed and properly taught,* to bring about higher-order thinking in education to be significantly greater than the capacity of any alternative approach. The case for this claim has not yet been made; the present study can be regarded as a kind of prologue to the making of such a case.

There is a second important (though not final) claim to be made in *Thinking in Education,* that is that the pedagogy of the "community of inquiry" should be the methodology for the teaching of critical thinking, whether or not a philosophical version of it is being employed.

And a third claim is that it is no accident that critical thinking is affiliated with such cognate terms as "criticism" and "criteria." These terms have to do with reasoning, evaluation, and judgment, and these in turn have to do with that higher-order thinking in which students are being encouraged to engage. Insofar as reasoning is a skill and a craft, it can be taught, studied, and learned. Insofar as judgment is an art, the community of inquiry provides an environment in which it can be practiced and acquired. Spinoza was being unduly grim when he remarked that everything excellent is as difficult as it is rare. We have to create a society in which excellence flourishes in diversity and in abundance. Upgrading the reflective element in education is a reasonable place to begin.

We have reached a point in American education where we must figure out how we can upgrade the entire educational process, and not just one or another of its parts. One of the things this means is that students must be participants in the upgrading. We may have the best criteria in the world for teaching, but if students perceive them as belonging to educators and not to them too, they will feel cheated and manipulated. Students have to be shown how to internalize adequate standards if they are to live by them. If we want them to regulate their thinking in a responsible way, if we want them to think for themselves, then we must see to it that they appropriate the values of the educational process as their own, just as they must appropriate the values of the democratic process if they are to live by that process.

Part I

Education for thinking

1 The reflective model of educational practice

There are three key models of private and public institutions in our society. The family represents institutionalized private values. The state represents institutionalized public values. And the school epitomizes the fusion of the two. As an amalgam of private and public interests, the school is no less important than the distinctively private or the distinctively public. In some ways it is the most important of all, because through it past and present generations deliberately and consciously attempt to stamp a design upon the future. Yet in all three institutions – family, government, and school – practice and policy conflicts abound, for each family and each government administration would like to shape succeeding generations in its own image, but the facts of social change – growth, regression, aimless or orderly drift – conspire to defeat such aspirations.

The school is a battleground because it, more than any other social institution, is the manufacturer of the society of the future, and virtually every social group or faction therefore aspires to control the school for its own ends. Not that this is generally acknowledged. The received opinion has it that the schools reflect the accepted values of their time; they are not to challenge such values or suggest alternatives to them. Many parents shudder at the notion that the schools will take it upon themselves to become initiators of social change, because they fear that this will merely mean that the schools will have been captured by this or that social faction seeking to impress its will upon the world.

If, then, the school is looked upon as the representative of all social factions rather than of any one in particular, it is able to retain its claim to legitimacy in a democratic society, because it will not have surrendered its claim to impartiality. On the other hand, it will tend to be under these circumstances a very conservative – even traditionalist – institution.

And this is, in fact, what the school is in our present society. As for the schools of education that prepare future teachers, they probably do not see themselves as suppliers of technical personnel to school districts that constitute the market for such personnel. Yet school districts specify what textbooks they want taught and how they want them taught, and it would be unlikely that they would hire prospective teachers who have been trained to teach very different books in very different ways. So schools of education justify their resistance to change on the ground that it would be a disservice to their students to prepare them any differently, despite the fact that few professors of education have full confidence in the methods of teacher preparation they employ. But schools of education are not alone in this; school districts excuse themselves on the ground that textbook and text publishers provide them with no feasible alternatives, and the publishers in turn point out that they are circumscribed by state departments of education and defended by the research that emerges from the schools of education in these same states. And so each factor sees itself as fixed in its position and helpless to change. For all practical purposes, therefore, critics from the outside are wasting their breath. Considerations like tests and texts and turfs – in short, economic and bureaucratic considerations – have locked the system in place so that, like a boat with a jammed rudder, it is only free to move about in circles.

Were these the only considerations, the situation would be much more dismal than it actually is. The allegiances that keep the members of the family cemented together are kinship, child-rearing necessities, the economic division of labor, and sexual interdependence. The primary governmental allegiance is to consensus, in the name of which virtually any military or economic policy can be justified. (The courts represent a partial exception to this generalization, since constitutionality and precedent must also be taken into account. But the laws followed by the courts are consensus-generated.) The schools, on the other hand, have a very different criterion to which they can appeal, and that is *rationality*.

Rationality as an organizing principle

There are, of course, many kinds of rationality. There is means–end rationality. An example is the corporation that sees its ultimate objective as profit and its various policies as means of maximizing profits. Another type of rationality has to do with the distribution of authority in a hierarchical organization. Examples are the military, the church, and the government. These may also be seen as mixed types. The army, for instance, is hierarchically organized yet is always prepared to seek military victory. The schools too are bureaucracies, with a rationalized distribution of authority, but their goal is the production of educated persons – persons who are as knowledgeable as they need to be and as reasonable as they can be helped to be.

Reasonableness is not pure rationality; it is rationality tempered by judgment. The schools, like the courts, are under a mandate of rationality, but in a democratic society we need reasonable citizens above all. How are we to educate for reasonableness?

It is not simply that the schools must themselves be rationally organized so that they can justify their organization and procedures to lay boards of education. It is not simply that they operate for the good of those they serve (in contrast to businesses, which operate for the profit of those who own or who manage them). It is that the students who pass through the schools must be reasonably treated in an effort to make them more reasonable beings. This means that every aspect of schooling must be, in principle at any rate, rationally defensible. There must be better reasons for using this curriculum, these texts, these tests, these teaching methods than for using alternatives to them. In every instance, the rationale is the same: Children brought up in reasonable institutions are more likely to be reasonable than children raised under irrational circumstances. The latter, as we know, are more likely to be those who grow up irrational and raise their own children irrationally. More reasonable schools mean more reasonable future parents, more reasonable citizens, and more reasonable values all around.

Can we educate for reasonableness without educating for thinking? This is the dilemma Kant was faced with. He sincerely wanted people to think for themselves, and he was ready to contemplate teaching them to do so while they were still children. But the thinking for oneself Kant had in mind was not the full-fledged engagement in inquiry that we advocate today; it was rather the voluntary obedience of each individual to universally generalizable principles.[1] Rationality for Kant was therefore very different from rationality for Socrates or Aristotle or Locke or Dewey.

Schooling without thinking

It is a fact often noted and commented on with regard to very young children as they begin their formal education in kindergarten that they are lively, curious, imaginative, and inquisitive. For a while, they retain these wonderful traits. But then gradually a decline sets in, and they become passive. For many a child, the social aspect of schooling – being together with one's peers – is its one saving grace. The educational aspect is a dreaded ordeal.

Since the child's first five or six years were spent at home, and since this did not seem to impair the child's intellectual energies, it seems strange to condemn the child's background for a subsequent loss of curiosity and imagination. It is more likely due to the nature of schooling. How are we to explain why the child's intellectual alertness is not extinguished in the often adverse circumstances of family or childcare life, while it is all too frequently damped down in the often congenial circumstances of the classroom?

One hypothesis that seems worth considering is that children learning to speak are in a situation even more mystifying and enigmatic than that of an immigrant in a foreign culture. The immigrant still has the use of his or her native tongue; the toddler has no language at all. But the child is surrounded by a world that is problematic through and through, a world in which everything invites inquiry and reflective questioning, a world as provacative of thought as it is of wonder and

[1] Kant's 1784 essay *What Is Enlightenment?* begins with a powerful statement of the need for a society in which we each think for ourselves instead of having guardians who do our thinking for us. But as the essay proceeds it is apparent that Kant has not grasped the necessity, in democratic institutions, of internal self-criticism. His later *Foundations of the Metaphysic of Morals* continues and systematizes this approach.

action. And of all the puzzling things in this world, none is more puzzling than one's own family and the bewildering regimen that its members follow and seek to impose upon the newcomer. The child finds this world extraordinary, but the uncanniness is evocative; it draws speech and thought out of the child. This development is further abetted by the prospect that the child's acquisition of speech will lead to a fuller integration into the life and practices of the family and the home.

What the child probably expects from the school is a surrogate home and a surrogate family – a surrounding that constantly stimulates thought and speech. Even when it is uncaring, as it often is, the home environment contains so much to be learned, so much to be experienced, that it represents a constant challenge to the very young child. What the child discovers in early elementary school, on the other hand, is a completely structured environment. Instead of events that flow into other events, there is now a schedule that things must conform to. Instead of statements that can be understood only by gleaning their significance from the entire context in which they occur, there is a classroom language that is uniform and rather indifferent to context and therefore fairly devoid of enigmatic intimations. The natural mysteriousness of the home and family environment is replaced by a stable, structured environment in which all is regular and explicit. Children gradually discover that such an environment is seldom an invigorating or challenging one. Indeed, it drains them of the capital fund of initiative and inventiveness and thoughtfulness that they brought with them to school. It exploits their energies and gives them back little in return. Before long, children become aware that schooling is enervating and dispiriting rather than animating or intellectually provocative. In short, schooling provides few natural incentives to thinking in the way that the home environment does. A drop-off in student interest is the natural consequence.

To teachers who have worked long and hard to become professionals in charge of primary school classrooms, these remarks may be hard to take. But they are not intended as accusations. Teachers do what they are taught to do, and by and large they do it well. What they are taught to do is likely to be where the problem lies, yet this is an area of education that is most taken for granted and most unlikely to be subject to reappraisal. Taking one's professional preparation pretty much for granted is normal academic practice.

Indeed, many teachers nowadays are aware that the constant insistence upon order and discipline can be stultifying and can destroy the very spontaneity that they would most like to cultivate and cherish. The solution does not lie in alternating periods of rigor and randomness: now paper-and-pencil exercises and now free play. The solution lies rather in the discovery of procedures that encourage both organization and creativity, such as having children invent stories and tell them to their classmates. As John Dewey puts it, "the problem of *method* in forming habits of reflective thought is the problem of establishing *conditions* that will arouse and guide *curiosity;* of setting up the connections in things experienced that will on later occasions promote the *flow of suggestions,* create problems and purposes that will favor *consecutiveness* in the succession of ideas."[2] A curriculum that itself lacks consecutiveness can hardly be a model for the child in his or her struggle to develop a sense of sequence. Children have a keen sense of what is going on, but they do not necessarily have a keen understanding of how things can be sequenced so that they will begin to build and grow on their own. This is why children need as textbooks narratives instead of sourcebooks of information, so that growth and development, with recurrent themes and variations, can be constantly before their eyes. Children need models both of reasonableness and of growth. The model of growth may be better provided by the curriculum and by the community of one's peers than by those who are already adult.

Normal versus critical academic practice

A distinction can be drawn between "normal" and "critical" academic practice. Let me say first, however, that by "practice" I mean any methodical activity. It can also be described as customary, habitual, traditional, and unreflective, but these do not convey as well as the term *methodical* the fact that practice is not random, unsystematic, or disorganized. Moreover, there is generally a sense of conviction about our attitude toward our own practice, just as we have a sense of conviction about our own opinions that is lacking regarding the opinions of others. It would not be indulging in caricature to say that *practice is to action as belief is to thought.* Beliefs are thoughts we are convinced of despite the fact that we do not continually question them; practice is what we do methodically and with conviction but without a conspicuous degree of inquiry or reflection.

It is often assumed that unreflective practice is irrational and even downright dangerous, but this need not be so and is generally not the case. Unreflective practices, like customs and traditions that prevail successfully in a given cultural context, are likely to continue to prevail as long as that context does not change. And even if the context does change — and change drastically — it may be that it is only the survival of those customs and traditions that holds the community together, as Durkheim has noted.[3]

In other cases, traditional practice may be unsuccessful but is continued anyway, either because no alternatives exist or because the viable alternatives have been decreed out of bounds and are therefore not even contemplated. Still another option is token examination of practice, which is what often takes place in educational contexts. This permits the practitioner to espouse the lofty notion that

---

[2] *How We Think* (New York: Heath, 1933), pp. 56–57 (italics in original). Dewey's most important educational works are *The Child and the Curriculum* (Chicago: University of Chicago Press, 1902), *Democracy and Education* (New York: Macmillan, 1916), and *Experience and Education* (New York: Macmillan, 1938). However, there are important statements in out-of-the-way places, like his critique of the avant-garde education of his day, to be found in Joseph Ratner (ed.), *Intelligence in the Modern World: John Dewey's Philosophy* (New York: Random House, 1939), pp. 616–26.

[3] Emile Durkheim, *The Division of Labor in Society* (New York: Macmillan, 1933).

unexamined practices are not worth performing while hewing in actuality to the maxim that performed practices are not worth examining.

A society that expends vast sums on research into certain modes of practice is generally considered to be dedicated to the improvement of such practice; again, this is not necessarily the case. For example, much educational research is engaged in for the explicit purpose of justifying or solidifying existing educational practice, and a good deal more has this consequence even though not carried out with this intent.[4] Nevertheless, the converse is also true. It is normal for a certain amount of educational research not aimed at improvement in educational practice to have the consequence of producing such improvement, just as it is normal for much research explicitly aimed at educational improvement to have only negligible consequences of a beneficial nature.

Despite the fact that instructional behaviors involve a fairly broad zone of discretion, the practice of teaching is normally institutionalized and tradition-bound. Teachers do make use of these areas of discretion and are very proud of their ability to do so. Nevertheless, such creative endeavors on the fringe of normal academic practice are insufficient to bring about large-scale changes in teacher behavior. This is partly owing to what Veblen has called the "trained incapacity" of teachers to reconstruct the role definitions impressed upon them in schools of education.[5] Even more so, it is a result of the isolation of the teacher in the classroom and the specious solidarity of the teacher corps. Innovation by a particular teacher is applauded and even welcomed by the principal in a particular school building, but it is taken for granted that such inventiveness is not likely to spread, and the chance that it might affect academic practice generally is considered highly remote.

No doubt teachers resent the way they seem to be disregarded when it comes to curricular innovations, and they come to recognize the enormous power wielded by the large textbook houses and the purchasing agreements of the larger states. On the other hand, the textbook publishers do not ignore teachers and their experience when it comes to the construction of new texts; it is simply that the publishers look for the best representatives they can find of normal academic practice, with the result that texts are generally written by professors with a limited command of practice, by teachers with a limited command of theory, or by huge crews of freelance writers. In any event, the result is the reinforcement of normal academic practice.[6] (The same pattern prevails with respect to the production and publication of tests.)

This brings us at last to steps to be taken to make normal practice critical. Four steps can be specified as stages of reflection on practice. They are (1) criticism of the practice of one's colleagues, (2) self-criticism, (3) correction of the practice of others, and (4) self-correction. The degree to which normal academic practice

[4] Cf. Donald Schön, *The Reflective Practitioner* (New York: Basic, 1983).

[5] See Thorstein Veblen, *The Higher Learning in America* (New York: Sagamore, 1957).

[6] Cf. Thomas Kuhn's trenchant analysis of the way texts are constructed and used in science education, in *The Essential Tension* (Chicago: University of Chicago Press, 1977), pp. 228–39.

has become critical depends upon the extent to which any or all of these factors are involved.

Reflection on practice may therefore involve the clarification of prevailing assumptions and criteria as well as of the consistency between such principles and prevailing practice. It may involve challenging these matters and not merely clarifying them. It may furthermore involve the active institution of changes and not merely the proposal of such changes. After all, reflection upon practice constitutes inquiry into practice, and effective inquiry includes appropriate interventions.

Academic practitioners are pressed to think critically on occasions such as these (in no particular order):

- When the work of a colleague is being read or reviewed
- When you serve on a committee that must make a judgment regarding a proposal from a colleague
- When a grievance is filed or must be acted on
- When students challenge the criteria by which courses are graded, the materials being taught, or the pedagogy being used
- When a grant proposal is being written or reviewed
- When judgments are made regarding school or campus conflicts, such as students vs. administration, administration vs. faculty, or faculty vs. students
- When you contrast your actual professional conduct with what you think it ought to be, or your school or profession with what you think it ought to be
- When you detect bias or prejudice in yourself or others
- When you search for alternatives to established but unsatisfactory practice
- When you find to be problematic that which others regard as non-problematic
- When you evaluate theory by means of practice and practice by means of theory
- When you acknowledge the implications for others of your professional conduct

The list could obviously be greatly elaborated. It tends to spell out some of the particular reasons we have for insisting that critical thinking must be self-corrective thinking, even if the attempted self-correction is unsuccessful.

Restructuring the educational process

In what follows, I shall assume that there are two sharply contrasting paradigms of educational practice – the standard paradigm of normal practice and the reflective paradigm of critical practice. The dominating assumptions of the standard paradigm are:

1. Education consists in the transmission of knowledge from those who know to those who don't know
2. Knowledge is about the world, and our knowledge of the world is unambiguous, unequivocal, and unmysterious
3. Knowledge is distributed among disciplines that are nonoverlapping and together are exhaustive of the world to be known
4. The teacher plays an authoritative role in the educational process, for only if teachers know can students learn what they know
5. Students acquire knowledge by absorbing information, i.e., data about specifics; an educated mind is a well-stocked mind

In contrast, the dominant assumptions of the reflective paradigm are:

1. Education is the outcome of participation in a teacher-guided community of inquiry, among whose goals are the achievement of understanding and good judgment
2. Students are stirred to think about the world when *our* knowledge of it is revealed to them to be ambiguous, equivocal, and mysterious
3. The disciplines in which inquiry occurs are assumed to be neither nonoverlapping nor exhaustive; hence their relationships to their subject matters are quite problematic
4. The teacher's stance is fallibilistic (one that is ready to concede error) rather than authoritative
5. Students are expected to be thoughtful and reflective, and increasingly reasonable and judicious
6. The focus of the educational process is not on the acquisition of information but on the grasp of relationships within the subject matters under investigation

It should now be clear that the reflective paradigm assumes education to be inquiry, whereas the standard paradigm does not. Hence there is disagreement about the conditions under which the process must take place, and there is disagreement about the goals to be targeted. There are differences in what is done and in how it is done. For example, in the standard paradigm, teachers question students; in the reflective paradigm, students and teachers query each other. In the standard paradigm, students are considered to be thinking if they learn what they have been taught; in the reflective paradigm, students are considered to be thinking if they participate in the community of inquiry.

I have been contrasting in very general terms the standard paradigm of normal practice with the reflective paradigm of critical practice. At this point I want to consider a number of cardinal features of the reflective paradigm. This brief outline will be done in very broad strokes; in a sense, the remainder of the book will be occupied with filling in the details. The key concepts with which I will be working are not precise, clear-cut, and technical; instead they are rather diffuse and contestable. They include such redoubtable stalwarts as inquiry, community, rationality, judgment, creativity, and autonomy, all of which have about them more than a whiff of traditional philosophy. These are, nevertheless, foundational concepts for any theory of education, and we had better confront them head on rather than risk becoming even more confused by trying to steer around them.

At the same time, I want to emphasize that concepts such as these, the principles that connect them, and the implications that flow from them are merely the abstract, theoretical side of critical practice. If we fail to come to grips with the practice – the ways in which reflective education can actually take place in the classroom – we will be just as likely to fall prey to misunderstanding as those whose lives are filled with practice and devoid of theory.

Education as inquiry

John Dewey was convinced that education had failed because it was guilty of a stupendous category mistake: It confused the refined, finished end products of inquiry with the raw, crude subject matter of inquiry and tried to get students to learn the solutions rather than investigate the problems and engage in inquiry for themselves. Just as scientists apply scientific method to the exploration of problematic situations so students should do the same if they are ever to learn to think for themselves. Instead, we ask them to study the end results of what the scientists have discovered; we neglect the process and fixate upon the product. When problems are not explored at first hand, no interest or motivation is engendered, and what we continue to call education is a charade and a mockery. Dewey had no doubt that what should be happening in the classroom is thinking – and independent, imaginative, resourceful thinking, at that. The route he proposed – and here some of his followers part company with him – is that the educational process in the classroom should take as its model the process of scientific inquiry.

Community of inquiry

This phrase, presumably coined by Charles Sanders Peirce, was originally restricted to the practitioners of scientific inquiry, all of whom could be considered to form a community in that they were similarly dedicated to the use of like procedures in pursuit of identical goals.[7] Since Peirce, however, the phrase has been broadened to include any kind of inquiry, whether scientific or nonscientific. Thus, we can now speak of "converting the classroom into a community of inquiry" in which students listen to one another with respect, build on one another's ideas, challenge one another to supply reasons for otherwise unsupported opinions, assist each other in drawing inferences from what has been said, and seek to identify one another's assumptions. A community of inquiry attempts to follow the inquiry where it leads rather than being penned in by the boundary lines of existing disciplines. A dialogue that tries to conform to logic, it moves

[7] C. S. Peirce, "The Fixation of Belief," in Justus Buchler (ed.), *Philosophical Writings of Peirce* (New York: Dover, 1955), pp. 5–22.

forward indirectly like a boat tacking into the wind, but in the process its progress comes to resemble that of thinking itself. Consequently, when this process is internalized or introjected by the participants, they come to think in *moves* that resemble its *procedures*. They come to think as the process thinks.

Sensitivity to what is problematic

Teachers may ask questions and students may answer them without either party feeling the least twinge of doubt or puzzlement and with hardly any real thinking taking place, because the process is mechanical and contrived. On the other hand, there are times when inquiry begins because what has been encountered – some aberration, some discrepancy, something that defies being taken for granted – captures our interest and demands our reflection and investigation. If, then, thinking in the classroom is considered desirable, the curriculum cannot present itself as clear and settled, for this paralyzes thought. The curriculum should bring out aspects of the subject matter that are unsettled and problematic in order to capture the laggard attention of the students and to stimulate them to form a community of inquiry.

Reasonableness

Insofar as it can, science attempts to be a model of rationality. It seeks to formulate laws to account for what occurs and to predict what will occur. It may even recognize a moral role for itself and attempt to make transformations where they are called for in order to make things better than they would have been without such intervention. But many aspects of the world – particularly those that deal with human conduct – cannot be dealt with or formulated with the precision characteristic of science. Approximations are needed, and we have to develop a sense of the appropriate rather than expect our thought and the shape of things to correspond exactly. We must be content to reach an equitable solution, not necessarily one that is right in all details. We must be satisfied with a sensible or reasonable outcome even if it is not strictly speaking a rational one. This is particularly true in the case of ethical disputes, for more and more we discover that the contested issues in these cases cannot be rationally resolved and that we must make compromises and employ trade-offs that allow each of the parties to save face and retain self-respect. Education can be seen as the great laboratory for rationality, but it is more realistic to see it as a context in which young people learn to be reasonable so that they can grow up to be reasonable citizens, reasonable companions, and reasonable parents.

Relationship and judgment

To judge is to judge relationships, either by discovering relationships or by inventing them. Few readers will have forgotten those essay-type examinations that

---

Characterizations

Judgments are settlements or determinations of what was previously unsettled, indeterminate, or in some way or other problematic. We can say that *inquiry* and *judgment* are generally related to one another as process and product, but the connection is not an exclusive one; some inquiries do not terminate in judgments, and some judgments are not the products of inquiry. Typically, however, the products of inquiry sum up and express the appraisive character of the inquiry process: Estimating produces estimates, portraying produces portraits, and analyzing produces analyses. As for *good* judgments, we often attempt to explain these as a happy admixture of critical and creative judgings. Such retrospective accounts can be useful and have their place, but it is likely that, in the long run, what makes good judgments good is their role in the shaping of *future* experience: They are judgments we can live with, the kind that enrich the lives we have yet to live.

Relationships. Thinking is a process of finding or making connections and disjunctions. The world is made up of complexes (evidently there are no simples) such as molecules and chairs and people and ideas, and these complexes have connections with some things and not with others. The generic term for connections and disjunctions is *relationships.* Since the meaning of a complex lies in the relationships it has with other complexes, each relationship, when discovered or invented, is a meaning, and great orders or systems of relationships constitute great bodies of meaning.

---

sought to elicit judgment by formulating an assignment beginning with the magic words "Compare and contrast." "Compare and contrast the historical impact of the American and French revolutions." "Compare and contrast the psychological theories of Piaget and Vygotsky." "Compare and contrast the artistic styles of Renaissance and Baroque painting." Obviously, the criteria in such cases are *similarity* and *difference,* but similarities and differences are kinds of relationships, just as are part–whole, means–end, cause–effect, and countless others. Every classification scheme establishes formal relationships for empirical entities. Every law, ever principle, bears a relationship, or more precisely a set of relationships, to the events to which it applies. Disciplines are only trivially the information they contain; more important, they are the structures of relationships into which such information is organized.

Thinking in the disciplines

According to Hirst, Dewey has it wrong when he talks about the logic of the inquiry process as having educational preeminence. He thinks that what education should take from science is not the process but the product. Scientific knowledge is a model of rationality. All scientific knowledge is contingent and must be justified by means of evidence or reasons. It is just such knowledge that students should be taught to aspire to. The knowledge that is the finished product of the inquiry process is logically organized, and the student must be educated to seek that organization so that no claims of fact will be made without evidence, no opinions will be proffered without accompanying reasons, and no judgments will be made without appropriately relevant criteria.[8]

What Hirst does acknowledge, however, is that, just as the student of foreign languages must aspire to think in those languages (and not merely be able to translate mechanically from one language to the next while thinking only in his or her own), so the recipient of a liberal education must aspire to think in the different languages that the disciplines represent. It is not enough to learn what happened in history; we must be able to think historically. "What we want is that pupils shall begin, however embryonically, to think historically, scientifically or mathematically; to think in the way distinctive of the particular subject involved."[9] But this is apparently as far as Hirst will permit himself to go in the direction of "effective thinking," and when confronted by the 1946 Harvard Committee report *General Education in a Free Society,*[10] which identifies the essential attributes of general education as the ability to think effectively, to communicate thought, to make relevant judgments, and to discriminate among values, he gives up on thinking and retreats to an invocation of "the public features of the forms of knowledge."[11]

Conversational apprenticeship

The infant growing up in the family is intrigued by the adventure of family conversation and learns to "recognize the voices" and to "distinguish the proper occasions of utterance" so as gradually to be initiated into the "skill and partnership" of this ongoing dialogue. When it is time for formal education, there is once again, as Michael Oakeshott puts it, "an initiation into the skill and partnership of this conversation in which we learn to recognize the voices, to distinguish the proper occasions of utterance, and . . . acquire the intellectual and moral habits appropriate to conversation. And it is this conversation which, in the end, gives place and character to every human activity and utterance."[12] Martin Buber, on the other hand, extols dialogue rather than conversation. (He classifies conversation, along with debate, friendly chat, and lovers' talk, as a mere spectre of

[8] Paul H. Hirst, "The Logical and Psychological Aspects of Teaching a Subject," in R. S. Peters (ed.), *The Concept of Education* (New York: Humanities Press, 1967), pp. 44–60.

[9] Ibid., p. 45.   [10] London: Oxford University Press, 1946.

[11] Paul H. Hirst, "Liberal Education and the Nature of Knowledge," in R. F. Dearden, P. H. Hirst, and R. S. Peters (eds.), *Education and the Development of Reason* (London: Routledge and Kegan Paul, 1972), p. 397.

[12] "The Voice of Poetry in the Conversation of Mankind," *Rationalism in Politics* (New York: Basic, 1962), p. 199.

dialogue.) Genuine dialogue occurs only where each of the participants "really has in mind the other or others in their present and particular being and turns to them with the intention of establishing a living mutual relationship between himself and them."[13] Ideally, the relationship between teacher and students has this character of face-to-face dialogue. It is at once a community exhibiting both apprenticeship and mutual respect and a workshop in which traditional skills are passed on from one generation to the other. Despite the obviously traditionalist emphasis in both Oakeshott and Buber,[14] their outlooks on education have had considerable influence on educational reforms in the final quarter of the twentieth century.

Autonomy

Not uncommonly, the reflective model of education is distinguished from the standard model on the ground that the primary objective of the reflective model is the autonomy of the learner. There is a sense in which this is correct: the sense in which autonomous thinkers are those who "think for themselves," who do not merely parrot what others say or think but make their own judgments of the evidence, form their own understanding of the world, and develop their own conceptions of the sorts of persons they want to be and the sort of world they would like it to be. Unfortunately, autonomy has often been associated with a kind of rugged individualism: the independent critical thinker as a self-sufficient cognitive macho type, protected by an umbrella of invincibly powerful arguments. In reality, the reflective model is thoroughly social and communal. Its aim is to articulate the friction-causing differences in the community, develop arguments in support of the competing claims, and then, through deliberation, achieve an understanding of the larger picture that will permit a more objective judgment.

This may suggest to some that the aim of the reflective model is achieved with production of the judgments just referred to. But this would be a misreading of the situation. The aim of the educational process is to help us form better judgments in order that we can proceed to modify our lives more judiciously. Judgments are not ends in themselves. We do not experience works of art in order to judge them; we judge them in order to be able to have enriched aesthetic experiences. Making moral judgments is not an end in itself; it is a means for improving the quality of life.

Higher-order thinking

Different commentators ascribe different properties to higher-order thinking, but in general what they seem to mean is thinking that is conceptually rich, coherently organized, and persistently exploratory. Each of these characteristics is controversial. It can be argued that higher-order thinking need not be conceptually rich, since it can be powerful, flexible, resourceful, and so on even when dealing with

---

[13] Ibid.   [14] Martin Buber, *Between Man and Man* (London: Kegan Paul, 1947).

materials that are ideationally rather superficial. The material need not be coherently organized, as in sprawling works of fiction that bewilder us by their amorphousness yet impress us with their insight. Nor does it have to be persistently exploratory, for it may be content merely to mirror reality rather than to investigate it.

I do not find these objections so solid and substantial as to outweigh the value of the three characteristics cited above. "Higher-order thinking," like a great many technical terms, can be a useful notion even if chronically infected with vagueness. The three traits just mentioned – richness, coherence, and inquisitiveness – can be thought of as those to which higher-order thinking always returns, not those from which it never deviates. But if the case of thinking under examination is significantly lacking in all of these traits, it is doubtful that it should be viewed as higher order.

Just as important as the question of what higher-order thinking is is the question of how to teach for it. At this point, I merely observe that the mistake currently being made with regard to teaching for higher-order thinking stems directly from the narrow assumptions that often prevail in educational research. These assumptions suggest that, since wholes are capable of being analyzed into parts, the assemblage of parts must precede the construction of wholes. In other words, the implantation of higher-order cognitive skills in students will result in higher-order thinking on their part. I would argue that, on the contrary, we should teach directly and immediately for higher-order thinking. The skills will take care of themselves, and if they do not, this is a matter for subsequent remediation. Direct teaching for higher-order thinking tends to be highly meaningful to students and teachers alike. It is therefore intrinsically rewarding. How, then, do we teach directly for higher-order thinking?

Having students do philosophy is an example of how higher-order thinking can be stimulated in the classroom, making use of the community of inquiry. But although philosophy may be a paradigm case, it is not necessary to employ philosophy in order to promote higher-order thinking. In each discipline, the community of inquiry approach can be used in order to provoke discussion and reflection about the subject matter of the discipline. Moreover, a critical thinking methodology can be used as a framework so that the discipline's content can be infused or metered into the discussion.

Higher-order thinking, it should be added, is not equivalent to critical thinking alone, but to a fusion of critical and creative thinking. It is particularly evident when the critical and the creative aspects support and reinforce each other, as when the critical thinker invents new premises or new criteria or when the creative thinker gives a new twist to an artistic tradition or convention. And higher-order thinking is resourceful and flexible thinking. Resourceful in that it has a sense of where to look for the resources it needs, and flexible in that it is able to range freely in deploying those resources so that they will be maximally effective.

HIGHER-ORDER THINKING

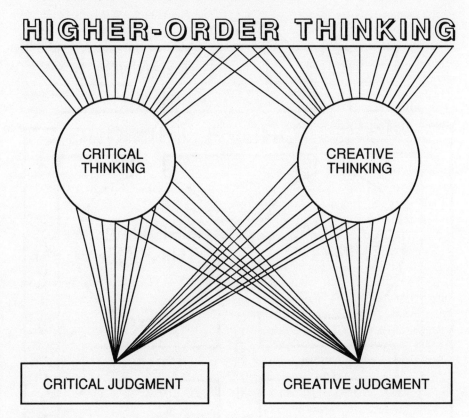

Figure 1

Figure 2 represents an effort to show the connectedness of the following considerations:

1. Higher-order thinking takes place under the aegis of two regulative ideas – truth and meaning
2. Higher-order thinking involves both critical and creative thinking
3. Critical thinking involves reasoning and critical judgment
4. Creative thinking involves craft, artistry, and creative judgment
5. There is no critical thinking without a modicum of creative judgment
6. There is no creative thinking without a modicum of critical judgment
7. It is not that the polishing of cognitive skills is the means by which higher-order thinking is improved but rather that higher-order thinking is the context in terms of which cognitive skills are improved
8. The community of inquiry, especially when it employs dialogue, is the social context most reliable for the generation of higher-order thinking

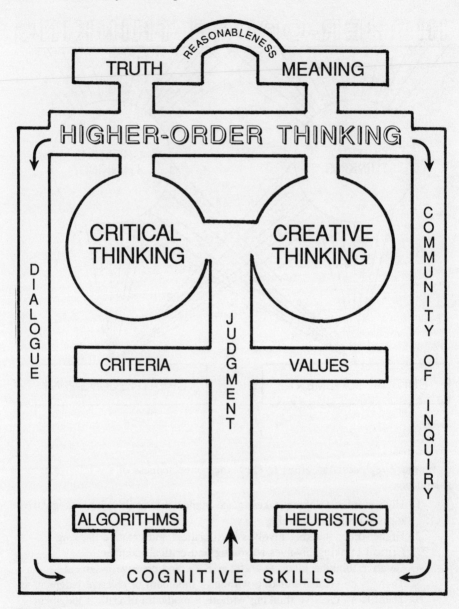

Figure 2

9. Algorithms are cognitive tools designed to reduce the need for creative judgment in critical thinking. As labor-saving devices, they can be useful, for they guarantee that, if properly employed, they will produce jus-

tifiable conclusions. They are ways of expediting inquiry that can be misleading when thought to be ways of terminating inquiry

10. Heuristics are approaches that aim to reduce the need for critical judgment in creative thinking. They represent assurances that, if the results of a particular operation are successful, the means used must have been justifiable. The danger they represent is that of failing to warn the user that the same use of means may result in other consequences, possibly quite harmful, in addition to the successful ones just cited

11. Criteria are highly reliable reasons that are appealed to in a community because they are recognized as governing factors in judgment

12. Values are matters of importance. Since people generally feel strongly about such matters, it is here that the affective element enters the thinking process. (Reasoning and feelings or emotions are not inimical to each other; emotions are as likely to enhance our reasoning as to obstruct it.) Since we feel strongly about matters of importance to us, our thinking about such matters is strongly emotion-laden

Complex thinking

I have been trying to draw some sort of picture that will be helpful in understanding what is meant by cognitive excellence. The notion of higher-order thinking is helpful here, along with the claim that such thinking represents the fusion of critical and creative thinking. I shall reserve until later the definitions of these twin pillars on which higher-order thinking rests, except to observe that they are not opposites of one another, as is commonly thought, but symmetrical and complementary.

We need to have some idea of what cognitive excellence involves because if we do not we will be unable to distinguish better thinking from worse thinking. We need to know, for example, cognitive excellence relies on creativity as much as rationality. (That this understanding of the matter is not widespread is attested to by the fact that critical thinking is received so much more favorably by the schools than is creative thinking.) Since the notion of higher-order thinking suggests to us how things ought to be rather than how they are, it is a normative rather than a descriptive concept.

Excellent thinking involves still a third component. Virtually everyone is familiar with the distinction between holding sound convictions without knowing the reasons or grounds on which such convictions rest and holding such convictions while at the same time being aware of the reasons and grounds that support them. The second way is more complex, but in the long run it is the more excellent form of thinking. *Complex* thinking, then, is thinking that is aware of its own assumptions and implications as well as being conscious of the reasons and evidence that support this or that conclusion. Complex thinking takes into account its own methodology, its own procedures, its own perspective and point of view. Complex thinking is prepared to recognize the factors that make for bias, prejudice, and

PROCEDURAL   SUBSTANTIVE
THINKING   THINKING

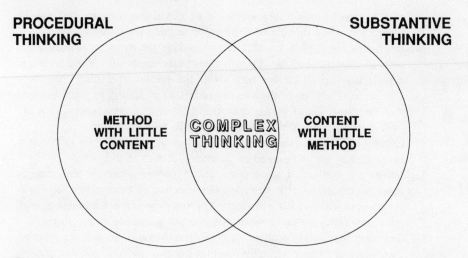

METHOD   COMPLEX   CONTENT
WITH LITTLE   THINKING   WITH LITTLE
CONTENT   METHOD

Figure 3

self-deception. It involves *thinking about its procedures* at the same time as it involves *thinking about its subject matter*. Just as in a discussion that takes place in a legislature there must be constant awareness of parliamentary procedure all the while that there is consideration of matters of substance, so in deliberative inquiry in the classroom there must be constant acknowledgment of the primacy of the methodology of such inquiry all the while that matters of substance are being discussed. It is because this is so seldom the case that bias and self-deception so frequently have free rein in classroom argumentation. The conversation is a ventilation of prejudices rather than a deliberative inquiry.

In its simple forms, then, thinking may be solely procedural or solely substantive. Thinking about logic or mathematics – or better, thinking logically about logic or mathematically about mathematics – is an instance of purely procedural or methodological thinking. Thinking solely about content, taking procedure wholly for granted, is wholly substantive thinking. The mixed mode created by the overlapping of these two simple forms is complex thinking. It is clear that what is here called complex thinking includes recursive thinking, metacognitive thinking, self-corrective thinking, and all those other forms of thinking that involve reflection on their own methodology at the same time as they examine their subject matter.

Excellent thinking, then, is higher-order, complex thinking and contains the components just described. This brings us back to the question of what can be done to produce such thinking. What can be done to make education more critical, more creative, and more appraisive of its own procedures? My recommendation is that, as a start, we add philosophy to the elementary and secondary school curriculum. Of course, such an addition will not be sufficient. More has to be done to strengthen the thinking that must occur within and among all the disci-

Characteristics of higher-order, complex thinking

Critical thinking	Creative thinking	Complex thinking
Governed by criteria	Sensitive to criteria (particularly binary)	Concerned with both procedural and substantive considerations
Aims at judgment	Aims at judgment	Aims at resolution of problematic situations
Self-correcting	Self-transcending[14]	Metacognitive (inquiry into inquiry); aims at improvement of practice
Sensitive to context	Governed by context	Sensitive to context

plines. And of course, when I speak of philosophy at the grade-school level, I do not mean the dry, academic philosophy traditionally taught in the universities.

There will no doubt be some who will say that the cure sounds worse than the disease. One can only wonder if they have looked lately at the patient. To be sure, schools everywhere stand accused because student knowledge is so scanty, but what is worse is that what little students know they hold so uncritically, and what little they reflect upon they reflect upon so unimaginatively. Students like these will not become the thoughtful citizens that robust democracies require, nor can they look forward to the productivity and self-respect that they themselves require as individuals. We unquestionably have the capacity to make such changes as need to be made. Whether we have the will to do so is far from clear. What is clear enough is that we must more thoroughly reexamine what we are doing. Such reflection upon practice is the basis for inventing improved practices that will invite, in turn, further reflection.

[14] I understand inquiry to be *self-critical practice*. In the case of so-called critical thinking, this entails *self-correction*. In the case of creative thinking, this involves the kind of thinking that seeks to go beyond or to *transcend* itself. Self-critical practice is therefore to be understood as dividing naturally into self-corrective practice and self-transcending practice.

2   Learning the craft of thinking

During the late 1960s and early 1970s, educators began to ask themselves a question something like this: If all education is simply the guidance of thinking into a discipline, why not teach thinking itself? It was hardly the first time such a question had been raised, nor was it surprising that skeptical answers were quickly forthcoming. One of the most acute and perceptive analysts of the thinking process at that time was the British philosopher Gilbert Ryle. But while Ryle acknowledged that there were specific thinking skills, he held that these could be cultivated only within specific academic disciplines. He scoffed at the notion that thinking was something that could taught as a separate subject. The late essays of Ryle on thinking were the crowning work of a long and distinguished career, and the position he took on the teachability of thinking was a posture most educators, had they been aware of it, might have been inclined to accept.[1] Nevertheless, even before Ryle's death in 1976, significant new developments were beginning to occur, developments that had a direct bearing on the teaching of thinking. Moreover, it is quite possible that, just as Ryle's late work represented a modification of the unrelenting behaviorism he had professed earlier, his skeptical stance regarding the teaching of thinking in the schools might have been revised had he lived to observe children engaged in conceptual inquiry in the classroom.

As it turned out, Ryle's views had little immediate influence on the controversy that began to develop in educational circles. Educators who were fed up with a system of schooling that, whatever its cosmetic packaging, was drearily centered on rote learning were beginning to argue that it would be a good thing if children were encouraged to think rather than being made to learn what their teachers before them had been made to learn. Some even advocated getting children to think for themselves.

Reasoning to the rescue

It is one thing to contend that better thinking is needed in the schools; it is something else again to provide a curriculum and a pedagogy capable of bringing about that result. Countless studies have been produced purporting to show how students

[1] Gilbert Ryle, *Collected Papers*, 2 vols. (New York: Barnes and Noble, 1971). A specific and extremely rich attempt on Ryle's part to connect thinking and education is to be found in his essay

26

think, how teachers teach, how business people brainstorm, and how scientists prepare and conduct experiments; but few of these studies of what is done have provided a clear picture of how teachers ought to teach in order to get children to think better – as they ought to think. Yet, as any reader of Edgar Allen Poe's "The Purloined Letter" will recall, the most obvious place of all is the place most likely to be overlooked. The discipline most concerned with the cultivation of rationality through improved reasoning and concept formation seemed the last discipline in the world to consult.

Better thinking in the classroom primarily meant better thinking in language, and that implied the need to teach reasoning, traditionally a subdiscipline of *philosophy*. Reasoning is that aspect of thinking that can be discursively formulated, subjected to evaluational criteria (there can be valid and invalid reasoning), and taught. It involves, for example, the drawing of sound inferences, the offering of convincing reasons, the flushing out of underlying assumptions, the establishing of defensible classifications and definitions, and the organizing of coherent explanations, descriptions and arguments. In general, it entails a sensitivity to the logical aspects of discourse that has not been cultivated in our present-day system of education.

Just how important is reasoning to academic success? Or, put in another way, just how damaging to academic success are deficiencies in reasoning? Let us go back to the early stages of the child's development – to the initial period of language acquisition. This is when the child learns to reason – although not by having been explicitly taught to do so. The essentials of logic, like the essentials of syntax, are so much a part of everyday language that to acquire proficiency in the language is at the same time to have acquired the logic and syntax dissolved in that language. The infant learning to talk puts subjects in front of predicates; provides objects for transitive verbs; infers that the denial of the consequent of a conditional implies the denial of the antecedent; describes, narrates, explains, and even functions metacognitively, making judgments as to the truth or falsity of statements.

All of this happens in the home, in the context of family communication, long before schooling begins to take place. If syntactical and logical skills have been properly acquired before kindergarten, they will serve us our entire lives, for this cluster of proficiencies is the platform or foundation on which our lives as rational creatures are constructed. All other things being equal, those who are fortunate enough to possess an intact and functional set of cognitive skills at the start of schooling may breeze through elementary school like strong swimmers mastering an undertow that carries off their comrades. They will welcome with enthusiasm the knowledge-rich disciplines they encounter in junior high and high school, for the skills they bring to such encounters are wholly adequate to the challenge. But what if they are not so fortunate?

"Thinking and Self-Teaching," in Konstantin Kolenda (ed.), *Symposium on Gilbert Ryle*, Rice University Studies, 58: 3 (Summer 1972).

Children who begin schooling with grammatical, spelling, and pronunciation deficiencies that teachers have been trained to correct will likely be corrected; children with deficiencies teachers cannot diagnose or remedy will likely continue to be plagued by malfunctioning in these areas throughout elementary school. When they reach adolescence, when there is an avalanche of heavy-content courses and they need these skills the most, they will find themselves going through a period where the acquisition of new skills is most difficult. If they should get as far as college, they will discover that they lack the rudimentary skills needed to make sense of the work demanded of them. As a matter of fact, college freshmen trying to cope with college-level assignments often find themselves struggling to do so with reasoning skills not much higher than those of middle-school or junior high school students.[2]

Insofar as adults are adapted to their environment, they can reason in it fairly well. The basic reasoning equipment possessed by adults is rather like a kit of tools. The chief difference between the adult's kit and the child's kit is that the adult may be better able to cope with complicated problems by structuring his or her activity as a series of reasoning steps. Each reasoning step may be fairly rudimentary, but when used in a sequence it can become quite powerful, just as a carpenter can build a house or a mechanic repair a car with quite simple tools that are serially and strategically deployed. (In general, the difficulty children experience with algebraic or geometric problems seems to be proportionate to the number of reasoning steps needed to deal with them.) The fact that an adult possesses vastly greater experience than does a child does not change the fact that their sets of elementary reasoning equipment are fundamentally similar. The adult's fund of acquired experience is all to the good, of course, provided that he or she has

[2] This comparison is based in part on the work of the New Jersey Department of Higher Education's Task Force on Thinking (see Edward A. Morante and Anita Ulesky, "Assessment of Reasoning Abilities," *Educational Leadership* 42:1 [September 1984], 71–4), and an unpublished report dated February 1986 of the Institute for the Advancement of Philosophy for Children. The Institute, which developed the New Jersey Test of Reasoning in conjunction with the Educational Testing Service, reported the following means based on its scoring of tests in schools throughout the United States:

Grade	No. of children tested	Average no. right out of 50 items	% correct	Standard deviation
4	2,411	31.07	62.14	10.13
5	7,719	33.99	67.98	10.15
6	3,912	31.60	63.20	13.19
7	2,658	33.28	66.56	10.22
8	1,728	34.12	68.24	9.99

The NJDHE research (unpublished), involving the testing of 845 freshmen in nine colleges (one a community college), revealed a mean score of 38.22 on the New Jersey Test of Reasoning, so that the average percentage right was 76.44. The mean for the 110 freshmen in the community college was lower than any of those reported for grades 4–8.

actually learned from it, but that may not always be the case. Some children do not seem to think better as they get older, and some may actually show a decline in reasoning skills. We simply do not know the extent to which experience (such as school experience) retards rather than fosters improvement in reasoning skill.[3]

To conceive of a thinker as orchestrating his or her thinking into a linear series of simple steps is, of course, an enormously oversimplified paradigm, because a human being, whether adult or child, is capable of engaging in a considerable variety of thought processes simultaneously. While you are driving your car in traffic, you are wondering if you turned off the stove, imagining the mess that awaits you when you get to your office, and remembering what your daughter told you as you left her at school, together with performing countless other mental acts and bits of reasoning.

Earlier, it was implied that proficiency in primary reasoning skills is related to school performance. This should be understood in the sense that the lack of these skills assures academic difficulties rather than that the presence of such skills is a sure sign of academic success. One can reason well and still not succeed academically: Many other factors can account for academic misfortunes. But the lack of reasoning skills is sufficient to produce failure.

If a child's reasoning is functioning at only three-quarters of full efficiency (and this is the level at which most fifth graders and many college freshmen seem to be functioning), how can his or her academic performance be other than mediocre? Yet it will be of little value just to drill children in this or that skill and try to improve it; the level of functioning of the entire reasoning process must be raised. What must be improved is each and every skill and the manner of synchronizing or orchestrating all of them. We must move the child toward 100 percent of full reasoning efficiency, and we should not expect less, just as we do not readily tolerate errors in spelling or syntax.

This goal is not illusory. It has already been shown that children taught reasoning through philosophy will show an 80 percent greater improvement in reasoning than children not exposed to philosophy.[4] Three years of improvement at a similar rate would be more than enough to give children a kit of reasoning tools that they could employ in both school and out-of-school situations.

It should not be thought that the purpose of such educational intervention is merely remedial. The larger and more important objective is to establish a regimen of sound thinking among children, a regimen that will not be simply remedial in function but preventive of unreasonableness. Nevertheless, why must it be thought of as an occasional intervention? Why not make it a regular and intrinsic part of the elementary and secondary school curriculum?

There is good reason for caution on this point. Education involves more than skill development. We may acquire a skill but may misuse it. For example, we may learn to use a knife skillfully and then proceed to employ it antisocially.

---

[3] We do not know why the means reported above are lower in grades 6 and 7 than in grade 5.

[4] Matthew Lipman, Ann Margaret Sharp, and Frederick S. Oscanyon, *Philosophy in the Classroom*, 2d ed. (Philadelphia: Temple University Press, 1980), App. B (pp. 217–24).

When surgeons acquire the identical skill, they acquire it in the context of the discipline of medicine, and insofar as that entire discipline is committed to healing, learn that their skills are never to be used inhumanely. The lesson is that thinking skills too should be taught in the context of a humanistic discipline to guard against the skills being misused. The most appropriate discipline, in this case, would be one that is committed to the furtherance of humanistic inquiry into significant but problematic concepts. Thus it is the humanities discipline of philosophy and not reasoning skills alone that should be taught as an integral part of the elementary and secondary school curriculum.[5] Philosophy is to the teaching of thinking what literature is to the teaching of reading and writing.

Coming to think in language

According to Jerome Bruner in his recent book *Child's Talk*, there are certain categories of prelinguistic experience that sensitize the child to corresponding aspects of language, with the result that these categories guide the language-acquisition process "both syntactically and semantically." Thus, Bruner contends that the initial cognitive endowment of the prelinguistic child provides the primitive conditions that not only serve to enable prelinguistic communication but that serve to prefigure linguistic communication. He specifies four examples of such readiness:

1. Readiness for purposive or goal-directed behavior
2. Readiness to engage in role reversibility (as in mother–child transactions) or in turn taking
3. Readiness to order experience systematically
4. Readiness to make abstract distinctions, such as between causal and noncausal acts, between states and processes, or between the specific and the nonspecific.[6]

Presumably Bruner has listed here only a small sample of the categories of readiness that are developed by the activities of the prelinguistic child. It is somewhat surprising that Bruner makes no mention of the likelihood that these categories sensitize the child to the *logical* as well as the syntactical aspects of language. The child's initial competence in developing these prelinguistic experiential categories should develop into logical competencies along lines that correspond to the categories. The first category, *goal-directed behavior,* might foreshadow and eventuate in such cognitive skills as sequencing, working with transitive relationships, means–end relationships, and process–product relationships.

The second category, *turn taking,* might prefigure such cognitive skills as working with symmetrical relationships, drawing comparisons, discerning and constructing similes and analogies, and translating from one domain of language

---

[5] The preceding pages are taken from "Philosophy for Children and Critical Thinking," *National Forum/Phi Kappa Phi Journal* 65:1 (Winter 1985), 18–19.
[6] Adapted from Jerome Bruner, *Child's Talk* (New York: Norton, 1983), pp. 23–31.

to another. The third category, which involves *systematic ordering,* would seem to lead to classifying, making predicative judgments, forming concepts, generalizing, exemplifying, noting similarities and uniformities, and recognizing such relationships as part–whole and degree–kind. The fourth category, the *making of abstract distinctions,* might involve defining, using criteria, employing contradictories, and seeking validity of inference.

Bruner's thesis, in the somewhat modified version just stated, helps explain how it is that the process of language acquisition in any society involves simultaneously acquisition of the elements of logic and of the competencies to perform the logical operations that thinking presupposes. It is not that the logic is dissolved in the syntax but that both the logic and the syntax are aspects of language that answer to the categorial requirements of the child's prelinguistic experience.

Roadblocks to the development of reasoning

Infants begin to explore, deliberate, infer, and inquire well before the acquisition of language. As verbal behavior emerges, it is both grammatical and logical; children acquire the rules of logic and grammar along with words and their meanings. By "rules" in this context is meant nothing more than those conditions of usage that suggest *suitability* to children. Conversation in the home encourages the child to prefer grammatical usages that conform to the linguistic conventions of the cultural environment. Likewise the child's gleanings of prevailing family usages and his or her interactions with the environment combine to motivate a preference for the making of valid rather than invalid inferences. The result is that children usually arrive at kindergarten having at least a rudimentary proficiency in both grammatical and logical usage.

In their early school years, children's occasional deviations from accepted grammatical usage will be subject to reproof and correction from their teachers. Teachers are prepared to listen for such deviations and promptly correct them. The same is not the case with children's awkwardness when it comes to reasoning. Teachers are seldom educated so as to be on the lookout for logical flounderings among their pupils or knowledgeable enough to correct such errors with confidence. It is taken for granted that primary reasoning skills are acquired along with language – in itself, not an unreasonable presupposition. But *it is also taken for granted that no provision need be made in the schools for diagnosing reasoning deficiencies or for correcting them* in the way that schools employ specialists in the diagnosis and correction of reading deficiencies.

This is not to be taken as the pejorative comment that teachers fail to model correct reasoning in front of their students or that they fail to involve students in inferential performances. The fact is that they do both without realizing it. Take such familiar teacher utterances as "I hear talking" or "I don't see any hands." Teachers do not make such assertions because they are seeking confirmation from the class about certain matters of fact. These remarks function as the minor premises of conditional syllogisms whose major premises are unstated (i.e. enthymemes). The students in even the earliest school grades are able to supply the missing premises ("If I hear talking, the class must come to a stop"; "If you know the answer, raise your hand"). Then, in keeping with the rules of conditional syllogisms, they draw the proper inferences ("If you know the answer, raise your hand. I don't see any hands. Therefore you must not know the answer."). Teachers are generally unaware of how valuable such utterances are for the sharpening of reasoning skills. Unfortunately, they are equally unaware of the steps to be taken when the demands of logic cause students to stumble.

When teachers are unable to recognize reasoning lapses in the classroom (inconsistencies, self-contradictions, etc.) or are unprepared to remediate those instances that they do recognize, children with primary reasoning deficiencies are condemned to go through school – and through life – coping as best they can with a world that expects and demands more logicality and rationality from them than they can muster. Somehow many of them manage to get by, but only barely. They may develop self-preserving techniques to camouflage their incapacities and thus pass them off as innocent and charming frailties, or avoid situations in which proficiency in reasoning is obligatory. Nevertheless, whenever we take it for granted that reasoning skills have been adequately learned in very early childhood and need no subsequent attention from the schools, we leave the children in question to sink or swim, and many of them do indeed sooner or later sink.

For educational purposes, the behavioral matrix of thinking is *talking,* and the matrix of organized thinking (i.e., reasoning) is *organized talking.* Ideally, early-childhood linguistic communication in the family prepares children for thinking in the language of the classroom, and that in turn prepares them for thinking in the languages of the disciplines. But since family communication is seldom all that it should be, disciplined, coherent conversation in the classroom must be provided as its replacement. The conversational community is the key to the smooth transition from life in the family to life in the rule-governed classroom.

Other transformations are, of course, involved – translations and substitutions must be made from the natural language we speak to the languages we read and write and thence to the languages of specific areas of academic study. Given these branchings, there should be little wonder that the natural logic that is so much a part of natural language should operate as a kind of deep structure with respect to the surface structures of the academic disciplines that the child eventually encounters. The built-in or "hard-wired" modules or competencies that the primary cognitive skills represent must proceed through a sequence of contextualizations, decontextualizations, and recontextualizations before the child is fully prepared to engage in performances displaying higher-level cognitive skills in a variety of academic disciplines.

What children are inclined to find particularly difficult are the transitions: From the language we speak, we are expected to translate into written language or to move from the English language into the symbolic language of mathematics. Nor are the difficulties always unilinear. The student who can with ease infer the conclusion of a syllogism formulated in letters may be quite perplexed when confronted with the same syllogism formulated in words. Yet we insist on children's learning the most elaborate systematization we can devise within each discipline while neglecting to provide them with the stepping-stones they need to move easily from one language to the next. For children to whom the rules of translation are not readily apparent, each new educational phase can be traumatic. (Why should algebra, for example, come as such a shock to so many students? Why cannot the transition to it be better prepared for? Surely children who are taught to detect and cope with ambiguity in their natural language are less likely to be puzzled by ambiguities in algebraic formulations. Likewise, children who have discussed and reflected upon the nature of questions in their natural language are prepared to understand $y = 7 + 9$ as functionally equivalent to the question "What is the sum of $7 + 9$?") Perhaps if the educators of prospective teachers and the developers of curricula would keep in mind the need always to provide the means for making such transitions, children would find successive contextualizations much easier to accomplish.

Since the importance of reasoning has been recognized for thousands of years, how could it have happened that the fostering of reasoning skills has been systematically omitted from the elementary and secondary school curriculum? No doubt philosophers, the custodians of the subdiscipline of logic, might have raised their voices more strenuously in favor of early philosophical instruction. Schools of education might have placed the fostering of dialogue and reflective thinking rather than learning and classroom management at the center of the preparation of teachers. Taxonomists of educational objectives might have recognized that the inquiry skills to which they give such prominence were unrealizable without the requisite language and reasoning skills. And psychologists eager to preserve reasoning as a peerless index of cognitive processing might have wondered about the ethics of proclaiming that reasoning could not be taught while knowing that, as a result, it would not be. But all of this may now be in the past. We seem to be in a situation that holds somewhat greater promise of success in the matter of improvement in reasoning skills.

How reasoning differs from the basic skills

It may be well to pause at this point in order to mention two very common misconceptions. The first has to do with the relationship between primary reasoning skills and the so-called basic skills, such as reading, writing, and computation. Reading, writing, and computation are indeed basic with reference to subsequent educational development, for without them we could hardly become proficient in the academic disciplines we begin to encounter in middle school and which are characteristic of secondary school and college education. We may also add speaking and listening. But reading, writing, speaking, listening and computation are incredibly complex and sophisticated megaskills. They are orchestrations of vast numbers of highly diversified skills and mental acts that have been developed previously. Reasoning is not another of these megaskills; it is not the fourth R. It is instead, with reference to the basic skills, foundational. It is fundamental to *their* development. Yet even this foundation, it turns out, is multi-level. One of the teacher's and the student's major tasks is to unpack and order the galaxy of cognitive components within reasoning that must be marshaled in even a single act of reading, writing, speaking, listening, or computation.

A second misconception is that, as we mature, our reasoning skills proliferate in quantity and improve greatly in quality. No doubt this is partially true, but it is not wholly so. Throughout our lives we rely to a very considerable extent on the same core of primary reasoning skills; the basic repertoire of reasoning skills of the adult is relatively unchanged from the child's. The situation is somewhat analogous to what prevails with respect to language acquisition. The number of words an individual can add to his or her vocabulary is virtually unlimited, but it can be predicted with certainty that the letters in each new word will be drawn from the identical repertoire – the twenty-six-letter alphabet. Thus, even when we engage in the most elaborate kinds of thinking – long deductive chains, highly abstruse theoretical constructions, and the like – familiarity is presupposed with a relatively small number of mental acts, reasoning skills, and inquiry skills upon which the more elegant and sophisticated thought operations are predicated. Without the ability to assume, suppose, compare, infer, contrast, or judge, to deduce or induce, to classify, describe, define, or explain, our very ability to read and write would be imperiled, to say nothing of our capacity to engage in classroom discussion, prepare experiments, and compose prose.

Orders of cognitive skills

There are many kinds of skills and many kinds of skill-like behaviors. In addition, there are many ways of arranging or ordering, of which only a few are pertinent here.

First, cognitive skills themselves. We speak of higher-order skills, but how are these to be differentiated from lower-order skills? One way is to see the skills somewhat as we see a series of powers (x, x^2, x^3 . . .). Thus, we have comparison of terms ("Wolves are like dogs"), comparisons of relationships among terms, or analogies ("Puppies are to dogs as kittens are to cats"), comparisons of analogies, and so on. Or we can have inferences from single premises (immediate inference), inferences from pairs of premises (syllogistic inference), inferences from arguments containing inferences from single or double premises or both, and so on. So one way of distinguishing lower-order from higher-order skills is through *hierarchies* of this kind, with the understanding that the hierarchy lies not so much in differences among the skills themselves as in their pyramiding.

A second aspect of the difference between lower-order and higher-order skills has to do with their *sequencing* and *coordination* with other skills. We often see this when we contrast people who are handy with tools and those who are not. It is not so much that the mechanic uses a wrench or screwdriver that much more skillfully than we do; it is that the mechanic knows how to coordinate and sequentialize and synchronize the use of tools far more effectively than we can. And add to that the greater knowledge and experience that mechanics bring to their use of very simple tools.

A similar situation prevails with respect to cognitive operations. For example, suppose I read a story about a robbery, and I infer (although it is not stated in the story) that the robber was a man. That inference in turn illuminates an underlying assumption that might not have come to light if I had not drawn that inference: I have evidently assumed that robbers are always male. Thus, there is a sequence of operations: A statement is made, an inference is drawn, an assumption comes to light.

Third, a somewhat different type of sequence occurs in cases where skills are *nested* – that is, where the earlier operations are subsumed or taken up into the later ones, so that instead of having a series of discrete skills that have been rationally sequenced for dealing with a particular problem, we have what more nearly resembles a single skill that evolves and expands in a cumulative fashion. Thus, when we move from immediate inference (inferring from a single premise) to syllogistic arguments (inferring from dual premises) and thence to chain-syllogistic arguments (where the conclusion of one syllogism becomes a premise of the next, and so on), we are in a sense dealing with the same skill all along but enlarging on it and varying it so that it becomes increasingly more powerful, increasingly higher-order. Another example of nesting is in analogical reasoning, where on the most elementary level we have a comparison of terms ("Fingers are like toes") and then a more elaborate comparison that includes the primitive stage just alluded to ("Fingers are to hands as toes are to feet"). Here, however, we note that an important variation has occurred. In the first case, we compared terms; here we are comparing relationships. We are saying that the relationships between the first pair of terms is similar to the relationship between the second pair of terms. On a still higher level, we can compare analogies themselves; for example, we may say that one projective map better resembles the sphere of the earth than another does. Still another example of nesting is what occurs fairly often in the dialogue of a community of inquiry. Someone makes a statement about which a *question* is raised. In time the questioner may begin to move from the question to the formulation of a specific *counterexample* and from the counterexample to a still more elaborate *counterargument*.

What is important about the sequencing and nesting of skills, of course, is that it makes possible an enormous increase in sheer power and efficiency. We see this illustrated in an elementary school science classroom when, to understand the principle of the pendulum, a teacher will hold a yardstick loosely at one end and tap it at the other. If the taps are regular and properly timed, the arc of the swings becomes progressively larger. So it is with cognitive skills: An effective curriculum will teach students how such skills can be employed cumulatively so that they reinforce each other.

Skills and meanings[7]

The primary incentive for acquiring speech is probably the power speech affords to express meanings and acquire them. It is not enough to be able to spit food out or pat the dog; the infant evidently wants to be able to say, "Nasty food" or "Nice doggie." Likewise, it is not enough merely to observe the sky; the infant evidently wants to be able to say that it is blue. To be able to predicate nastiness of the food, niceness of the dog, and blueness of the sky – in short, to be able to make logical judgments – is a significant achievement. But at the same time the infant wants to know what other people mean by *their* verbal expressions, such as "The dog is dirty," the clue to which is usually given by the adult's facial expression. Our animal inquisitiveness is rapidly transformed into a lust for *meaning* – to acquire meaning and to express it through interpersonal communication. The acquisition of meaning gains added momentum through acquiring the ability to read, while the expression of meaning is enhanced by acquiring the ability to write.

It is not that the literary skills traditionally emphasized by language arts teachers are not "thinking skills." (The phrase is redundant; all skills involve thinking, and nothing can be a skill that does not involve thinking.) But these literary skills do not play the meaning-acquisitive role that reasoning and inquiry skills play in the reading process. Violations of the reasoning operations result directly in losses of meaning to the writer or reader, while violations of syntactical and spelling rules do not necessarily cause such losses.

To insist upon the primacy of meaning in motivation will be thoroughly unsurprising to those who have all along stressed comprehension as the chief incentive to children in getting them to read or to read better. What the primacy of meaning in motivation does spotlight, however, are those rudimentary activities that are more directly involved in meaning acquisition and those that are less so. By way of illustration of this point, let us consider some errors:

Error	*Comment*
1. "Thirty-five divided by seven equals four," said George.	George's error involves a violation of conventions and procedures within the system of arithmetic.
2. Ruth left a note saying, "Us going to the stor."	Ruth has violated English syntax and spelling conventions, although she manages to convey the same meaning she would have conveyed had she written without errors.

[7] This section is taken from my essay "The Seeds of Reason," originally published in Ronald T. Hyman (ed.), *Thinking Processes in the Classroom: Prospects and Programs* (New Jersey Association for Supervision and Curriculum Development, 1985), pp. 1–15.

3. Gary remarked, "Gems are defined as ordinary stones."

Gary's failure to define "gems" correctly rests on his failure to classify them correctly as precious rather than as nonprecious. As a result, the defining term ("ordinary stones") does not have the same meaning as the term to be defined ("gems"). Because Gary does not perceive the lack of synonymity, he fails to convey the meaning he attempts to convey.

4. Sally said, "All detectives are interested in crime and all criminals are interested in crime; therefore all detectives are criminals."

We may assume the premises of this syllogism to be true, but then we discover that, owing to its formal invalidity, it fails to preserve the truth of its premises in its conclusion.

5. "The French word *chat*," said Tom, "means, in English, *an informal conversation.*"

Tom's translation of the French word for *cat* into the English *chat* fails to preserve the French meaning by finding an equivalent English meaning.

6. The item in the reading comprehension test reads as follows: "The main idea of the statement 'One of the most alarming statistics in recent years has been the rapidly rising number of fires' is that false alarms are costly and dangerous, rather than that there are more fires now than there used to be."

This passage betrays a faulty understanding of the way the original statement is to be translated into a more colloquial (but still English) locution. The resulting lack of synonymity can also be described as a failure to preserve meaning.

These examples provide us with an opportunity to make two distinctions. The first is between errors that violate *meaning* and errors that do not. The second is between operations that preserve *truth* and operations that preserve meaning.

With regard to the second distinction, consider the cases of Gary, Sally, and Tom. Sally's syllogism failed to preserve the *truth* of its premises. Gary's definition failed to preserve the *meaning* of the term to be defined. And Tom's translation failed to preserve the *meaning* of a French word by failing to select an equivalent English word.

Now, in the light of these distinctions, let us reconsider the item on the reading comprehension test. The error is one that violates meaning but is independent of the question of truth, since we are expected to understand and correctly translate false statements just as we are expected to understand and correctly translate true ones. What lesson does this hold for us?

Strictly speaking, the truth-preserving process is *inference* and the meaning-preserving process is *translation*. Reading comprehension presupposes skill in translating not from one language to another but from one domain of a language to another domain of the same language, as when we read a passage in formal prose and then say what it means in colloquial language. But while the truth of the passage under translation is not at issue, the operations by means of which the translation is made may be inferential and hence truth-preservative.

There is, of course, a broader and narrower sense of reading comprehension. The broader sense involves a collaboration between author and reader that results in a common product that goes beyond what the author has stated or implied. I am deliberately putting aside this quite valid sense of meanings as generated by the act of reading and am restricting myself to the narrower sense employed by the constructor of tests of reading comprehension. These test-constructors apparently take into account only (1) whether or not the reader understands what the passage *states*, (2) whether or not the reader infers what the passage *implies*, and (3) whether or not the reader *grasps the underlying assumptions* on which the passage is based. All three of these considerations presuppose skills that are primarily logical in character. (1) Understanding what the passage states is held to be achieved when the reader can identify a second passage whose meaning is equivalent to the meaning of the first. In this sense, to understand is to recognize *identity* in the form of *synonymity*. (2) To infer correctly what a passage implies is obviously a logical procedure, whether it is formal and syllogistic or informal and linguistic (in the sense that "John beat Mary badly at cards" implies that "John beat Mary at cards"). (3) To grasp underlying assumptions is to ask what the premises might be if a given assertion were to be the conclusion of a valid argument; once again, logical procedures are involved.

The question, of course, is not whether we can show *identity* of meaning but whether we can show *similarity* of meaning. Take the case of the fourth-grade child who was asked, in a Philosophy for Children class, what it would be like to be the only person on earth and who replied, "It would be like being the only star in the sky." What the child noted was a telling likeness between the person alone in an empty world and the star alone in an empty sky. She evidently found the relationship between the person and the world much like the relationship between the star and the sky; in other words, she discovered a relationship of similarity between two part–whole relationships. And this is precisely what constitutes analogical reasoning: the finding of similar relationships among other relationships. The child's answer is impressive evidence that she has grasped the meaning of the question.

Reading comprehension can therefore be said to rest upon the formal skills of deductive inferential reasoning and upon such skills as analogical reasoning. It is likely that reading comprehension will be more effectively improved if these primary reasoning skills are strengthened than if attention is paid to syntactical lapses, vocabulary weaknesses, spelling deficiencies, and a lack of stylistic appreciation. This is because reasoning skills contribute directly to the reader's acquisition of meaning, and it is access to meaning that most effectively motivates the reader to continue pursuing the reading process. Teachers of reading and language arts insist that they teach thinking, and they do. But if we examine the skills they stress (the ones they grade for), it is clear that the emphasis is on the skills that are not meaning-bearing rather than on the semantic skills that are.

This is true not only of teachers of reading and language arts. In each elementary school discipline, education textbooks bend over backwards to cite thinking skills and to urge their fostering by the teacher because of the relevance of such skills to the mastery of the material, whether in science, math, or social studies. Consider a representative approach in education – for example, the eighth edition of *Social Studies for Children*, by John U. Michaelis.[8] Michaelis is a respected educator who has been concerned with the development of cognitive processing in educational contexts and who is the coauthor of *A Comprehensive Framework of Objectives*.[9] His advocacy of thinking skills in a social studies framework is clear and explicit. He presents four modes of thinking: critical thinking, creative thinking, decision making, and problem solving and inquiry. These four approaches intersect with a knowledge base derived from other thinking skills: remembering, interpreting, comparing, gathering data, and classifying.

Michaelis says that concepts must be developed to supplement the knowledge base. Examples he gives of concepts are conjunctive, disjunctive, and relational. The strategies of concept formation include defining, distinguishing examples from nonexamples, listing–grouping–labeling, and "problem solving or inquiry." He lists, as skills to be emphasized, generalizing, inferring, predicting, hypothesizing, analyzing and synthesizing information, and evaluating. For each skill, a few hints are given as to the kinds of questions the teacher should ask in order to foster the skill, and then the text turns to other important matters. Judging from this text, it is as if only a quick brush-up or tune-up is needed to get these skills operating and plugged into the discipline.

The fact is that elementary school teachers, like teachers at every other level, are in no position to read the now-obligatory chapter on thinking skills that virtually all new textbooks such as this one by Michaelis contain and to operationalize the taxonomies of skills set forth. Indeed, many teachers become rebellious and vow not to be distracted from their lesson plans by futile efforts to strengthen skills that students should have brought with them on school opening day. It may be somewhat useful to a teacher to have a neat new definition of inference if they are to be answered correctly, but teachers must be extraordinarily naive to believe that such hints even remotely prepare them to strengthen the inferential proficiencies of those students who perform uncertainly when inference is called for. And the educators who prepare such teachers in schools of education must be extraordinarily naive to believe that an educational process that fails to provoke students to think can be successful at making them think better.

[8] Englewood Cliffs, N.J.: Prentice-Hall, 1985, pp. 233–63.
[9] John U. Michaelis and Larry B. Hannah, *A Comprehensive Framework of Objectives* (Reading, Mass.: Addison-Wesley, 1977).

Four major varieties of cognitive skills

For educational purposes, the most relevant skill areas are those relating to inquiry processes, reasoning processes, information organizing and translation. It is likely that very small children possess all of these skills in a rudimentary way. Education is therefore not a matter of cognitive skill acquisition but skill strengthening and improvement. In other words, children are naturally disposed to acquire cognitive skills, just as they naturally acquire language, and education is needed to strengthen the process.

Inquiry skills

By "inquiry," I mean self-correcting practice. I do not call a behavior inquiry if it is merely customary, conventional, or traditional – that is, simply practice. But if the supervening practice of self-correction is added to that practice, the result is inquiry. I do not think this definition of inquiry is too broad just because it spans the behavior of the exploring infant and that of the exploring scientist. The fumbling, groping infant, trying to guess where the ball went – perhaps under the sofa – is engaged in considering alternatives, constructing hypotheses, testing, and other forms of behavior that will gradually become recognizable as "intelligent."

Inquiry skills, like the other varieties of cognitive skills, are continuous across age levels. The differences, from childhood to old age, are much more of degree than of kind. It is primarily through inquiry skills that children learn to connect their present experiences with what has already happened in their lives and with what they can expect to happen. They learn to explain and to predict and to identify causes and effects, means and ends, and means and consequences as well as to distinguish these things from one another. They learn to formulate problems, estimate, measure, and develop the countless proficiencies that make up the practice associated with the process of inquiry.

Reasoning skills

Knowledge originates in experience. One way of extending it, however without recourse to additional experience, is through reasoning. *Given what we know, reasoning permits us to discover additional things that are the case.* In a soundly formulated argument, where we begin with true premises, we discover an equally true conclusion that "follows from" those premises. Our knowledge is based upon our experience of the world; it is by means of reasoning that we extend that knowledge and defend it.

One of the merits of logic is almost purely educational. To students eager to vaunt their newfound relativism, it provides a superb reminder that what may be true for one may not be true for all, that not everything follows from everything else, and that relativism does not necessarily exclude objectivity. What logic does beautifully is demonstrate to incredulous students that rationality is possible, that there is such a thing as logical correctness or validity, and that some arguments are better than others.

In Plato's day, inference had something living and fresh and surprising about it, and we have attempted to explain this away by saying that it must have been because, to Socrates and Plato, logic was so *new*. But this was only part of the matter. The vitality of reasoning then was much more closely connected to the nature of *dialogue*. When we think by ourselves, rather than in conversation with others, our deductions are derived from premises we already know. As a result, the conclusion we infer is totally unsurprising. But when no person knows all the premises, as is often the case in dialogue, the reasoning process has much more vitality, and the conclusion can come with considerably more surprise.

Information-organizing skills

For purposes of cognitive efficiency, we have to be able to organize the information we receive into meaningful clusters or units. These conceptual clusters are networks of relationships, and since each relationship is a unit of meaning, each of the alternative networks or clusters is a web of meanings. Three basic types of informational clustering are the sentence, the concept, and the schema. There are however, also organizational *processes* that are not merely parts or elements of a larger whole but are global ways of formulating and expressing what we know. I am thinking here of narration and description, very comprehensive skills that can take into account the whole of an experience and break it down into its constituents, whether viewed sequentially or simultaneously.

Sentences. These, rather than individual words, are *basic contexts of meaning*. They are larger units than, say, the relationship between any two words in a sentence, but they are elementary as contrasted with such larger units as paragraphs and arguments. It is true that individual words have reference to things in the world, but they make sense only when organized with other words and when understood in the context of the language as a whole.[10]

When we deal with reasoning, we are primarily preoccupied with relationships among sentences. We tend to forget, therefore, how great an achievement an individual sentence can be for the language learner. What goes on in a sentence is

---

[10] I take it that the most elementary unit of meaning is a relationship. In this sense, since words have semantic or referential relationships to things in the world, words participate in and partake of the meanings of those relationships. (Obviously, I hesitate to say that the relationship, and hence the meaning, is in cases of this sort in the connection between the word and the thing referred to. Rather, the relationship spans the word and the thing it refers to in an overarching way so as to include and comprise them in the meaning. In other words, I see connections as interactional and words as transactional. Cf. John Dewey and Arthur F. Bentley, "A Trial Group of Names," in *Knowing and the Known* [Boston: Beacon, 1949], pp. 287–312.) But I see no conflict between this and the assumption that the sentence (because it includes a complex nesting of linguistic and not just referential relationships) is in a better position to be taken as the basic unit of meaning. Cf., for example, Michael Dummett, "Meaning and Understanding," in *The Interpretation of Frege's Philosophy* (Cambridge, Mass.: Harvard University Press, 1981), pp. 74–82.

no less exciting than what goes on among sentences. Some writers, for example, say something different in each sentence they construct, so that we comprehend the whole of what they say only by understanding each of the sentences in the order in which they are presented. Other writers write epigrammatically or aphoristically, so that each of their sentences intimates something of the sense of their work taken as a totality. Nietzche's sentences are something like this. And there are still other writers whose individual sentences are fairly atomistic in content, so that their larger compositions are like mosaics with each of the tiny units united with every other by means of a consistent texture or style. We readily recognize Hemingway in the repetitions and adjectival choices of a sentence such as "The cows were big, gray, striped-flanked antelope with ridiculously small heads, big ears, and a soft, fast-rushing gait that moved them in a big-bellied panic through the trees."[11]

Sentences are the basic building blocks of reading and writing, and they may be of many kinds: questions, exclamations, commands, assertions. From the point of view of traditional logic, assertions or statements are of the greatest interest; each statement is said to represent a judgment. An example of an elementary logical judgment is "All mice are rodents."[12]

Concepts. When we cluster things in terms of their similarities, we are said to have a concept of them. As Rom Harré says, concepts are the vehicles of thought, entities by means of which thought is carried on.[13] Analysis of concepts involves clarifying and removing ambiguities, as in Figure 4, an example by Katz and Fodor. In another example, students are presented with a targetlike map; two concentric areas, identified by a pair of antonyms, are separated by a "fuzzy area." The students are given a list of words that they are to distribute as appropriately as possible among the three areas. The synonyms in the inner zone are to contribute to the massed meaning in that zone, while the unique meaning of each term is to be found by contrasting it with its synonyms. This method was suggested by J. L. Austin.[14]

Schemata. There can be no doubt that working with concepts is more efficient than trying to deal with each and every entity in the work independently. But concept formation and concept analysis may be very hard work. Many students, confronting an assigned number of pages in a text, find themselves drained of energy as they attempt to grasp and understand the concepts that the author uses with such facility.

[11] *The Green Hills of Africa* (New York: Scribner, 1935), p. 138.
[12] John Dewey argues, in contrast, that "all particular propositions are relational," and propositions about the relationships among kinds are also relational – logically, if not verbally. See *Logic: The Theory of Inquiry* (New York: Holt, 1938), pp. 307–9.
[13] "The Formal Analysis of Concepts," in H. J. Klausmeier and C. W. Harris (eds.), *Analysis of Concept Learning* (New York: Academic Press, 1966), p. 3.
[14] *Philosophical Papers*, 3d ed. (New York: Oxford University Press, 1979), pp. 94–5.

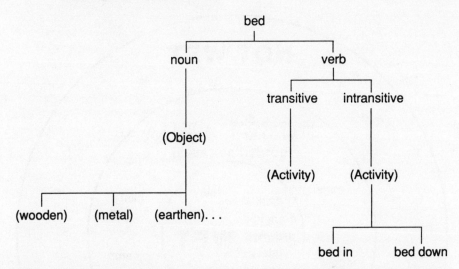

Figure 4 (adapted from Jerrold J. Katz and Jerry A. Fodor, "The Structure of a Semantic Theory," in Katz and Fodor [eds.], *The Structure of Language* [Englewood Cliffs, N.J.: Prentice-Hall, 1964], p. 485)

On the other hand, there are organizing systems that impart energy rather than soak it up. An example is the schema; an example of a schema is a narrative, such as a story. Narrative organization, in contrast to expository organization, tends to unfold as it is explored. As it unfolds, it gathers momentum and energy and transmits this to the reader. It is not simply the sequencing of information that makes this possible. It is made possible by the organic relationship that the parts have to one another and to the whole. This is in contrast to the jigsaw part–whole relationship found in a technical text. Additionally, the narrative form readily encompasses affective strands as well as cognitive ones, and this further intensifies the reader's interest and attentiveness.

Schemata are dynamic rather than static. They represent an active requiredness that urgently demands completion or equilibrium. A work of art in the process of being created exhibits this demand character; so does an organism when it resists or rejects what it finds alien to it and accepts what it can tolerate or find congenial. But whatever a schema (such as a story) incorporates is bound to affect and modify the whole of that schema.[15]

When we employ schemata in perceptions we tend to impose structure on what we observe. An example is the three-dimensional structure of space that we impose on the blur of perceptions with which we begin our postnatal experience of the world. This is what makes the three-dimensional renderings of space by artists

[15] See the discussion of schemata in Chapter 4 below. For an understanding of the organic nature of schemata, Paul Schilder, *Image and Appearance of the Human Body* (London: Routledge, 1935), is indispensable.

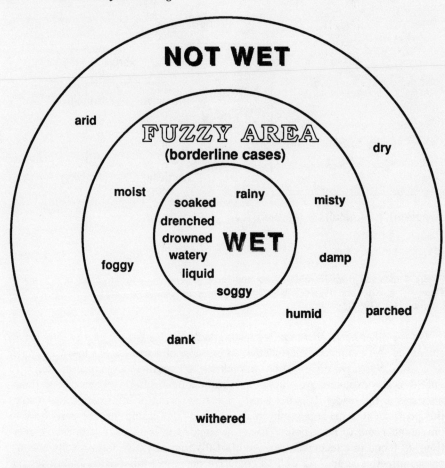

Figure 5 (from Matthew Lipman and Ann Margaret Sharp, *Wondering at the World* [Lanham, Md.: University Press of America, 1986], pp. 74–5)

intelligible to us. However, there are times when we impose schemata upon the world gratuitously, as when we impute to whole social groups characteristics common to only a few of their members. In cases of prejudice, which is what I am describing, it is difficult to correct the matter simply by direct communication or instruction, for the power of the schema to resist radical reconstruction is very great.[16]

Description and narration. These are not simply ways of organizing information; they are ways of organizing and expressing experiences. But at the same time

[16] For more on the role of schemata in contributing to ethnic stereotypes, see M. Rothbart, M. Evens, and S. Fulero, "Recall for Confirming Events: Memory Processes and the Maintenance of Social Stereotypes," *Journal of Experimental Social Psychology* 15 (1979), 343–55.

Characterizations

Inquiry is a self-corrective practice in which a subject matter is investigated with the aim of discovering or inventing ways of dealing with what is problematic. The products of inquiry are judgments.

Reasoning is the process of ordering and coordinating what has been found out through the inquiry. It involves finding valid ways of extending and organizing what has been discovered or invented while retaining its truth.

Concept formation involves organizing information into relational clusters and then analyzing and clarifying them so as to expedite their employment in understanding and judging. Conceptual thinking involves the relating of concepts to one another so as to form principles, criteria, arguments, explanations, and so on.

Translation involves carrying meanings over from one language or symbolic scheme or sense modality to another and yet retaining them intact. Interpretation becomes necessary when the translated meanings fail to make adequate sense in the new context in which they have been placed. *Thus, reasoning is truth-preservative, and translation is meaning-preservative.*

---

they are capable of organizing the informational content of such experiences, they are also modes of transmission.

Authors think in flights and perchings. There are details on which our thought rests long enough to permit a description. These details are perchings. Then there are flights of thought as we move from observation to observation or from idea to idea or from premises to conclusions. As we read what the author has written, our thought tends to recapitulate the flights and perchings of the author's thought. If the author's thought pauses to examine and describe something, we become absorbed in that description. If then the author's thought takes wing, ours may do the same, as when we breathlessly follow a narrative so closely that our thinking keeps pace precisely with the unfolding of the story.

Translation skills

We usually think of translation as a process in which what is said in one language is then said, without loss of meaning, in another. By "language" here is meant natural languages like Spanish and Chinese. But translation is not limited to transmission of meaning from one natural language to another. It can occur among different modes of expression, as when a composer attempts, by means of a tone poem, to tender literary meanings in musical form, or a painter tries to give a title to her work that will be true to the painterly content. No doubt all translation involves an element of interpretation; preservation of meaning is not always assigned the highest order of priority by those doing the translating. But the fact remains that translating skills enable us to shuttle back and forth *among* languages, and this may be no less important than discovering or constructing meanings *within* a given language.

One of the values of learning formal logic is that it requires the learning of rules for the standardization of everyday language so that the complexities of ordinary discourse can be reduced to the simplicities of logical language. This does considerable damage to meaning, but it demonstrates to students that natural language has an underlying musculature that makes possible such pushings and pullings as are involved in inference, causal expressions, and the like, and that natural language can be translated into this rudimentary but powerful logical language. Thus the rules of logical standardization form a paradigm of translation as well as a model that encourages students to carry their thinking proficiencies over from one discipline to the next.

In a pluralistic world composed of diverse communities, some of which overlap others or are nested within others, and each of which has commitments, some of which are local and particularized and others universal, it becomes more and more important to articulate and specify what precisely is being translated into what, what is being converted into what. It is impossible to have an ethics or politics of distribution unless we are clear about the values or meanings involved in the transactions with which we are concerned.

Economic terms like "exchange" and "distribution" have to be employed here, because thinking is a form of productivity, and this entails problems that extend far beyond questions of patents, copyrights, and permissions. For if thinking is a form of productivity, then communal deliberations can be seen as resulting in communal judgments, and a fresh appraisal is needed to determine our entitlements to public or private, shared or unshared values. All the more reason, then, to cultivate skills in the schools.

When thinking is understood as a kind of productivity, then translation can be understood as a form of exchange. When we translate from poetry into music, as a composer does in writing a tone poem, or from body language into ordinary language, we are exchanging and preserving meanings. Indeed, just as reasoning is that form of thinking that preserves *truth* through change, so translation is that form that preserves *meaning* through change.

Is teaching reasoning worthwhile?

Just a few years ago, the mammoth testing organizations were assuring us that reasoning could not be taught. This was a self-serving move. Significant portions of their tests involved reasoning, and if they could convince the schools that reasoning was unteachable, there would be no need to worry about the schools preparing students to do better on the tests by teaching them reasoning.

All that is now in the past. Today the testing organizations are clamoring to be allowed to teach teachers how to teach children thinking skills. Their approach does not inspire confidence; it is generally the mechanistic and atomistic approach deplored elsewhere in these pages.

One thing might be mentioned, however, as deserving of careful consideration. When the testing organizations are asked whether it would not be helpful to teach students reasoning, their answer is to cite the evidence they have obtained about testing for reasoning. This shows that there is a very high correlation between student performance on reasoning tests and reading comprehension tests – so high, in fact, that it threatens to cease being a fraction and approaches unity.

Now, a high correlation may not mean very much for practical classroom purposes. Vocabulary and I.Q. correlate highly, but no one suggests raising I.Q.s by teaching children vocabulary. The vocabulary performance is merely symptomatic of the intelligence level. The role of the latter is causal.

However, this situation may not be analogous with the correlation between reasoning and reading comprehension. We do not know that one of this pair is causal and the other symptomatic. For example, if reasoning and reading were *both* taught to students, might the results not be better than if reading alone were taught?

The fact is that we do know this to be the case,[17] but the testing organizations would rather it were not so because they feel threatened by it. Hence the bland dismissal of the teaching of reasoning on the ground that the results correlate highly with reading. The possibility that the teaching of reasoning could be highly worthwhile in and of itself jeopardizes the experience and expertise of all of those who now purport to be teaching reading, teaching reading teachers, testing for reading proficiency, and so on. It is indeed a sad situation, and one that many educators and psychologists seem determined to ignore. At the same time, it must be acknowledged that there are many educators and psychologists who have a very clear sense of the direction in which reform in education has got to go. What remains to be seen is whether these reformers will coalesce into a critical mass. For example, a prominent educator summarized pithily what he would tell the president if he were a consultant:

Research has discredited the idea that learning consists of the transmission of knowledge to students by teachers, texts, or computers. Instead of being viewed as consumers of information and skills, students should be seen as producers of knowledge and learning capabilities. (If students were thought of as producers of knowledge, teachers would be seen as

---

[17] Several dozen experiments have now been performed and reported with regard to Philosophy for Children, a program that incorporates the teaching of reasoning among its goals and objectives. Virtually all of these show significant improvement in reasoning. For example, in Dr. Virginia Shipman's 1978 experiment in Newark, N.J., the gains made by experimental students, as compared with students in control classes, were 80% greater in reasoning, 66% greater in reading, and 36% greater in mathematics proficiency. (See Lipman et al., *Philosophy in the Classroom*, pp. 217–24, for a description of the experiment.) For a summary of all experimental research to date on Philosophy for Children, see Supplements 1 and 2, "Philosophy for Children: Where We Are Now," *Thinking: The Journal of Philosophy for Children* 6:4 [1987], S1–S12; 7:4 [1988], S1–S20.

managers of learning experiences. Their job would involve more than maintaining discipline, providing students with interesting material, and efficiently directing them to the right answer. It would mean putting students into situations where they could learn to use knowledge they already have, to relate that old knowledge to new in systematic and reflective ways, to organize seemingly unconnected pieces of information, and to assess their conclusions before settling on them – even if the conclusions were correct.[18]

Additionally, says this educator, we have to think about applying current research to the reform of teaching and curricula. We would then see that the so-called basic and higher-order skills could be dealt with simultaneously rather than sequentially and that "higher-order skills are within the grasp of almost all children – at all ages. Problem-finding capabilities would be stressed even more than problem solving. Opportunities to learn with and from others would be emphasized. Also, curricula should emphasize "generative knowledge," ideas and theories that help students organize and learn other knowledge. Needless to say, these points corroborate many of claims made in this book.

[18] Willis D. Hawley, "Looking Backward at Education Reform," *Education Week*, November 1, 1989, pp. 32, 25.

3   The cornucopia of cognitive performance

Several years ago Ray Nickerson, speaking at an Association for Supervision and Curriculum Development conference, suggested that the appropriate way of expressing the relationship between creative and critical thinking was not so much to show them in cooperative opposition (like the halves of a pair of scissors or pliers) but as coordinates, so that any given proportion of critical and creative thinking could be mapped or diagrammed (see Fig. 6). Although this is very helpful, I do not mention it because I want to plot the various ways in which creative and critical thinking can be combined, useful as that might be. I mention it, rather, because it seems to me fairly uncontroversial that good thinking – what is likely to be referred to as higher-order thinking – is a combination of both components, the critical and the creative.

When I speak of higher-order thinking, I mean *excellent* thinking, because it seems to me that, to be helpful to teachers, we need to show how thinking is to be evaluated and not merely how it is to be classified. The approach that is generally accepted is that of Bloom: There is a pyramid or hierarchy of skills, at the apex of which are analysis, synthesis, and evaluation.[1] Now, if by "analysis" is meant critical thinking, if by "synthesis" is meant creative thinking, and if by "evaluation" is meant judgment, these might well be called the components of higher-order thinking.

Nevertheless, Bloom's approach suggests that there is a fixed hierarchy of skills, regardless of context. As a result, many researchers have taken a more context-specific approach. Here I have in mind in particular the work of Ennis,[2] Quellmalz,[3] and Resnick.[4] The reason a taxonomy of skills (or "strategies") cannot be hierarchical "in general" is that such hierarchies are meaningful only with respect to particular contexts. For example, it is important to distinguish (1) the

---

[1] Benjamin S. Bloom et al. (eds.), *Taxonomy of Educational Objectives,* vol. 1: *Cognitive Domain,* (New York: McKay, 1956).

[2] Robert H. Ennis, "A Taxonomy of Critical Thinking Dispositions and Abilities," in Joan Boykoff Baron and Robert J. Sternberg (eds.), *Teaching Thinking Skills: Theory and Practice* (New York: Freeman, 1987), pp. 9–26.

[3] Edys S. Quellmalz, "Developing Reasoning Skills," in ibid., pp. 86–105.

[4] Lauren B. Resnick, *Education and Learning to Think* (Washington, D.C.: National Academy Press, 1987), p. 46.

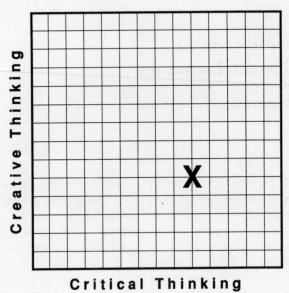

Figure 6

order in which skills are to be presented in a cognitive curriculum from (2) an evaluational ranking of such skills and both of these from (3) a "natural" or "stage" sequence of such skills. In constructing a curriculum, which is of necessity sequential, we have to present the skills in a certain order, and this order has to be arrived at logically.

A curriculum developer tries to begin with primitive skills, move on to skills that build upon primitive skills, and proceed to skills that build upon skills that build upon primitive skills. This results in a sequence that starts with primary or foundational skills like comparing, distinguishing, and connecting (which are called lower-order simply because they come first). It moves on perhaps to classification, seriation, analogical reasoning, and immediate inference (called middle-order because they build on the first order), and then arrives at, say, syllogistic reasoning and the use of criteria (called higher-order because they build largely on the second order).

Now, as I have said, this curricular sequence is not to be confused with the values we set on the skills in a particular context. In a particular moment of medical research, what may be of paramount value involves a comparison of the similarities and differences resulting from the use of two serums; what is of the lowest curricular order (comparing) is then found to have the highest functional value. Nor is this uncommon. As in sports, skills are powers, and the skill that decides the game in one instance may be virtually absent in the next.

I have been arguing for a contextual, nonhierarchical approach to excellence in thinking. As I see it, no cognitive skill is, in itself, better than others, just as words are, by themselves, neither right nor wrong. In both instances it is the context that determines what should be considered better and what should be considered worse.

At the same time it must be acknowledged that many of the terms used by Bloom to identify what he calls educational objectives come out of the vocabulary of educational psychology and bear a rough correspondence to philosophical usage. Thus, as I have already pointed out, "analytic" and "synthetic" are analogous to critical and creative aspects. of higher-order thinking. It may also be the case that "evaluation" is understood to be similar to judgment and that "comprehension" is much the same as what has traditionally been called understanding. Mention of these similarities may help readers translate from one vocabulary to another, but it is not intended to suggest that the hierarchical and the nonhierarchical approaches are equivalent.

It is also possible to claim that individual aspects of higher-order thinking, such as the critical or the creative, display gradations of better and worse. For example, Richard Paul distinguishes between "strong sense" (or good) critical thinking and "weak sense" (bad) critical thinking.[5] Critical thinking in the strong sense, according to Paul, involves the thinkers in discovering and rejecting their own prejudices and self-deceptions. In the weak sense, it involves nothing more than the technical perfecting of isolated cognitive skills. This characterization, that critical thinking is good when it is self-correcting but bad when it is self-serving, can be built into its definition, as will be discussed.

Thinking as internalized communication

Since we are concerned with education for higher-order thinking, it is obviously of great importance that we fashion curricula and pedagogies that educate for judgment. We can best do so if we make use of those elements of educational theory that have proven most sound in practice. I am thinking here of such notions as that an individual's thinking is to a considerable extent an *internalization* of what has been going on in the group or groups in which that individual participates. This movement from the social to the individual is exemplified in the child's acquisition of the parent's language and in the child's appropriation of the meanings of the culture into which he or she has been born. We must begin, therefore, with considering thinking as a social fact and with asking ourselves what sort of a social fact it is. This in turn should help us arrive at a better understanding of how to strengthen the kinds of teaching that will strengthen student thinking.

For George Herbert Mead, social communication occurs when a group shares similar meanings, and this occurs, prototypically, when the attitude I assume toward the gesture I make toward you is the same as the attitude you assume in

---

[5] "Some Vocabulary and Distinctions," in "31 Principles of Critical Thinking," unpublished (Sonoma State University). See also Debbie Walsh and Richard Paul, *The Goal of Critical Thinking: From Educational Ideal to Educational Reality* (American Federation of Teachers, n.d.).

response to my gesture.[6] Take an example: You are attempting to feed an infant, and so you offer her a spoonful of food. She opens her mouth, and in the same moment so do you. You respond to your ongoing gesture in the same way she responds to it; the meaning of the gesture is shared between you. Social communication has occurred, and a community has been created.

As children grow up, they internalize – replicate in their own thinking – the processes of communication they discover in their families. If the classroom is to retain continuity with the home, it must to some extent replicate the communicative community that the home represents for the child. If the classroom is to go beyond that continuity, it must give special support to the child's disposition to inquire by becoming not merely a community of communication but also a community of inquiry. Here are how some of the characteristic behaviors of the community of inquiry look when they are internalized by individual members:

Characteristic behaviors of the community	*Internalized individual behaviors*
Members question one another	Individuals question themselves
Members request of each other reasons for beliefs	Individuals reflect on their reasons for thinking as they do
Members build on one another's ideas	Individuals build on their own ideas
Members deliberate among themselves	Individuals deliberate in their own thinking
Members offer counterexamples to the hypotheses of others	Individuals anticipate counterexamples to their own hypotheses
Members point out possible consequences of one another's ideas	Individuals anticipate possible consequences of their own ideas
Members utilize specific criteria when making judgments	Individuals use specific criteria when making judgments
Members cooperate in the development of rational problem-solving techniques	Individuals follow rational procedures in dealing with their own problems

And so with countless other cognitive acts and processes: They begin in each of us as adaptations of group behaviors. And since thinking is individual emulation of social norms and social conduct, the more rational the social or institutional conduct, the more rational will be the internalized reflection. A community that has institutionalized patterns of criticism among its members prepares the way for those members to become more self-critical, self-controlled, and autonomous.

It should be added that the notion of autonomy is a thorny one and should be approached with great caution.[7] Obviously, it is connected with such attractive

---

[6] *Mind, Self and Society* (Chicago: University of Chicago Press, 1934), pp. 135–40, 150–60.

[7] For a careful consideration of the concept of autonomy, see R. F. Dearden, "Autonomy as an Educational Ideal," in S. C. Brown (ed.), *Philosophers Discuss Education* (Totowa, N.J.: Rowman and Littlefield, 1975), pp. 3–18. "To be autonomous," says Dearden, "is very much a matter of degree.

concepts as self-government, self-regulation, and self-correction, but there is always the danger that autonomous individuals or groups will think themselves totally self-contained and will proceed to ignore all outside influences. This becomes autonomy with a vengeance; it culminates in our believing in the myth of our own infallibility. Thus a nation that thought of itself as autonomous would proceed to ignore criticisms from its peers in other parts of the world because it would be confident that it need listen only to its internal critics, if it listens to any.

Some social interpretations of critical thinking

One theorist of critical thinking, Connie Missimer, has argued that the prevailing view of critical thinking too readily takes for granted the criteria of the autonomous "Individual View" and rejects the criteria of the "Social View."[8] True, there are some criteria they have in common. Both involve a search for reasoned judgment, where the judgment is relevant to and does not contradict the evidence on which it rests. And both assume the existence of objective knowledge. But here the agreement ends.

The individual view, Missimer says, conceives of critical thinking as logically sound, unbiased, impartial thinking, the product of a fair-minded person. The individual, discrete act of critical thinking can therefore be judged in ahistorical isolation. The social view, on the other hand, refuses to consider acts of critical thinking in isolation from the historical context in which they occur. Critical thinking is not just the construction of the perfect argument; it is thinking that takes the range of alternatives into account and compares their evidence. The social view is longitudinal, seeing each argument presented in time as a feature of the historically emerging consciousness of humanity.

The individual view, Missimer argues, likes to see itself characterized by such words as "appropriate" and "reasonable" (as in Harvey Siegel's definition of critical thinking as thinking that is "appropriately moved by reasons"[9] or in Robert Ennis's definition: "reasonable reflective thinking concerning what to believe or do").[10] Such definitions are circular, she observes; they rest on the assumption

Unlike being six feet tall, married, or a British citizen, whether a man is quite simply autonomous or not is something which we will often quite rightly refuse to say. And our hesitation will be related to at least three dimensions of variability: the extent to which he shows initiative in forming judgments of his own, the firmness with which he then adheres to those judgments, and the depth of ramifying reflection which lies behind the criteria which he employs in making those judgments" (pp. 9–10). Obviously this is quite similar to my contention that thinking is higher-order to the degree to which it involves sound judgment. For a later article in which Dearden describes autonomy as the ability to make independent judgments and to reflect critically on those judgments, see his "Autonomy and Intellectual Education," *Early Child Development and Care* 12:3/4 (1983), 211–28.

[8] "Why Two Heads Are Better Than One: Philosophical and Pedagogical Implications of a Social View of Critical Thinking,"*Proceedings of the Philosophy of Education Society,* 1988, pp. 388–402.

[9] *Educating Reason* (London: Routledge, 1988), p. 41.

[10] "A Taxonomy," p. 10.

that reasonableness involves logicality, but logicality alone is insufficient to produce impartiality. In the course of the ongoing conversation of human beings with one another, many contrasting or conflicting arguments are thrown into the pot, and few of these are logically consistent with one another. Yet they are all parts of a larger whole, according to Missimer, and so coherence rather than consistency may have to be our foundational criterion. "The Social View, therefore deliberately eschews the requirement of reasonableness or appropriateness at each step of the way. Maverick ideas count as good critical thinking, so long as they are supported by reasons and placed in association with related arguments so we can judge the adequacy of their evidence." [11] Missimer concludes that the individual and the social views of critical thinking are incompatible. The social view encourages the judgment of adequacy in the light of alternative arguments; the individual view does not. The social view can declare a piece of critical thinking good even though considering its assumptions incorrect or its conclusion unjustified. Unlike the individual view, the social view involves "stereoscopic" thinking. Since many perspectives are better than one as far as the obtaining of genuine knowledge is concerned, the stereoscopic view is, Missimer insists, the superior one.

Missimer's analysis is a useful corrective to the frequently encountered conception of critical thinking as the Quest for the Perfect Argument. We are, after all, a deliberating community – what Karl Popper has called an "open society" [12] – and it is unlikely that there is any point of view so favored and so privileged as to provide, all by itself, an Authoritative Perspective, a "God's eye" view that would shelter a Perfect Argument. We are left with the view, previously alluded to, that objectivity is multifaceted, with each perspective serving to corroborate or supplement or negate what is revealed from this or that other perspective. The social view of critical thinking advanced by Missimer does not erase the individual view, but instead compels us to recognize a larger panorama of perspectives.

Another version of the social view of critical thinking – one quite different from Missimer's – is that of Fred M. Newmann. What we call critical thinking, Newmann contends, is simply one version of higher-order thinking. [13] Where lower-order thinking is mechanical, routine, and constrained, higher-order thinking is expansive; it is a response to challenge, and it constitutes a challenge to others. "Higher-order thinking requires special mental effort: the resolution of conflicting views, tolerance for uncertainty and ambiguity, self-criticism, independence of judgment (rather than dependence upon authorities), serious consideration of ideas that may challenge conventional wisdom or doctrine" (p. 63). To achieve these results, Newmann urges that we adopt a pedagogy that helps chil-

[11] "Why Two Heads Are Better Than One," p. 392.
[12] *The Open Society and Its Enemies*, 2 vols. (Princeton, N.J.: Princeton University Press, 1962).
[13] "Higher Order Thinking in the High School Curriculum," *NASSP Bulletin*, May 1988, pp. 58–64. (See also "Higher Order Thinking in the Teaching of Social Studies: Connections between Theory and Practice," in James F. Voss, David N. Perkins, and Judith W. Segal [eds.], *Informal Reasoning and Education* [Hillsdale, N.J.: Erlbaum, 1990]).

dren to become less passive; such a pedagogy should become an official criterion for formal teacher evaluation.

To fight student passivity and stimulate students to engage in higher-order thinking, Newmann urges a reduction in the number of topics and subjects they must learn. This means that tests requiring survey knowledge would be given a relatively low priority in school testing, new instructional materials would be available to replace survey-type texts and tests, and the connections between courses would be stronger, since "taking a host of unrelated courses only accentuates the tendency toward superficial coverage" (p. 63). What links Newmann's conception of higher-order thinking with the social view of critical thinking is his advocacy of a "schoolwide culture of thoughtfulness." This of course echoes a view that Seymour Sarason was courageously pushing in the early 1970s – that thinking is not something that happens only in class. [14] As Newmann puts it, "Principals must find ways to reward students and staff . . . for showing that they have used their minds well in both official and unofficial tasks" if a schoolwide climate of thoughtfulness is to be developed (p. 64).

It should be noted that for both Missimer and Newmann, critical or higher-order thinking is to be identified only in relation to its particular, concrete setting. To Missimer, this setting is historical, so that what would be considered a case of critical thinking in one historical setting might not be in another. To Newmann, the setting is more likely to be the personal history of the individual thinker, so that, for one person, "trying to understand and follow a bus schedule may require higher-order thought, but for another, the same task will be routine" (p. 60).

Missimer and Newmann are both attempting to broaden the notion of critical thinking by insisting that it always be located in its setting. Their formulations differ, however, in a way that is reminiscent of Karl Mannheim's distinction between relativism and relationism. [15] For Mannheim, relativism is "a product of the modern historical-sociological procedure which is based on the recognition that all historical thinking is bound up with the concrete position in life of the thinker." Relationism, on the other hand, is an alternative solution to the problem of what constitutes reliable thinking. Both relativism and relationism constitute rejections of absolutism, but relationism connects each particular act of thinking now with the life situation of the thinker, as relativism does, but with the historical position of the thinker, just as all spatial observation must take into account the spatial position of the observer. All spatial and temporal acts are therefore to be understood relationally when they open out into the wider context of a universe that can be viewed from an infinite number of standpoints and where there is no single fixed, authoritative standpoint. They are to be understood relatively when they are understood in the light of the personal history and life situation of the

---

[14] Cf. Seymour B. Sarason, *The Culture of the School and the Problem of Change* (Boston: Allyn and Bacon, 1971), and equally his *Schooling in America: Scapegoat and Salvation* (New York: Free Press, 1983).

[15] *Ideology and Utopia: An Introduction to the Sociology of Knowledge* (New York: Harcourt Brace, 1936), pp. 78–83.

actor. In the light of Mannheim's distinction, Missimer's account of critical thinking is relational, whereas Newmann's is relativistic. Yet both should be understood as attempting to broaden the notion of critical thinking and make it more flexible and accountable.

Combating absolutistic thinking: relativism or relationism?

It is thanks to the cosmopolitan thinking of the bourgeoisie, says Karl Marx, that we have been rescued from the "idiocy of rural life." Presumably, this remark is intended not as a slur on the intelligence of farmers but as an attempt to show that the more local and provincial our outlook is, the more likely we are to consider it universally true and absolute. Both relativism and relationism, in the sense in which Mannheim uses these terms, are attempts to overcome the narrowness and rigidity of absolutistic thinking. One strategy for doing so is the delocalization of thinking, making it multiperspectival instead of having it emanate from a single point of view. Another strategy is to reduce or eliminate reliance upon ideologies, those great masses of predigested thought that are the popular substitutes for thinking for oneself. I shall take Richard Paul's writing as a prototype of the first strategy and Mannheim's work as a prototype of the second.

Paul distinguishes between "monological thinking" – thinking that is conducted exclusively from one point of view or within one frame of reference – and "multilogical thinking" – thinking that goes beyond the single frame of reference or point of view.[16] Monological problems are those that we can solve by restricting ourselves to a single frame of reference. Many technical problems are of this sort. Multilogical problems require more than a single point of view: They require dialogical thinking that represents an exchange between different points of view. When dialogical thinking is conducted in order to test the strengths and weaknesses of opposing points of view, Paul calls it dialectical thinking.

To Paul, critical thinkers "in the weak sense" are those who do not hold themselves to the same intellectual standards to which they hold opponents, who tend to think monologically, who fail to empathize with other points of view, and who use the intellectual skills of critical thinking selectively and self-deceptively to foster and serve their vested interests (at the expense of truth). In contrast, critical thinkers "in the strong sense" are those who hold themselves and those they agree with to the same intellectual standards to which they hold those they disagree with, who are capable of seeing truth in their opponents' points of view, who are able to think multilogically and dialogically, who are able to detect their own self-deceptive reasoning, and who endeavor to live in accordance with the critical tenets of their own thinking. Critical thinking is thus, for Paul, an ongoing fight against dogmatism, narrow-mindedness, and intellectual manipulation, and a critical society is one that abstains from indoctrination and rewards reflective questioning, intellectual independence, and reasoned dissent.

[16] "Some Vocabulary and Distinctions."

It is clear that Paul conceives of critical thinking as the primary weapon of the forces of enlightenment in their struggle with the forces of darkness, and he is particularly effective at needling those whose critical thinking is tepid but who nevertheless conceive of themselves as daring and provocative. He recognizes that human beings generally have a boundless capacity for self-deception and are biased in favor of their own point of view as they are prejudiced against the perspectives of others. (This is not to deny that there are many cases of reverse bias, where we condemn our own perspective and uncritically accept that of others.)

Paul's outlook is therefore one that accepts the need for conflict. He envisages the world as the scene of innumerable intellectual struggles, in which bigotry, intolerance, and indoctrination do battle against rationality, autonomy, and empathy. But if Paul wants us to throw ourselves into the fray, Mannheim wants us first to understand it. In his analysis of ideological thinking, Mannheim is attempting to dissect uncritical reflection and at the same time to lay bare the different levels of our understanding of such thinking. Mannheim sees the peoples of the world as locked in a variety of conceptual rivalries, of which the most formidable is ideological warfare. Like Freud, Mannheim would like us to purge ourselves of our self-serving rationalizations and confront ourselves as we really are. The index of our success in such a venture is the degree to which we can penetrate to the profounder levels of the conception of ideology itself as we move toward a thoroughly disenchanted, undistorted mode of understanding, one that Mannheim identifies with "the sociology of knowledge."[17]

The first step we take in this effort to raise our consciousness with regard to the nature of ideological thinking is, according to Mannheim, to understand our opponent's thinking in psychological terms – that is, in relation to the opponent's biography and needs and life situation. We are then able to see through our opponent's conscious lies and unwitting distortions, calculated attempts to dupe others, and unconscious self-deceptions. We discover how this ideological screen keeps the opponent even from recognizing his or her real interests.

The second step we take, says Mannheim, is to see our opponent as part of a group or society, so that the opponent's thinking is seen as simply a particular expression of that society's characteristic way of thinking. Once again, we move to understand the society's thinking in terms of its particular history and in terms of its unique needs and interests. Our understanding is now more broadly based, but it is still *relative* to the particular background of the society whose thinking we are analyzing.

Our third step is to dispense with the social-psychological diagnosis by which we seek to explain a society's ideology in terms of its particular needs and interest. Instead, we begin to formulate correspondences between given social structures and particular ideological patterns. We are no longer concerned to perceive

---

[17] *Ideology and Utopia*, pp. 55–77.

these correspondences as lies or distortions, whether conscious or unconscious, since we see each pattern of ideological or uncritical thinking as a necessary manifestation of a particular type of social organization under particular historical conditions.

The fourth and final step is one we take when we have the courage to subject not just our adversary's point of view to this kind of ideological analysis, but our own as well. It is only when we have gone through these four stages of ideological penetration that we can hope to arrive at a genuinely critical and objective assessment of the nature of thinking. Only this demystified reflection, in which all motives are unmasked and bared, can be truly critical. It is in this sense that Mannheim and Paul agree on the nature of critical thinking: It is thinking from which all bias, egocentricity, and self-deception have been eliminated. It is thanks to this kind of analysis that the regulative idea of rationality takes on new and fresh significance as one of the guiding ideals of education.

Algorithmic versus heuristic thinking

Those who concern themselves with the theory of thinking often make a distinction between thinking that is *algorithmic* and thinking that is *heuristic*. The touchstone of the first is method and of the second, results. An algorithm provides a track or procedure along which our thinking can move. An example is formal logic. Logical thinking is thinking that is methodologically faultless. This systematic correctness logicians identify as validity. The logical thinker infers conclusions from premises or perhaps supplies a premise to an argument when one is missing. The person who starts from true premises and thinks logically will necessarily arrive at true conclusions. And so the method is one by which we can trace out the implications of what we know while preserving its truth.

On the other hand, the heuristic approach is not fastidious about methods; it focuses on results. It would appear that this is what Edward de Bono has in mind when he distinguishes "vertical" from "lateral" thinking.[18] Vertical thinking is mechanical, unimaginative, and uncreative. Lateral thinking is successful, productive, creative thinking. De Bono tells a little story that provides a revealing look at his approach. A boy who is considered the village idiot, when offered his choice between two coins, always chooses the bigger rather than the more valuable one. As the boy explains to a sympathetic visitor, if he were always to select the more valuable coin, people would stop giving him the choice. As we see, the boy is concerned solely with results – in this case, making a bit of small change. If this requires a wily deception on his part, so be it.

Let me hasten to add that the heuristic approach does not require deception, wily or otherwise. Any means that produce the sought-for consequences are acceptable. There are no criteria here to require that the means be consistent, ethically or aesthetically, with the ends. There are two readily apparent dangers when we concentrate on results and are indifferent to means. The first is that we find

---

[18] "Critical Thinking Is Not Enough," *Educational Leadership* 42:1 (September 1984), 16–17.

ourselves in the position of asserting that the end justifies the means, which is a position of slippery expediency. The other danger is that heuristic thinking too often provides the consequences we want along with additional consequences we don't want. If we kill off the rats by means of the rat poison we spread about the house, and in the process kill off the cat, too, can what we have achieved really be called success?

Critics of heuristic thinking concede that it is hospitable to creativity but vulnerable to amoralism. It represents for them the triumph of the aesthetic over the ethical. Or else they see it as an illegitimate effort to transfer what may work in a large corporation to the elementary school classroom. The emphasis on success does not sit well with their feeling that children should be taught principled rather than unprincipled thinking, that they be other-regarding as well as self-regarding creatures, that they have a sense of proportion with regard to the difference between long-range goals and immediate gratification. They wonder if the kinds of criteria that prevail at the board meetings that de Bono typically cites are the same criteria we should teach children in the elementary school. Are we, then, forced to choose between the heuristic approach to thinking, creative but unprincipled, and the algorithmic approach, principled to be sure, but with a rigor that at times approaches rigor mortis? We might give three answers.

The first is that the pictures I have presented of the two approaches are one-sided caricatures. When combined, when the emphasis is on means as well as on ends, on methods *and* consequences, the kind of thinking one gets is quite unobjectionable. I think this reply is all right as far as it goes, but it doesn't go very far, and it surely provides us with little basis for distinguishing between ordinary and higher-order thinking.

A second response would be to retain the portrayal of algorithmic and heuristic thinking as extremes and to try to discover between them a more wholesome and constructive middle path. This is what I perceive Eugene Garver to be doing in his study of the thought of Machiavelli. Garver would like to show that *prudential* thinking falls between algorithmic and heuristic thinking. He is aware, however, that it is often difficult to distinguish between thinking that is prudential and thinking that is merely clever and self-interested. He is aware also that the prudential thinker, attempting to be always in tune with the prevailing circumstances, has no more character than a chameleon has color. "In both rhetoric and practical efficacy," he remarks, "success seems to be bought at the price of losing one's self."[19] Socrates, who is never in tune with the times, has ample character, while the Machiavellian prince, whose character is always in tune with the times, has no character at all. To Garver, then, "the problem of good practical conduct, as opposed, especially, to good artistic performance and good theoretical understanding, is to see how constancy of character can be consistent with the adaptability to circumstances it sometimes seems to require."[20] While I can understand

---

[19] *Machiavelli and the History of Prudence* (Madison: University of Wisconsin Press, 1987), p. 7.
[20] Ibid.

Garver's contention that prudent people of good character are likely to abstain from the more noxious versions of algorithmic or heuristic thinking, his reliance upon the notion of prudence seems to me questionable. Prudence is too frequently associated with cautious self-interest for it to be very useful in coming to grips with the nature of higher-order thinking in education.

It seems to me that instead of directing most of our efforts toward the development of algorithms and heuristics, useful as this may be, we would do better to concentrate on the improvement of reasoning and judgment. The improvement of reasoning involves persistent practice in distinguishing logical from illogical discourse, the acquisition of logical principles, and learning how to apply such principles to actual practice in academic matters and in life generally. The improvement of judgment involves getting students to make and to evaluate judgments of practice in a never-ending continuum of judgment, so that the judgments made gradually become more and more reliable and enlightening.

The reason courses in elementary school philosophy have traditionally been thought to be extraneous or superfluous is that reasoning and judgment have not been considered to be important educational goals. The moment their importance is recognized, the indispensability of philosophy leaps into prominence. Philosophy is not very relevant to a situation in which being a teacher is a matter of knowing the right questions to ask and being a student is a matter of knowing the right answers to give in reply. But once the fact is faced squarely that this method does little to improve reasoning and judgment, which are actually of cardinal importance to education, and once the fact is faced that a process that does not produce reasonable and judicious persons does not deserve to call itself educational, we are much closer to acknowledging that only the steady and continuous practice of philosophy, added to the school curriculum from kindergarten on up, is likely to satisfy these requirements.

Good judgment is a microcosm of higher-order thinking. Indeed, we sometimes speak of it as "balanced judgment," meaning that it has that desirable combination of the critical and creative to be found in all excellent cognitive processing. But we need to examine judgment more closely.

Relationships: the bearings of judgment

Judgments are judgments of relationships. If there were such a thing as a completely isolated point, one which had no connection with anything else, no context, and no internal character, we would be unable to make any judgments about it. Relationships provide judgments with their bearings and orientation as well as, ultimately, their meaning. We judge by comparing things with one another or with ideal standards. Every comparison involves a discernment of similarities and differences, and each such discernment is a judgment.

To say that all judgments are of relationships or connections does not mean that judgments can do no more than reveal connections. They may reveal them, or they may create them. Some judgments detect a difference; some make a difference. Some detect a similarity that already exists; others shape a resemblance where none had existed.

To say that all judgments are of relationships, and only of relationships, is to contrast them with other aspects of mental life. Consciousness, for example, must always be about something and can be about anything. But judgments fix upon relationships with the same necessity that arcs subtend angles.

In view of the one-to-one correlation of relationships and judgments, a taxonomy of relationships might be an efficient way to devise a classification of judgments – something that would be invaluable for curriculum development in the cognitive aspects of education. For if it is indeed the case that all mental activities involve judgment and that whether thinking is of a higher or lower order depends upon the degree of judgment involved, then it evidently follows that, if we wish to develop curricula that will strengthen higher-order thinking, we must have judgment-strengthening opportunities (and exercises) at every step of the way. The only way children will learn to make better judgments is by being encouraged to make judgments frequently, to compare them, and to discover the criteria by means of which the better are to be distinguished from the worse.

Thus, there is no grade level, in a K–12 curriculum, at which it would be improper to ask children to provide "good reasons" for their stated opinions or to discuss what they may be assuming to be the case when they draw a particular inference or to assess the relationships between parts and wholes or means and ends. Judgment is bound to be involved at every educational level, whether we approach matters descriptively, as in classification ("What sort of thing is this?"), or normatively, as in evaluation ("Is it a good example of this kind of thing?"). Every time we have recourse to an algorithm, we have to make a judgment as to whether it is the appropriate algorithm to use, whether we are employing it properly, and so on. For example, we may know how to reason syllogistically, but we still have to make judgments about the truth of the premises, and we still have to make judgments about the relevance of such abstract reasoning to natural-language situations or contexts. The construction of a satisfactory geometrical proof requires judgment, just as the construction of a satisfying English sentence does. By examining such a sentence in terms of the judgments that went into its composition – judgments of syntax, of style, of contextual relevance, of word choice and word order – we can determine the level of thinking it expresses.

There are, of course, three general kinds of relationships that a curriculum must incorporate: symbolic relationships (e.g., linguistic, logical, and mathematical relationships), referential relationships (i.e., those between symbolic terms or systems and the world they refer to), and existential relationships (i.e., connections among things in the world).[21] To fail to introduce children to these three kinds of relationships is to consign them to a concreteness of mental life that they

---

[21] Gregory Bateson's insistence that the judgment of difference is essential to mental functioning is not unreasonable:

may never transcend and that is bound to handicap them terribly when they attempt to move in the direction of higher education.[22] After all, the more we enter into a discipline, the more we find it to involve conceptual schemes that are essentially relational, consisting of historical relations, linguistic relations, causal relations, stylistic relations, social relations, and the like. The more relational the curriculum, the more coping with it demands higher-order thinking.[23]

We may conceive of education as instilling knowledge, where by "knowledge" we mean retention by the child of some set of learned contents, and so E. D. Hirsch and others draw up their lists of what every culturally literate person should know. These disconnected bits of information may or may not be typical of what an educated person should know, but being educated is hardly just a matter of possessing knowledge. Education should provide meaning, and if it fails to do so, it is an overall failure.

But what are meanings? Surely they are connections, relationships. What is unconnected is irrelevant, as a disconnected electrical appliance is a useless appliance. To compel children to memorize mere content is to deprive them of opportunities to discern relationships and form judgments; it is to make their school experience meaningless. On the other hand, to provide such opportunities is to encourage them to think for themselves, make judgments, and engage in higher-order thinking.

The pedagogy of judgment

In his discussion of intellectual strengths, or virtues, Aristotle remarks: "What is called judgment . . . is the right discrimination of the equitable. . . . Sympathetic judgment is judgment which discriminates what is equitable and does so correctly; and correct judgment is that which judges what is true."[24] So judgment is needed to distinguish the equitable from the inequitable and the false from the true. But judgment itself rests on sound understanding, and the way to arrive at sound understanding is through deliberation. (It should be added that, for Aristotle, "un-

In fact, wherever *information* – or *comparison* – is of the essence of our explanation, *there*, for me, is mental process. Information can be defined as a *difference that makes a difference*. A sensory end organ is a comparator, a device which responds to difference. Of course, the sensory end organ is material, but it is this *responsiveness to difference* that we shall use to distinguish its functioning as "mental."

This is quoted from Gregory Bateson and Mary Catherine Bateson, *Angels Fear: Towards an Epistemology of the Sacred* (New York: Macmillan, 1987), p. 17. The notion that every difference makes a difference is of course a cardinal tenet of pragmatism – particularly the pragmatism of William James, whose *Principles of Psychology* examines the relationships of resemblance and difference in rich detail. It is worth adding that, in the eighteenth century, differences alone were detected by judgment; similarities were detected by *wit*. (Cf., for example, the impressive *Practical Education* of Maria and Richard Edgeworth [1st American ed., New York: Hopkins, 1801].)

[22] Cf. John Dewey, *Logic: The Theory of Inquiry* (New York: Holt, 1938), pp. 400–4.

[23] See A. Leon Pines, "Toward a Taxonomy of Conceptual Relations and the Implications for the Evaluation of Cognitive Structures," in Leon H. T. West and A. Leon Pines (eds.), *Cognitive Structure and Conceptual Change* (New York: Academic Press, 1985), pp. 101–29.

[24] *Nichomachean Ethics* VI. 10, 11, in Richard McKeon (ed.), *The Basic Works of Aristotle* (New York: Random House, 1941), pp. 1031–3.

derstanding only judges''; it is "practical wisdom" that issues commands.[25] And both understanding and practical wisdom are sharpened by deliberation. Deliberation is inquiry that has not yet reached the stage of assertion; it is correctness of thinking, and it involves reasoning.) It does not seem to be far-fetched to say that, according to Aristotle, if we want students to exercise good judgment, we should strengthen their understanding, and if we want them to understand, we should encourage them to deliberate. Aristotle recognizes that, in the main, human experience is too complex and incoherent to allow us to make exact judgments. We must extrapolate, make approximations, compromise on the expedient and appropriate rather than on what is theoretically right, and make judgments even when we are uncertain. It is through deliberation, then, that we learn to become reasonable and judicious. And if Aristotle is right, it is deliberation that we must install in our classrooms if we want to encourage higher-order thinking.

Deliberating on issues in preparation for the making of judgments is something done by groups as well as by individuals. By fostering deliberation in the classroom, we provide opportunities for the members of the class to internalize the process and to deliberate individually rather than collaboratively.

The pedagogy of judgment requires that adequate attention be paid to *procedures,* as in any other practical field. Health care, for example, insists upon proper medical procedures; the preparation of nurses involves their learning how to take patients' temperatures, draw blood, and perform many other seemingly routine but nonetheless highly important activities. Likewise, the strengthening of students' judgment involves practice in a wide variety of procedures, some of which can be quite crucial. Take the following:

1. *Prejudice reduction.* Students need to be given practice in avoiding the making of premature judgments, in identifying circumstances in which the temporary suspension of judgment is called for, and in taking a non-judgmental stance when this is appropriate. Exercises should be performed that force stereotypical assumptions to the surface. This can be done by having students consider deductive inferences such as "He's British; he must be reserved" or "He's reserved; he must be British" and having them identify the underlying presuppositions.

2. *Classification.* Here, exercises may be employed that move from clear-cut cases to fuzzy cases. Students need continual practice in grouping, classifying, and categorizing. The sortings need to be not only of physical things but also of activities, mental acts, abstract concepts – anything that will give them practical experience in making judgments of inclusion and exclusion.

3. *Evaluation.* Students need to be introduced first to evaluative practices in various trades and crafts so as to familiarize them with the grounds

---

[25] Ibid., 10 (McKeon, p. 1031). Cf. E. A. Peel, *The Nature of Adolescent Judgment* (New York: Wiley-Interscience, 1971), p. 18: "Understanding is not enough. The ultimate measure of education is its power to bring about more effective thinking and action. . . . Usually we face possible alternatives, as in making personal or political judgments, none of which is unambiguously better than others. We need judgment and also the readiness to act on that judgment."

of ranking as a practical activity, as for example the rankings done by apple growers, meat processors, and dairy workers. Consideration should also be given to grading and ranking in sports, in the arts, and in education.

4. *Criterion identification.* Ample practice must be provided in working with reasons so students understand the role they play in justifying whatever is made, said, or done. Criteria can then be identified as governing or decisive considerations in any attempt to justify a classification or an evaluation.

5. *Sensitization to context.* Students should be given ample opportunity to distinguish among contexts that are largely similar but contain slight but significant differences.

6. *Analogical reasoning.* This involves the converse of sensitization to context, in that it calls for practice in identifying features that are quite similar in contexts that are conspicuously different. It also calls for practice in relational reasoning based upon these resemblances.

7. *Self-correction.* Individuals and groups seeking to strengthen their judgment making should practice questioning others and themselves, offering counterexamples and counterarguments and looking for disconfirming evidences or testimonies. They should recognize the potential value of dissent in the community as a possible basis for correction of errors as well as the value of falsification as a method of identifying vacuous truths.

8. *Sensitization to consequences.* All students, and not just those who tend to be impulsive or tactless, should be given practice in anticipating the possible consequences of what they propose to do. They should be assisted in learning to what extent the meaning of what they do will be made up of the consequences of those actions.

9. *Adjusting means and ends.* To some, this involves the whole of rationality; in any event, it is surely one important strand. But practice is needed not only in adjusting means and ends to one another but in seeing each as flexible, as means-in-view and as ends-in-view, rather than as fixed.

10. *Adjusting parts and wholes.* If adjusting means and ends emphasizes the value of consistency, adjusting parts and wholes emphasizes the value of coherence. Practice in each comes from dealing with such questions as "What sort of world do I want to live in?" and "What sort of person do I want to be?"

Some educational requirements

At this point I want to summarize some of the points I have been trying to make and some of the points I now want to begin to make:

(1) I take it that in a democratic society there is a maximum premium on the cultivation of reasonableness. The goal of education should therefore be the development of reasonable individuals.

(2) Reasonableness certainly does not exclude cultural literacy, but neither does it specify such literacy in terms of a particular set of contents. We are rapidly moving toward a multicultural world. To the extent that any one culture insists that it is of exclusive importance, the remaining cultures become endangered species and are threatened with extermination. With cultural as with biological species, we have an obligation to preserve the natural variation we have inherited. As we work to develop multicultural literacy, we will be faced with the need for painful trade-offs, but this is better than a cultural imperialism that denies non-Western European ethnic groups access to their cultural heritage. All past cultures have been products of cultural diversity; they cannot be sustained, respected, and nurtured in an atmosphere intolerant of such diversity. If a world community is to be born, multicultural literacy can contribute significantly to its delivery.

(3) Education for reasonableness entails the cultivation of higher-order thinking. By "higher-order thinking" I mean the combination of critical and creative thinking.

(4) By "critical thinking," I mean thinking that is self-correcting, sensitive to context, guided by criteria, and conducive to judgment.[26] The twin pillars of critical thinking are reasoning and judgment.

(5) Reasoning is thinking that is either determined by rules that have been approved by judgment or guided by criteria in a way that necessarily involves judgment.

(6) Judgments are settlements or determinations that emerge during the course of or at the conclusion of a process of inquiry.[27] A favorite (but by no means the only) route to judgment is that via the enhanced understanding that is itself the result of deliberation.[28] Every act, every assertion, every work of art is a judgment that contains subsidiary judgments. These acts, assertions, and works of art are distinctly human products, and each expresses or represents the individual who engaged in that doing, saying, or making, just as each constitutes an appraisal or evaluation of the world of that individual.[29] Judgments are not determined by

---

[26] Matthew Lipman, "Critical Thinking – What Can It Be?" *Educational Leadership* 46:1 (September 1988), 38–43.

[27] Cf. John Dewey: "Judgment as final settlement is dependent upon a series of partial settlements. The judgments by which propositions are determined are recognized and marked off linguistically by such words as *estimates, appraisals, evaluations*. In resolution of problems that are of a looser quality than legal cases we call them *opinions* to distinguish them from a warranted judgment or assertion. But if the opinion held is grounded it is itself the product of inquiry and in so far is a judgment" (*Logic*, p. 122).

[28] In the *Nicomachean Ethics*, Aristotle remaks that "that excellence in deliberation . . . is rightness with regard to the expedient – rightness in respect both of the end, the manner, and the time. . . . If, then, it is characteristic of men of practical wisdom to have deliberated well, excellence in deliberation will be correctness with regard to what conduces to the end of which practical wisdom is the true apprehension" (1142b). And further, "What is called judgment, in virtue of which men are said to 'be sympathetic judges' and to 'have judgment,' is the right discrimination of the equitable" (1143a). McKeon, pp. 1031–2.

[29] For Justus Buchler, there are three modes of judgment: the active, the assertive, and the exhibitive, the positive criteria for which are the morally good, the true, and the aesthetically good. In each of

rules, even though what is done in accordance with rules nevertheless must be accompanied by judgment. Judgments are generally guided by criteria, but the specific identity of these criteria depends upon the context. In critical thinking contexts, criteria may be principles, definitions, canons, axioms, standards, reasons – the list is endless. In creative thinking contexts, any judgment or set of judgments can serve as a criterion by means of which the making of some further judgment can be guided, as the second brush stroke in a painting is guided by the position, color, and texture of the first, the third is guided by the first and second, and so on.

(7) Those who educate for reasonableness guide themselves by two major criteria: rationality and creativity, and these are the regulative principles of, respectively, critical thinking and creative thinking.[30]

(8) Rationality is the guiding principle of practices that are rule- and criterion-governed, that accept as provisionally true the outcome of valid inquiry procedures, and that engage in the *self-corrective adjustment of means and ends.*[31]

(9) Creativity is the guiding principle of practices that are sensitive to context, that find meaning in the outcomes of valid construction procedures, and that focus upon the *innovative adjustment of parts and wholes.*

(10) There is a tendency in some quarters to equate reasonableness with being conciliatory or ready to compromise, and while these are not unrelated, to focus upon them would be to form a one-sided picture. Critical and creative thinking are both rigorous and venturesome; as their product, reasonableness is unlikely to be merely edifying or wimpish. If boldness and imagination are what the world's problems call for, it would be unreasonable to tolerate a moment longer an educational system that espouses good thinking but everywhere tolerates as normal practice what is, in fact, both uncritical and uncreative.

Children will not be encouraged to think well by endless engagement in superficial logic-chopping or in mindless research innocent of any guiding hypotheses. They need arenas of academic freedom similar to those in colleges and universities, where there is no barrier in principle to imaginative speculation or to the cultivation of audacious hypotheses. Unfortunately, the existence of such arenas in

these three modes – doing, making, and saying – we produce judgments as products: "Depending upon which essential aspect of the human process is emphasized, utterance may be seen as production or as judgment. Man produces (a) by acting in relation to the integrities among which he finds himself, (b) by contriving new integrities, and (c) by propositionally structuring integrities in order to affirm or test his suspicions. He is the creature that judges the complexes of nature by producing in these three modes" (*Metaphysics of Natural Complexes* [New York: Columbia University Press, 1966], p. 23).

30 See Matthew Lipman, "Philosophy and Creativity," *Philosophy Goes to School* (Philadelphia: Temple University Press, 1988), pp. 173–90.

31 Cf. Alan Gewirth, "The Rationality of Reasonableness," *Synthèse* 57 (1983), 225–47. Gewirth holds that rationality consists in means–end calculation of the most efficient means to our ends (which are usually taken to be self-interested), whereas reasonableness consists in equitableness, whereby we respect the rights of others as well as our own. Gewirth attempts to show that, where reasonableness and rationality conflict, reasonableness is rationally superior.

higher education can do relatively little to counteract the habits of intellectual timidity that students bring with them from elementary and secondary school. Academic freedom does not guarantee higher-order thinking, although it is a valuable condition of such thinking, as is sunlight for plants. The cultivation of cognitive excellence requires an appropriate curriculum and pedagogy. Sunlight alone is not enough.

4   Cognition, rationality, and creativity

It has already been suggested that higher-order thinking is a blend of critical and creative thinking, that critical thinking involves creative judgment and creative thinking involves critical judgment, and that the comparative "height" of higher-order thinking may be proportionate to the degree to which sound judgments are involved. The first two contentions seem to me to be relatively uncontroversial; the third does not. There are those for whom good critical thinking is represented by an extreme of analytic precision or logical rationality; others may maintain that really good creative thinking is represented by an extreme of pure intuition or imagination. Nevertheless, if we examine the documents that are considered major products of critical intelligence, we find them shot through with creative judgment. If we examine the works of art that are highly esteemed, we are struck by the amount of sheer knowing and thoughtfulness they contain, not to mention their obvious craft and calculated organization. We will look in vain for the magistrate who has never found a case without extenuating circumstances requiring judicious consideration or for an artist who has never been anything but intuitive and spontaneous.

On the one hand, then, we have a coursing of critical judgment through creative thinking and of creative judgment through critical thinking. On the other hand, we have critical and creative thinking interpenetrating one another to form higher-order cognition. Each type calls forth the other and then responds to the other's response to that calling forth. It is this exciting interplay, which in turn animates intermeshing schemata, that largely accounts for the driving dynamism of higher-order thinking.

This pattern of mounting energy and propulsion is what is often neglected in efforts to teach for higher-order thinking, because such efforts fail to prepare thinkers to develop cognitive momentum. Where students have no sense that anything has been left out or is incomplete, they have no need to go beyond the information given. In contrast, the partial, the fragmentary, and the problematic taunt us to complete them or resolve them. The developing story or scenario haunts us, even as we watch it or listen to it, with the portents it hints at or develops. To make higher-order thinking happen in the ordinary classroom, there needs to be reliance upon highly charged materials such as narrative provides and upon a highly charged pedagogy such as the community of inquiry represents. It is asking too much of teachers to demand that they replace the predictable order of the classroom with suspense or that they magically draw knowledge out of mystery or that they invent philosophical exercises that children can do, although this is not to say that they cannot respond to these challenges with considerable capability. But the chief burden of evoking higher-order thinking from students resides with the curriculum and the classroom community of inquiry. To put it more succinctly, higher-order thinking in the classroom rests largely on higher-quality dialogue.

The texture of the dialogue is woven of a warp that is logical and analytical and a woof that is intuitive and imaginative. We see this in the word-by-word, sentence-by-sentence interplay of the dialogue, as the penetrating analytical question is parried by means of a fresh hypothesis or by an even more probing question or by a paradox, so that the voice of reason causes the voice of experience to surface, the voice of experience evokes the intuitive voice, and so on. Higher-order thinking involves not just a dialogue of words but a dialogue of styles of thought, of methods of analysis, of epistemological and metaphysical perspectives. Expecting dialogue to emerge from the purely critical or purely creative is like waiting for the sound of one hand clapping.

Resnick's conception of higher-order thinking

I doubt that any other current researcher has confronted as resolutely as Lauren B. Resnick the task of defining higher-order thinking. In the book she prepared for the National Research Council, she has set forth the traits that she feels are distinctive of such thinking, and she sums them up in this fashion:

Higher order thinking involves a cluster of elaborative mental activities requiring nuanced judgment and analysis of complex situations according to multiple criteria. Higher order thinking is effortful and depends on self-regulation. The path of action or correct answers are not fully specified in advance. The thinker's task is to construct meaning and impose structure on situations rather than to expect to find them already apparent.[1]

What I take to be the key terms here are *judgment, criteria, self-regulation,* and *meaning.* There are also important adjectives: *elaborative, nuanced, complex,* and *multiple.* And there are rather mysterious phrases, such as "construct meaning" and "impose structure," that beg to be unraveled. These tasks will be addressed in this and in later chapters of this book.

It might be useful to look at a somewhat expanded account Resnick provides of higher-order thinking and to comment briefly on each point:[2]

1. "Higher order thinking is *nonalgorithmic.* That is, the path of action is not fully specified in advance."

Comment: Insofar as higher-order thinking is creative, it is of course nonalgorithmic. But insofar as it is critical, it may employ algorithms for particular purposes.

[1] *Education and Learning to Think* (Washington, D.C.: National Academy Press, 1987), p. 44.
[2] Ibid., p. 3.

Thus a person engaged in higher-order thinking might have recourse to a logical algorithm as a safeguard against fallacious reasoning, but this need not significantly lower the quality of the thinking. Moreover, the use of algorithms is compatible with an unending train of judgments. Take the case of a recipe, which is certainly an algorithm of sorts. A beginning cook might follow the recipe mechanically, as though the instructions left nothing to discretion. A professional chef, on the other hand, might conceive of the recipe as a theme calling for inventive variations and would make creative judgments galore. Thus, in playing chess or in exploring a jungle, the paths of action are not fully specified in advance, but an individual tactic may be algorithmic even though the large-scale strategy is improvisational. It might be better, therefore, to say that higher-order thinking is *predominantly* nonalgorithmic.

2. "Higher order thinking tends to be *complex*. The total path is not 'visible' (mentally speaking) from any single vantage point."

Comment: Here Resnick describes the thinking as complex, whereas later she speaks of it as involving "the analysis of complex situations." There seems to be some waffling here, some indecision as to whether it is the thinking itself that is complex or that which is thought about. This may be an occasion to make a general point with regard to the possible confusion of situational components, but I will postpone this discussion for now and take it up with regard to point (9).

Resnick's comment here is particularly interesting. She explains "complex" as "not 'visible' from any singe vantage point." In other words, she chooses to understand complexity as less a matter of a high degree of intricacy or complication than as a matter that can be grasped only if it can be observed from a number of vantage points. Now, one of the characteristics to be noted in the deliberations of a community of inquiry is that such deliberations are multifaceted. Different discussants see the matter differently, but together they see it more objectively than any one individual can see it from his or her point of view.

Perhaps it will be said that vantage points, like dispositions, are the properties of thinking persons, not of the thinking they do. But this is another way of saying that the complexity to which Resnick refers reveals itself in the varied *perspectives* of the community of inquiry, in the diverse *aspects* of the problem under investigation, and in the *many-faceted* nature of the thinking itself.

3. "Higher order thinking often yields *multiple solutions,* each with costs and benefits, rather than unique solutions."

Comment: This is in fact a corollary of the preceding point. A single problem has many aspects, each of which must be given particular attention on the way to any overall resolution. Thus, a jury, in the course of its deliberations, must arrive at many settlements of individual points before it can achieve that overall settlement represented by its verdict. And medical researchers are familiar with the saying that "there isn't one big step; there are just lots of little ones" en route to conquering a disease.

Consequently, any consistent course of action recommended or engaged in by higher-order thinking will involve many subsidiary judgments. But Resnick is pointing out that higher-order thinking involves also a search for alternatives that can be contrasted with one another. Often there are many possible solutions to a problem. The significant judgment to be made has to do with selecting the best among alternatives. The poet whose manuscripts reveal how many alternatives she rejected before she finally settled on a particular word is an example of this aspect of higher-order thinking.

4. "Higher order thinking involves *nuanced judgment* and interpretation."

Comment: That higher-order thinking intimately involves judgment is something I have repeatedly insisted upon. That such judgment is nuanced means, presumably, that it is responsive to the subtler similarities and differences to be found in the subject matter itself or that it is a product of the refined distinctions invented and insisted upon by the thinker. When scientific investigators speak of a theory as "elegant," they are referring to the aesthetic satisfaction they obtain in contemplating it, quite apart from its explanatory power. But a powerful theory does not have to be elegant or nuanced in order to be a product of higher-order thinking.

5. "Higher order thinking involves the application of *multiple criteria,* which sometimes conflict with one another."

Comment: This may be the most substantial of Resnick's nine points. First, it should be noted that a criterion *is* a criterion only insofar as it functions in such a way as to guide the making of judgments. And so, although judgment is mentioned explicitly only in point (4), it is implicitly present also in point (5).

Just why higher-order thinking involves multiple criteria is something Resnick does not explain, but the answer is suggested by her reference to costs and benefits in point (3). Responsible thinkers will not ordinarily employ one criterion without the others. And different alternatives are important because each may satisfy different criteria differently: Some may satisfy weaker but not stronger criteria; others may satisfy stronger but not weaker criteria.

Furthermore, one may take into consideration, in addition to run-of-the-mill criteria, *metacriteria* and *megacriteria.*[3] For example, a person assessing an analogy may employ such metacriteria (criteria for evaluating criteria) as accuracy and simplicity and such megacriteria (extremely general criteria) as truth and meaning, in addition to the usual criteria of similarity and difference.

There are therefore different criteria for judging different aspects *of* the problem, for judging different approaches *to* the problem, for judging the problem in terms of greater or lesser degrees of generality, and for judging the criteria we employ in making the judgments above. Higher-order thinking involves at least these varieties of criteria.

6. "Higher order thinking often involves uncertainty. Not everything that bears on the task at hand is known."

---

[3] The two terms introduced here are discussed at somewhat greater length in Chapter 6.

Comment: Resnick says "often," so this can hardly be an essential feature of higher-order thinking. The word "often" suggests that these nine criteria are involved to different degrees. Perhaps it might be best to say that, for any given instance, a quorum of these criteria is applicable, but just how many are needed to form a quorum is not specified.

Another thing: Is it the thinking that is uncertain or the person doing the thinking? Perhaps higher-order thinking might be better described as thinking that is tentative, probative, provisional, exploratory, questioning. And it is these things because it must deal with a world that is itself problematic, one that forces problematic character upon us.

"Not everything that bears on the task at hand is known," she adds. We do not know everything, and we know that we do not know everything. Yet it is creative ignorance, creative emptiness that drive us to discover and invent.

7. "Higher order thinking involves *self-regulation* of the thinking process. We do not recognize higher order thinking in an individual when someone else 'calls the plays' at every step."

Comment: More precisely, it involves *self-correction*.[4] Self-regulation is closer to self-monitoring. Inquiry is not merely self-regulating practice; it is self-correcting practice. But perhaps what Resnick is emphasizing here (judging from the second sentence) is that there is an element of *autonomy* or *self-government* in higher-order thinking. In any event, both critical and creative thinking, the components of higher-order thinking, are fundamentally *self-corrective*.

So as to guard itself from untruth, critical thinking seeks to discover if it can be falsified. Creative thinking, on the other hand, seeks to guard itself from vacuity or meaninglessness. It therefore aims at warding off or eliminating whatever fails to provide meaning. If critical thinking can be said to seek veracity, creative thinking seeks its own integrity in the form of soundness or validity. If critical thinking is self-correcting, creative thinking is self-validating.

8. "Higher order thinking involves *imposing meaning*, finding structure in apparent disorder."

Comment: Two moves are suggested here, to be employed when we confront what seems to be a disorderly situation. We can probe beneath the surface and perhaps discover a structure that would otherwise have remained hidden. Or we can forcibly impose a structure on the chaos. Either way, whether we discover structure or invent it, we convert meaninglessness into meaningfulness.

---

[4] The notion that members of a community that practices criticism will be able to internalize that practice as self-criticism and will then be in a position to move from self-criticism to self-correction is derived from "Ideals of Conduct," in Charles Hartshorne and Paul Weiss (eds.), *Collected Papers of Charles Sanders Peirce*, 8 vols. (Cambridge, Mass.: Harvard University Press, 1965–6), vol. 1, pp. 591–615. The strategic move here is from epistemological fallibilism to ethical fallibilism. It is the common text of the community of inquiry that makes possible the shift from epistemological inquiry to ethical inquiry.

Meaning, then, is tied to structure, and structures are composed of relationships. Higher-order thinking involves a proliferation of judgments, each of which represents a connection made, a comparison carried out, or a sorting effected. The more numerous the connections we make in our thinking, the thicker the texture of meanings such thinking will possess.

9. "Higher order thinking is *effortful*. There is considerable mental work involved in the kinds of elaborations and judgments required."

Comment: Surely this is an oversimplification, if not a category mistake. The amount of effort expended has relevance only in proportion to the difficulty and significance of the task undertaken. Higher-order thinking is hardly likely to occur in a case in which someone expends great effort to perform a task of minimal difficulty and significance.

In any event, it seems desirable to distinguish, for purposes of analysis, the thinker from the thinking, the thinking process from the product of that process, and the problem being addressed from the inquiry project that addresses the problem.

(a) *The thinker and the thinking.* When we characterize a piece of music, we want to be sure it is the music we are describing and not the composer of that music. When we characterize a plant, we want to be sure we are describing the plant and not the gardener. So with thinking. When we talk about, for example, "critical dispositions," these are tendencies *of the thinker,* not of the resultant thinking.

(b) *The process and the product.* Just as we distinguish between the process of cooking and the food cooked by that cooking, so we distinguish between the thinking process and the thoughts produced by that process. A tortuous process may produce clear thoughts and straight reasoning, and a transparently clear process may produce thoughts that are muddy and muddled.

(c) *The problem and the project.* Problems have different levels of difficulty, and the inquiry projects that investigate such problems mobilize energies at different levels. But we should not confuse the difficulty of the problem under investigation with the difficulty of the problem of organizing the inquiry project.

Consider the circumstances: Schrag's reply to Resnick

In a rather testy response to Resnick's book, Francis Schrag complains that her efforts to distinguish higher- from lower-order thinking remain quite unsatisfactory. To Schrag, we cannot grade the level of thinking unless we know the difficulty of the task and the resources the thinker has available for it. And even if we can identify the moves needed for one kind of domain, it does not follow that the thinker will have similar proficiency when operations are transferred to some other domain:

Consider an analogy with territorial exploration. Within a particular kind of terrain – rocks, for example – we do "grade" the degree of difficulty of different routes, *assuming* a climber of average ability and experience. Although a particular route may look very hard or very easy to the untutored, there is a difference between appearance and reality. Consider two routes up a cliff, one graded as slightly more difficult than the other (for the average climber) but neither of extreme difficulty, and consider two climbers – a world-class expert and a complete novice. Will the expert be challenged more by the tougher route than the novice by the slightly easier one? Almost certainly not. Nor will the "climbing operations" performed by the two climbers be identical even if both successfully scale the cliff, for the expert will almost certainly be able to employ "moves" not in the novice's repertoire. Finally, although we can rate the level of difficulty of rock climbs relative to each other with some confidence, we cannot reliably rate them relative to routes through deserts or tropical forests.[5]

If we know what the intellectual tasks are, says Schrag, we will be able to estimate how challenging such tasks will be to thinkers with whose skills we are familiar. Yet despite his acknowledgment that thinking might be a performance comprising moves and operations, he wants us to pay attention to the conditions and circumstances under which such performances take place.

Schrag is right to call our attention to the relevant circumstances. We should not ask whether an alleged fallacy is really a fallacy or whether a particular statement is true; we should ask under what circumstances it is or is not a fallacy and under what circumstances the statement is or is not true. But even if we understand the challenge that, say, Beethoven represented for Schubert, if we understand the compositional problems Schubert posed for himself, and if we know the skills he brought to the task, we are not exempted from analyzing the music itself.

Thinking is in many ways a performing art, and in some ways it is a creative art. As a performer, the musician may be guided primarily by the criterion of faithfulness to the score, while as a creative artist, his or her central criterion may be originality. Likewise with thinking. We may ponder a text, trying to discover its intrinsic meaning, so that we resemble performers, or we may invent a new hypothesis or write an ingenious essay, with the result that we very much resemble composers. In analyzing thinking we have to keep both dimensions in mind.

A merit of Schrag's critique is that it calls attention to the fact that all judgments are relational. We must judge the relationship between the intent and the actual performance, between the challenge and the response, between the design and the execution, and so on. Thinking does not occur in a vacuum but in concrete situations. It must always be evaluated relative to the circumstances in which it occurs. An illustration of this is to be found in a frequently cited anecdote from William James. He wanted to determine if his dog could distinguish between James intending to go for a walk and James behaving identically but not intending to go. The dog had always been eager to accompany James, but on this occasion the dog failed to move when James went through his preparations. At last James discovered that when he meant to go for a walk he would automatically shake the drawer in which he kept some change to see if it was locked. On this occasion,

[5] Francis Schrag, "Are There Levels of Thinking?" *Teachers College Record* 90:4 (Summer 1989), 534.

this was the one bit of behavior he unwittingly omitted. The dog realized the omission and what it signified.

Cognitive operations, moves, and skills

Critical thinking is one of the components of higher-order thinking, and reasoning is one of the components of critical thinking. As we have just seen, reasoning can in turn be thought of in one sense as being composed of symbolic *operations* and in another sense as being composed of the cognitive *moves* by which those operations are performed. Thus, *implication* is a logical operation in which, in a valid argument, the premises can be said to imply the conclusion. Inference, however, is a cognitive *move* in which someone actually *draws* the conclusion from the premises. Thus, in reading, we may fail to infer what is being implied in one paragraph, just as we may incorrectly infer what is not implied in another.

It would be pleasant to report that every move has its corresponding operation and every operation its corresponding move. But things are not so simple, and the example of implication and inference is, unfortunately, the exception rather than the rule. (For example, is contradiction a symbolic operation or a cognitive move?) Yet, although there may not be corresponding pairs of operations and moves in any consistent fashion, it is possible to conceive of logic, in its broad sense, as the locus of operations and to conceive of rhetoric as the general locus of moves. It might furthermore be conceivable that informal logic is the specific locus of *logical* moves – and indeed, this seems to be what Aristotle had in mind in the *Topics,* where he is investigating under what circumstances a particular logical performance is called for and under what circumstances it is not called for. Thus, informal logic is not primarily concerned with persuasive effectiveness, as rhetoric is, but with the appropriateness of particular logical performances. Should this particular instance of analogical reasoning be judged proportionate and equitable, or should it not? Under what circumstances are ambiguity and equivocation permissible, and under what circumstances are they not?[6]

The distinction between operations and moves is not limited to reasoning, of course. The patient is likely to think of an operation in terms of the changes it makes in his body, while a surgeon may think of it in terms of the moves that constitute its performance. We observe a tilled field as a pattern of ridges and furrows; the farmer may think of it as an exercise in plowing.

---

[6] For more on informal logic, one would do well to consult J. Anthony Blair and Ralph H. Johnson, "The Current State of Informal Logic," *Informal Logic* 9:2–3 (Spring and Fall 1987), 147–52. Among the pioneer works in this area are Michael Scriven, *Reasoning* (New York: McGraw-Hill, 1976); Stephen Toulmin, Richard Rieke, and Allan Janik, *An Introduction to Reasoning* (New York: 1979); and Chaim Perelman, *The Realm of Rhetoric* (Notre Dame, Ind.: University of Notre Dame Press, 1982). Model examples of specialized studies are Robert H. Ennis, "Identifying Implicit Assumptions," *Synthèse* 51 (1982), 61–86; Trudy Govier, "Ad Hominem: Revising the Textbooks," *Teaching Philosophy* 6 (1983), 13–24; and David Hitchcock, "Enthymematic Arguments," *Informal Logic* 7:2 (1985), 83–97.

Characterizations

Cognitive operations are discoverable relationships that components of symbolic systems have to one another. Premises will *imply* a conclusion, so logical implication is a cognitive operation. An arc will *subtend* an angle, so subtending is a geometrical operation. And so symmetry and asymmetry, transitivity and instransitivity are discoverable properties of the components of conceptual schemes or symbolic systems. They are epistemological rather than psychological.

Cognitive moves and performances are psychological acts whereby certain cognitive operations are carried out. Sometimes these acts have specific names, as when we say that a thinker *infers* a conclusion from a set of premises or *draws* a distinction or *makes* a judgment. A performance is therefore a psychological act that corresponds to a particular cognitive operation. But many of our mental (i.e. psychological) acts do not bear a one-to-one correspondence with specific operations. For example, when we surmise or hypothesize, we are engaged in making cognitive *moves* that are at least partially open. Analogously, an actor speaks the lines written for him, and a player in a game plays the position assigned to her; the actor *performs* the part, while the player makes appropriate *moves*.

Cognitive skills represent the capacity to make cognitive moves and performances *well*. It is true that moves are more improvisational than performances and involve greater inventiveness or creativity. Nevertheless both are necessary, just as composers and performers of music are both necessary.

Performances and moves can be made well or badly, depending upon the criteria and standards we apply to them. For example, dancers in training will perform choreographic acts that are standardized components of classical technique, and the dance teacher will then criticize the performance. In a hospital setting, there are medical acts to be performed; nurses and doctors generally refer to these acts as *procedures*. Carrying them out is a matter of performance.

A *skill* is the capacity to organize moves and procedures so as to achieve a sought-after result. It is not unusual to find that the criteria by which skills are judged have been conventionally agreed upon, as in figure skating, where judges employ ten criteria, each graded numerically.

To learn a craft requires becoming conversant with a number of skills and with their orchestration so as to achieve a given end. In a sense, moves and skills and crafts are all teachable – in the sense that the operations and techniques they embody can be taught, and the moves and skills and crafts themselves can be acquired through apprenticeship.

As we ascend from moves to skills and from skills to crafts, the judgment component is augmented, but the judgments remain critical because the criteria are explicit and the task remains one of working from a given repertoire of means in order to achieve a given end. Yet as the degree to which judgment is involved continues to increase, a marked qualitative change begins to occur. The role of judgment begins to shift as we move from skill to craft; more and more judgment comes to be seen as the end or goal of the process rather than solely as a means to an end. This occurs because the notion of a fixed end has begun to crumble as we near the condition of art, and we find ourselves in a situation in which ends are no longer foreseeable. We engage in creative inquiry without knowing where it will lead but confident that we will be satisfied with the settlement, determination, or product toward which we are moving.

What I have been describing is the process by which craft is transcended and the project in which we are engaged approaches the condition of art. When a furniture maker produces a sofa, the craft component consists in organizing wood and fabric and glue and design, as well as other materials and considerations, so as to produce an object that is comfortable to sit in and not unpleasing to the eye, or whatever the criteria the furniture maker must satisfy. But when an *artist* produces a sofa or chair, though it may resemble greatly the product of craft, there is no assurance which criteria (if any) guided its construction, so that it is not at all clear (in contrast to the product of craft) how it is to be evaluated. We find works of craft comfortable to live with because they do not challenge us to find criteria by which we might assess them; such criteria are generally established by tradition or convention and are unproblematic.[7] But the mystery of a work of art lies precisely in the fact that we do not know what to make of it. In time, relevant criteria may surface, and the relationships they establish with the work will be freighted with meaning.

Although this account began with *moves* and ended with *meaning*, this sequence has been employed only for purposes of analysis. As a matter of fact, schooling should employ just the reverse sequence. What must first be established is the human setting – the community in which each being can be a person. What must next be established is the process by which judgment is to be cultivated, including the generation and appreciation of art. It is in such an atmosphere, in which students can grasp the connection between the moves and skills they are expected to learn and the meanings they would like to acquire, that successful learning and thinking can be expected to take place. Nature has seen to it that very young children are natural inquirers. They will prosper as students when they find assurances that the school is an environment hospitable to inquiry and to the formation of human communities, when they sense that the affinities they feel for their fellow students need not be repressed and that their efforts to understand will be encouraged rather than frustrated.

---

[7] Cf. Robin G. Collingwood, "Art and Craft," *The Principles of Art* (Oxford: Clarendon Press, 1937), pp. 15–28.

The boundaries of skill

Philosophers have always been suspicious of talk of skills and have insisted that intelligent making, saying, and doing are not reducible to a repertoire of skills. Once we know what is to be done, we may do it either skillfully or unskillfully, but how do we know what is to be done? This is not a matter of skill, Aristotle tells us, but a matter of understanding. Understanding is "about things which may become subjects of questioning and deliberation,"[8] and it is the understanding that enables us to make judgments; that is, to decide what is appropriate in a given situation. To have judgment is "the right discrimination of the equitable," and the equitable is "a correction of law where it is defective owing to its universality."[9] So according to Aristotle, it is not skill that governs the adaptation of rule and case to one another or means to ends, but judgment.

For Kant, Aristotle did not go nearly far enough in distinguishing between that which governs and that which obeys. When reason acts in a self-serving fashion, it makes use of skills in accordance with "hypothetical imperatives," so that if a certain end is desired, then the appropriate means for obtaining that end can be specified and skills can be learned to facilitate the desired result. But this is all contingent, Kant argues. Nothing requires me to recognize that some ends are more important than others, and I am left free to indulge myself however I choose. It is only when we bring our "good will" or moral character into play that we invoke the *categorical* imperative and choose to do what we would like everyone to have to do in our situation. There is only one moral criterion, according to Kant: Only actions done solely for the sake of the moral law are good.[10] When we follow a *hypothetical* imperative, Kant says, even if we are acting *as* duty requires, we are not acting *because* duty requires, and our actions lack moral worth. Skilled performances are precisely of this kind; they lack moral worth to the extent that they are contingent and self-serving.

A contemporary version of the disparagement of talk of skills, if not of skills themselves, is to be found in W. A. Hart's "Against Skills."[11] Hart is nauseated by educational jargon according to which everything becomes a matter of skill: language skills, social skills, moral skills, skills of relevance, skills of loving and caring, skills of leadership, religious skills, imagining skills, and perhaps even skills for coping with innovation and skills of humility. Take reading, Hart says. It is not just a matter of mechanically mastering the left-to-right convention or of decoding the look and sound of the words. Reading involves skills, he argues, but it is not itself a skill. Comprehending and appreciating significance cannot be

[8] Aristotle, *Nicomachean Ethics*, 1143a, in Richard McKeon (ed.), *The Basic Works of Aristotle* (New York: Random House, 1941), p. 1032.

[9] Ibid., 1137b (p. 1020).

[10] Immanuel Kant, *Groundwork of the Metaphysics of Morals* (New York: Harper and Row, 1964).

[11] Hart's article appeared originally in *Oxford Review of Education* 4:2 (1978), 205–16. It was reprinted in *Thinking: The Journal of Philosophy for Children* 5:1 (n.d.), 35–44.

skills because "it is open to argument whether one has 'read' a certain passage correctly." In order to be able to read well, says Hart, "you have to be able to bring something to your reading. But what you have to bring isn't skills; it's yourself."

An analogous situation prevails with regard to learning to speak, Hart says, and he invokes Wittgenstein. Learning to speak is not mastering a technique or acquiring a skill; it is coming to have something to say. At least this is Rush Rhees's interpretation of Wittgenstein.[12] But Hart is not satisfied with our merely participating in the conversation; we have to bring a perspective of our own. We have to bring *ourselves*, and to do this we must *be* someone. Learning to speak is not a matter of what we can skillfully do, but of who we are. If we keep this in mind, we see that skills are peripheral; they are at one remove from the person exercising them. But thinking, reading, and loving are not to be put at one remove from our humanity; according to Hart, they *are* our humanity. The narrating of great writers like D. H. Lawrence is not external and manipulative; great writers concentrate on exploring what they have to say and let the language take care of itself. (I wonder if, by this criterion, Hart would consider Flaubert a great writer.)

There is a definitely Kantian ring to Hart's argument. I have some problem with the dualism whereby he exiles skills to a peripheral realm outside the human, just as I have difficulty swallowing Kant's separation of the technological and the moral; it gives rise to the myth of "value-free" science and technology. It seems to me that to vest morality wholly in persons and to divest it wholly from methodologies, procedures, and institutions is the way to go if we want to compound our problems rather than resolve them.

But Hart's critique is not to be shrugged off. He is right to insist on a difference between the mastery of the mechanics of reading and what goes on in comprehension, appreciation, interpretation, and evaluation. The first involves technical skills, the criteria for which we know in advance. But in the second instance we are not sure what the criteria are, and this is why Hart says that what a passage says is "open to argument."

Hart's comments on Wittgenstein also bear out, I think, what was expressed at the end of the preceding section with regard to the order of priorities that schooling should establish. There must first be establishment of the human setting – a community of inquiry; second, there must be demonstration that the function of the community is to deliberate and arrive at (or suspend) judgments; and third, schooling should establish the environment in which to cultivate skills and acquaint students with procedures. Children learn their first language readily because they are born into a family, which is a form of life that calls forth the learning of language. Children will more readily learn what the schools have to teach *if* the schools too begin by immersing them in a form of life – the community of inquiry – that will stimulate them to respond as persons. From the very

[12] Rush Rhees, *Discussions of Wittgenstein* (London: Routledge and Kegan Paul, 1970), pp. 81–3, 89.

first, then, young readers should be taught to evaluate what they read and to argue for their interpretations rather than be confronted with years of mechanical reading before they can be entrusted with the formation of critical judgments.

It should be added that Hart's invocation of Wittgenstein cuts in two ways. There is the Wittgenstein for whom it is the form of life – and not the criteria – that seems relevant, that dictates the form our judgments are to take. But there is also the Wiggenstein (in *On Certainty*) who ponders the question of the relative worth of skills versus rule-gained behavior and comes down on the side of skills. How can we help seeing, in this crucial disjunction, how Kant contrasts acting *as* duty requires and acting *because* duty requires? To Kant, we are virtuous only if we consciously obey the moral law; we are not virtuous if our action happens merely to coincide with rule-governed behavior. But Kant's disjunction, I think is too severe: Skill represents a third choice, in which the rule is completely internalized by the practitioner and dissolved in the skill itself. In a sense, skills transcend Kant's distinction, because they represent conduct in which we act both ways, *as* the rule requires and *because* the rule requires.

This leads me in turn to reject Hart's rigid dichotomy between the technical and the human. Skill does not have to fall on either side of the fence. The violinist who plays a sonata skillfully is not therefore doing something that has no relevance to what is human. The very existence of the score presupposes a human product and a human performance. We can no more separate the humanity of the *product* from the person than we can separate the humanity of the creative *process* from the person.

From craft to creativity

It is common to talk as though critical and creative thinking were different kettles of fish. It might be better to say that the process is not all that different in the two cases, but the circumstances are changed. An airplane engine, to use an analogy, operates in the same way whether it is idling or racing, whether the gears are engaged or disengaged, whether the plane is taxiing or flying. To be sure, there is a difference as far as the passengers are concerned; in one case we are standing still; in a second, we are rolling; in a third, we are winging our way through the air. But this is only because the brakes are locked or unlocked, the propellers are feathered or unfeathered, and the ailerons are in one position or another. So with our thinking; A mind at work is a mind at work. Whether the mind is engaged with fact of fancy is less a matter of how it works than of how and toward what is directed. Children turn their minds to the toys at hand or to the stuff of reverie, to sand and pebbles or to dreams and imaginings. It is only as they grow up that their minds develop a disposition toward the one kind of thinking and an indisposition toward the other.

The shift is most noticeable in the case of judgment, for judgment remains judgment even though there is shift from critical to creative judgment or from creative to critical. It is a bit like classic tragedy, as Aristotle describes it; there is

(1) reversal of the situation – "a change by which the action veers round to its opposite" – and (2) recognition – "a change from ignorance to knowledge, producing love or hate between the persons destined by the poet for good or bad fortune" (*Poetics* X.3–XI.4; McKeon, pp. 1465–6). So critical judgment, where the criteria are taken for granted as reliable or are subjected to continual scrutiny, may pass over into creative judgment, where the criteria deemed to be relevant are themselves controversial or even seemingly nonexistent. There is a loss of boundaries, a shift from definiteness to openness; the action veers round to its opposite and we move from actual into possible worlds.[13]

The move from the critical to the creative is, in effect, the move from skill to art, from a situation in which ends control the deployment of means to one in which ends and means surface and submerge, move together, play off each other, and then retreat. It is the move from guidance by rules and criteria to an existentialist landscape in which no landmarks are given, yet every act *claims* to be a landmark, claims to establish that precedent which all succeeding acts are to follow.[14] And so creative judgments are free in the sense that there is no known criterion they cannot defy (at their peril, of course), but they are responsible in the sense that they cannot help serving as examples for other judgments. It is in this sense, I think, that we might most profitably interpret Kant's remark that not rules but examples are "the go-cart of judgment."[15] Each judgment is a kind unto

---

[13] Consider these remarks by Frank Smith:

> Writing may not be superior to speech for the communication of information which I have argued neither speech nor the brain itself is very good at in any case. But writing is infinitely more efficacious than speech in another respect. It is superbly more potent in creating worlds. . . .
>
> Writing enables us to explore and change the worlds of ideas and experience that the brain creates. This is the enormous power and attraction of writing, I feel, especially for children – until something happens to persuade them that writing does not have this power at all.
>
> The power of writing is not initially lost upon many children. A child writes "The dog died" and is astounded at what has been accomplished. The child has put the dog into the world that did not exist before – created a world that would not otherwise have existed –and then has killed the dog. None of this can be done in any other way. And if the child is contrite, a stroke of the pen is all that is required to bring the dog to life again, something else again that would be difficult to accomplish in any other way.

"A Metaphor for Literacy: Creating Worlds or Shunting Information?" in David R. Olson, Nancy Torrance, and Angela Hildyard (eds.), *Literacy, Language and Learning: The Nature and Consequences of Reading and Writing* (Cambridge University Press, 1985), p. 207.

[14] Jean-Paul Sartre, *Existentialism* (New York: Philosophical Library, 1947), pp. 11–61.

[15] For Kant (as for Aristotle), understanding is prior to judgment. Aristotle seems to believe that the understanding instructs judgment, at least in a general sense: "For when the thing is indefinite the rule also is indefinite, like the leaden rule used in making the Lesbian molding; the rule adapts itself to the shape of the stone and is not rigid, and so too the decree is adapted to the facts" (*Nichomachean Ethics* 1137b; McKeon, p. 1019). But Kant argues that while the understanding is itself instructed, it is unable to turn around and instruct judgment:

> If understanding in general is to be viewed as the faculty of rules, judgment will be the faculty of subsuming under rules; that is, of distinguishing whether something does or does

itself. Nor should we ignore the profoundly empirical implication of this dictum, whether we relate it formally to the role of precedent or informally, as in Justice Oliver Wendell Holmes's remark that "experience is the life of the law." For it is also the life of art.

The sense of freedom as spontaneity involves either the absence or the suppression of criteria. But how are criteria to be dispensed with? Without them, nothing can be discriminated or determined, classified or evaluated, compared or contrasted. With them, on the other hand, we have only an infinite regress of criteria for the selection of criteria, a paradox as notorious as those of Zeno.

One way of assuring spontaneity is to eliminate the infinite regress of criteria. How? Simply by fiat – by claiming to have outlawed it. This is a move that has found much favor among some "post-modern philosophers," such as Richard Rorty, who is eager to dispense with absolutes and recognize the provisional nature of all criteria. Here are two vehemently argued statements of his position:

> The really exasperating thing about literary intellectuals, from the point of view of those inclined to science or to Philosophy, is their inability to engage in such argumentation – to agree on what would count as resolving disputes, on the criteria to which all sides must appeal. In a post-Philosophical culture this exasperation would not be felt. In such a culture criteria would be seen as the pragmatist sees them – as temporary resting places constructed for specific utilitarian ends. On the pragmatist account, a criteron (what follows from the axioms, what the needle points to, what the statute says) *is* a criterion because some particular social practice needs to block the road of inquiry, halt the regress of interpretations, in order to get something done. So rigorous argumentation – the practice that is made possible by agreement on criteria, on stopping places – is no more *generally* desirable than blocking the road of inquiry is generally desirable. . . .
>   . . . there is nothing deep down inside us except what we have put there ourselves, no criterion that we have not created in the course of creating a practice, no standard of rationality that is not an appeal to such a criterion, no rigorous argumentation that is not obedience to our own conventions.[16]

Rorty's claim is that we have good pragmatic reasons for calling a halt to the infinite regress of criteria: We have to get on with our work and our lives. Kant's problem is that if he makes judgments totally spontaneous, totally unguided by rules or criteria, they will turn out to be anarchic, meaningless, and absurd. He needs to show, therefore, how a rule-determined spontaneity is possible – or how at any rate, a seemingly rule-determined spontaneity is possible.

> not stand under a given rule. General logic contains, and can contain, no rules for judgment. [For] if it sought to give general instructions how we are to subsume under these rules, that is, to distinguish whether something does or does not come under them, that could only be by means of another rule. This in turn, for the very reason that it is a rule, again demands guidance from judgement. And thus it appears that, though understanding is capable of being instructed, and of being equipped with rules, judgement is a peculiar talent which can be practised only, and cannot be taught.

> The quotation is from the second edition of the Kemp Smith translation of Kant's *Critique of Pure Reason* (London: Macmillan, 1933), pp. 171–2. The square brackets are in the translation.

[16] Rorty, "Pragmatism and Philosophy," in Kenneth Baynes, James Bohman, and Thomas McCarthy (eds.), *After Philosophy: End or Transformation?* (Cambridge, Mass.: MIT Press, 1987), pp. 59, 60. In an essay in the same anthology, Hans Blumenberg describes the stipulated termination of the regress of criteria as the "principle of insufficient reason."

An account of how Kant might have defended himself on this point is put forward by David Bell.[17] Bell argues that Kant's theory of judgment assumes a *principle of spontaneity* – a principle that "outlaws, in other words, any theory according to which, in general, criteria are applied on the basis of the application of criteria, judgments are made in accordance with prior judgments, rules are followed on the basis of prior rules, and so on."[18] There are to be no intermediaries between ourselves and our thoughts; our relationship to our judgments is therefore immediate and direct. At the very center of our rational and cognitive capacities, then, there is an inescapable blindness on the basis of which we understand, judge, and act. Just as it has been said ironically that for Santayana "there is no God and Mary is His mother," so for Kant there are ultimately no laws and our judgments conform to them.

When we read Max Weber's "Politics as a Vocation," we think back to Kant as Kant himself, fashioning this doctrine, must have thought back to Luther. For Weber, when we deal with politicians who invoke "the ethic of ultimate ends" rather than the "ethic of responsibility," nine times out of ten we deal with windbags. And yet, Weber says, with Luther in mind:

It is immensely moving when a *mature* man – no matter whether old or young in years – is aware of a responsibility for the consequences of his conduct and really feels such responsibility with heart and soul. He then acts by following an ethic of responsibility and somewhere he reaches the point where he says: "Here I stand; I can do no other." That is something genuinely human and moving. And every one of us who is not spiritually dead must realize the possibility of finding himself at some time in that position.[19]

And so there are times when, with our backs to the wall, we *must* make judgments, and we do what we think we have to do, even though we may have run out of reasons. This is when critical judgment perforce becomes creative judgment. If critical thinking is thoroughly accountable, in the sense that it can cite the rules and principles that guided it or goaded it, creative thinking is thinking that is less accountable but no less responsible. In creative thinking we are, as Sartre says, "alone, with no excuses."[20]

Directly opposed to the heroic conception of creative judgment offered us by the Kantian/existentialist/postmodern tradition is the temperate empiricism of David Hume. Although Hume appears to be restricting his remarks to the prerequisite conditions for aesthetic appreciation, he conceives of these as a criterion of aesthetic judgment, and he goes so far as to suggest that both artistic and critical expertise rest ultimately on experience: "In a word, the same address and dexterity which practice gives to the execution of any work, is also acquired by the same means in the judgment of it."[21] For Hume, normative judgment is a matter

[17] David Bell, "The Art of Judgment," *Mind* 96 (April 1987), 221–44.
[18] Ibid., p. 226.
[19] "Politics as a Vocation" is to be found in H. H. Gerth and C. Wright Mills (eds. and trans.), *From Max Weber: Essays in Sociology* (New York: Oxford University Press, 1946), p. 128.
[20] *Existentialism*, p. 59.
[21] "Of the Standard of Taste," in Matthew Lipman (ed.), *Contemporary Aesthetics* (Boston: Allyn and Bacon, 1973), p. 31.

of bestowing praise or blame by means of ethical or aesthetic terms that are seem-ingly objective facades for our approval or disapproval. A judicious critic has to have (1) strong, sound senses, so that the work of art will be adequately perceived and scrutinized; (2) delicacy of feeling, so as to respond to the subtler nuances of the work; (3) a capacity for comparison, so as to grasp the qualities of the work in proportion to the qualities of comparable works; (4) the benefit of practice, of experience with many works of art under many different circumstances; (5) an absence of prejudice, making allowances for cultural differences; and (6) good sense – a sound understanding of the fittingness of the work in question to attain its end or purpose.

What is true of "just taste" in the critic, according to Hume, is also true of the inventive judgment of the artist: "The persons introduced in tragedy and epic poetry must be represented as reasoning, and thinking, and concluding, and act-ing, suitably to their character and circumstances; and without a judgment, as well as taste and invention, a poet can never hope to succeed in so delicate an undertaking."[22] And so there are principles that the artist must be guided by. They are not principles given by intuition in advance of experience, but principles born of experience. They are "general observations concerning what has been universally found to please in all countries and in all ages."[23] Artistic creation is confined by the rules of art, and these rules are nothing but experience-based generalizations about what pleases. Some irregular writers have pleased in spite of their violations of these rules, but only because their works have possessed other sources of pleasure. Whatever is found to please cannot be a fault, however unex-pected and unaccountable the pleasure it produces. Pleasure, then, to Hume, is the criterion that guides the critic and the artist alike, and the rules that guide aes-thetic judgment are the laws of what human beings take pleasure in, about which every new and successful work of art may have something to teach the rest of us.

Somewhere between the rationalism without rules of Kant and the empiricism with rules of Hume is the rationalistic empiricism of Diderot. When Diderot speaks of perceptual beauty, he sounds like Hume. When he speaks of the intrinsic beauty a thing might have for any possible viewer – the beauty it has in itself – he reminds us of Kant. When he analyzes aesthetic judgment in terms of relation-ships, he brings Leibniz to mind.

According to Diderot, judgments of beauty are judgments of relationships. Our intellectual faculties, taking into account our needs as human beings, provide us with notions of order, arrangement, symmetry, mechanism, proportion, and unity. These ideas come from experience and are as positive, distinct, clear, and real as those of length, width, depth, quantity, and number. We also have ideas of appro-priateness and inappropriateness that are deprived from experience. Thus, the concept of beauty is tied in to the concept of relationships (*rapports*), and there are three kinds of beauty because there are three kinds of relationships. The first are the relationships that are intrinsic to a thing as we understand it, not as we

[22] Ibid., p. 33.   [23] Ibid., p. 27.

perceive it in relation to other things. These objective relationships are those that would be discernible by all possible beings and consist of the order and arrangement of the thing's constituent parts. These are what constitute intrinsic or objective beauty. Second are those relationships that emerge from perception of the thing as compared with other things, as when we compare this rose with other roses or with a fish. From these are derived comparative beauty or, as Diderot calls it, relative beauty. Objective, intrinsic beauty awakens in us the very idea of relationships; comparative or relative beauty is the name given to everything that calls forth appropriate relations with the things with which they are necessarily compared. There is yet a third kind of relationship – intellectual or fictional relationships that are attributed to things, as when the sculptor imagines the finished work of sculpture in the block of marble.[24]

Obviously, I have barely touched upon these theories of aesthetic judgment and what they imply for creativity. Kant's especially is enormously more complex than I have suggested. But perhaps enough has been said to indicate three of the many perspectives from which the problem of creative judgment can be viewed. What we have seen with regard to aesthetic judgment can help us better understand creative thinking, for each creative judgment is a minuscule version of such thinking. In each creative judgment, the inventive conduct is guided by the qualitative context. So too in creative thinking generally: It is the artist's awareness of and appreciation of the pervasive quality of the creative situation as a whole that sets the stage for the creative performance. An example is the case of photographers, for such artists must be thoroughly immersed in and attuned to the situations in which they find themselves at the moment they click the shutter.

Sovereign schemata

I have already indicated that critical thinking is shot through with judgments that can be called, without apology, "intuitive," and creative thinking is shot through with judgments that exhibit rationality by being rule-guided or rule-determined.[25] I have also argued that one account of judgment can be constructed in accordance with which the changeover from critical to creative is primarily one of changing circumstances. As an example, take an ethical act such as shaking hands with

[24] Denis Diderot, "Treatise on Beauty," in Lipman (ed.), *Contemporary Aesthetics*, pp. 10–23.

[25] An excellent example of the recognition of the intuitive element in scientific thinking is provided by Patrick Suppes in *Probabilistic Metaphysics* (Oxford: Blackwell Publisher, 1984), pp. 216–17. Suppes ridicules what he calls "the fantasy of explicit formality" with its elimination of all intuition and cites instead the need for "continual intuitive decisions about relevance, timeliness, significance, etc." He also makes a case for cognitive apprenticeship, rather than direct instruction, as the preferred mode of training for judgment. Rather than being algorithmic, such a pedagogy, he says, "will depend upon the kinds of complicated, indirect and subtle methods already familiar in the training of many different physical and mental skills." Another very helpful treatment of the intuitive mode of cognition is to be found in Rudolf Arnheim, "The Double-Edged Mind: Intuition and the Intellect," in Elliot Eisner (ed.), *Learning and Teaching the Ways of Knowing* (Chicago: University of Chicago Press, 1985), pp. 77–96.

someone. One can perform such an act *because* conventional rules of conduct require that one do so, or one can shake hands (as with an adversary) *in spite of* the conventions that frown on such an act. In the latter instance, one's performance assumes an ethically creative aspect.

So there is a sense in which there is a continuity between critical and creative thinking, in which they flow into and permeate each other, in which all creative thinking contains an element of rational, methodical calculation and all critical thinking contains an element of intuitive spontaneity. But the coin, like most coins, has two sides, and the other side displays the discontinuity between the two forms of cognitive processing. In this sense, what we do when we draw a conclusion by applying a principle to a case is radically different from what we do when we sketch a profile or change a word in the draft of a poem. At the risk of inviting confusion by using a much overused word in yet another sense, I might say that creative thinking is in a minor sense logical but in a major sense *dialogical*. That is, being cognitively inventive has much more in common with a conversational inquiry than it does with the drawing out of a series of inferences. The assertions we make when we think critically are warranted by reasons or by evidence or, better still, by both. But creative judgments are responses – at first to our own experience and subsequently as responses to those responses, just as a dialogue among persons is inaugurated with a comment that is a response to a situation and triggers in turn a series of replies one to another, following the argument where it leads.

Argument is a form of inquiry, and in inquiry we follow the inquiry where it leads. But what controls and determines the trail that lures us on? According to Dewey, it is the felt quality of the problematic situation that guides us. Whether we are scientific investigators or practicing artists, it is the unique and specific feel of the enigmatic context in which we find ourselves.[26] When we speak of the "initiative" of inquirers, we tend to forget how much of their behavior is evoked from them by the mysterious circumstances in which they find themselves and to which their investigation is a response.[27]

Insofar as the process of inquiry yields an outcome, the quality of the process will be expressed by that outcome, almost as if it were wrung out of the process and precipitated into the product. The uniqueness of the guiding quality will therefore be expressed in the way the product displays its own individuality. In the case of works of art, this individuality, like our own, entitles the works to be known by proper names rather than by the common names of classes. As the art object is generated, its individuality becomes more pronounced, more sharply defined. As it grows, its unique contextual quality exerts a more and more powerful pull upon the creative thinker and becomes a guiding criterion upon which subsequent creative judgments are based.

[26] *Logic: The Theory of Inquiry* (New York: Holt, 1938), pp. 68–9.
[27] Cf. Matthew Lipman, "Natural Obligation, Natural Appropriation," in *Journal of Philosophy* 56:5 (1959), 246–52.

George Yoos has called this individuality the "primary aspect" of an art object, and he argues that as it develops, the work of art comes to serve "as a standard for itself." In a sense, then, this is another theory in which critical judgment of the work can find no criteria external to the work by means of which it can be understood or evaluated and hence must have recourse to a criterion internal to the work. Since the primary aspect of each work is unique, it is only to it that comparisons can be made when the critic appraises this or that detail: The meaning or success of each part can be grasped only in relationship to its individuality as a whole.

Yoos's contention that "until the primary aspect sets a standard for us, we have no standard to measure the degree to which the discrete values accrue to the work of art"[28] is a challenging and persuasive one, and it is helpful in understanding critical judgment. What about creative judgment? I should imagine that artists, critics, and investigators continue to be under the authority of the creative situation as long as the creative activity continues. However, the increasingly specific and distinctive individuality of the product represents an alternative authority and perhaps even a dissonant one. Hence there is the governing criterion of the creative context and the emerging criterion of the artistic product, so that the artist must shuttle dialogically between these or must work out some kind of compromise with regard to them.

It has been suggested by Ernst Gombrich that if we are going to choose one criterion as dominant or sovereign, then we must either exclude other criteria completely or tolerate them. (He calls these the principle of exclusion and the principle of sacrifice.) To Gombrich, the principle of exclusion is simple, primitive, almost brutal. Examples are the absence of ornament in functionalism and the absence of symmetry from abstract expressionism. But, says Gombrich, "the mature artist will never sacrifice more than is absolutely necessary for the realization of his highest values. When he has done justice to his supreme norm other norms are allowed to come into their own."[29] In creative thinking, then, one of the problems is to move without stumbling from acceptance of regulation by the individuality of the creative process to acceptance of regulation by the individuality of the created product while attempting to satisfy both criteria as far as possible. This mutual adjustment of guiding criteria is another example of the way in which creative thinking is dialogical. This leads in turn to our consideration of schemata and how they become authoritative.

Schema theory and creative thinking

The advent of schema theory in recent years suggests an even more complex dialogical interpretation of the creative thinking process. While the notion of a schema goes back at least to Kant, it first appears in the twentieth century in the

[28] "A Work of Art as a Standard of Itself," *Journal of Aesthetics and Art Criticism* 26 (Fall 1967), 81.
[29] *Norm and Form: Studies in the Art of the Renaissance* (London: Phaidon, 1966), p. 97.

neurological work of Sir Henry Head[30] and then in F. C. Bartlett's powerful probing of human memory.[31] But Bartlett's approach conflicted with the dominant theory of British empiricism and was almost universally rejected. One who did not reject it was the neurologist Paul Schilder,[32] and Schilder's work in turn influenced Merleau-Ponty's study of body imagery.[33]

Bartlett has now been resuscitated by cognitive psychologists, and schema theory is much in vogue. This is how one of the leading proponents of the theory, David E. Rumelhart, sees the matter:

A schema, then, is a data structure for representing the generic concepts stored in memory. There are schemata representing our knowledge about all concepts: those underlying objects, situations, events, sequences of events, actions and sequences of actions. A schema contains, as part of its specification, the network of interrelations that is believed to normally hold among the constituents of the concept in question. A schema theory embodies a *prototype* theory of meaning. That is, inasmuch as a schema underlying a concept stored in memory corresponds to the *meaning* of that concept, meanings are encoded in terms of the typical or normal situations or events that instantiate that concept.[34]

Schemas, therefore, encompass both knowledge and meaning. Each schema is a living, shifting matrix that is modified throughout by each new increment of knowledge or meaning, for the relevance of each increment is established by reference to the schema into which it is incorporated. Schema theory enables us to attain a better realization of how human judgment is guided by human understanding. Consequently, it throws light on the nature of creative thinking.

The recognition that there are schemata in mental functioning represents an important development in that it constitutes a significant step beyond the comparatively static structures of Gestalt theory – even though Gestalt itself was relatively dynamic when contrasted with traditional theories based on association. The traditional approach had been atomistic and mechanical, conceiving of experience as comprising psychic bits and pieces, such as sensations, that somehow managed to stick together, like burrs, to form our impressions of things; these things again came together and made up the picture we had of the world. It was a theory that made the person a mere spectator rather than an active agent. Gestalt theory, in contrast showed that wholes are not necessarily just aggregations of

---

[30] See Henry Head, *Studies in Neurology,* vol. 2 (London: Hodder and Stoughton, 1920), as well as Henry Head and G. Holmes, "Sensory Disturbances from Cerebral Lesions," *Brain* 34 (1911), 102–254.

[31] *Remembering* (Cambridge University Press, 1932).

[32] *The Image and Appearance of the Human Body* (London: Routledge, 1935).

[33] Maurice Merleau-Ponty, *Phénoménologie de la perception* (Paris: Gallimard, 1945; tr. as *Phenomenology of Perception* [London: Routledge and Kegan Paul, 1962]). I must admit that I now look back ruefully on not seeing to it that my long paper "The Concept of the Schema," which was written in 1949 and accepted by Merleau-Ponty for publication in *Les Temps Modernes* in 1951, was actually published.

[34] "Schemata: The Building Blocks of Cognition," in Rand J. Spiro, Bertram C. Bruce, and William F. Brewer (eds.), *Theoretical Issues in Reading Comprehension* (Hillsdale, N.J.: Erlbaum, 1980), p. 34. For a brief historical résumé, see William F. Brewer and Glenn V. Nakamura, "The Nature and Function of Schemas," in Robert S. Wyer, Jr., and Thomas K. Srull (eds.), *Handbook of Social Cognition,* vol. 1 (Hillsdale, N.J.: Erlbaum, 1984).

parts, but that the structure of a whole could dominate and govern the disposition of parts, arranging them to suit the formal requirements of the whole.

Indeed, *requiredness* came to be something of a watchword in Gestalt theory, standing as it did for the imperative "demand character" of a context or situation. What was needed next was a schema theory, in which the requiredness was not of a static situation but of a dynamic, onward-moving process. It is not simply that the ongoing process of experienc*ing* is controlled and directed to a very considerable extent by cumulative, funded past of what we have experien*ced*. It is that this funded past is itself composed of countless schemata, ranging from huge in size to microscopic, and that these go on more or less autonomously, like movies making themselves, until they are brought momentarily into focus by the dominant perception of the moment. Most important, perhaps, the schemata conjure up our expectations, and to a very great extent we perceive what we expected to perceive. The most flagrant example of this is the way in which our prejudices (which are among our most vicious schemata) control our perceptions and convince us that we have just observed a clear instance that confirms our unclouded and disinterested generalizations from experience.

I have already referred to Dewey's conception of the way inquiry is guided by the pervasive quality of the creative situation, and I have spoken of the conventional understanding of the artist's being guided by the pervasive quality of the developing art object. But each of these is capable of being understood as schematic processing; both process and product are schemata that incorporate judgments and are altered by judgments. Now, if there are also cognitive schemata of which we are not conscious but that operate at the same time as the process and product schemata and, indeed, mediate between them, then what we are dealing with are multiple schemata. It is a community of schemata whose deliberations provide the understanding that in turn provides the cognitive environment in which our judgments take place.

The notion of dissociated (unconscious) schemata that are constantly at work on their own idiosyncratic problems is hardly unfamiliar. William James used to say that we learn to ice skate during the summer. Our failures of the previous winter are reviewed and amended over the summer without our even realizing it, so that in the next winter we suddenly find ourselves skating. The theory also helps explain the breaking out, in dreams, of highly complicated and innovative thoughts or images that can hardly have been assembled on the spot. Constantly working schemas could prepare ideas and scenarios in advance and have them ready for inclusion in ongoing dream sequences – or for ongoing creative thinking. There may be countless such schemata at work at any one time – volcanoes of the mind.

Building with and on ideas

The relevance of schema theory to thinking skills curricula has been insightfully pointed out by Marilyn Jager Adams. After observing that transfer is the primary criterion of the success of a thinking skills program, she notes that content-specific programs are too deeply embedded to permit transfer and content-free programs too isolated to produce it. This leads her to observe that "*if* the goal of the course is to teach thinking, that is, if it is to develop a schema that is about thinking, then the course should very consistently and very unambiguously be about thinking."[35]

There is further observation by Adams that underscores the relationship between schema theory and the Philosophy for Children approach to the teaching of higher-order thinking. The use of children's readers in the form of novels provides, she says, the "freedom to introduce, reintroduce and elaborate each logical process across a diversity of real-world situations, simultaneously ensuring that all such instances will be remembered together, in the single evolving schema for the novel as a whole." In short, Philosophy for Children courses "are designed to build on themselves both thematically and . . . logically. In combination, these two features must enhance the likelihood that the resulting product, in the student's mind, will be a single, contextually rich, but thematically integrated and logically well-articulated schema. From the perspective of schema theory, this is the ideal."[36]

If we continue to view this matter from the perspective of schema theory, we see that each novel in the curriculum is a schematic product that at the same time embodies in its content the schema of an ongoing process of critical inquiry. This novel then serves as a model for the thinking and deliberation of the children in the classroom. Classroom practice seeks to emulate the ongoing inquiries in the fictional schemata, and classroom dialogue evokes inventive thinking from the participants. Indeed, it has a Gestalt character that *requires* their participation and their creative contributions. (The educational power of this demand character should not be overlooked.)

When children together build a house of blocks, there is a recognition that as the house begins to take shape it begins to lead a kind of life of its own to which some construction ideas are appropriate and others are inappropriate. Each added block restructures the developing house and slightly alters its demand character. New ideas are thereby evoked, which the house may or may not tolerate. What is important, in any case, is that the children are building with ideas as well as with blocks, they are building on each other's ideas as well as on each other's blocks, and they are together learning to take into account the creative requiredness of schemata they themselves create.

Intervention and innovation

Since our concern here is with the creative aspect of higher-order thinking, we should keep firmly in mind the principle that the kind of outcome we get will be directly related to the kind of intervention we employ. Some types of intervention

[35] "Thinking Skills Curricula: Their Promise and Progress," *Educational Psychologist* 24:1 (1989), 34.
[36] Ibid., p. 37.

will draw very little creativity from the student, while others may be able to evoke a great deal.

Consider an analogous situation. We want young children to become conversant with and creative in the visual arts. What should we do? Option 1 might be to show them paintings by great artists and suggest that they copy such works. Needless to say, this option is in little danger of success. Option 2 might be reasoned out this way: Young children have no conception of what constitutes a work of art or how to construct one. And of course they are wholly unskilled. Let us begin, therefore, by teaching them the skills they need to engage in artistic composition, and gradually we will teach them to orchestrate these skills so that eventually the time may come when they will put them all together and create whole paintings. We should not hold our breath about the outcome of Option 2. The children will have perished of boredom by the time we think they might be ready to be creative. Option 3 is the approach we generally employ. We encourage the children to begin with wholes: whole finger-paintings, whole drawings, whole watercolors, paintings, and so on. We may gradually work the skills in, showing them how to shade and how to achieve three-dimensional perspective. But the point is that we do not prejudge their ability to construct unified and coherent works from the very beginning. This is what they find meaningful and enjoyable to do; this is what they are motivated to do. Why should we force either of the first two options on them?

A similar situation prevails, it seems to me, with respect to the encouragement of higher-order thinking. We can present students with examples of higher-order thinking, such as selections from major philosophers, and request that they compose works modeled on these selections. Or we can stress the critical thinking aspect and rehearse the students in cognitive skills in preparation for the eventual employment of these skills. Or, finally, we can construct an environment in which higher-order thinking comes naturally once students find themselves seriously engrossed in a dialogue about things that matter to them. It is in such a situation that rationality and creativity are repeatedly evident, as students find themselves reflecting, reasoning, and devising original ideas, despite the fact that they have not previously engaged in such discussions.

It seems hardly necessary to point out that the last approach is fully compatible with the "cognitive apprenticeship" model of education[37] in which students can have thinking modeled for them by others, and in particular by the teacher. They need coaching as they prepare their individual presentations. They may also need opportunities for reciprocal teaching[38] and cooperative learning.[39] After all, in

---

[37] Cf. Allan Collins, John Seely Brown, and Susan E. Newman, "Cognitive Apprenticeship: Teaching and the Craft of Reading, Writing and Mathematics," *Thinking: The Journal of Philosophy for Children* 8:1 (n.d.), 2–10.

[38] A. S. Palincsar and A. L. Brown, "Reciprocal Teaching of Comprehension-Fostering and Monitoring Activities," *Cognition and Instruction* 1 (1984), 117–75.

[39] Robert E. Slavin, "Cooperative Learning," *Review of Educational Research* 50:2 (Summer 1980), 315–42.

thinking in language, as in thinking in paints, we cannot teach someone else to be creative. We can only create an environment in which students find it possible to teach themselves to be creative.[40]

If we try to understand terms like "thinking" and "creativity" very broadly, we could put the matter this way: Thinking is making connections, and creative thinking is making new and different connections. This is not far from the notion Charles Spearman put forward, in *Creative Mind* (1930), that creative thinking occurs when, out of the conjunction of two or more relationships, an additional relationship emerges. The community of inquiry is a social matrix that generates social relationships, thereby setting the pattern for a variety of cognitive matrices that generate fresh cognitive relationships. But both components must be in place: the community component and the inquiry component.

Distinctive characteristics of higher-order thinking

Education should aim to produce reasonable, judicious, and creative individuals. There are many who object to such a goal, on the ground that it emphasizes method at the expense of content – it exaggerates the importance of how one learns and underestimates the importance of what one needs to know. I think that those who raise this objection are in error. It is true that we can be knowledgeable without being reasonable, judicious, or creative; we can be staid and pedantic ignoramuses. It is not unusual to find people who are learned but reason poorly and lack judgment. But I cannot imagine anyone being reasonable without acquiring the amount of content a reasonable person ought to have. If knowing too little is injudicious, then surely that is something a judicious person will endeavor to avoid. I see no reason, therefore, to alter my contention that the schools should primarily aim at the production of persons who can reason well, have good judgment, and are disposed to think in new ways. Now, if this is the goal of education, then whatever is the kind of thinking that is conducive to this goal, *that* is higher-order thinking. This still leaves us in the dark about how to recognize higher-order thinking when we encounter it. And even if we do arrive at some characterizations that will help us recognize the different degrees of excellence in the order of thinking, we have to make provision for the fact that some populations (for instance, children) may be very high in terms of one criterion, such as creativity, while not being outstanding in the others.

Furthermore, what assumptions are we to make with regard to the thinking episodes among which we want to make our discriminations? Should we treat them as we would any natural entity, or as acts of conduct, or as works of art, or as states of consciousness, or as something still other? If we were to treat them as we would any natural entity, Buchler's categories might be helpful. If we were to treat them as thinking episodes or states of consciousness, Peirce's phenomeno-

---

[40] Gilbert Ryle, "Thinking and Self-Teaching," in Konstantin Kolenda (ed.), *Symposium on Gilbert Ryle*, Rice University Studies 58:3 (Summer 1972), reprinted in *Thinking: The Journal of Philosophy for Children* 1:3–4 (n.d.), 18–23.

logical categories would be very suggestive. And if we were to treat them as we would anything susceptible to aesthetic criticism, then Beardsley's canons would give us a starting point and a sense of direction.

An advantage of employing Beardsley's aesthetic criteria is that they presuppose the creativity requirement, for they are designed for use with artistic products that presumably exhibit creativity. An advantage of using Peirce's phenomenological criteria is that they are designed explicitly for judging thinking events. An advantage of using Buchler's metaphysical criteria is that they are designed, in the broadest sense, to apply to anything.

Beardsley's three canons of art criticism are *complexity, unity,* and *intensity.*[41] All specific reasons in the sphere of aesthetic criticism rest on these generic criteria. It is these three factors whose presence is aesthetically "good-making" and whose absence is aesthetically "bad-making." It seems, however, that unity and complexity, like the dialectically related concepts of the one and the many, are simply two sides of the same coin – what might be called unity-in-complexity, or *e pluribus unum.* The differences of degree in question are differences in the intensity of this single factor.

Peirce's three categories of mental experience are quite different.[42] They consist of *quality, brute fact,* and *lawfulness.* The qualities he refers to are exemplified by "red, bitter, tedious, hard, heartbreaking and noble." By "brute fact" (this is my word, not his), he means pure, raw actuality – what is happening here and now or then and there: the unreasoning causal sequence of things. Lawfulness is the general character of things, their tendency to conform to a general rule and therefore to be predictable. It seems that Peirce's second and third categories, brute fact or actuality and lawfulness or intelligibility, admit of degrees and therefore could usefully characterize gradations of thinking. But the first category, quality, is presumably not a matter of degree (all qualities stand on the same footing) unless we add the further criterion of intensity.

For Buchler, there are no elements, no simples, no basic sentences, no irreducible elements at which inquiry must inevitably terminate.[43] Whatever is, is a "complex," encloses some complexes, and is enclosed by still others. (If in Peirce all qualities stand on the same level, in Buchler all complexes stand on the same level.) But Buchler does suggest a differentiating factor, and that is scope. Complexes differ in *scope,* and scope is determined in turn by *comprehensiveness* and *pervasiveness.* These, then, are the factors that govern the gradation of complexes.

I do not propose here to add to this list nor to attempt to boil it down to a smaller number. Instead, it might be worthwhile to assemble these three sets of

[41] Monroe C. Beardsley, *Aesthetics: Problems in the Philosophy of Criticism* (New York: Harcourt Brace and World, 1958), pp. 464–70.
[42] C. S. Peirce, "The Principles of Phenomenology," in Justus Buchler (ed.), *The Philosophy of Peirce* (New York: Dover, 1955), pp. 74–97.
[43] Justus Buchler, *Metaphysics of Natural Complexes* (New York: Columbia University Press, 1966), pp. 30–40.

candidates and try them out as the factors governing the differentiation of higher-order from lower-order thinking:

(1) Higher-order thinking tends toward complexity. It tries to steer clear of simplistic formulations or solutions. Indeed, it is actually challenged by what is complicated and problematic; it feels, in Yeats's words, "the fascination of what's difficult." Complexity here implies variety, infinite diversification, and individuation that call forth higher-order thinking.

(2) Higher-order thinking tends to display *unity*, i.e., integrity and coherence. It is not content to wallow in complexity but seeks out ways to reduce complexity to sets, orders, kinds, families, and classes. It looks for the threads that bind the riotous diversity of things together. Even then the unity looks simple, it is a simplicity wrought out of a full awareness of diversity. Even a scene of turmoil can have its coherence, and creative thinking may be full of turbulence on its way to resolution.

(3) Higher-order thinking is prepared to be compelled by evidence. It refers to or represents the world outside itself, and it does so in a way that conveys the brute actuality of that world. This is not to say that higher-order thinking cannot on occasion deal solely with ideas, thoughts, and concepts, but even when it does, it does so in terms of their impact on us due to their vitality. Higher-order thinking often involves a recognition of causal or logical compulsions or necessities that thinking of a lesser order is content to skirt or to disparage.

(4) Higher-order thinking tends to seek *intelligibility*. On the one hand, this suggests that such thinking looks for the general and uniform character of events that makes for their predictability and hence for their lawfulness. On the other hand, intelligibility suggests a search for meaning. (I do not insist here on discursive meaning. Music does not have to be translated into words in order to be meaningful.)

(5) Higher-order thinking tends to display *qualitative intensity*. All thinking, whether of a higher or a lower order, is characterized by qualities that are unique. Each thinking episode has is own distinctive quality. Slackness, monotony, insipidity are just as authentic, in their own way, as the active, the alert, and the energetic, as the light from a match is as genuine a light as one from a beacon. The difference is not of quality but of the intensity of the quality.

(6) Higher-order thinking generally exhibits largeness of *scope*. It has a broad range of applicability. It is comprehensive and pervasive. Yet it does not leave internal richness behind; it is compact rather than abstract. A parable or a proverb may have the same scope as an epic poem or a novel.

Internal texture of higher-order thinking

Dialogue is surely not the only index of higher-order thinking, for there are silent inventors and poets and scientists whose behavior is overt evidence of thinking of the very highest order. Nor is this formulation a satisfactory index, for their behavior is not a facade behind which thinking lurks mysteriously; their behavior bespeaks their thinking just as verbal behavior bespeaks thinking. Our bodies are not marionettes whose strings are pulled by the thoughts in our minds; making and saying and doing are all forms of conduct in which we think. Nevertheless, in the context of the school, communication is largely linguistic communication. The body language of the teacher is noted by the students, and that of the students is noted by the teacher, but there is an effort to convert all such signs into words. Words are the main currency of communication, and meanings are exchange values.

The texture of higher-order thinking is not glassy smooth. It is coarse and nubbly, consisting as it does of a vast number of mental acts, each performed with some skill and each eventuating in some microscopic determination or judgment. I could liken it to a piece of chamber music in which the instruments are in dialogue with each other and with the score and where each note and notation are obviously the products of the composer's deliberations, so that each written and played note is a judgment judged. (For example, the instrumentalists may want to decide for themselves whether they want to play a movement in the tempo called for by the composer. They make a judgment of the appropriateness of the composer's judgment.)

The case of literature is still more complex. Not only is every word written by the author the product of a mental act of some sort, but literature also contains descriptions or characterizations of the mental activities of the fictional characters. If Henry James writes, "Isabel surmised that Caspar already knew . . . " his compositional acts result in portrayals of the mental acts and states of those characters.[44] (Indeed, his prose represents the ebb and flow of consciousness much more than it does the movements of physical presences.) And so the texture of the literary work of art is built up of layer upon layer of mental activity into which the reader is then introduced and from which the discourse in the community of inquiry takes its cues.

Higher-order thinking, then, is rich in mental acts, which may cooperate or collide with one another as we build upon each other's ideas or compete with each other intellectually or criticize each other's reasons in the course of our deliberations. There is also an interplay between nonverbalized mental acts and verbalized mental acts, or between mental acts and speech acts. And there is an additional interplay between mental acts and mental states. Thus inquiring involves a suspension of believing, and doubting involves a suspension of knowing. Our rather passive mental states are constantly being challenged or disrupted by our critical or creative mental acts.[45]

---

[44] Cf. Sharon Cameron, *Thinking in Henry James* (Chicago: University of Chicago Press, 1989).

[45] I have made comparatively few references to the vast literature produced by cognitive psychologists on the topic of thinking. But I should single out for mention, among the works I have found most useful, Mary Henle, "On the Relation between Logic and Thinking," *Psychological Review* 69 (1962), 366–78; Philip N. Johnson-Laird and P. C. Wason, *Thinking: Readings in Cognitive Science* (Cambridge University Press, 1977); George Lakoff, *Women, Fire, and Dangerous Things: What Categories Reveal about the Mind* (Chicago: University of Chicago Press, 1986); R. E. Nisbett and L. Ross, *Human Inference: Strategies and Shortcomings of Social Judgment* (New York: Prentice-Hall, 1980); and Howard Gardner, *The Mind's New Science* (Cambridge, Mass.: Harvard University Press, 1988). For a very useful overview of the dialectic between rules and patterns or between the

Every mental act is a minute performance of sorts: It involves some degree of skill, it can be done well or badly, and it eventuates in a minuscule judgment. Thus, if, as Leibniz suggests, the roar of the sea that we hear is in fact composed of countless *petites perceptions,* so our macroscopic judgments are composed of countless microscopic ones. Nor is it different with our raw experience of the world. Just as we now acknowledge that our observations are inevitably theory-laden, so we must acknowledge that our gross experience, so largely consisting of perceptions, is in fact made up of perceptual judgments, which are in turn modified by our assumptions, our values, our purposes, and the contexts in which those judgments occur.

The contrast between mental acts and mental states is largely a matter of the degree of cognitive initiative involved. We can think of these differences of degree as stretching across a range or order, with raw sensations and feelings at the one end, cognitive acts at the other, and mixed modes in between (see table). The instances cited in the table are merely intended as examples, of which a great many more could be cited. The point is that higher-order thinking involves percolation of these mental states and acts that in turn escalates the level of thinking involved. Thus we may *generalize* ("All cats are mortal") and then *exemplify* ("Sam is a cat"), so that we are now in a position to *infer* ("Sam is mortal"). All three statements are, of course, judgments.

Higher-order thinking in the schools

Suppose now that I have the responsibility for evaluating the educational offerings in a particular school in order to determine whether education for higher-order thinking is going on as claimed. Certainly I would pay little attention to humdrum homework assignments that required little originality and offered few rewards for initiative or for independent thinking. But I would look closely at the quality of the student artwork and at poetry and prose compositions, and I would pay particularly close attention to student deliberations over open-ended issues. If, then, I

---

critical and the creative, similar in many ways to the present study, see Howard Margolis, *Patterns, Thinking, and Cognition: A Theory of Judgment* (Chicago: University of Chicago Press, 1987). Margolis suggests use of a "cognitive ladder," in which each step takes us to a more sophisticated level of information processing:

Step 1: simple feedback
     2: pattern recognition
     3: learning
     4: choice
     5: judgment
     6: reasoning
     . . . .
     7: calculation

In the ladder, "each step is seen as a refinement or extension of what is already available at the previous step, never a basic restructuring of how things work at the previous steps" (p. 43).

Sensations and feelings/ affective states	Affective/ cognitive states	Cognitive states	Cognitive states/ acts	Cognitive and metacognitive acts
Being joyous	Loving	Knowing	Wishing	Supposing
Being sad	Liking	Doubting	Guessing	Hypothesizing
Being anxious	Fearing	Understanding	Associating	Reviewing
Being melancholy	Hating	Realizing	Conceding	Surmising
Etc.	Envying	Appreciating	Refusing	Choosing
	Hoping	Accepting	Assuming	Distinguishing
	Believing	Being skeptical	Remembering	Deciding
	Caring	Etc.	Preferring	Discriminating
	Respecting		Etc.	Inferring
	Etc.			Defining
				Questioning
				Classifying
				Explaining
				Generalizing
				Instantiating
				Etc.

Degree of cognitive initiative   ————————————————————————⟶

were to keep in mind the criteria just reviewed, I would be inclined to ask questions such as these:

1. Is the complexity of the thinking in this instance proportionate to the complexity of the problem under discussion?
2. Is the coherence of the thinking sufficient to make sense of the topic under discussion, despite its complexity?
3. Does the thinking in this instance suggest a genuine awareness of the world as it is in fact and of the need to relate theory to practice?
4. Does the thinking in this instance try to discover meaning in what would otherwise be meaningless? Does it seek to explain what is explainable?
5. Is the thinking in this instance distinctive and intense, or is it ordinary and vapid?
6. Does this thinking exhibit scope – i.e., does it have internal richness, and does it extend to a variety of contexts?
7. Does this thinking reveal reasoning where reasoning would be appropriate?
8. Does this thinking arrive at sound determinations or judgments?
9. In matters in which it is not under compulsion, is this thinking imaginative and free, or is it dull and stale?

The inquiry into higher-order thinking will be pursued in subsequent chapters by examining its major components, critical and creative thinking, in more detail. It will then be possible to examine the conditions underlying such thinking in the classroom.

Part II

Seeking standards for classroom thinking

5   Enter the critical thinking movement

During the 1980s there was a constant drumbeat of criticism of the educational process from such persons as Secretary of Education William Bennett, his assistant Chester Finn, and the director of the National Endowment for the Humanities, Lynne Cheney. Bennett even came to office vowing to preside over the demolition of the very department he headed, so deplorable did he consider its activities.

These were not, of course, voices from the left crying out against social and economic injustice. They were conservatives critical of existing institutions – a rather different breed from the usual run of conservatives. One might even speak of them as educational fundamentalists.

Their complaint, in a nutshell, was that Americans were poorly served by the educational system, because those emerging from the system knew little, or nothing worth knowing. Consequently, they concluded, the entire system of schooling was in crisis.

The response of those in the lower echelons of education – teachers and administrators alike – was to draw up their wagons in a circle and exchange volley for volley with their attackers. They ridiculed the naive lists of items that every educated person should know (as drawn up by E. D. Hirsch of cultural literacy fame) and cited mountains of educational research in defense of what they were doing. In brief, they behaved the way members of most professions behave when attacked: They found little amiss in their practice but much to be desired in the circumstances under which that practice had to be carried out.

The schools sought to exonerate themselves, in other words, by contending that the crisis, if indeed there was one, lay not in them but in the society of which they were a part. Students were being taught the right things in the right ways, but they just weren't learning. They were too distracted by television, drugs, sex, family discord, and peer pressures. Textbook writers worked hard to compress the essentials of a vast subject between the covers of a book, and teachers worked hard to convey those essentials to their students. Unfortunately, many teachers seemed to be saying, we live at a time in which the factors keep multiplying that tend to make such knowledge seem irrelevant. We no longer live in a time in which education is valued for its own sake. It has value today, most students seem to feel, only as a ticket to enter the job market with a few acceptable credentials.

Consequently, it is disposable, like a paper cup – something you acquire for only as long as you need it and throw away when you are done with it. But the knowledge one gets in the schools, students feel, is not relevant to life; it is relevant only to the tests that bar one from entering or permit one to enter life. Once a test has been taken, the knowledge needed for it can be forgotten with no more regret than one has in throwing away the paper cup.

Such, at any rate, is the defense many teachers offer when confronted with the accusations of the educational fundamentalists. When the fundamentalists charge, "You don't teach well because you don't know your own subjects well enough! All you know is what you got from those wretched methods courses in the schools of education!," the teachers summon up their dignity and reply haughtily, "We know our subjects quite well enough, thank you. But we are today in the position of the teachers of Latin and Greek a hundred years ago. The times are passing us by. Who needs to read for meaning or write grammatically in an era of MTV? How can the histories of Rome and Greece seem relevant to our students when their parents don't bother to vote? It is not we who have lost our way but the world we live in."

The underlying assumption of both the defenders of the schools and their critics is that the purpose of education is to instill knowledge. It is taken for granted that great bodies of knowledge exist and that these can be summarized and transmitted to students. The controversial issue as both educational fundamentalists and teachers see it has to do with how well the job of transmission is being accomplished. And if it is not being done well, why not? In a sense, then, the combatants share similar assumptions and indeed belong to the same educational tradition. But meanwhile, in that same decade of the 1980s, something else was happening.

How we got to where we are

During the Carter administration and before, back to the Kennedy administration, a great deal of money was allocated to the National Institute of Education for research. For a while in the 1970s, there had been a hold on these funds, but then there was a brief period of clear sailing until the weather closed in once again in the early 1980s. In the Teaching and Learning Division of the National Institute of Education in the late 1970s and early 1980s, there was a sense of an era coming to an end and a desire to make an important gesture, to do something significant before it was too late. Dissatisfaction with Piagetian orthodoxy was beginning to emerge. The most stirring influences seemed to be Vygotsky and Bruner, and the magic words were *thinking* and *cognitive skills* and *metacognition*.

And so, under the leadership of Susan Chipman and Judith Segal and Robert Glaser, all of the NIE, a conference was called to take place at the Learning Research and Development Center of the University of Pittsburgh. Its ostensible goal was "to examine educational practices and scientific investigation concerned with students' abilities to understand, reason, solve problems, and to learn. The plan for the conference was to bring together cognitive researchers, program developers, and teachers of cognitive skills to provide mutual advice and to discuss their theories, findings, and recommendations."[1] Among the program developers present were Reuven Feuerstein, Jack Lochhead, Edward de Bono, Martin Covington, and I. Among the cognitive psychologists were Philip Johnson-Laird, John Bransford, Robert Siegler, James Greeno, Robert Sternberg, Jonathan Baron, Susan Carey, and Jerome Bruner. Still others came from educational psychology and related fields: Carl Bereiter, Beau Fly Jones, David Perkins, Donald Meichenbaum, and Allan Collins. It would be a ground-breaking, exhilarating experience for all participants, and it would set the stage, it was hoped, for a new era in which thinking would play a leading role in the educational process.

The conference did usher in a new era, but it also ended one. It was a smashing coda for a certain phase of the NIE's activities, and then the NIE lapsed into silence.

But enough had been done to send a responsive shiver through the educational research community. People began talking about teaching for thinking. At first, many of them saw it as merely ancillary to teaching for learning. Before long, however, there were those, such as Lauren Resnick, who identified thinking as the very heart of the educational enterprise, even though they were reluctant to assign learning a less important role.

One place where the idea of teaching for thinking did have a special impact was in the editorial offices of *Educational Leadership*, a powerful opinion-shaping journal published by the Association for Supervision and Curriculum Development and aimed at educational administrators. The journal's managing editor, Ron Brandt, together with his colleagues, began to welcome articles on the teaching of thinking skills, and by 1984 they were able to devote the first of several issues to that theme.[2] Before long, hardly an educational periodical remained that had not recognized and welcomed the sexy newcomer to the educational scene. And soon teachers and professors alike were insisting that all along they had been teaching for thinking; nothing new was really required of them.

Some educators perceived, however, that the problem was bigger than this. Of course traditional education involved thinking, they acknowledged. But the *quality* of such thinking was deficient. What was needed was not merely teaching for thinking, but teaching for *critical* thinking.

Some more recent origins of critical thinking

Critical thinking? What in the world was that?

No one seemed to know where the term had originated, nor did anyone seem to care very much. Some guessed that it was connected with a textbook, *Critical Thinking*, by Max Black, published in 1952.[3] Black's book obviously represented

---

[1] Robert Glaser, Preface to Judith W. Segal, Susan F. Chipman, and Robert Glaser (eds.), *Thinking and Learning Skills*, vol. 1 (Hillsdale, N.J.: Erlbaum, 1985), p. x.

[2] *Thinking Skills in the Curriculum*, Educational Leadership 42:1 (September 1984).

[3] 2d ed., Englewood Cliffs, N.J.: Prentice-Hall, 1952. Also worthy of mention is a still earlier milestone: Edward Glaser's *Experiment in the Development of Critical Thinking* (New York: Columbia University Press, 1941).

a genuine effort on the part of a logician to make logic more accessible to students. Others guessed it was related to the work of an equally respected logician in Great Britain, Susan Stebbing, whose *Thinking to Some Purpose* was another attempt to demonstrate the practical value of logical thinking.[4]

But there was another work published in this period that may have lent an even greater impetus: Monroe Beardsley's *Practical Logic*.[5] Beardsley was a philosopher with great sensitivity to literary values, and at the same time he was quite taken by the language-oriented approaches to logic of Frege and Wittgenstein. He had also been an English teacher at one time. Not surprisingly, therefore, Beardsley's book was an ingenious interweaving of logic, grammar, rhetoric, and writing. His work had widespread educational implications, as might have been expected from someone who greatly admired the work of John Dewey. To students who might otherwise have been paralyzed by the logical exercises and examples that had descended from ancient times, Beardsley brought a breath of fresh air: sparkling new exercises that made logical practice a pleasant challenge rather than a dreary task. So Beardsley's work was relevant: to the interests of students, to the language they spoke, and to the world they lived in.

Other authors of logic textbooks often made a fetish of the truth values of propositions and seemed to be fascinated with truth tables, whose function seemed to many students to be at times quite counterintuitive. Beardsley was more concerned with meaning than with truth, as befits someone immersed in the problems of aesthetic criticism. For this reason, he gave considerable attention to matters of translation, which were meaning-oriented, and not just to matters of inference, which were truth-oriented. (You could say that the conclusion of a deductive inference preserves the *truth* of the premises from which it is derived, while a good translation preserves the *meaning* of the original text from which it is derived.) It is hardly necessary to point out that the translation skills and procedures emphasized by Beardsley held great promise for those attempting to improve reading comprehension, since reading involves translation from the thought and language of the writer into the thought and language of the reader.

I do not mean to give the impression that Beardsley and Black were the first American logicians to be associated with the development of critical thinking. That honor may very well belong to Josiah Royce, an eminent philosopher in his own right, an idealist, and, late in his life, a pragmatist. Royce's *Primer of Logical Analysis for the Use of Composition Students*, which apparently fell stillborn from the press in 1881, was admirable in its mastery of formal logic, but its exercises were stuffy and musty, and it could hardly have been of much help to composition students. Like most in the critical thinking field, however, Royce had a strong sense of social accountability, and he wanted to show that logic was educationally useful. In this he was drawing on the earlier work of the German logician Sigwart and the British logician Venn (the latter the inventor of the famed Venn diagrams, so helpful to beginning students of class logic who are

---

[4] Harmondsworth: Penguin, 1939.   [5] Englewood Cliffs, N.J.: Prentice-Hall, 1950.

visually oriented and so puzzling to those who are not). Moreover, Royce's philosophy of community, in part derived from Plato and Hegel and in part from Charles Sanders Peirce, had powerful implications for education. For Royce, the community is a community of interpretation – a meaning-sharing, meaning-creating community – just as for Peirce it had been a community of inquiry in which even logic itself was seen as an essentially social enterprise. It was G. H. Mead who, a generation later, picked up these threads of social origins and social responsibility and wove them into a communal theory of communication and of the self. Mead's social interpretation of behaviorism still influences those in the critical thinking and informal logic movements who recognize in the social impulses of the child perhaps the most powerful motives for education and for becoming reasonable.[6]

Dewey and the Deweyans

Dewey had been a student of Peirce's at Johns Hopkins in the 1870s, and there can be no doubt that the concept of pragmatism invented by Peirce became the guiding force for Dewey's sweeping philosophical endeavors up until the middle of the twentieth century. Peirce was a man of enormous originality. Indeed, he was too continuously creative ever to have time to construct a system or to spell out the practical implications of his ideas (even while maintaining that the meaning of his ideas lay precisely in their practical implications). What Dewey took from Peirce was not a doctrine but a method, and that method he proceeded to apply to science, to art, to logic, to education, and to many another area of learning.

Dewey's interest in education began early, in the last two decades of the nineteenth century. Historians of philosophy have tended to make much of his original attachment to Hegel, but his early monographs on Leibniz and Darwin display his immense excitement as a result of encountering their writings. The mid-nineteenth-century educational scene focused on the decline of the classics and the vigorous bid of science for a place in the curriculum. To Dewey, this was a triumph of the flexible, adaptable method of inquiry over the adapted but inflexible deference to classical humanism. He never thereafter rescinded his allegiance to science as "the method of intelligence," his equation of scientific inquiry with inquiry in general, or his conviction that the reconstruction of education along the lines of inquiry was the desirable way to proceed. Our society could not be fully civilized and our schools could not be fully satisfactory, Dewey thought, until students were converted into inquirers and thereby prepared to be participants in a society likewise committed to inquiry as the sovereign method of dealing with its problems.

But it must be remembered that Dewey was also a psychologist, and when he addresses himself to educational matters there is always a subtle blending of his

[6] *Mind, Self and Society* (Chicago: University of Chicago Press, 1934).

approaches to education as a psychologist and as a philosopher. His psychological approach is presented most straightforwardly in *How We Think*, first published in 1903. Here Dewey traces the natural history of scientific inquiry back to its origins in everyday problem solving. He attempts to show that early peoples, when they discovered their conduct to be blocked in some way or other, were able to evolve an algorithm for problem solving based on a history of success in the use of that algorithm. On sensing a difficulty, they would note that something they had been taking for granted, some belief they had assumed to be true, could no longer be counted on as reliable. It would be necessary to define the problem, convert wishes into possibly desirable outcomes, form hypotheses as possible ways of achieving ends-in-view, imaginatively consider possible consequences of acting on these hypotheses, and then experiment with them until the problem was resolved. The blockage would be removed, and a new belief could be taken for granted. This algorithm for problem solving, drawn from *descriptions* of everyday human behavior, when combined with scientific inquiry becomes *prescriptive,* and we glide, by imperceptible steps, from what *is* (or *was*) to what *ought to be*. Little wonder that contemporary cognitive psychologists, in their desperate quest for a problem-solving paradigm, fastened on Dewey's model with the alacrity with which medieval Christianity fastened upon the naturalistic philosophy of Aristotle!

And yet the very same book, *How We Think*, set out the distinction Dewey made between ordinary thinking and something called reflective thinking, by which Dewey meant thinking that is aware of its causes and consequences. To know the causes of ideas – the conditions under which they are thought – is to liberate ourselves from intellectual rigidity and to bestow upon ourselves that power of choosing among and acting upon alternatives that is the source of intellectual freedom. To know the consequences of ideas is to know their meaning, for as Dewey, pragmatist and follower of Peirce, was convinced, their meaning lies in their practical bearings, the effects they have upon our practice and upon the world. To many in the critical thinking movement today, it was Dewey's emphasis on reflective thinking that was the true harbinger of critical thinking in this century.

Scarcely a decade later, Dewey's major work in education appeared. *Democracy and Education* continues the appeal for education fashioned on the model of scientific inquiry, but the emphasis upon thinking *in* education is strengthened. We have got to learn how to teach children to think for themselves if we are to have a democracy worth having. The thinking individual is as important as the inquiring society. It is as if Dewey had begun to suspect that democracy and inquiry were not natural allies, although with effort they could be made compatible with one another.

To many a contemporary reader, Dewey's vision of the relationship between democracy and education is a powerfully persuasive one. There are hints aplenty that community is the middle term or link between scientific method and democratic practice. But there is a difficulty lurking in Dewey's approach that did not become apparent until much later. The problem is that thinking may be no more a natural ally of science than democracy is. The differences are papered over in *How We Think*, but the fact is that for many students of the matter, reaching all the way back to Plato, excellent thinking is conceived of as philosophical thinking, and philosophy and science are independent ventures in no way reducible to one another. Therefore, if good thinking is to become a prime objective of the classroom, is it to be along the lines of scientific inquiry or philosophical inquiry?

This is a question Dewey never takes up. His love of philosophy is utterly beyond question, but he seldom addresses himself to the problem of what it is, aside from an occasional essay or the throwaway remark that it is "the general theory of education." Consequently, some of those who have been inspired by Dewey's vision have argued for philosophy in the schools as the route to the improvement of student thinking. But many, including a good number of those who also consider themselves Deweyans, have rejected that approach and have adopted other routes of implementation.

Most ill-starred of these ventures was "progressive education," which appeared over the horizon in the 1920s and in a decade had so disappointed Dewey that he wrote *Experience and Education* in denunciation of it. Another effort to keep faith with Dewey was the "reflective education" movement of the 1950s under the leadership of Ernest Bayles, H. Gordon Hullfish, Lawrence Metcalf, and others. In one sense it was an unsuccessful movement. It failed to provide curricula that would pass the teacher's thinking along to the student. But in another sense it can be considered successful, in that schools of education that are concerned only with reflective teachers and are indifferent to whether the thinking process is instilled in the student have adopted this approach and proclaim that they are now "teaching for critical thinking." A prime example was the sound educator Louis Raths, who attempted, reasonably enough, to use the Deweyan problem-solving algorithm as a format for "teaching for thinking."[7] For Dewey – and for Raths – such an approach could be helpful in distinguishing better values from worse. But when Raths was unable, for reasons of health, to continue with his work, his followers took over and transformed his approach into "values clarification," in which no value was to be considered better or worse than any other. So what began as a model of critical thinking had before long become a model of uncritical thinking.

Another contribution of considerably greater substance, came from B. Othanel Smith and Robert Ennis, whose edition *Language and Concepts of Education*,[8] supplemented by Israel Scheffler's *The Language of Education*,[9] was among the earlier efforts in the United States to examine the linguistic and logical aspects of education. In 1963, Ennis published in the *Harvard Educational Review* "A Definition of Critical Thinking,"[10] an article that was destined to have widespread influence on the developing concept of education for thinking. With his strong

---

[7] Louis E. Raths, Selma Wassermann, Arthur Jones, and Arnold Rothstein, *Teaching for Thinking* (1967), 2d ed. (New York: Teachers College Press, 1986).

[8] Chicago: Rand McNally, 1961.   [9] Springfield, Ill.: C. C. Thomas, 1978.

[10] 32:1 (1962), 81–111.

background in logic (he was the author of *Logic for Teachers*,[11] a fine logic text, but one that said little about how logic might best be taught), he has continued to tinker with his definition of critical thinking in order to give it the logical power and educational relevance it undoubtedly requires. He now defines the term as "reasonable, rational thinking that helps us decide what to believe and do." This formulation continues to have great popularity, more so than any of its competitors. To nonphilosophers especially it seems to hit the nail square on the head.

In searching for the distinctive Deweyan contributions to the critical thinking movement, we cannot limit those contributions to his ideas concerning reflective thinking. It should not be forgotten that Dewey makes a strong case in *Experience and Nature*[12] for a conception of philosophy as criticism. (It is this conception of philosophy that Beardsley continues in his major work, *Aesthetics: Problems in the Philosophy of Criticism* [1958].) Dewey locates philosophy as a special non-scientific form of cognition that is concerned with the judgment of value as a unique form of inquiry – a judgment of judgment, a "criticism of criticism" (p. 398). Those who see little connection between critical thinking and philosophy would do well to reread the final chapter of Dewey's major work in metaphysics to which I have just referred.

Analytic skills and cognitive objectives

The British, meanwhile, must have seen little connection between the emergence of critical thinking in the United States and their own interest in developing an analytical philosophy of education. They were unaware of the practical implications that their philosophical work would have: The first British text in critical thinking did not appear until 1988. (It was Alec Fisher's edited volume *Critical Thinking: Proceedings of the First British Conference on Informal Logic and Critical Thinking*.)[13]

Nevertheless, a series of public lectures given at the University of London in early 1965 had devoted itself to the conceptual and logical aspects of teaching and learning, and the lecturers were the foremost figures in the area of philosophical reflection on the educational process: R. S. Peters, D. W. Hamlyn, Gilbert Ryle, and Michael Oakeshott. Two years later, Peters edited a collection, *The Concept of Education*,[14] of which these talks formed the core. Additional articles were supplied by, among others, Paul Hirst and R. F. Dearden, the Americans Israel Scheffler and Max Black, and the Australian John Passmore. Passmore's article, "On Teaching to Be Critical," was the last in the collection but the first to recognize the need to operationalize the theoretical discourse that prevailed in the other contributions. His article remains to this day a sparkling exemplar of critical thinking theory. It deals effectively with the question of cognitive skills and even more effectively with the dispositions that critical thinkers need to have or to develop.

[11] Englewood Cliffs, N.J.: Prentice-Hall, 1969.   [12] 2d ed., LaSalle, Ill.: Open Court, 1929.
[13] Norwich: University of East Anglia, 1988.   [14] New York: Humanities Press, 1967.

Mention of cognitive skills brings us to another highly relevant portion of the academic background out of which the critical thinking movement emerged. In the 1950s, educational discussions and practice were filled with reference to "behavioral objectives" in the classroom. At the University of Chicago, Benjamin Bloom and his colleagues asked themselves, "What about cognitive objectives?" and "What about the skills needed to achieve those objectives?" Thus was born *Taxonomy of Educational Objectives*, vol. 1: *Cognitive Domain*, edited by Bloom and others,[15] which to many a professor of education and many a teacher was to be the last word in education in the last half of the twentieth century. The book was and remains useful despite the glaring absence (one might even say the critical absence) of the objectives of logical reasoning. But one of its most influential aspects was the hierarchy it proposed. Mere memory (of inert knowledge) was consigned to the lowest status. Ascending, one found comprehension, analysis, synthesis, and, at the apex of the pyramid, evaluation. To many an observer of the educational scene, this appeared to be a landmark move toward critical thinking; knowledge had been downgraded and evaluative thinking upgraded, and this may well be what Bloom and his cohort had intended. One could carp at the details of the hierarchy (Nelson Goodman was to argue, much later, that evaluation was a developmental, instrumental process, not a summative one).[16] But the way seemed much clearer than before to the installation of critical thinking as a major objective of the educational system.

In education, the twists and turns of fate are especially chancy, however, and what happened to Bloom was something like what had happened to Dewey a half-century before with the advent of progressive education. Dewey discovered that his ideas, when dropped suddenly into an educational context unprepared for them, were interpreted as and transformed into something quite contrary to his intentions. The context into which Bloom's ideas were dropped was that of sovereign Piagetianism, the dominant force in child psychology from the 1930s through the 1970s. For most of his life (his views relaxed some in his final years), Piaget had maintained that the mental existence of young children was "concrete" – perceptual and affective. They could not be entrusted with abstract ideas, which, in their ignorance, they distorted and misunderstood. Education was a matter of getting time to shuck off their childish ways of thinking and acquiesce in the truth – that is, the way adults understood things. It might have to be late secondary school or even college before students could be expected to handle ideas.

When Bloom's concepts penetrated the Piagetian empire in education, they were accorded an interpretation that allowed them to blend in perfectly with Piaget: The hierarchy was to be understood as a theory of developmental stages. Children's concrete thought processes in their early years allowed them to perform little more than memory tasks, but they could ascend, stage by stage, until finally they would arrive at the adult level, the pinnacle of the entire process, the evaluational stage.

---

[15] New York: McKay, 1956.   [16] *Languages of Art* (Indianapolis: Bobbs-Merrill, 1968), p. 262.

The net effect was to preclude teaching critical thinking to children. Given the longitudinal, developmental interpretation, young children were not capable of monitoring their own thought, of giving reasons for their opinions, or of putting logical operations into practice. It was only in the late 1970s, with the exhaustion of the "back to basics" movement, that educators were prepared to reexamine their assumptions about knowledge and thinking and that psychologists could reexamine theirs about Piaget and Vygotsky. And it was only in the 1970s that educators began to suspect that students were in fact abstraction-deprived and that this might be remedied by teaching them reasoning through philosophy and philosophy through reasoning.

The emergence of informal logic

The critical thinking movement's momentum was increased considerably in the late 1970s with the formation of the enterprise known as informal logic. For some time, a dissident group of logicians had been calling for a logic that was more attuned to natural language and that would be better adapted than classical logic or symbolic logic to help students reason more effectively. Toward this end, a conference was held at the University of Windsor in Canada in 1978, and this in turn produced the *Newsletter of Informal Logic* (later to become the *Journal of Informal Logic*). The very first issue of the *Newsletter* announced the credo of the group: "Our conception is very broad and liberal, and covers everything from theoretical issues (theory of fallacy and argument) to practical ones (such as how best to display the structure of ordinary arguments) to pedagogical questions (how to design critical thinking courses; what sorts of material to use)."[17] Among those who participated in the Windsor conference were men who remain in the forefront of informal logicians: Ralph Johnson and J. Anthony Blair (coeditors of the *Newsletter*), Howard Kahane, Michael Scriven, Douglas Walton, Robert Ennis, and Alex Michalos. Indeed, Scriven's role in the formation of the informal logic movement was virtually that of a founding father, and in his contribution to the conference he contended that the movement would "save philosophy" and "would manifest itself in the improved teaching of basic skills."[18]

The phrase "informal logic" may well have commenced with Gilbert Ryle's use of it in his article "Formal and Informal Logic,"[19] and there can be no doubt that the analysis of natural language by Wittgenstein, Austin, and Ryle had done much to prepare the way for an informal logic movement. The contributors to this movement are too numerous to mention, but among those who sought to build bridges between linguistic analysis and critical thinking by way of informal logic one would have to mention Paul Grice, Stephen Toulmin, Robert Fogelin, C. L. Hamblin, and Rupert Crawshay-Williams, in addition to Michael Scriven. Informal logic is now in a very productive phase, with a considerable number of text-

---

[17] Ralph Johnson and J. Anthony Blair, in *Informal Logic* 1:1 (July 1978), 1.
[18] In ibid., p. 5.   [19] *Dilemmas* (Cambridge University Press, 1966).

books being published every year and with a continuing affirmation of its kinship to critical thinking.

While in some ways informal logic was very new, in other ways it was very ancient. We will put aside for the moment its roots in ancient philosophy, particularly in Aristotle (just as we leave aside, for the time being, the roots of critical thinking in Socrates and the Sophists). Nevertheless, the study of rhetoric did not terminate with antiquity but has been a living tradition through to the present day, and many of those in the critical thinking and informal logic movements owe more than a little of their inspiration and skill to that tradition. Indeed, if Continental philosophy is to be linked to the rise of critical thinking, one of the firmest of connections is the work on rhetoric and argumentation of such writers as Chaim Perelman, Paul Ricoeur, I. A. Richards, Arne Naess, Hans Blumenberg, Hans-Georg Gadamer, and Jacques Derrida.

In a sense, informal logicians and rhetoricians attack the same problem from different directions, and in the best of all worlds could be expected to meet somewhere in the middle, like the crews building a tunnel by starting at either side of a river. Both are examining claims to reasonableness (and therefore are concerned with the theory of rationality). But the informal logicians move toward a new conception of reasonableness by broadening and refining the concept of logic, while the rhetoricians do so by examining writing that is not or does not appear to be formally logical, in an effort to determine what justification such prose may claim to have to being reasonable. Moreover, both are inclined to focus on argumentation, but the one group emphasizes the persuasive force of argument while the other emphasizes its logical force.

Other conversations, other voices

Just as rhetoricians and informal logicians support critical thinking from different directions, so philosophers tend to emphasize the reasoning component in critical thinking, while nonphilosophers (particularly scientists) tend to emphasize the problem-solving (or "decision-making") component. The "problem-solving approach" in scientific, professional, and technical education is not particularly new; it has been used for decades, especially in schools of engineering but also in mathematics, physics, chemistry, biology, and medicine. Of more recent vintage are generalized rather than specialized problem-solving courses and theories. A conference, "Problem-Solving and Education," held at Carnegie-Mellon University in 1978 gathered many cognitive researchers together to compare their approaches to the theory and methods of problem solving. Some were more optimistic than others about the possibility of finding generalized problem-solving processes by going beyond the memorization of specific heuristics based on knowledge in specific domains. Among the more hopeful have been those cognitive psychologists, like Raymond Nickerson and Allan Collins, who have been using computers to test theories of problem solving and who as a result are now developing educational theories of "cognitive apprenticeship."

Still another connection can be traced, although it may be more tenuous: one between critical thinking and applied philosophy. The applied philosophy movement did not organize itself until the mid 1980s. In Britain it has attracted such luminaries as Richard Hare and A. J. Ayer, but in the United States there appears to be somewhat greater reluctance by those in so-called pure philosophy to cross over in support of a branch of philosophy prepared to get its hands dirty by dealing with the practical issues of life. There are now several journals dealing with applied philosophy and publishing papers exhibiting the impact of philosophical thinking upon problems in education, business, law, health care, ecology, and government.

It might seem that Philosophy for Children could be a version of critical thinking best placed under the rubric of applied philosophy: It is a clear example of philosophy applied to education for the purpose of producing students with improved proficiency in reasoning and judgment. There are, however, some significant differences, not the least of which is that other forms of applied philosophy represent an intervention by philosophers with the aim of clarifying or resolving problems faced by nonphilosophers, whereas Philosophy for Children is an intervention that aims to get students to do philosophy themselves.

Finally, there are those in the field of education itself who were among the first to champion critical thinking. Hilda Taba, James Shaver, Philip Phenix, Freeman Butts, and Thomas Greene come to mind, as well as, more recently, Arthur Costa, Ron Brandt, and Barry Beyer.

I have concentrated on those who have contributed positively to the development and promotion of critical thinking in education, with the result that I have not dealt with those whose concern has been more adversarial. This is something a comprehensive history of the critical thinking movement will have to do. However, it would be useful to take note, in passing, of John McPeck's *Critical Thinking and Education*, which takes critical thinking to task for attempting to teach thinking as a separate subject instead of conceding that thinking is completely discipline-specific and can be fostered only within the context of individual disciplines. A running debate has taken place, in consequence, between McPeck and those, such as Robert Ennis and Richard Paul, who defend the notion of teaching generic skills in separate, free-standing courses.[20] While many points made by McPeck against critical thinking have some validity, he seems to be clearly in the wrong with regard to his contention that all teaching of thinking must be discipline-specific, for he ignores the flagrant counterinstance of philosophy. The fact that philosophy and logic do exist, together with the fact that these are normative disciplines concerned with specifying what excellence in thinking ought to be – these facts are in themselves a refutation of McPeck's rejection of the notion that there is a discipline specifically devoted to the teaching of thinking as an autonomous activity.

[20] See John E. McPeck, *Critical Thinking and Education* (New York: St. Martin's, 1981); Richard W. Paul, "McPeck's Mistakes," *Informal Logic* 7:1 (Winter 1985), 35–43; John E. McPeck, "Paul's Critique of *Critical Thinking and Education*," ibid., pp. 45–54.

This has been no more than a thumbnail sketch of the recent sources of the critical thinking movement. It is a movement that has had some difficulty in deciding on its own identity – for example, its relationship to philosophy on the one hand and to creative thinking on the other. But its attempt to overcome this difficulty is a major reason for its value to us.

6   A functional definition of
        critical thinking

Outstanding among the intellectual virtues treasured in the ancient world were knowledge and wisdom. Knowledge was needed for cases in which the required decisions could be made by rational means, such as the relationship between causes and effects or between means and end. But wisdom was necessary for cases that were rationally undecidable and where what had to be relied on instead were Solomonic judgments.

In highly stable, tradition-bound societies, knowledge was often conceived of as a stockpile of truths transmitted from the older to the younger generations. It was thought of as a body of eternal verities, perennially applicable to an unchanging world. In times of change, however, traditional knowledge was likely to become inapplicable or obsolete. What was emphasized instead were intellectual flexibility and resourcefulness. Wisdom was cultivated, by the Stoics and others, in preparation for whatever might happen, whether for good or for ill.

We no longer divide things up the way the ancients did. With modern experimental science, the mountains of knowledge accumulated in the past are no longer looked upon with awe. And the notion of wisdom seems more remote than ever.

On the other hand, we are ready to acknowledge that past experience is not always a reliable guide to the future, with the result that judgments of probability must be made. Yet it is precisely in cases like these that we are most prone to jump to conclusions and to make sweeping generalizations that reveal our biases and prejudices. Nor is our logical understanding infallible, since logic fits our everyday language and the world that surrounds us only imperfectly. We are constantly called upon to make reasonable judgments that neither our reason nor our experience prepares us to make.

In recent years, we have become more conscious of the profound abyss separating the thinking that the schools have prepared us to do and the decisions that we are called upon to make in everyday life. And we have become aware of how dangerous it is to hold uncritically such knowledge as we do possess. Consequently, there has been a turn in recent education toward something called critical thinking.

If we are to foster and strengthen critical thinking in the schools and colleges, we need a clear conception of what it is and of what it can be. We need to know

114

its defining features, its characteristic outcomes, and the underlying conditions that make it possible. Let us begin with outcomes.

The outcomes of critical thinking are judgments

If we consult current definitions of critical thinking, we cannot help being struck by the fact that the authors stress the *outcomes* of such thinking but generally fail to note its essential characteristics. What is more, the outcomes that are specified tend to be limited to *solutions* and *decisions*. Thus, one writer defines critical thinking as "the mental processes, strategies and representations people use to solve problems, make decisions and learn new concepts."[1] Another conceives of critical thinking as "reasonable reflective thinking that is focused on deciding what to believe and do."[2]

These definitions provide us with insufficient enlightenment; the outcomes (solutions, decisions, acquisitions of concepts) are too narrow, and the defining characteristics (reasonable, reflective) they suggest are too vague. For example, if critical thinking is whatever thinking it is that results in decisions, then deciding what doctor to go to by picking a name at random out of a phone book would have to count as critical thinking. *We must broaden the outcomes, identify the defining characteristics, and show the connection between them.*

It was suggested earlier that the present concern for critical thinking is reminiscent of the ancient concern for wisdom. It would be worthwhile to return briefly to that point. What is wisdom conceived to be? Phrases commonly taken to be synonymous are "intelligent judgment," "excellent judgment," and "judgment tempered by experience." We can hardly fail to notice how the term *judgment* keeps cropping up.[3]

But what is judgment? Here again, recourse to equivalent expressions suggests that it is the forming of opinions, estimates, or conclusions. It therefore includes such things as solving problems, making decisions, and learning new concepts, but it is more inclusive and more general.

As for wisdom, it is generally explained that those who are wise exercise *good judgment*. What is the difference between mere judgment and good judgment? This distinction is not an unfamiliar one; we commonly distinguish between mere singing and singing well, between mere living and living well. Nor is it unusual to distinguish between mere thinking and thinking well.

The line of inquiry we have been following is one that shows good judgment to be the modern descendant of the ancient notion of wisdom and to be, at the same

---

[1] Robert Sternberg, "Critical Thinking: Its Nature, Measurement, and Improvement," in Frances R. Link (ed.), *Essays on the Intellect* (Alexandria, Va.: ASCD, 1985), p. 46.

[2] Robert H. Ennis, "A Taxonomy of Critical Thinking Dispositions and Abilities," in Joan Boykoff Baron and Robert J. Sternberg (eds.), *Teaching Thinking Skills: Theory and Practice* (New York: Freeman, 1987), p. 10.

[3] For a penetrating discussion of judgment, see Justus Buchler, *Toward a General Theory of Human Judgment* (New York: Columbia University Press, 1951).

time, the chief characteristic of critical thinking. Perhaps the point we have come to, where we want to know how ordinary judgment and good judgment are different, is a good place to pause and consider some illustrations.

Wherever knowledge and experience are not merely possessed but *applied to practice,* we are likely to see clear instances of judgment. Architects, lawyers, and doctors are professionals whose work constantly involves the making of judgments. The same is true of composers, painters, and poets. It is true of teachers and farmers and theoretical physicists as well; all of them have to make judgments as part of the practice of their occupations and their lives. It is again true of any of us when we are in moral situations: We have to make moral judgments. There are practical, productive, and theoretical judgments, as Aristotle would have put it. Insofar as we make such judgments well, we can be said to behave wisely.

Good professionals make good judgments about their own practice as well as about the subject matter of their practice. A good doctor not only makes good diagnoses of patients and prescribes well for them but also makes good judgments about medicine and his or her ability to practice it. Good judgment takes everything relevant into account, including itself.

A judgment, then, is a determination – of thinking, of speech, of action, or of creation. A gesture, such as the wave of a hand, can be a judgment; a metaphor like "John is a worm" is a judgment; an equation like $e = mc^2$ is a judgment. They are likely to be *good* judgments if they are the products of *skillfully performed* acts guided or facilitated by appropriate instruments and procedures. If we now look at the process of critical thinking and identify its essential characteristics, we will be in a better position to understand its relationship to judgment. I will argue that critical thinking is *thinking that* (1) *facilitates judgment because it* (2) *relies on criteria,*[4] (3) *is self-correcting, and* (4) *is sensitive to context.*

Critical thinking relies on criteria

We suspect an association between the terms "critical" and "criteria" because they resemble each other and have a common ancestry. Also, we are all familiar with book, music, and film critics, and it is not uncommon to assume that those among them whose criticism is considered excellent are those who employ reliable criteria.

We are also aware of a relationship between criteria and judgments, for a *criterion* is often defined as "a rule or principle utilized in the making of judgments." It seems reasonable to conclude, therefore, that there is some sort of logical connection between critical thinking and criteria and judgment. The connection, of course, is to be found in the fact that critical thinking is skillful thinking, and skills themselves cannot be defined without criteria by means of which allegedly skillful performances can be evaluated. So critical thinking is thinking that both employs criteria and can be assessed by appeal to criteria.

[4] Useful discussions of the nature of criteria are to be found in Michael Anthony Slote, "The Theory of Important Criteria," *Journal of Philosophy* 63:8 (April 1966), 221–4, and Michael Scriven, "The Logic of Criteria," *Journal of Philosophy* 56 (October 1959), 857–68.

Furthermore, it might be profitable to consider what uncritical thinking might be. Surely it suggests thinking that is flabby, amorphous, arbitrary, specious, haphazard, and unstructured. The fact that critical thinking can rely upon criteria suggests that it is well-founded, structured, and reinforced thinking. It seems to be defensible and convincing. How does this happen?

Whenever we make a claim or utter an opinion, we are vulnerable unless we can somehow back it up. We should therefore ask ourselves questions such as these: "When our opinions come under fire, to what do we appeal?" "When our claims are contested, what do we invoke?" "When our assertions are not convincing, what do we cite to strengthen them?" In attempting to answer questions like these, we are led to see that claims and opinions must be supported by reasons. What is the connection between reasons and criteria?

Criteria *are* reasons; they are one kind of reason, a particularly *reliable* kind. When we have to sort things out descriptively or evaluationally – and these are two very important tasks – we have to use the most reliable reasons we can find, and these are classificatory and evaluational criteria. Criteria may or may not have a high level of public acceptance, but they have a high level of acceptance and respect in the community of expert inquirers. The competent use of such respected reasons is a way of establishing the objectivity of our prescriptive, descriptive, and evaluative judgments. Thus, architects will judge a building by employing such criteria as *utility*, *safety*, and *beauty*; magistrates make judgments with the aid of such criteria as *legality* and *illegality*; and presumably critical thinkers rely upon such time-tested criteria as *validity*, *evidential warrant*, and *consistency*. Any area of practice – like the examples just given of architectural practice, judicial practice, and cognitive practice – should be able to cite the criteria by which that practice is guided.

The intellectual domiciles we inhabit are often of flimsy construction; we can strengthen them by learning to reason more logically. But this will help little if the grounds or foundations upon which they rest are spongy. We need to rest our claims and opinions, as well as the rest of our thinking, upon a footing as firm as bedrock. Relying on sound criteria is one way of putting our thinking on a solid foundation.

Here, then, is a brief list of the sorts of things we invoke or appeal to and that therefore represent specific kinds of criteria:

- Standards
- Laws, bylaws, rules, regulations, charters, canons, ordinances, guidelines, directions
- Precepts, requirements, specifications, gauges, stipulations, boundaries, limits, conditions, parameters
- Conventions, norms, regularities, uniformities, covering generalizations
- Principles, assumptions, presuppositions, definitions
- Ideals, purposes, goals, aims, objectives, intuitions, insights
- Tests, credentials, factual evidence, experimental findings, observations
- Methods, procedures, policies, measures

All of these are instruments that can be employed in the making of judgments. They are part of the apparatus of rationality. Isolated in categories in a taxonomy, as they are here, they appear inert and sterile. But when they are at work in the process of inquiry, they can function dynamically – and critically.

It has already been noted that by means of logic we can validly *extend* our thinking; by means of reasons such as criteria, we can justify and *defend* it. The improvement of student thinking depends heavily on students' ability to identify and cite good reasons for the opinions they utter. Students can be brought to realize that for a reason to be called good it must be *relevant* to the opinion in question and *stronger* (in the sense of being more readily accepted or assumed to be true) than the opinion in question.

Since the school or college is a locus of inquiry, procedures employed therein must be defensible, just as job applicants are provided with specifications for hiring or promotion. When assigning grades to students, teachers must be prepared to justify the grades by citing the reasons – that is, the criteria – that were employed in arriving at the judgments at issue. It will hardly do for the teacher to claim that a judgment was arrived at intuitively or to say that criteria were unnecessary and irrelevant. Critical thinking is *cognitive accountability*.[5] When teachers openly state the criteria they employ, they encourage students to do likewise. By providing models of *intellectual responsibility*, teachers invite students to assume responsibility for their own thinking and, in a larger sense, for their own education.

This does not mean that all aspects of our lives are always and necessarily occasions for inquiry. There are things we prize that we may not care to appraise; there are people we esteem whom we may not want to estimate. Where the harm done to intimacy and privacy outweighs the benefits to be derived from such evaluations, the call for criteria and standards may well be ignored. In any event, if there are matters about which we do not care to reflect publicly, the drawing of such boundary lines should be of our own choosing.

Metacriteria and megacriteria: banisters of the mind

When we have to select among criteria, we must of course rely on other criteria to do so. Some criteria serve this purpose better than others and can therefore be said to operate as *metacriteria*. For example, when it was earlier pointed out that

[5] I see no inconsistency between urging "cognitive accountability" (e.g., feeling an obligation to supply reasons for stated opinions) and urging the development of intellectual autonomy among students. If providing students with cognitive skills is a form of empowerment, such increased powers entail increased responsibilities, especially to and for oneself. There are times when we cannot let other people do our thinking for us, and we must think for ourselves. And we must learn to think for ourselves by thinking for ourselves; other people cannot instruct us in how to do it, although they can put us in a community of inquiry where it becomes a relatively easy thing to do. The point is that students must be encouraged to become reasonable for their own good (i.e., as a step towards their own autonomy) and not just for our good (i.e., because the growing rationalization of the society requires it).

criteria are especially reliable reasons and that good reasons are those that reveal strength and relevance, this is another way of saying that *reliability, strength,* and *relevance* are important metacriteria. Others that might be cited are *coherence* and *consistency.*

Some criteria are of a very high level of generality and are often presupposed, either explicitly or implicitly, whenever critical thinking takes place. Thus, the notion of knowledge presupposes the criterion of *truth,* and so wherever something is said to be knowledge, the claim also being made is that it is in some sense true. In this sense, philosophical domains such as epistemology, ethics, and aesthetics do not dictate the criteria relevant to them; it is rather the other way around: The criteria define the domains. Epistemology consists of judgments to which truth and falsity are relevant; ethics comprises judgments to which right and wrong are relevant; and aesthetics contains judgments to which beautiful and not-beautiful are relevant. *Truth, right, wrong, just, good, beautiful* – all of these are regulative ideas of such vast scope that we should probably consider them *megacriteria.* And they in turn are instances of the great galactic criterion of *meaning.*

Criteria as bases of comparison

One of the primary functions of criteria is to provide a basis for comparisons. When an isolated, context-free comparison is made and no basis or criterion is given (as is the case in, say, "Tokyo is better than New York"), confusion results. Or if several competing criteria might be applicable (as when someone says, "Tokyo is larger than New York," and we don't know whether the speaker means larger in area or larger in population), the situation can be equally confusing. Just as opinions should generally be backed up by reasons, comparisons should generally be accompanied by criteria or expressed in contexts that can be as illuminating as criteria.

Sometimes criteria are introduced informally and extemporaneously, as when someone remarks that Tuesday's weather was good compared with Monday's, while Wednesday's weather was bad compared with Monday's. In this case, Monday's weather is being used as an informal criterion. The same is the case if someone says, "Compared with a dog, an elephant is large, but compared with a dog, a mouse is small"; this case also involves the informal, impromptu use of criteria. Even figurative language can be understood as involving the use of informal criteria. Thus, such open and closed similes as "The school was like an army camp" and "The school was as regimented as an army camp" use the army camp as an informal criterion against which to measure the orderliness of the school.

On the other hand, when criteria are considered by an authority or by general consent to be a basis of comparison, we may speak of them as "formal" criteria. When we compare the quantities of liquid in two tanks in terms of gallons, we are employing the unit of the gallon on the say-so of the Bureau of Standards. The gallon measure at the Bureau is the institutionalized paradigm case to which our gallon measure is comparable.

So things can be compared by means of more or less formal criteria. But there is also the distinction between comparing things with one another and comparing them with an ideal standard, a distinction Plato addresses in *The Statesman*.[6] For example, in grading test papers, we may compare a student's performance with the performances of other students in the class (using "the curve" as a criterion), or we may compare it with the standard of an error-free performance. In baseball, we may compare pitchers' averages with one another, or we may compare their performances with what is entailed in pitching a perfect game – a no-hit performance.[7]

The indispensability of standards

"Standards" and "criteria" are often used interchangeably in ordinary discourse. It would appear, however, that standards represent a vast subclass of criteria. It is vast because the concept *standard* can be understood in many different ways. There is the interpretation cited in the preceding paragraph, where we were talking about an ideal standard or standard of perfection. There are, in contrast, standards as minimal levels of performance, as in the oft-heard cry, "We must not lower our standards!" There is a sense in which standards are conventions of conduct: "When in Rome, do as the Romans do" provides a conventional standard for our guidance. There is also the sense in which standards are the units of measurement defined authoritatively by a Bureau of Standards.

There is, of course, a certain arbitrariness about even the most reliable standards, such as units of measurement, in that we are free to define them as we like. We could, if we liked, define a yard as containing fewer inches than it now does. But the fact is that we prefer such units, once defined, to be unchanging; they are so much more reliable that way. When concepts are vague, arbitrariness may be unavoidable. Thus the concept of maturity is vague; it lacks clear cut-off points. But once the voting age is set at, say eighteen, a precise decision procedure is available for deciding who is and who is not eligible to vote.

Criteria – and particularly standards among them – are among the most valuable instruments of rational procedure. Teaching students to recognize and use them is an essential aspect of the teaching of critical thinking.

[6] The Stranger remarks to Young Socrates, "We must posit two types and two standards of greatness and smallness. . . . The standard of relative comparison will remain, but we must acknowledge a second standard, which is a standard of comparison with the due measure" (*Statesman* 283e, in Edith Hamilton and Huntington Cairns [eds.], *Plato: The Collected Dialogues* [Princeton; N.J.: Princeton University Press, 1961], p. 1051).

[7] For a contemporary interchange regarding comparison of things with one another versus comparison of things with an ideal, see Gilbert Ryle, "Perceiving," *Dilemmas* (Cambridge University Press, 1966), pp. 93–102, and D. W. Hamlyn, *The Theory of Knowledge* (London: Doubleday and Macmillan, 1970), pp. 16–21.

Critical thinking is self-corrective

Much of our thinking moves along uncritically. Our thought unrolls impressionistically, from association to association, with little concern for either truth or validity and with even less concern for the possibility that it might be erroneous.

Among the many things we may reflect upon is our own thinking. We can think about our own thinking, but we can do so in a way that is still quite uncritical. And so, granted that "metacognition' is thinking about thinking, it need not be equivalent to critical thinking.

The most characteristic feature of inquiry, according to C. S. Peirce, is that it aims to discover its own weaknesses and rectify what is at fault in its own procedures. Inquiry, then, is *self-correcting*.[8]

One of the most important advantages of converting the classroom into a community of inquiry (in addition to the undoubted improvement of moral climate it brings about) is that the members of the community begin looking for and correcting each other's methods and procedures. Consequently, insofar as each participant is able to internalize the methodology of the community as a whole, each is able to become self-correcting in his or her own thinking.

Critical thinking displays sensitivity to context

An astute copyeditor going over an essay prior to publication will make innumerable corrections that can be justified by appeal to recognized canons of grammar and spelling. Idiosyncratic spellings are rejected in favor of uniformity, as are grammatical irregularities. But stylistic idiosyncrasies on the author's part may be treated with considerably greater tolerance and sensitivity. This is because the editor knows that the style is not a matter of writing mechanics; it has to do with the context of what is being written as well as with the person of the author. At the same time, thinking that is sensitive to context involves recognition of

1. *Exceptional or irregular circumstances.* For example, we normally examine statements for truth or falsity independent of the character of the speaker. But in a court trial, the character of a witness may become a relevant consideration.
2. *Special limitations, contingencies, or constraints* wherein normally acceptable reasoning might find itself prohibited. An example is the rejection of certain Euclidean theorems, such as that parallel lines never meet, in non-Euclidean geometries.
3. *Overall configurations.* A remark taken out of context may seem to be flagrantly in error, but in the light of the discourse taken as a whole it appears valid and proper, or vice versa.

[8] C. S. Peirce, in "Ideals of Conduct," *Collected Papers of Charles Sanders Peirce*, ed. Charles Hartshorne and Paul Weiss (Cambridge, Mass.: Harvard University Press, 1931–5), vol. 1, discusses the connection between self-correcting inquiry, self-criticism, and self-control.

Taking Turns

There are times when people engage in sharing. For example, they go to a movie and share the pleasure of looking at the movie together. Or they can share a piece of cake by each taking half.

In other cases, however, simultaneous sharing is not so easily accomplished. If two people ride a horse, someone has to ride in front. They can take turns riding in front, but they can't both ride in front at the same time. Children understand this very well. They recognize that certain procedures must be followed in certain ways.

For example, ask your students to discuss the number of ways they "take turns" in the classroom during the ordinary day. They take turns washing the blackboard, going to the bathroom, going to the cloakroom, and passing out the papers. On the playground, they take turns at bat, they take turns lining up for basketball, and they take turns at the high bar.

Ask your students what they think the connection is between "taking turns" and "being fair." The resulting discussion should throw light on the fact that sometimes being fair involves the way children are to be treated simultaneously, while at other times it involves the way they are to be treated sequentially. For example, if it is one child's birthday and there is going to be a party with cupcakes, there should be at least one cupcake for every child. This is being fair simultaneously. Later, if you want to play "Pin the Tail on the Donkey," children should sequentially take turns in order to be fair. (The prospect of everyone *simultaneously* being blindfolded and searching about with a pin boggles the mind.)

EXERCISE: When is it appropriate to take turns?

	Appropriate	Not Appropriate	?
1. Pam: "Louise, let's take turns riding your bike. I'll ride it Mondays, Wednesdays, and Fridays, and you ride it Tuesdays, Thursdays, and Saturdays."	☐	☐	☐
2. Gary: "Burt, let's take turns taking Louise to the movies. I'll take her the first and third Saturday of every month, and you take her the second and fourth Saturday."	☐	☐	☐
3. Jack: "Louise, let's take turns doing the dishes. You wash and I'll dry."	☐	☐	☐

	Appropriate	Not appropriate	?
4. Chris: "Okay, Louise, let's take turns with the TV. You choose a half-hour program, then I'll choose one."	☐	☐	☐
5. Melissa: "Louise, what do you say we take turns doing our homework? To-night I'll do yours and mine, and to-morrow you can do mine and yours."	☐	☐	☐
6. Hank: "Louise, I hate to see you struggle to school each day, carrying those heavy books! Let me carry yours and mine today, and you can carry yours and mine tomorrow."	☐	☐	☐

4. *The possibility that evidence is atypical.* An example is a case of over-generalizing about national voter preferences based on a tiny regional sample of ethnically and occupationally homogeneous individuals.
5. *The possibility that some meanings do not translate from one context or domain to another.* There are terms and expressions for which there are not precise equivalents in other languages and whose meanings are therefore wholly context-specific.

With regard to *thinking with criteria* and *sensitivity to context*, a suitable illustration might be an exercise or assignment that involves the application of a particular criterion to a set of fictional situations. Suppose the criterion in question is *fairness*, which is itself a way of construing the still broader criterion of justice. One form that fairness assumes is *taking turns*. Look at an exercise taken from *Wondering at the World*,[9] the instructional manual accompanying *Kio and Gus*,[10] a Philosophy for Children program for children nine to ten years old.

The students performing this exercise are applying the criterion of *turn taking* (that is, *reciprocity* or *fair play* or *justice*) to half a dozen specific situations requiring sensitivity to context. Classroom discussion should be able to distinguish between those situations in which the procedure of turn taking is appropriate and those in which it is dubious. When exercises like these are employed in a community of inquiry setting, the stage is set for critical thinking in the classroom. It is not the only way to accomplish this, needless to say. But it is one way.

[9] Matthew Lipman and Ann Margaret Sharp, *Wondering at the World* (Lanham, Md.: University Press of America and IAPC, 1986), pp. 226–99.
[10] Matthew Lipman, *Kio and Gus* (Upper Montclair, N.J.: IAPC, 1982).

Professional education and the cultivation of judgment

It should be evident now why law and medicine were cited earlier as likely places to look for exemplary instances of critical thinking. Medicine and law both involve the flexible application of principles (criteria) to practice (judgment), extreme sensitivity to the uniqueness of particular cases (context sensitivity), refusal to allow either principles or facts to become Procrustean beds to which the other is to be fitted, and a commitment to tentative, hypothetical, self-correcting procedures as befits a species of inquiry (self-correction). Both judges and doctors recognize the importance of being judicious: of making good judgments in the carrying out of their practice. Law and medicine at their best illustrate what critical thinking can be and ought to be. It remains for educators to design appropriate courses in critical thinking and to help teachers and professors recognize the critical thinking elements in their present practice that need to be strengthened.

What, then, is the relevance of critical thinking to the enhancement of elementary school, secondary school, and college education? Why are so many educators convinced that critical thinking is the key to educational reform? A good part of the answer lies in the fact that we want students who can do more than merely think; it is equally important that they exercise good judgment. It is good judgment that characterizes the sound interpretation of a written text, the well-balanced and coherent composition, the lucid comprehension of what we listen to, and the persuasive argument. It is good judgment that enables us to weigh and grasp what a statement or passage states, assumes, implies, or suggests. And this good judgment cannot be operative unless it rests upon proficient reasoning skills that can assure competency in inference as well as upon proficient inquiry, concept-formation, and translation skills. If critical thinking can produce an improvement in education, it will be because it increases the quantity and quality of meaning that students derive from what they read and perceive and that they express in what they write and say.

The infusion of critical thinking into the curriculum carries with it the promise of the academic empowerment of the student. Once this is recognized, it will be necessary to come to grips with the question of the best way to bring about such infusion. In the meantime, it will be well to keep in mind that students who are not taught to use criteria in a way that is both sensitive to context and self-corrective are not being taught to think critically.

Last, a word about the employment of criteria in critical thinking to facilitate good judgment. Critical thinking, as we have seen, is skillful thinking, and skills are proficient performances that satisfy relevant criteria. When we think critically, we are required to orchestrate a vast variety of cognitive skills, grouped in families such as reasoning skills, concept-formation skills, inquiry skills, and translation skills. Without these skills, we would be unable to draw meaning from a written text or from a conversation, nor could we impart meaning to a conversation or to what we write. But just as in an orchestra there are such families as the woodwinds, the brasses, and the strings, so there are these different families of cognitive skills. And just as within each orchestral family there are individual instruments – oboes and clarinets and bassoons, each with its own standard of proficient performance – so there are families of cognitive skills, like induction, questioning, and analogical reasoning, that represent particular kinds of proficient performances in accordance with relevant criteria. We are all familiar with the fact that an otherwise splendid musical performance can be ruined if so much as a single instrumentalist performs below acceptable standards. Likewise, the mobilization and perfection of the cognitive skills that go to make up critical thinking cannot neglect any of these skills without jeopardizing the process as a whole.

This is why we cannot be content to give students practice in a handful of cognitive skills while neglecting all the others that are needed for the competency in inquiry, in language, and in thought that is the hallmark of proficient critical thinkers. Instead of selecting and polishing a few skills that we think will do the trick, we must begin with the raw subject matter of communication and inquiry – with reading, listening, speaking, writing, and reasoning – and we must cultivate whatever skills the mastery of each process entails. When we do this, we come to realize that only philosophy can provide the logical and epistemological criteria that are now lacking in the curriculum.[11] This is far from saying that these are the only skills and criteria that are lacking, but they do represent a significant proportion of what is needed to make student thinking more responsible.

At the same time, it should be evident that, just as individual skills are not enough, the orchestration of skills is not enough either. Critical thinking is a normative enterprise in that it insists upon standards and criteria by means of which critical thinking can be distinguished from uncritical thinking. Shoddy work may be due less to a lack of skill than to the worker's having low standards, an insufficient commitment to quality, and a lack of judgment.[12]

Of course, psychologically oriented studies of critical thinking are often considered normative in the sense that the behavior of the "most successful" thinkers is described and recommended as a model for the way one ought to think. But this is a narrow and precarious base on which criteria and standards are to be set. Consider how much more broadly based in human experience are the logical criteria that guide our reasonings. Or consider the craft standards that prevail in the arts, crafts, and professions in contrast to the questionable implications of successful problem solving in this or that experiment. If critical thinking is to be insisted upon in education, it will have to develop conventions and traditions of cognitive work and cognitive accountability, which teachers will readily recommend to their students. It is not enough to initiate students into heuristic and algorithmic procedures; they must also be initiated into the logic of good reasons, the logic of inference, and the logic of judgment.

[11] An earlier version of the preceding portion of this chapter appeared in *Educational Leadership* 16: 1 (September 1988), 38–43, under the title "Critical Thinking – What Can It Be?"

[12] This point has been well made by Mark Selman in "Another Way of Talking about Critical Thinking," *Proceedings of the Forty-third Annual Meeting of the Philosophy of Education Society, 1987* (Normal, Ill., 1988), pp. 169–78.

7   Criteria as governing factors in critical thinking

What follows is a continuation of the introduction I have been offering to the problem of criteria. As such, it does not deal with the more profound controversies over the nature of criteria that have rocked philosophy since the time of Plato and that were represented by Sextus Empiricus's essay "The Dilemma of the Criterion." Nor does it concentrate, for that matter, on the complex technical issues that crop up whenever the methodology of classification or evaluation is in the spotlight. Students need to know a great deal more about criteria and their role in judgment than they have been told. This is because all of us, whether students or nonstudents, have a right to understand the nature of the powers that govern us, and criteria are among those governing factors. If when we shop we are unaware of the interrelationships between the criterion of price and the criterion of quality, our vulnerability as consumers is intensified. If as students we do not know the criteria by which we are graded, our intellectual vulnerability is intensified. If as job applicants we do not know the specifications of the job for which we are applying, we are in no position to present our qualifications effectively. If criteria are governing factors in our lives, we need to know more about them. Ignorance about criteria is closely linked to cognitive servility. Knowing this, unscrupulous advertisers make sure to cite criteria in terms of which their products come off well, but at the same time they make sure not to cite criteria of great importance that might undermine their claims.

Criteria as appropriate and decisive reasons

As reflective beings, we have our reasons for what we say and do. As critical thinkers, we have our criteria. Criteria form a subset of reasons, but they are reasons of a particularly effective variety. Just as a lever can rest on anything but is especially useful when it rests on a fulcrum, so our actions and statements carry more weight when they rest on criteria rather than on just any kind of reason.

Another way of putting this is that in the making of a judgment there may be many considerations, and as we deliberate upon each of these considerations, it is likely we will develop, for each one, a reason for judging in this way rather than that. But many of these considerations may be of only trivial significance. Rea-

126

sons that are of momentous importance with regard to the matter at hand, reasons that are therefore *decisive,* are criteria.

How does a reason emerge from the ranks and come to be considered a criterion? Here an analogy with political experience may be helpful. To hold political office, someone has to be (1) deemed eligible for that office, (2) nominated, and (3) elected. The first represents a test of relevance; the second is likely to be based upon the person's record of past achievements; the third is a measure of the person's strength as a candidate vis-à-vis the strength of the competitors. Likewise with a criterion: A reason (1) that is especially relevant to an ongoing inquiry, (2) that has a record of reliability, and (3) that is especially forceful is likely to be chosen to serve as a criterion.

For example, we are introduced to Mary and Martha, and we note that they have some resemblance. We wonder if they are sisters. Someone says, "They have the same last name." That is, of course, a reason for thinking they may be sisters, but it is not decisive. Someone else says, "They are the daughters of the same parents." That is decisive, for it will settle the matter unless some counterexample is found. It is decisive because it expresses a definitive consideration. It is more than an ordinary reason; it is a criterion. It is eminently relevant, reliable, and forceful.

This does not mean that criteria must resemble definitions. What gives definitions their great power as criteria is their exclusiveness. If in wondering whether to classify a snail as a mollusc I can appeal to its definition, I have selected a criterion that has exclusive jurisdiction over the matter in question. But there are other ways of being exclusive. Suppose I say, "I will take my umbrella *only if it is actually raining.*" In this case I have stipulated a condition that can serve exclusively as a criterion. The fact that *it is raining* assumes the sovereign role in guiding my judgment.

It appears then that, just as in the election of office holders the first task is the stipulation of eligibility conditions, so in the election of criteria from the ranks of reasons the first task is the stipulation of relevance conditions. (This is where informal logic makes perhaps its most significant contribution. Formal logic deals with the soundness or unsoundness of arguments, not with their relevance or irrelevance. That the premises of an argument are true in no way guarantees that the argument is relevant to the inquiry at hand. Informal logic, in contrast, is particularly sensitive to contextual considerations; in some ways it might be accurate to say that relevance is at the heart of all of its activities.)

The second concern in selecting criteria is to establish a criterion's plausibility as a candidate by considering its record of performance – that is, its reliability. The third is to consider the criterion's strength as a candidate by examining any claims as to its preferability to other candidates. Thus, a reason can come to be a criterion only by passing a series of trials to determine its fitness to be a criterion. If, then, criteria are reasons that are especially fitted to be employed in the circumstances in question, it would not be amiss to say that the critical thinker is not merely one who is "appropriately moved by reasons," as Harvey Siegel puts it, but one who is appropriately moved by *appropriate* reasons.[1]

More on metacriteria

I want to return at this point to the comparison I was making earlier between the selection of metacriteria and the choice of candidates for a position. I suggested that there were – not in a clear-cut way but roughly – three steps to the process: determination of eligibility, determination of applicable experience, and determination of comparative strengths among candidates. Thus, in the selection of metacriteria we first want to know if the proposed metacriterion is *relevant;* we then want to consider its vitae, as it were, and determine from its record of past service its *reliability;* and third, we want to evaluate its *strength.*

(1) *Relevance.* A criterion is relevant to an impending determination if it is pertinent to the subject matter under investigation and appropriate to the context in which the judgment is to take place. There are, of course, degrees of lesser and greater relevance. A criterion's relevance is increased if it can be shown that it has at least partial jurisdiction over the matter in question, and it can be increased greatly if it can be shown that it has exclusive jurisdiction over that matter.[2]

Ascertaining irrelevance can be a tricky matter. It is clear enough that square mileage, while relevant when it comes to judging the size of a country, is not relevant for judging the quality of a poem. But if we were to insist that only spatial criteria be employed for spatial matters and only temporal criteria for temporal matters, we would very quickly run up against the fact that ordinary usage insists otherwise; people say things like "We live a half-hour from town" and "We have only thirty minutes of fuel left on the plane."

To some philosophers, these are metaphorical usages, and metaphors represent category mistakes. Nevertheless, if a description of what happens in one mode of experience is best formulated in terms borrowed from another mode of experience, then the criteria by which the description is judged will also have to be

---

[1] *Educating Reason* (London: Routledge, 1988). Siegel has significantly elaborated on his understanding of the phrase "appropriately moved by reasons" in his article "Teaching, Reasoning, and Dostoyevsky's *The Brothers Karamazov*," in P. W. Jackson and S. Haroutunian-Gordon (eds.), *From Socrates to Software: The Teacher as Text and the Text as Teacher* (Chicago: National Society for the Study of Education, 1989), pp. 115–34.

[2] In dealing with criteria, I have confined the discussion of relevance to the matter of *jurisdiction over.* A criterion having no jurisdiction over a given domain would, then, strictly speaking, be irrelevant to it. But a broader, more encompassing understanding of relevance is nevertheless highly desirable, and one such definition has been offered by D. Wilson and D. Sperber: "Let us say that, other things being equal, the relevance of a proposition increases with the number of the contextual implications it yields and decreases as the amount of processing needed to obtain them increases" ("Inference and Implicature in Utterance Interpretation," in Terry Myers, Keith Brown, and Brendan McGonigle [eds.], *Reasoning and Discourse Processes* [New York: Academic Press, 1986], p. 249). It is also useful to consult, in the same volume, the critique by Y. Wilks, "Relevance and Beliefs," pp. 265–70.

borrowed. Thus if "He has on a *garish* necktie" fails to represent what I see as accurately as does "He has on a *loud* necktie," then I may need to employ criteria that are pertinent to the "auditory" aspect of the experience as well as to the visual. Indeed, the whole field of metaphor, and of figurative language generally, looms as a constant and formidable challenge to our efforts to distinguish neatly between relevant and irrelevant criteria.

(2) *Reliability.* Like politicians, criteria must run on their records and attempt to convince us of their trustworthiness. Of course, even a demonstrably reliable criterion may let us down, but it is not likely to do so often. Criteria are, after all, means or instruments to be employed, and their reliability stems from their history of sustained success in producing desirable consequences. Inches and minutes, like grades of meat and shoe sizes, represent measurement and evaluational aspects of normal practice. It is when we forget the enormous investment of feeling and habit involved in normal practice that we think it an easy matter to get people to switch over to Centigrade instead of Fahrenheit or to a metric currency. Reliability therefore involves more than ease of calculation; it takes into account whatever testimony human experience has to offer.

(3) *Strength.* When Aristotle talks of the "intellectual virtues," it is clear that he means intellectual powers or, better still, *strengths.* Similarly, if we were to speak of the virtues of a metacriterion, we would mean its strengths compared (a) with the strengths of alternative metacriteria and (b) with the degree to which the guidance of a criterion in the making of the judgment in question is required. The differences of degree here can be enormous. Some judgments can be made virtually without recourse to reasoning. We may call such judgments intuitive or uncritical or other apparently disparaging epithets, but the point is that the contexts in which such judgments are made place a low value on rationality or on the use of criteria. We say we like it, and that is the end of the matter. At the other end of the scale are those judgments that are so weak by themselves that almost any criterion they might appeal to would be better than none at all. Often we try to bolster judgments that are intrinsically weak by appealing to the eminence of their source. We say, "That is good because *he* likes it," and we think that is the end of the matter.

But these are extreme cases, and in between we are likely to find that the criterion appealed to has only slightly greater strength than the judgment would have if it stood alone, as when a judge is guided in her decision by a precedent in an appeals court or when we cease to enumerate precedents and cite instead the legal reasoning that may be elicited from precedents.

I am not alleging that these three metacriteria – relevance, reliability, and strength – are the only or even the best metacriteria for the selection of criteria that we are likely to be able to find. Perhaps others would do as well or better. I am merely remarking that these are metacriteria typical of normal rational practice.

Still, I do want to argue that there are no meta-metacriteria. There is only the vast domain of criteria, of which some serve for a time to help select others and therefore become, for a while, metacriteria. But there is no permanent hierarchy; in the eyes of God, as the saying goes, all criteria stand on the same footing.[3]

Criteria, relationships, and judgments

Judgments appraise or pronounce upon relationships, but they are guided by criteria. Criteria are parts of the procedure – part of the methodological apparatus of inquiry; relationships are part of the subject matter that get taken up into and become part of the judgment itself. If I assert that India is geographically larger than Pakistan, my criterion is *area*, but the relationship which the judgment expresses is *is larger than*.

In teaching students the logic of judgment, one must see to it that they become acquainted with the use of criteria and that they recognize the function of relationships in that use. This is why cognitive practice in the early elementary school years begins with the making of comparisons, for this involves the discernment of similarities and differences and the making of connections and distinctions. Eventually the students begin to understand why there can be no such things as distinctions without differences of connections without connectednesses, and this leads them to recognize that there are no judgments without relationships.

It is of the very nature of judgments to correlate with relationships, as it is of the very nature of arcs to subtend angles. One might say, therefore, that judgments are known by the relational company they keep, and if we were to want a typology of judgments, the easiest course to take might be a classification of the relationships those judgments would subtend, such as those shown in the accompanying table.

Family	Time	Value	Space
is a cousin of	is later than	is better than	is farther away than
is a sister of	is earlier than	is superior to	is closer than
is the father of	is the day before	is worth more than	is larger than
is the aunt of	is the day after	is cheaper than	is rounder than
is the wife of	is slower than	is no better than	is more angular than

Touch	Taste	Sound	Color
is softer than	is more bitter than	is louder than	is bluer than
is rougher than	is sweeter than	is softer than	is redder than
is fluffier than	is saltier than	is more shrill than	is more purple than
is smoother than	is tastier than	is more harsh than	is lighter than
is greasier than	is more sour than	is more on key than	is darker than

[3] Cf. Walter R. Fisher, in "Toward a Logic of Good Reasons," *Quarterly Journal of Speech* 64 (1978), 376–84: ". . . any evaluative system is circular. . . . Thus, my concern is not to avoid circularity; it is to increase the diameter of the circle that contains 'good reasons' " (p. 377). On this point, see also Abraham Kaplan, *The Conduct of Inquiry: Methodology for Behavioral Science* (San Francisco: Chandler, 1964), pp. 362–3.

Weight	Feelings	Actions	Character
is heavier than	is happier than	is clumsier than	is more stubborn than
is lighter than	is angrier than	is more restless than	is more courageous than

Cause–effect	Means–end	Part–whole	Class–members
is the cause of	is designed to	is part of	is a member of
is the result of	is intended to	participates in	belongs to the class of
brings about	is meant to	is involved in	is a
makes	is made so that	belongs to	is one of

A metaphysics can be constructed that bases itself on the one hand on human judgment, and on the other hand the presence of relationships in nature. It sees relationships as clustering together in orders, but it stops short of claiming that everything in nature is related to everything else or that nature is the order of all orders.[4] A metaphysical account such as this provides a hospitable cognitive environment for a theory of critical thinking that envisages all such thinking as aimed at the making of judgments and all such judgments as involving the disclosure or fabrication of relationships.

What can serve as a criterion?

In principle, the answer to the question above is "Anything." In practice, however, the field is not quite so open, and the metacriteria we employ see to it that a great many candidates are rejected because they are irrelevant, unreliable, weak, or some or all of these together.

Even so, the logic of criteria is amazingly tolerant of a great jumble of instances. Criteria can be facts, principles, values, bases of comparison, and countless other sorts of things. All criteria need to do is satisfy the metacriteria.

Thus, consider the statement of fact when used as a minor premise: "If he confessed, then he's guilty." "He confessed, all right!" "Well, then, he's guilty!" The fact that he confessed is evidently relevant; confession is a fairly reliable piece of evidence; and it is fairly strong as well. But the argument is not conclusive, because the major premise is so shaky. On the other hand, consider "If this liquid turns litmus red, it's an acid." "Hey, the litmus is turning red! Sure enough, the liquid must be an acid!" Here we have a factual minor premise and a much stronger major premise. Given the truth of the major premise, the event referred to in the minor is sufficient to warrant drawing the conclusion. This suggests that criteria may be most effective in facilitating judgments when they can work together as premises.

But whether taken separately or locked together to form a strong, multipremise argument, criteria are higher-order reasons. They appear to be more conclusive

[4] I am of course referring to Justus Buchler's splendid four-book enterprise (all published in New York by Columbia University Press): *Toward a General Theory of Human Judgment* (1951), *Nature and Judgment* (1955), *The Concept of Method* (1961), and *Metaphysics of Natural Complexes* (1966).

than ordinary reasons, and this is why we turn to them and appeal to them when we are in need of settlements or determinations. Yet there are no common or essential traits that all criteria share. Anything can be a criterion that functions decisively as the inquiry process moves toward the making of a judgment. A criterion is whatever performs the operation of decisively facilitating the settlement of deliberations.

Having acknowledged that anything can serve as a criterion, I will now review briefly some of the things that often do serve in that capacity. These are a few of the things to which people customarily appeal:

Shared values

Values are matters of importance, and we try to settle our disputes by appealing to matters of importance that we hold in common. St. Thomas says somewhere that if there is a controversy between Christians and Jews, appeal should be made to the Old Testament; if it is between Christians, appeal should be made to the New Testament; and if it is between Christians and nonbelievers, appeal should be made to reason. To some extent, all appeals to authority are in effect appeals to shared values, but it would be an oversimplification to say they are only this.

It is worthwhile noting that when it comes to the making of value-guided judgments, the values in question tend to split up into ideal and actual varieties; it is the relationship between the two that the judgment expresses. Thus, the judgment that drinking milk helps make healthy children *is guided by* the criterion of the ideal value of health and the criterion of the actual value of milk; the judgment *expresses* the nutritional relationship between these two values.

Precedent and convention

Are the appeal to precedent and the appeal to convention two different things or parts of the same thing? "When in Rome, do as the Romans do" is clearly a conventional criterion, but is the convention itself anything but a summary statement of precedents in Roman conduct? So David Lewis takes it to be.[5] (Another way of putting this would be to say that both precedent and convention are components of any appeal to normal practice.)

Lewis sees conventions as appeals to precedent that further the great work of human coordination. This suggests that one vast area of criteria-as-conventions is measurement. After all, we often coordinate our activities with one another through agreed-upon standardizations, and standardization generally involves the use of measures. These are, for the most part, stipulated systems of demarcation that make it possible to mark off qualitative differences in nature in terms of

---

[5] In *Convention* (Cambridge, Mass.: Harvard University Press, 1969), Lewis speaks of conventions as regularities that just about everyone in a given population conforms to and expects others to conform to. The source of the agents' mutual expectations is precedent. See pp. 35–41 and 78–9.

quantitative degrees.[6] There can be no doubt that the appeal to measurability has been one of the most powerful moves in the whole chess game of the legitimation of judgments and that measures are among the most potent of criteria.

Common bases of comparison

"You can't compare apples and oranges," people remark. But of course you can if you can find shared respects, such as weight, that admit of such comparisons. Things may be ever so different, but they are still likely to be comparable in some fashion or other. (Indeed, the power of similes and metaphors often lies in their identifying some previously unnoticed similarity among things that are obviously in a great many ways very, very different.) The identification of shared parameters, respects, or bases of comparison is sometimes the only foothold we can find for the judgments we need to make. "But he's your brother!" we cry out in despair when all else has failed – and sometimes it works.

Requirements

Often we stipulate in advance what is to be made or said or done, and these specifications ("specs") act as criteria, as in hiring and promotion, in materials requisitions, and in the case of criterion-referenced tests. In following algorithms, the applicable criterion is simply methodological rigor – what in logic is termed validity. In following heuristic approaches, the applicable criterion is simply success.

Perspectives

A perspective is an area of concern with a distinctive point of view and a distinctive fund of experience. If in a controversy over, say, vivisection, someone invokes what he or she terms "an ethical perspective," then in effect the area of concern called ethics is being introduced in order to perform a criteriological function. Often different perspectives lead to the making of different judgments. To one person, for whom the ethical perspective is primary, a tawdry part of the city should be demolished. For another, whose point of view is aesthetic, the same part of the city may be considered colorful and therefore ought to be preserved.

Principles

Principles are relatively simple conceptual formulations of relatively complex sets of existential relationships. They provide our best understanding of how things have been connected and how, apparently, they *must* be connected. For example,

---

[6] See the magisterial ch. 15, "Measurement," in Morris R. Cohen and Ernest Nagel, *An Introduction to Logic and Scientific Method* (New York: Harcourt Brace, 1934), pp. 289–301.

in classical economics, a principle (or "law") is said to connect supply and demand. (Normative principles are recommendations for the ways things *ought* to be connected.) People are said to "stand on" principle rather than appeal to it, as if principled thinking rests on some kind of bedrock. But principles have no claim to intrinsic superiority as criteria; they must meet the same metacritical criteria as all other candidates.

Rules

If values *influence* us and requirements *guide* us when we judge, rules *tell* us, *command* us, *goad* us into judging in conformity with them. To be guided by a rule in the making of a judgment is to use the most direct and unsubtle procedure available.

The distinction between categorical and hypothetical rules is a tenuous one. In practice, so-called categorical rules are simply collapsed or truncated hypothetical rules. Rules are always domain-specific and contingent upon contextual considerations.

Rules are the residue of normal practice. The practice regulates the rules, and the rules regulate the practice; it is a circular procedure. It is thus that normal practice (e.g., primitive agriculture) aims at social rationalization – the virtual elimination of all behavior that is not rule-governed. There are even rules governing the introduction of innovative rules.

Standards

Our standards are our criteria for indicating the degree to which we expect our criteria to be satisfied.[7] We may recognize correct spelling as a criterion in the grading of essays, but we may be very tolerant of spelling errors. In other words, we have a relevant criterion here but low standards. Since criteria are either relevant or irrelevant, and standards tend to be either high or low, we can have (1) the optimal situation of relevant criteria and high standards; we can have (2) relevant criteria and low standards (the prevailing situation); we can have (3) irrelevant criteria and low standards; or we can have the worst-case scenario: (4) irrelevant criteria and high standards.

Definitions

Definitions are useful in the standardization of discourse and the coordination of inquiries. They serve as starting points for inquiries that are fundamentally classificatory in nature and function as criteria for helping decide questions of inclu-

[7] This notion comes from Stanley Cavell, "Criteria and Judgment," in *The Claim of Reason* (New York: Oxford University Press, 1979), p. 11. I am indebted also to Roger A. Shiner's "Canfield, Cavell and Criteria," *Dialogue* 22 (1983), 253–72, and to John V. Canfield (ed.), *The Philosophy of Wittgenstein: Criteria*, vol. 7 (New York: Garland, 1986).

sion and exclusion. They are also suggestive when we are puzzled as to which word to use in a given context. Nevertheless, dictionary definitions must be taken with great caution, and teachers are prudent when they advise students to "consult" dictionaries rather than appeal to them. Beginning readers are particularly likely to find dictionary definitions treacherous; they are generally better off trying to hypothesize what the unknown word means in context instead of having the dictionary tell them what it means out of context.

Facts

Judgments often hinge upon facts, because so often it is a fact that is the pivot of a course of events:

> Two roads diverged in a yellow wood,
> And sorry I could not travel both
> And be one traveler, long I stood
> And looked down one as far as I could
> To where it bent in the undergrowth;
>
> Then took the other, as just as fair,
> And having perhaps the better claim,
> Because it was grassy and wanted wear

The two roads make their claims upon the traveler, but one was a bit grassier and "wanted wear." Indeed, the difference was so slight that Robert Frost tells that, as for wear, they were "really about the same." And yet "that has made all the difference."[8] Of course, it bears repeating that there are two intersecting influences here: The grassier road needs the traveler's footsteps, and so there is a fact but also a requiredness that bears upon the judgment. These criteria converge and reinforce each other; in another instance, they might have been in competition and neutralized each other. The world offers us a great deal that can serve as criteria, but it is under no obligation to make criteria compatible.

Test results

Tests are interventions aimed at obtaining sample bits of evidence on the basis of which judgments can be made. Those searching for oil first drill several test wells. Doctors administer tests for evidence of disease or injury. Teachers employ tests to ascertain levels of student proficiency. These experimental probes are everywhere relied upon in order to buttress the decision-making process. The test results may be taken to be merely informative, suggestive and illuminating, or compelling and decisive. When decisions are guided by test results, such results function as criteria even when the data itself is unimpressive. (Administrators who have to make decisions generally feel that some criteria, even weak ones, are better than none at all.)

[8] "The Road Not Taken," *The Complete Poems of Robert Frost* (New York: Holt, Rinehart and Winston, 1970).

Purposes

That human beings are often governed by their purposes would be hard to dispute. To a great extent, rationality consists in fashioning procedures and instruments by means of which those purposes can be achieved as well as in modifying purposes to make them consonant with what is available by way of instruments and procedures. Our chances of achieving our goals are greatest when we see to it that our ends-in-view and means-in-view are consistent with one another. In all cases that involve the arrangement of future conduct, purposes are governing factors.

A purpose, however, is not a motive. Motives are the engines by which we are driven. In Aristotle's language, they are efficient causes that force us ahead, while purposes are final causes that draw us onward. What makes purposes special if they are to be granted the status of cause is that they are also reasons.

They are, in particular, the kinds of reasons that primarily guide rather than justify. Tom's purpose – to rob Bill – does not justify Tom's robbing Bill. Tom's purpose leads him to shape his life as he does, to make the decisions he does, to perform the acts he does; it hardly matters whether we condemn that purpose or condone it – it functions as a fundamental organizing principle for Tom.

As such, it is a criterion. As such, it controls not only the making of broad life plans but even the making of narrow and precise judgments, such as those involved in measurement. It is here that purposes clearly serve as *standards,* for they determine the degree of tolerance we display for deviations from precision. The launching of a rocket must be on time in a way that children's arrival at school need not be. We have different purposes in these cases, and these lead to different standards of punctuality. And so our purposes not only serve as criteria for making judgments but also as standards for determining the degree to which we expect those criteria to be satisfied.

The assessment of performance

The twelve examples of criteria categories just given are not exhaustive. Nor should they be confused with the things we apply criteria *to* – the things that we expect to *satisfy* criteria.

Consider credentials. Credentials are generally not criteria; they are the sorts of things we might supply in order to meet certain criteria. Thus, when abroad, I carry my passport and visas because these will satisfy the criteria established in various countries for adequate identification. Credentials lend credence to our claims to be who we purport to be.

Likewise, performances are behaviors to which criteria are applicable, but they are generally not themselves criteria. Thus, we may have certain criteria by means of which we judge an actor's performance, and we may have specific standards of acceptability for each criterion. The actor's performance is considered proficient to the degree to which he satisfies or exceeds the standards we have set for each criterion.

Some proficiencies are matters of competence; others are matter of skill. Competencies are developed; skills are acquired. We crawl, we toddle, we walk, these are developing competencies. (We would hardly say that a child is a "skilled walker.") On the other hand, we learn to be skillful dancers or singers. Finally, there are some proficiencies, such as ones in the use of language, where competencies and skills intermesh. No doubt we apply both criteria and standards to both developed and acquired behavior, as when we say that a child lacks competence in walking or a person lacks skill in singing.

By means of a particular cognitive criterion, such as *consistency,* we can assess the degree of a person's cognitive skillfulness with respect to that criterion. We will know that we are dealing with someone who lacks skill in terms of that criterion if, for example the person asserts a conditional statement ("If it's a rat, then it's a rodent"), ("It's not a rodent"), and proceeds to draw the conclusion that denies the antecedent ("It can't be a rat"). You cannot do this and be consistent.

Community experience: the seedbed of criteria

Go back for a moment to the Frost poem. What was critical, it seemed, was the fact that one path was grassier and needed more to be walked on. But what needs did the traveler bring to that point where the roads diverged? It has been said that Frost's poem "was a slightly mocking parody of the behavior of Frost's friend, Edward Thomas, who used to choose a direction for their country walks, then, before they had finished, berate himself for not having chosen a different, more interesting way." But Frost, it is added, did not approve of "romantic 'sighing over what might have been.' "[9] And so it is not necessarily that this fact or this judgment shapes your whole life, for it may be that your whole way of life – whether it be romantic or otherwise – shapes the selection of the facts and judgments by which you are influenced.

Yet it is more than your personal way of life. It is, Stanley Cavell argues, the way of life – the "form of life," as Wittgenstein calls it – of the community to which you belong. There is a background of pervasive and systematic agreements among us that Wittgenstein sometimes calls conventions and at other times calls rules. But this agreement in criteria is not what coordinates our judgments. It is rather our shared form of life that coordinates our judgments, and this in turn produces an agreement with regard to criteria. Wittgenstein offers us a startling reversal:

Now the whole thing looks backwards. Criteria were to be the bases (features, marks, specifications) on the basis of which certain judgments could be made (non-arbitrarily); agreement over criteria was to make possible agreement about judgments. But in Wittgenstein it looks as if our ability to establish criteria depended upon a prior agreement in judgments.[10]

---

[9] Richard Ellmann (ed.), *The Norton Anthology of Modern Poetry* (New York: Norton, 1973), p. 196n.

[10] Cavell, "Criteria and Judgment," p. 30.

And yet, Cavell concludes, the establishment of criteria is not altogether superfluous, because they are "after the fact." By our proclaiming (and not merely predicating) our criteria, the process of judging becomes more open, less private and arbitrary. Establishing criteria allows us to *settle* judgments publicly by declaring what the points at issue are in various judgments and then making them final (on a given occasion):

That is a practice worth having; human decisions cannot wait upon certainty. But it is therefore one which can be abused. In assuming the burden of finality in the absence of certainty, an authority stakes the virtue of its community; if its judgments are not accepted as scrupulously fair, in its criteria and in its application of criteria, the community is shown to that extent not to provide a secure human habitation for its members.[11]

An so, just as Peirce had argued that "logic is rooted in the social principle" and that logicality embraces the whole community, so Wittgenstein and Cavell argue that community may precede judgment and judgment may precede the selection of criteria, bizarre as this may seem from the point of view of rationality.

A similar reversal takes place (apparently contrary to common sense) in creative thinking, where judgments precede the formation of criteria or themselves act as criteria. The artist and the inventor are neither following rules nor consciously making them, but the judgments they make are responsive to other judgments they or others have made, and will likely provide their communities with criteria for subsequent aesthetic judgments.

Critical and creative thinking are therefore in some ways (not in all ways) startling reversals of one another, like figure–ground reversals, and nowhere so remarkably as in the reversibility of criteria and judgments. For if community forms the context with which the process begins, it also characterizes the product with which it ends.

Consider a jazz combo improvising. Its innovative judgments are not shaped by criteria but by the sovereign influence of the jazz community. This is the community with which its creative thinking begins. But as instrumentalists play, it is evident that the improvisations of each are addressed to the others, and it is to these that the others respond, so that gradually the texture of the work assumes the form of a dialogue, of face-to-face communication – in fact, of a community. Indeed, the work of art generally is a community of judgments whose internal communication with one another contains the thinking we try to grasp in the form of aesthetic "meaning." The work of art is, then, a model of community – of a community of inquiry – in that the dialogical quest or process that has led up to it is precipitated into the dialogue internal to the product.

We can summarize here by saying that in the kind of thinking over which rationality presides, logicality is preeminent, whereas in the kind of thinking over which creativity presides as the aegis, dialogicality is preeminent. In educating for higher-order thinking, opportunities for the practice of both components must be amply provided.

[11] Ibid., p. 31.

In what Alvin W. Gouldner calls "the culture of critical discourse," good speech is speech that can make its own principles explicit and is oriented to conforming to them rather than stressing context sensitivity and context variability. The culture of critical discourse

> is also relatively more *reflexive,* self-monitoring, capable of more meta-communication, that is, of talk about talk. . . . More importantly, the culture of critical speech forbids reliance upon the speaker's person, authority or status in society to justify his claims. . . . From now on, persons and their social positions must not be visible in their speech. Speech becomes impersonal. Speakers hide behind their speech. Speech seems to be disembodied, de-contextualized and self-grounded.[12]

The quest for critical thinking is evidence that enterprises considering themselves devoted to rationality will seek to upgrade the quality of rationality in those enterprises. But this is not where it ends. The quest for critical thinking is likely to mean a search for reasons of greater and greater leverage – that is, for higher-order reasons – and this in turn may make criteria a glamorous elite among logical operators. That seems to be the inference to be drawn when teachers urge students to emulate professionals and found their thinking upon firm criteria.[13]

Finally, a word about teaching students *about* the role of criteria as governing factors in classification and evaluation as well as *how to* use criteria for these purposes. This is the sort of practical as well as theoretical knowledge that the present curriculum, at whatever level, fails to offer. A course in assessment should be a module of every social science curriculum, so as to provide students – particularly at the junior high school level – with essential information and practice about how professional and craft judgments are made and how students can utilize criteria in the making of judgments in their own lives. But the entire educational process is going to have to do a better job of cultivating students' reasoning and judgment proficiencies: It cannot be the responsibility of a single independent course.

[12] *The Future of Intellectuals and the Rise of the New Class* (New York: Seabury, 1979), p. 29.
[13] Ludwig Wittgenstein, *Philosophical Investigations* (Oxford: Blackwell Publisher, 1953). See in particular I, para. 242. Needless to say, virtually all of Wittgenstein's writings allude in one way or another to the problem of criteria. A remark like this, in *On Certainty,* is characteristic: ". . . some propositions are exempt from doubt, are as it were like hinges on which those turn" (para. 341). What better description of the mode of operation of criteria could there be than that they are the hinges on which our judgments turn?

The issues I have been reviewing are those which are generally taken for granted in discussions of criteria, for it is at about this point that philosophical examinations of the nature of criteria generally begin. A sustained backward glance would start with Plato, who is persistently intrigued with the topic, while a focus on the near distance would take into account such works as Urmson's "On Grading" (*Mind* 59 [1950], 145–69) and Crawshay-Williams's *Methods and Criteria of Reasoning* (London: Routledge and Kegan Paul, 1957), particularly pp. 26–40 and 235–62. The Urmson article has been persistently seminal, as is shown by two of its impressive progeny: Bruce Vermazen's "Comparing Evaluations of Works of Art," in W. E. Kennick (ed.), *Art and Philosophy,* 2d ed. (New York: St. Martin's, 1979), pp. 707–18, and George Dickie's *Evaluating Art* (Philadelphia: Temple University Press, 1988), particularly ch. 9, "Comparison and Specificity." It is in the latter piece that Dickie articulates the notion of criteriological matrices or grids by means of which comparisons of works of art with respect to particular criteria can be facilitated.

Complex thinking: combining the declarative and the procedural

It cannot be said that those who write about critical thinking generally acknowledge the importance of criteria in guiding such thinking. They are aware that their recommendations of how critical thinking ought to take place are *normative*, but they do not generally specify the criteria in terms of which such recommendations are offered.

It would be easy enough to show this with regard to some of the more diffuse articles on critical thinking, but let me address instead one of the more solid and trenchant accounts. I am referring to Arnold B. Arons's article on the ways critical thinking might be given greater emphasis in undergraduate science education. He begins by accepting the distinction between declarative and procedural or operative knowledge. Declarative knowledge consists of facts; operative knowledge involves understanding where the declarative knowledge comes from and what underlies it. Operative knowledge also involves "the capacity to use, apply, transform or recognize the relevance of declarative knowledge in new situations."[14] Now, it seems to me that this distinction between declarative and procedural or operative knowledge is a useful one. And if I now review the statement I have just made, it seems evident that I am guiding myself by certain criteria, such as *useful* (i.e., utility), *true*, and *correct*. For the information called "fact" is indeed fact if it can be subsumed under the criterion of truth; the procedures involved in operative knowledge are presumably judged in terms of their *correctness*; and the distinction between declarative and true satisfies the criterion of *utility*. Thus, the generalizations we make about critical thinking, generalizations on the broadest levels, are themselves aligned with criteria that we accept and to which we customarily appeal.

The same thing might be done with the ten "thinking and reasoning processes that underlie analysis and inquiry"[15] that Arons cites. These are quite useful, and I shall summarize them here, letting readers see for themselves how these recommendations appeal implicitly to such procedural criteria as appropriateness, consistency, plausibility, validity, and relevance and to such conceptual criteria as evidence, observation, inference, fact, induction, and deduction:

1. Consciously raising the questions What do we know . . . ?, How do we know . . . ?, Why do we accept or believe . . . ?, What is the evidence for . . . ? when studying some body of material or approaching a problem
2. Being clearly and explicitly aware of gaps in available information and being able to tolerate the resulting ambiguity and uncertainty
3. Discriminating between observation and inference, between established fact and subsequent conjecture

---

[14] " 'Critical Thinking' and the Baccalaureate Curriculum," *Liberal Education* 71:2 (1985), 142.
[15] Ibid.

4. Recognizing the necessity of using only words of prior definition, rooted in shared experience, in forming a new definition and of avoiding technical jargon
5. Probing for the implicit, unarticulated assumptions behind a line of reasoning
6. Drawing inferences from evidence and recognizing when firm inferences cannot be drawn
7. Performing hypothetico-deductive reasoning; i.e., given a particular situation, applying relevant knowledge of principles and constraints and visualizing, in the abstract, the plausible outcomes that might result from various changes we can imagine being imposed on the system
8. Discriminating between inductive and deductive reasoning
9. Testing our own reasoning for internal consistency, thereby developing intellectual self-reliance
10. Being self-conscious about our reasoning: recognizing the processes we are using, selecting those most appropriate, and providing the basis for conscious transfer of reasoning methods from familiar to unfamiliar contexts

Arons condemns the shakiness he has observed among future teachers in regard to arithmetical reasoning, their failure to understand the most fundamental scientific concepts, and their incapacity to deal with historical reasoning (they concentrate instead on historical "facts"). But he emphasizes that it is the weaknesses he condemns, not the teachers:

I wish to emphasize most strongly that the teachers whose incapacities I describe are *not* the ones to be blamed for this situation. The input terminals to the feedback loop of my metaphor reside in *our* hands at the colleges and universities. *We* are the ones who perpetuate the mismatch and fail to provide remediation of disabilities and enhancement of abstract reasoning capacities at the opportunities *we* control. *We* are the ones who made the teachers as they are.[16]

I shall have more to say later about the responsibility of the university for the situation in the schools.

Toward complex thinking: enlisting philosophy in the curriculum

I want to conclude this chapter by pointing out that Arons's distinction between the declarative and the procedural or operative is highly useful for bridging the gap between higher-order and complex thinking. The characterization of complex thinking that I have already offered is "the combination of substantive and procedural thinking." Arons has suggested that this is the combining of declarative knowledge and operative knowledge, and I have already shown critical and creative thinking to be components of higher-order thinking. I think the picture of *higher-order, complex* thinking can now, with Arons's help, emerge somewhat more clearly.

[16] Ibid., p. 154.

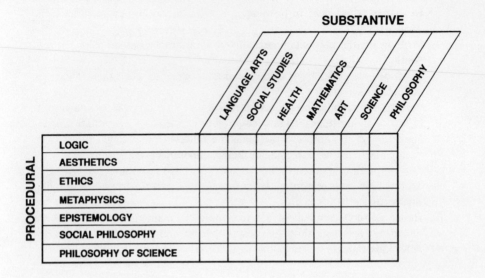

Figure 7

Consider what happens when philosophy is added to the curriculum. The consequence is not that the other subjects are weakened by being squeezed into smaller times slots. It must be seen rather that philosophy is a miscible subject that permeates the other disciplines and enriches them (fig. 7).

This should help us understand how systematically philosophy and the other disciplines interpenetrate so as to bring about complex rather than narrow and parochial thinking that fails to make judgments about human life.

I do not say that *only* the addition of philosophy to the curriculum can bring about complex thinking in education. Any discipline that supplements the teaching of the thinking in that discipline with teaching of the thinking about (or methodology of) the thinking in that discipline is engaged in encouraging the kind of thinking I have here been calling complex. But while it is important for a discipline to be open with students about its own methodology – its assumptions, its definitions, its idiosyncratic understandings, its self-image, its reasonings, and its criteria – I have to think that this is just the beginning of a movement in the direction of philosophy. We need *both* philosophy in the curriculum and complex thinking in the other disciplines.

8   Criteria as the hinges of practice

There are certain pivots, joints, and hinges that all practice turns on, whether it is self-correcting practice or not. They are often called standards: community standards, craft standards, professional standards, standards of common decency, and the like. In short, they are norms, and it is to these norms that people appeal when they claim that there are certain ways in which things "ought" to be done. The mores of a society are normative in that they specify how marriages, burials, property transactions, and the teaching of the young are to be carried out, and they can, if necessary, be articulated and codified as laws or principles – that is, as explicit criteria. Practice is methodical, and it is by one method or another that human activities are coordinated.

All societies endeavor to impress upon very young children certain modes of thought and behavior that are deemed essential to the continuity of those societies. Seldom are these children assured, even at adolescence, that the indoctrination was only for the very young and that they are now to use their own judgment in these matters. It is more likely that as these individuals enter adolescence they will be greeted by benevolent adults who will announce that they are there to help these young people decide what to believe and do. This rite of passage often involves a verbal acknowledgment that the young people have developed to a point where their thinking and conduct can be guided by criteria rather than by brute insistence upon conformity. This therefore raises a question as to whether the lives of these young people will continue to be regulated by unspoken social mandates or whether preparations will now be made for them to be independent and autonomous thinkers who can participate responsibly in a variety of communities within the larger society.

Critical thinking and the inculcation of belief

No one has labored more strenuously than Robert Ennis to advance critical thinking. We should therefore give him our attention when he tells us that critical thinking is aimed at helping us decide "what to believe and do." His choice of *believing* and *doing* is revealing, because believing and doing happen to be the targets of normal academic practice. School (so the thinking goes) is a place where we learn the right things to believe and where we learn to act accordingly.

143

Actually, the maxim is not couched in such blunt terms. It is said rather that school is a place where we learn the right things to know, but the inference is clear: If we have somehow been made to know something, then we have been compelled to believe it. And we can be counted on to act in accordance with our beliefs. Reading Ennis's definition of critical thinking, one has the uncomfortable feeling that this is precisely the language a late-twentieth-century society would employ if it wanted to ensure the acceptance by students of the more or less official ideologies of that society; it would do so under the guise of helping them think for themselves, helping them be more rational, and so on.

If we turn from normal academic practice to the inquiry paradigm of academic practice, we note that there is no longer a need to inculcate a set of substantive beliefs disguised as "knowledge." Instead, students are asked to accept in a tentative, provisional way the methodology of inquiry. This is the procedure that has been adopted by the inquiring community of which they are members. There are innumerable situations to be inquired into, and from countless ongoing inquiries there emerge a variety of settlements or verdicts, some fairly firm, representing what is "warrantedly assertible." For schoolchildren, what is in doubt may be friends and grades; for adult citizens, it may be inflation and the environment. It is because of the highly problematic nature of these issues that the general populace needs critical thinking. People need critical thinking in order to help them assess knowledge claims by distinguishing the stronger from the weaker, but that is a far cry from employing critical thinking in order to decide "what to believe." Critical thinking simply helps us avoid thinking uncritically and acting unreflectively.

Indeed, critical thinking is, if anything, even more valuable with respect to essentially contestable concepts and perennial arguments than it is with respect to matters for which there are acceptable decision procedures. When it comes to such questions as whether what has just been conceived is a human being, what the attitude of human beings toward animals and the rest of nature should be, and whether you can rightfully terminate your own life, it is obvious that, while the debates may move as slowly as glaciers so that progress is imperceptible, they nevertheless do move.

If the purpose of critical thinking is not to help us decide what to believe, what can that purpose be? Insofar as the question of knowledge and belief is concerned, I would say that the role of critical thinking is defensive: to protect us from being coerced or brainwashed into believing what others want to compel us to believe without our having an opportunity to inquire for ourselves. There are great and powerful forces ranged against the individual in every society – the political, the military, and the economic are the most obvious examples – and their aim is often to get us to acquiesce without reflection in the views they want us to have. The armor of skepticism that critical thinking can provide is not an impervious one as far as any given individual is concerned, but in a populace so armored it could be decisive. I think we are much better off construing critical thinking as nurturing in students a tentative skepticism than as nurturing in them a set of beliefs of dubious long-term reliability. Critical thinking can help us decide what claims *not* to believe.

Ennis's twin targets – belief and action – represent a misreading of the nature of education characteristic of the very popular confusion between education and schooling. It is schooling, not education, that insists that we be conventional and conform in our thought as well as in our behavior. What education insists upon, in contrast, is that we be reasonable and exercise good judgment while remaining cautious and open-minded with regard to beliefs.

It will be said, no doubt, that there is no basis for claiming that inquiry and belief are mutually incompatible (except, of course, for the belief in inquiry itself). But we cannot continue to believe that which is the subject of inquiry. When inquiry begins, it is because evidence has surfaced that constitutes grounds for suspension of belief, and until the inquiry is concluded, skepticism is the order of the day. The progressive self-correction that inquiry entails and the numerous settlements that are reached along the way progressively reduce the grounds for such skepticism. With the conclusion of the inquiry episode, when the problem has been resolved, there will be a renewed opportunity for belief, but it will be a reconstructed and chastened belief as a consequence of the inquiry that has just taken place.

Some will be quick to dismiss reasonableness and judgment as "mere process" or "mere method" and will decry the lack of attention to "content." It must be acknowledged that content is indispensable for the fostering of good judgment. Thus, if we want students to have good historical judgment, we will have to expose them to history; if we want them to have good literary judgment, we will have to expose them to literature; and if we want them to have good ecological judgment, we will have to expose them to ecology. But here precisely is where the mode of teaching – the mode of critical educational intervention – makes such a difference. If *all* we want is for the students to learn history or literature or ecology, little improvement in judgment can be expected. But if we understand that we are teaching them history critically *in order to* improve their historical judgment and not merely to provide them with grounds for patriotism, then content assumes its rightful place alongside method, neither inferior to it nor superior to it.

In point of fact, there is no way around teaching specific disciplinary contents (unless it is teaching *among* the disciplines as well as *within* them). If critical thinking essentially involves *sensitivity to context*, then it is only by direct encounters with particular contents that we can discover the contexts to which we should be sensitive. Unless we come up against the specificity of particular contents, their undeniable, inescapable *thisness*, we have little to become sensitive *to*. It is the irreducible particularity or individuality of specific disciplinary contents that demands scrupulous student attention. And to such encounters students must be taught to bring the self-correcting method of inquiry.

Finally, it is no less important that students engaged in academic practice come to understand the criterion dependency of all judgments and the judgment dependency of all inquiry. We tend to think of criteria as esoteric logical devices thinly populating some remote epistemological Olympus. We forget that criteria are applicable to every mental act, even where such acts do not themselves involve the conscious employment of criteria in their making. The person who exclaims, "Shakespeare's poetry is glorious" may or may not be aware of taking into account the differences between Shakespeare and Bacon, between poetry and prose, between "is" and "was," or between "glorious" and "flamboyant," but subsidiary judgments such as these undergird the judgment expressed in the proposition, and these subsidiary judgments are guided by their own proper criteria. Nouns may be primarily classification devices, adjective and adverbs evaluation devices, and verbs both, but in any case, whether it is a matter of classification or of evaluation, such usages are judgments and are therefore criterion-dependent. But the exact nature of the criteria to be selected will itself depend upon whether the inquiry in question is under the aegis preponderantly of rationality or of creativity.

Alternative approaches to teaching practical reasoning

Practice ranges from dull, mindless, habitual routine to dull, mechanical competence. When, however, practice comes to be permeated with critical thinking, so that we reflect critically on what we do before, while, and after we do it, mere practice becomes self-correcting practice, and self-correcting practice is inquiry.[1]

First, what are the purposes that critical thinking is presumed to be able to help us achieve? I would say they are better thinking, better performance, and better problem solving. The first of these is primarily a means to the attainment of the second and third. Thinking critically will not only produce better problem solving, but it will also produce better problem deterrence and problem avoidance. It will not only help bring about improved performances, but it will also enable us to select and concentrate on those areas in which achievement is more worthwhile.

These three purposes express themselves in three types of critical thinking programs. In the first group are programs devoted to cognitive improvement through the enhancement of logicality and rationality. In the second group are programs that aim at improved levels of skilled performance – academic achievement, athletic achievement, artistic achievement, moral achievement, and so on. In the third group are programs that attempt to strengthen the student's ability to recognize and resolve problems. It is not, of course, that these three purposes are so different that the programs follow strictly separate paths; there is a great deal of overlap. Nevertheless, the emphasis of the first group is upon sound reasoning; the second emphasizes adroit performances that satisfy explicit criteria, and the third stresses the rapprochement of ends and means. Another way of putting this would be to say that programs of the first sort put their emphasis on the guidance of practice by reasons, the second on the guidance of practice by criteria, and the third on the guidance of practice by hypotheses and consequences.

---

[1] Cf. John Dewey on judgments of practice in *Essays in Experimental Logic* (Chicago: University of Chicago Press, 1917), pp. 183–216.

The guidance of practice by reasons

Certain aspects of Philosophy for Children's "ethical inquiry" approach would be typical here. Consider this version of that approach:

Children are very much aware that certain acts are generally disapproved of and others are given social approval. They are also aware that the teacher carries moral authority, and they generally do not feel in a position to question that authority. This means that ethical inquiry, which involves a certain amount of thinking for oneself about moral issues, is very difficult to bring about in the classroom setting. If for example, one child hits another, students are fully aware that hitting is considered wrong and that the teacher will condemn the act. Therefore, the children have no opportunity for inquiry into the situation that prompted the act. Let us, however, consider an alternative scenario in which the teacher is concerned to decenter both the act and his or her authority in order to invite the class to think about what happened and therefore to assume some responsibility for the decision that must be made with regard to it. Thus, instead of immediately condemning the act, the teacher might inquire in an impartial manner what reasons the child might have had for hitting another. Suppose the child says, "I didn't like his looks." The teacher may then turn to the class and ask, "Is that a good reason?" The members of the class may now proceed to weigh the *reason rather than the act.* They may very well chorus, "No, *that's* not a good reason." Alternatively, the child may say, "He pulled a knife on me!" and the class will have to deliberate about *that* reason. The point is that the children will learn that all ethical acts must have reasons and that it is well to think of the reason before one engages in the act, because if one does not, one must face the moral censure of one's peers.[2] This is not decision making by mere consensus. The guidance we receive is from a critical community that weighs the reasons for actions and not just the actions in isolation.

The normal objection to this approach is that it shifts the basis of moral authority from the strong position of the teacher to the weak position of the class. In a sense, this is certainly true. The aim is to decenter the burden of moral responsibility by removing at least some of it from the teacher. But the teacher's position is not as strong, in the eyes of the students, as it appears to be to us. The teacher's moral authority rests on his or her being an adult and not on being an expert in ethical decision making. The students may respect the teacher's managerial efficiency, but this is not the same as respecting the teacher for being able to offer a rational justification for praise of this action or condemnation of that one.

As a matter of fact, the teacher's situation is intimately familiar to each of us, because we are in it every day. We may reiterate to ourselves over and over again that overeating is wrong, smoking is wrong, drinking is wrong, and so on, yet we persist in doing the very things we condemn. So with children. They are as aware

---

[2] This paragraph is quoted from Matthew Lipman and Ann Margaret Sharp, "How Are Values to Be Taught?" in *Ethics in Education* 9:2 (November 1989), 2–3.

as the teacher is that lying, stealing, and hitting are condemned by adults as wrong, and they may not disagree with the judgment. Their problem is to avoid *doing* what they consider to be wrong.

If we have learned anything at all about the success of adult group therapy sessions, it is that groups are not content merely to examine the *explanations* of the behaviors they agree in condemning. Eventually they must explore the *reasons* for and against such behaviors, for only then can participants assume responsibility for themselves. The same is true with children. Merely to prohibit certain behaviors is insufficient. Merely to explain them causally is insufficient. Children must be encouraged to discuss and deliberate about the reasons such conduct is problematic – to us and to themselves – so that they can proceed to determine what they deem right or wrong based on reasoned justifications.

Criterion-based performance

Now consider a different situation: A member of the school swimming team has entered a national competition for diving. She has been practicing for months and reviewing her practice with her coach. She has also been prepping herself with regard to the criteria that the judges will employ, and she recognizes the need to set very high standards for each criterion. In many ways her performance will be responsive to and guided by these criteria. This is again an "ethical inquiry" approach, especially if the whole team and the coach have, as a community, discussed the relationship of relevant criteria and standards to their swimming and diving practice.

The guidance of practice by hypotheses and consequences

This approach is a descendant of Dewey's "problem-solving" procedure, first outlined in *How We Think*.[3] Here is a contemporary version of it:

Eight steps to solutions

1. Encourage your child to look for signs of different feelings and to express them. Example: "I feel upset."
2. Help your child encapsulate the problem into a statement: "I feel upset *because Todd is teasing me.*"
3. Assist your child in deciding on a goal, such as "I want Todd to stop picking on me."
4. Don't provide answers. Help your child list multiple solutions of his or her own, such as "I could hit Todd or yell at him."
5. Enable your child to anticipate possible consequences of each approach: Q: "What would happen if you hit Todd?" A: "I'd get into more trouble or Todd could get hurt."

[3] Revised ed. (Boston: Heath, 1933).

6. Help your child decide on the best solution. "I'll yell at Todd." Should an inappropriate approach begin to emerge, offer an opinion without squashing the child's creativity. Don't wait until after a decision has been made to express your opposition.
7. Assist your child in planning when or how the decision might be executed. Help anticipate obstacles that could occur: "What might happen that could make yelling at Todd not work?" A child who can foresee possible problems is less discouraged by any roadblock that might occur.
8. Have your child try out the solution and evaluate its effect. End by inviting your child to "let me know how it worked out."[4]

Note what is involved in each of these steps:

1. Expression of *feeling* that there is a problem
2. Identification of *cause* of feeling (*formulation* of problem)
3. Choice of desired *end*-state or goal (formulation of *purpose*)
4. Identification of *means* (devising of *hypotheses*)
5. Anticipation of *consequences*
6. Selection among *alternatives*
7. Devising *plan* of operations
8. *Evaluation* of effects

This strikes me as being a sensible algorithm: an eight-step sequence of procedures that need to be employed in dealing with problematic situations. Putting such an algorithm into operation would likely be an effective demonstration of rational conduct.

To many people, thinking like this seems to come naturally. But in fact to many others it is much more difficult than it looks. Each of the eight procedures requires considerable skill; combining them properly requires even more skill. And although the algorithm looks reasonable and commonsensical, whether we do in fact utilize it in daily life is hardly self-evident. Certainly an impulsive, unreflective child might be expected to have some difficulty with it. It is therefore useful to learn from Elias and Clabby, the proponents of this approach, that experimental testing has shown it to be significantly successful.

In general, with regard to cognitive algorithms of this type, whether designed for therapeutic or for educational purposes, we would do well to integrate them into broad-gauge efforts to enhance reflection, raise consciousness, and sharpen cognitive skills, rather than use them all by themselves. Some of the stages of the algorithm specifically involve reasoning, and virtually all involve judgment. Without continued practice in critical, creative, and complex thinking, the algorithm could be of far less value than it otherwise promises to be.

[4] This eight-step procedure is quoted from "How to Teach Decision-Making to Kids," *U.S. News and World Report*, April 21, 1986, p. 64, a discussion of the problem-solving approach of Maurice J. Elias and John F. Clabby. See also Elias and Clabby, "Teaching Social Decision Making," *Educational Leadership*, March 1988, pp. 52–5, and George Spivack and Myrna Shure, *The Social Adjustment of Young Children* (San Francisco: Jossey-Bass, 1974).

It seems to me that the problem-solving, decision-making approaches of Spivack and Shure and of Elias and Clabby are more likely to be successful when they are part of a comprehensive pedagogical approach aimed at improving children's inquiry, reasoning, information organizing, and translation skills. It is precisely this overarching approach that philosophy provides. Other programs emphasizing problem solving can be made to fit very well into philosophy, although philosophy is too extensive to serve as a component of one of them. Some skeptics are apt to see this as a kind of curricular imperialism. Raising spectres of this kind, however, is not likely to be very profitable. We have seen what education *without* philosophy is like. It is time to see what it is like *with* philosophy.

Practical reasoning behaviors

The question most frequently asked by teachers expected to teach for critical thinking is "How can I tell when I am teaching for critical thinking and when I am not?" Revealingly, the question is itself a demand for criteria.

The definition I have offered is a kind of bridge over four supporting piers: self-correction, sensitivity to context, criteria, and judgment. What a teacher would like to know is what classroom behaviors are associated with each of these categories.[5] And even if the teacher does observe these behaviors separately, does it follow that he or she is applying the definition?

We can take up the supporting concepts one by one:

Self-correction

Examples of associated behaviors

   a. Students point out errors in each other's thinking
   b. Students acknowledge errors in their own thinking
   c. Students disentangle ambiguous expressions in texts
   d. Students clarify vague expressions in texts
   e. Students demand reasons and criteria where none have been provided
   f. Students contend that it is wrong to take some matters for granted
   g. Students identify inconsistencies in discussions
   h. Students point out fallacious assumptions or invalid inferences in texts
   i. Students identify the commission of fallacies in formal or informal reasoning
   j. Students question whether inquiry procedures have been correctly applied

[5] A number of instruments are available to evaluate the thinking of elementary school children. Although there appear to be none that effectively evaluate children's judgment, there are some that concentrate more or less successfully on children's reasoning. I would cite here the *New Jersey Test of Reasoning Skills* (Upper Montclair, N.J.: IAPC, 1983). For an instrument to evaluate possible changes in teacher attitudes toward students' cognitive potentials, there seems to be very little available other than the *Cognitive Behavior Checklist* (Upper Montclair, N.J.: IAPC, 1990).

Acquiring sensitivity to context

  Examples of associated behaviors

  a. Students differentiate among nuances of meaning stemming from cultural differences
  b. Students differentiate among nuances of meaning stemming from differences in personal perspectives or points of view
  c. Students recognize differences due to language differences, disciplinary differences, and differences of frames of reference
  d. Students contend to establish authenticity and integrity of interpretations of texts
  e. Students contest accuracy of translations
  f. Students point out how definitional meanings are modified by contextual circumstances
  g. Students note changes in meaning due to alterations of emphasis
  h. Students recognize changes in meaning resulting from shifts in speakers' intentions or purposes
  i. Students note discrepancies between present situation and seemingly similar past situations
  j. Students search for differences between seemingly similar situations whose consequences are different

Being guided (and goaded) by criteria

  Examples displayed by students

  a. Shared values, such as ideals, purposes, goals, aims, and objectives
  b. Conventions, such as norms, regularities, uniformities, and precedents or traditions
  c. Common bases of comparison, such as shared respects, properties, or characteristics
  d. Requirements, such as precepts, specifications, stipulations, and limitations
  e. Perspectives, including areas of concern, frames of reference, and points of view
  f. Principles, including assumptions, presuppositions, and theoretical or conceptual relationships
  g. Rules, including laws, bylaws, regulations, charters, canons, ordinances, and directions
  h. Standards – criteria for determining the degree of satisfaction needed to satisfy a criterion
  i. Definitions: assemblages of criteria that together have the same meaning as the word to be defined
  j. Facts: what there is, as expressed in warranted assertions

k. Tests: probes or interventions for the purpose of eliciting empirical findings
l. Purposes: aims, goals, or objectives by means of which developments can be appraised as on target or off target

Judgment

Examples displayed by students

a. Settlements of deliberations
b. Verdicts of trials of inquests
c. Decisions, as by administrators, executives, parents, teachers, etc.
d. Determinations: conclusive findings of investigative proceedings
e. Solutions to actual or theoretical problems
f. Classifications or categorizations
g. Evaluations of performances, services, objects, products, etc.; assessments
h. Distinctions, in the form of negative predications
i. Connections, in the form of affirmative predications
j. Deliberate, intentional makings, sayings, or doings

It should be pointed out that the examples of criteria and judgments listed above are examples of *types*; for greater specificity, we would have to turn to a taxonomy such as the excellent one by Ennis that I mentioned before. Obviously, it is no small task to prepare teachers to recognize the behavioral instances as well as the types of instances that are to be encouraged to operationalize the definition of critical thinking. Indeed, to do so effectively would require a recasting of a considerable portion of the programs by which teacher preparation is now carried out. Yet it will take a far-reaching reform such as this to bring about the emergence and maintenance of critical thinking in the classroom.

Teaching for bridging, transfer, and translation

One of the problems of present-day education is that students acquire bits of knowledge that, like ice cubes frozen in their trays, remain inert and incapable of interacting with one another. Consequently, educational reformers have placed a premium on helping children construct bridges from one knowledge domain to another, such as by discovering intervening variables, middle terms, missing links, and the like by means of which disparate domains can be connected. Emphasis has also been placed on the development of generic skills that are not specific content areas but are transferrable from one domain to another. Finally, there has been a search for ways of treating various domains as symbolic systems, languages, or communities, so that translation procedures that would enable students to translate the contents of one domain into another can be learned.

An example of bridging can be taken from classificatory reasoning. If we present students with a completion exercise such as "All Londoners are ____ ; All ____ are British; therefore, All Londoners are British," they are not limited to a single answer, but the students are of course required to find a middle term that will link those who are residents of London with those who are British. Alternatively, one might give students bridging practice by offering them a term such as "residents of England" and asking them what domains it connects. It is then possible to move to other concepts, asking such questions as "What do sunspot activity and precipitation have in common?" and "What domains does barter connect?"

Examples of transfer are amply provided by David N. Perkins and Gavriel Salomon, who distinguish between "low road" and "high road" transfer.[6] We are engaged in low-road transfer when, being already proficient in driving an automobile, we find it relatively easy to learn to drive a truck. The skills needed to drive the truck are sufficiently congruent to those needed to drive the car that we can readily extrapolate from the one situation to the other. In the case of high-road transfer, the two domains are not closely related but far apart. It may take a metaphor to establish a connection between them. When Shakespeare uses the phrase "summer's lease," we are forced to connect the brief tenancy that summer has during the course of a year with the tenancy one has in the apartment one rents or in the life one lives. The carryover from such disparate domains is of course far richer (if more tenuous) than that linking the world of cars and the world of trucks.

In the case of translation, the paradigm case is translating from one natural language to another. We find that knowledge of a root language like Latin makes it easier for people to learn French or Spanish than it would be if they had no such preparation. Or there is Aristotelian logic, which aims to furnish us with a highly simplified but universal language. Or there are parallel constructions, as in the arts, where musical and poetic structures can be compared, or painterly and photographic treatments of nature, or architectural and sculptural treatments of masses in space.

No doubt all three of these strategies – bridging, transfer, and translation – require of students facility with analogical reasoning. The connections that have to be established may be readily evident or far-fetched, but whatever the degree of difficulty they present, preparation for making them requires intense immersion in analogical practice. This is a skill developed in the arts and humanities as well as in the sciences. It is the most generic of the creative skills and the most imaginative of the analytic skills. The intellectual flexibility and resourcefulness needed to engage in successful translation and transfer will occur only when analogical practice is cultivated with the same feverish intensity we now reserve for the learning of say, arithmetic.

What makes higher-order thinking good?

Critical thinking, I have argued, is thinking that is governed primarily by criteria in order to make a rational judgment, and in a previous section I listed some examples of the kinds of criteria by which a given instance of thinking might be

[6] "Teaching for Transfer," *Educational Leadership,* September 1988, pp. 22–32.

identified as critical. While both critical and creative thinking are context-sensitive, a major point of difference is that critical thinking is guided mainly by discursively formulable criteria, whereas creative thinking is governed mainly by the nondiscursive quality of the situation in which the creative inquiry is taking place. Inasmuch as this situation is identical with the context of the inquiry, we may say that creative thinking is context-governed and not merely context-sensitive.

Since higher-order thinking is a product of both critical and creative thinking, this would seem to suggest a hopeless détente or standoff between criteria and context as the court of highest appeal. But in fact, as anyone who has participated in or witnessed a first-rate dialogue can attest, such a confrontation does not generally occur. Instead, there is an interaction between the discursive and the nondiscursive, between the critical and the creative, such that the discursive aspects of the problematic situation are referred for guidance to criteria, while nondiscursive aspects are situationally guided. Thus, when we say that we are following the inquiry where it leads, we mean that we are taking our cues from the situation itself as it develops and unfolds. The novelist does this in letting himself be guided by the demands of the plot, the painter does this in letting herself be guided by the emerging requirements of the painting. W. H. Auden puts it well when he says:

In the earlier stages of composition, the poet has to act like a Greek tyrant; the decision to write this phrase rather than that must be largely his, for the demands of the poem are as yet inarticulate or contradictory. As composition proceeds, the poem begins to take over the job of ruling itself; the transeunt rule of the poet gets weaker and weaker until, in the final stages, he is like the elected representative of a democracy whose duty it is to listen to and execute the demands of the poem, which now knows exactly what it wishes to be. On completion, the poem rules itself immanently, and the poet is dismissed into private life.[7]

I do not mean that in instances of higher-order thinking some participants assume a wholly critical posture while the stance of others is wholly creative, although this may conceivably happen. It is much more likely that all participants contribute to both the critical and the creative aspects of the dialogue, just as they do in their individual reflections.

Nor is it likely that we will ever be able to sort these elements out sufficiently to enable us to distinguish them clearly from one another. We must accept the fact that there is no such thing as pure critical or pure creative thinking. There is just thinking, and higher-order thinking is the order that blends the critical and the creative.

How then do we distinguish higher-order thinking from thinking that is of lesser quality in the same order? The matter might be expressed figuratively by saying that the quality of the thinking is not the sum of the creative and critical factors but is instead its product. But this is still inadequate. When it comes to the critical/creative order of thinking, what counts for better?

[7] "Squares and Oblongs," in Ruth Nanda Anshen (ed.), *Language: An Inquiry into Its Meaning and Function* (Port Washington, N.Y.: Kennikat, 1957), p. 177.

From the standpoint of heuristics, the answer is clear: The more a form of thinking advances the inquiry, the better it is. But from the standpoint of algorithmics, a different answer is clear: The more purely a form of thinking embodies the methodology of inquiry, the better it is. What are we to say about these different senses of cognitive excellence?

The hidden pivots of cognitive excellence

I think we need to distinguish here, as Dewey does, between the *instrumental* and the *consummatory*. Either a given episode of thinking can be considered insofar as it serves as a means to some desirable experiential consequence or it can be considered insofar as it is satisfying for its own sake. It may therefore have means value or end value. But it would be an oversimplification to say no more than this, because what is primarily a means may also provide immediate satisfaction (a person might enjoy driving a car for its own sake and not simply because it takes her where she wants to go). And what is primarily an end may nevertheless function, in a larger means–end continuum, as a means to some still further end (a person's enjoyment of music might play an instrumental role in his obtaining a job in a music store).

And so with episodes of thinking. We can consider the deliberations of a panel of judges solely with regard to the way these lead up to and produce a verdict, or we can consider them solely with regard to the enjoyment they provide when considered for their own sake. The first type of consideration involves an analysis of the relationships between *means and ends*; the second type involves an analysis of the relationships between *parts and wholes*.

Thus, in considering the deliberations of a group of students, legislators, jurors or whatever solely from a consummatory point of view, we would take into account the participatory performances of each member as skilled contributions to the whole, much as we would assess the performance of an orchestra in terms of the skills of each instrumentalist and the coordination of all of them as parts contributing to and making up an expressive whole.

The relationship between parts and wholes is fundamental to aesthetic experience and to the consummatory phase of all experience. The relationship between means and ends is fundamental to ethical analysis and to the ethical aspect of all experience. When it comes to the matter of judging cognitive excellence, we begin to see that the hidden pivots of such judgments are binary concepts like instrumental/consummatory, means/ends, and parts/wholes. Reliance upon binary concepts is, of course, characteristic of creative rather than critical thinking. This indicates that the judgment of cognitive excellence is more likely to be the product of creative than of critical inquiry.

Criteria as gauges of value

In thinking critically we are endeavoring to think not just reasonably but judiciously. That is, we are attempting to mediate among different arguments from different points of view, and at the same time we are attempting to be sensitive to the unique context in which we find ourselves (in other words, the merits of the case) while yet being loyal to the ideals and principles to which we are committed.[8] In the process, our thinking is guided by both criteria and values.[9] But these are not mutually exclusive. Instead, as in a Venn diagram, there are some of each and then there are some that are both.

Take a simple case of product evaluation as an instance of critical thinking. The shopper in the grocery store is trying to satisfy two kinds of *needs:* his felt lunchtime hunger and his known nutritional requirements. To understand nutrition, we must take into account two kinds of *values:* the ideal value of health and the actual nourishment offered by the particular foods in the store. Nutrition represents the relationship between the actual value and the ideal value.[10] To understand this, the shopper has only to look at the chart printed on the container. Say that the stuff in the container is yogurt. The protein content of the yogurt

[8] For Aristotle, the major premise of a syllogism generally embodies knowledge, while the minor premise embodies practical experience. When we have both ("Light meat is wholesome" and "Chicken is light meat"), we simply do what is logical, not *because* logic commands it but *as* logic commands. We simply eat chicken (see *Nicomachean Ethics,* 1141b; McKeon, p. 1029).

[9] Actual values – or at least what are here called actual values – resemble what Spinoza calls true goods:

> Man conceives a human character much more stable than his own, and sees that there is no reason why he should not himself acquire such a character. Thus he is led to seek for means which will bring him to this pitch of perfection, and calls everything which will serve as such means a true good. The chief good is that he should arrive, together with other individuals if possible, at the possession of the aforesaid character. (The Chief Works of Benedict de Spinoza, tr. R. H. M. Elwes [London, 1887], II, 1ff.)

For Dewey, there are ideals, and there are actual forces in society that move to approximate those ideals. There is the movement of law toward justice, of medicine toward health, of science toward truth, and so on. Dewey finds the *relationship* between these swelling movements and the ideals that draw them on awesomely impressive. See Joseph Ratner (ed.), *Intelligence in the Modern World: John Dewey's Philosophy* (New York: Modern Library, 1939), p. 1025.

[10] Charles Taylor argues that there is good and bad practical reasoning. The good model represents a "reasoning in transitions":

> It aims to establish, not that some position is correct absolutely, but rather that some position is superior to some other. It is concerned, covertly or openly, implicitly or explicitly, with comparative propositions. We show one of these comparative claims to be well founded when we can show that the *move* from A to B constitutes a gain epistemically. This is something we do when we show, for instance, that we get from A to B by identifying and resolving a contradiction in A or a confusion which A relied on. . . . The nerve of the rational proof consists in showing that this transition is an error-reducing one.

A bit further on, Taylor tells us that the bad model of practical reasoning,

> rooted in the epistemological tradition, constantly nudges us towards a mistrust of transition arguments. It wants us to look for "criteria" to decide the issue, i.e., some considerations which could be established even outside the perspectives in dispute and which would nevertheless be decisive. But there cannot be such considerations. My perspective is defined by the moral intuitions I have, by what I am morally moved by. If I abstract from this, I become incapable of understanding any moral argument at all. You will only convince me by changing my reading of my moral experience, and in particular my reading of my life story, of the transitions I have lived through – or perhaps refused to live through. (Charles Taylor, *Sources of the Self* [Cambridge, Mass.: Harvard University Press, 1989], pp. 72–73)

will be listed on the carton. But it will be listed in two ways: in terms of the actual weight of protein in grams and in terms of the percentage this weight represents of the daily minimum requirement for protein of a normal human being. Now, this daily minimum requirement is the nutritional requirement to be met; the percentage represented by the yogurt in the carton is the degree to which the protein therein satisfies the criterion. (An example of a low standard of nourishment would be a daily intake of protein representing only 20 percent of the minimum requirement.)

The shopper takes all of these considerations into account, the decisive ones being the criteria.[11] The judgment is made and can readily be defended by citing the considerations as justifying reasons. Nor should we be too quick to refer slightingly to this example as merely a case of rational consumerism. It is a homely instance, to be sure, but any attempt to approximate or achieve an ideal value through means that are actual values consistent with the ideal is an instance of the construction of goodness, where what is to be done is the criterion that guides the actual making and doing.

With respect to thinking, we can again distinguish between actual and ideal values. There is the actual value of critical thinking and the ideal value of rationality; there is the actual value of creative thinking and the ideal value of creativity; there is the actual value of judgment and the ideal value of wisdom. The dynamic forward movement that steers the actual process of medicine in the direction of health or science in the direction of truth or art in the direction of beauty is *inquiry*. It is inquiry that guides processes that would otherwise be blind toward ideals that would otherwise be static and effete. Inquiry is not itself the relationship between actual and ideal values; it is the process that reveals that relationship.

Then too, the distinction between criteria and values is a fuzzy one. Both guide judgments; both can function as ends; both can function as means. We see this particularly clearly when we consider such "regulative ideas" as rationality and creativity. Surely each of these is something we very much prize and esteem

It is difficult to imagine how one could identify a contradiction without a criterion of contradiction, or how one could identify an epistemic gain without a criterion of epistemic gain. In short, it is difficult to understand how, even when we do not count wholly on criteria, we are to operate wholly without them. Nevertheless, Taylor's point is well taken insofar as he can be understood as saying that practical reasoning that depends upon the use of criteria (what I call critical thinking) is good practical reasoning, while practical reasoning that tries to employ criteria but is in fact guided by our value intuitions is misguided and bad. He is asking us not to confuse the role of context-driven creative thinking with the role of criterion-driven critical thinking when it comes to value inquiry. The point I am making is that value inquiry requires both critical and creative thinking and rests on values as well as on criteria.

[11] For a useful analysis of the role of values and criteria in influencing and guiding judgments, see Thomas S. Kuhn, "Objectivity, Value Judgment and Theory Choice," *The Essential Tension* (Chicago: University of Chicago Press, 1977), pp. 320–39. A more recent analytic work is Allan Gibbard, *Wise Choices, Apt Feelings: A Theory of Normative Judgments* (Cambridge, Mass.: Harvard University Press, 1990). See in particular the chapter "Communities of Judgment," pp. 233–52.

(thereby suggesting that it is a value) and something by means of which we attempt to appraise what we prize and to estimate what we esteem, thereby indicating that it is a criterion.

It seems hardly necessary to point out that human beings are much more in accord with regard to what they consider values than with regard to what they consider instances of such values. We all, or virtually all, subscribe to rationality, but whether or not this particular instance is a case of rationality is likely to produce widespread disagreement. We may all deplore lying, but whether or not this particular verbal behavior could be called a lie may produce a convulsion in the community. This is why values are not enough; this is why they have to be complemented with criteria – so that we can tell what counts for an instance of the value in question. In this sense, criteria are for the thinker what calipers are for the machinist or tape measures for the home builder. They are independent dependable instruments that enable these workers to coordinate their activities efficiently. Their value lies in the way they help us implement our other values.

Criteria and experience

I have devoted so much attention to criteria – this chapter and the preceding two – because I see recourse to criteria as a powerful procedure wherever a claim is laid to cognitive accountability. Nevertheless, criteria are not infallible; they are the products of experience and can be overthrown by experience. Practically speaking, they are surrogates or stand-ins for authoritative voices in the community, and all the fuzziness that characterizes the distinction between legitimate and illegitimate authority among persons is likely to attend similar distinctions when applied to criteria.

Although criteria have an undeniable authority with regard to thinking, I would not want to exaggerate their importance in other domains, such as experience, life, and nature itself. Much of nature proceeds unthinkingly and proceeds, therefore, without reasons, standards, or norms of any kind. As for our experience, it is shaped by our judgments as our judgments are shaped by our criteria, and yet shape is not everything. There is also the qualitative substance of our experience to be taken into account: this joy here and now, this searing grief, this mischievous glance, this contemptible act, this soaring aria, this exquisite taste. These qualitative aspects of experience are not innocent of criteria; it is because we have criteria that we know how much they count. Yet without such experiences the criteria themselves would be worthless.

9 The strengthening of judgment

Expertness in judgment is generally thought to be the result of principle or of practice. Principled judgments are those guided by standards, criteria, and reasons. Teaching students to make principled judgments therefore focuses upon having them learn the principles by which their judgments are to be regulated. Judgments of practice, on the other hand, are the products of experience, and students are expected to arrive at expertness by profiting from their experience as they gradually make their judgments better and better.

Now, both of these approaches are on target. True, in theoretical fields the emphasis will be on the acquisition of principles; in fields populated by artisans, craftspersons, and artists the emphasis will be on practice; and in professional and technological fields the emphasis will be approximately equal. Obviously, both approaches are necessary. The question is – and here what I have primarily in mind is the formation of judgment in *educational* contexts – are they sufficient?

Before proceeding to deal at some length with this question, I am aware of another that interposes itself. It is a question many educators would feel inclined to ask, and the reasoning would run something like this: "Why are we spending all this time talking about judgment? Judgment is in no way a recognized area of educational responsibility. It has never been. Children come to us to learn – to acquire knowledge. How well or badly they apply that knowledge is up to them. Granted, we have neglected the teaching of reasoning. But we need not apologize for failing to teach judgment. No one has offered to show us how to do it in a school context, and it is doubtful that anyone ever will."

Parents have been inclined to accept this argument, although not without a little grumbling. To the extent that they are aware of their children's poor judgment, they are likely to think that it is they, the parents, who have failed and not the schools. Are the children impulsive, irresponsible, prejudiced toward others? These frailties, parents have been told, are defects of character, and such defects are attributable to home upbringing rather than to schooling. But this explanation leaves the parents frustrated. Even if they accept the responsibility that has been thrust upon them, they see no way out except with the school's help. The school, whether it likes it or not, has become a surrogate home, and the development of judgment is now a task for which there must be shared accountability.

Some parents are inclined to think that the improvement of children's judgment can be achieved by more effectively implanting in them strict codes of traditional values. But others shake their heads and say, "Perhaps, but the nub of the matter is judgment, and this is where we have to do better. Our youngsters have to learn to distinguish the authentic from the phony, the profound from the superficial, the justified from the unwarranted. They have to learn that the world they inhabit is not always candid with itself, so that violence against the innocent and helpless is only reluctantly defined as injustice, while victims are routinely told that they are the authors of their own suffering. If the schools could do more to teach our children to exercise better judgment, it would protect them against those who would inflame them with prejudice and manipulate them through indoctrination. It would make them better producers and consumers, better citizens, and better future parents. So why not education for better judgment?"

To many, this question will seem a plaintive one, similar to the one posed by Henry Higgins: "Why can't a woman be more like a man?" But the problem children have – of making sense of the world, making judgments about it, and acting accordingly – is a profoundly serious one. We like to think of ourselves as "firm" when we retort that the schools have never taught for judgment and are not going to start doing it now – until we recall Bertrand Russell's mocking comment, "I am firm, you are stubborn, he is pig-headed." We are going to have to teach for better judgment, so we had better set about figuring out how to do it.

Judgment as critical and judgment as creative

We should not assume, to begin with, that the improvement of children's reasoning will necessarily result in their having better judgment, just as it cannot be assumed that better judgments will necessarily be followed by better actions. We are in the area of likelihood here, not necessity.

The reasonableness we want to cultivate in students is, to be sure, the result of a combination of reasoning and judgment , but the relationship between the two is highly complex. Probably – we are not quite sure how – there is a kind of osmosis by means of which they flow into each other, so that at least some judgment informs all reasonings and at least some reasoning informs all judgments. Or, as Santayana might have put it, all judgments have a kernel of reasoning and all reasonings have judgment as their natural fruition.

Creative and critical judgment together enable us to get a handle on things, the way the jaws of a pair of pliers converging from opposite directions enable us to get a firm grip on a physical object. An example (for third and fourth graders) would be an exercise in the assessment of analogies, where the students are asked to rank or grade a series of analogies. The analogies range from shallow to insightful and so represent a range of judgments whose creativity is controversial. The students' evaluative judgments, for which they are asked to provide reasons, represent the critical jaw of the pliers. These are some of the items:

1. Thoughts are to thinkers as shoes are to shoemakers
2. Giggling is to laughing as whimpering is to crying
3. Words are to stories as seeds are to flowerbeds
4. Ideas are to children as memories are to adults
5. Taking home a report card is like removing a Band-Aid from an open wound
6. Putting sauerkraut over your pizza is like putting chow mein in your milkshake
7. Trying to teach someone by means of a test is like trying to put air in a bicycle tire by means of a pressure gauge

Students of nine or ten years of age welcome opportunities to assess figures of speech that are presented to them, but in addition they are prolific inventors of fresh analogies, metaphors, and similes. They must learn to employ this newfound creative initiative judiciously. Carried to an extreme, it can result in the atrophy of critical judgment, an outpouring of inventiveness that lacks all sense of direction or responsibility.

These extremes are not at all hard to find; they are quite prevalent. Critical thinking often moves in the direction of the construction of algorithms that eliminate the need for judgment, while creative thinking may move in the direction of heuristics such that all that counts is success and not the means by which it is achieved. Algorithms, in the extreme, represent reasoning without judgment, while heuristics, in the extreme, represent judgment without reasoning.

If educators concede that the schools must cultivate both reasoning and judgment, then they must grant the importance of two pedagogical moves. The first is that students encountering discrepancies that perplex them should be encouraged to find principles from which these puzzling events would follow as unsurprising and a matter of course. For example, the students are puzzled by the fact that litmus paper, when placed in this unknown liquid, turns red. They then learn that litmus paper will behave this way if and only if it is placed in an acid. The students now see that the behavior of the litmus paper is no longer an anomaly: It follows *as a matter of course* from the general principle they have now acquired.

The second pedagogical move is one that encourages creativity by encouraging students to preserve the element of surprise. The surprising fact opens the door to new discoveries and still further surprises. If critical thinking tends to eliminate surprise by seeing the perplexing event as something that happens quite as a matter of course, creative thinking tends to escalate surprise by seeing the surprising event as merely the first in a rapidly expanding series of surprises.

The critical judgment therefore contrasts with the creative judgment in a way that can perhaps be best summarized by considering the questions to which they are typically the answers. The characteristic discourse of critical thinkers aims at the articulation of judgments that respond to the query "What, precisely, is the question?" The characteristic conduct of creative thinkers, on the other hand, seems to be guided by the query "Now that I have invented this surprising thing, to what surprising but previously unasked question is it the answer?" Thus, the critical thinker looks for answers in the form of questions that will point the way to the elimination of inquiry. The creative thinker looks for questions in the form of answers that will lead to the perpetuation of inquiry. Teachers who wish to strengthen judgment must encourage both forms of thinking and convergence of the two forms.

The juncture of the universal and the particular

If a group of college students were to be asked what comes to mind when they hear such phrases as "logical reasoning" and "logical judgments," they might well reply by citing such examples as these:

1. All Greeks are human.
   All humans are mortal.
   Therefore, all Greeks are mortal.
2. If someone is a man, then he's mortal.
   Socrates is a man.
   Therefore, Socrates is mortal.

These are, for the average student, prototypes. They differ in a variety of ways. One way is worth noting here: In the first case the premises and the conclusion are universal, whereas in the second case the universality in the premises yields to particularity in the conclusion. The student may be inclined to interpret the difference as indicating that the reasoning in the first case is universal and theoretical, whereas in the second it exhibits the application of the universal to the particular. The first case is seen as issuing in a universal judgment; the second issues in a particular judgment. The second case is therefore seen as closer to critical thinking, because it involves the use of theoretical understanding in the making of a practical decision or determination.

Now, logical judgments are only one kind of judgment; there are countless other kinds. And logical reasoning is only one kind of reasoning. There are part–whole reasoning and means–end reasoning, for example. And indeed, whenever we perform work on what we know, whenever we seek to extent it or defend it or coordinate it, we are involved in reasoning.

If we are concerned to strengthen reasoning and judgment in education, it has to be, it seems to me, this enlarged sense of reasoning and this diversified sense of judgment as creative and as critical, as particular and as universal. I have not sought to conceal my own preference for the formation of classroom communities of inquiry that reflect on intrinsically interesting materials, such as conceptually rich stories, and then try to construct such stories themselves. This provides an outlet both for the students' impulse to analyze for the sake of understanding and for their impulse to emulate the thinking people they encounter in their reading by thinking like them.

We have until now been holding to the notion that reading and writing should be taught in the context of language and literature – and rightly so. But if we are to stress the analytical as well as the creative, if we are to stress the universal as well as the particular, then it seems to me we have to teach reading and writing – along with reasoning, speaking, and listening – in the context of the humanities generally and in the context especially of English and philosophy.

Philosophy contains, along with many other things, a core of concepts. These concepts are embodied or illustrated in all of the humanities, but it is in philosophy that they are analyzed, discussed, interpreted, and clarified. Many of these concepts represent profoundly important human values, such as truth and meaning and community. In fact, it can be argued that philosophy is the conceptualizable, teachable aspect of human values generally, just as craft is the conceptualizable, teachable aspect of art. Without philosophy, there is a tendency for the behaviors these concepts represent to remain unarticulated and mute. One reads Homer and accepts Agamemnon as just. But what is justice? Only a philosophical discussion can provide the process of dialogical inquiry that properly responds to this question.

Now, there is no reason why such concepts as those just referred to cannot be presented first in literary form, embodied and concrete, and then taken up in more abstract form for discussion and analysis. Indeed, if we want to get students to confront the relationship between the universal and the particular, we must get them to examine both a particular friendship – say, between Achilles and Patroclus or between David and Jonathan – and friendship in general. Likewise, they must not be allowed to rest content with this or that particular instance or variety of truth. We must get them to push on and consider if there is such a thing as truth in general, or "the truth."

Elementary school philosophy provides a forum that enables children to reflect upon their values as well as upon their actions. Thanks to these reflections, children can begin to see ways of rejecting those values that do not measure up to their standards and of retaining those that do. Philosophy offers a forum in which values can be subjected to criticism. This is perhaps a major reason for its exclusion, until now, from the elementary school classroom, and a major reason for its now, at last, being included. Consider, for example, the value of *toleration*. As long as one group in a society is in an authoritarian position, other groups will plead with it to be tolerant, and tolerance in this instance is put forward as an unambiguous virtue. But if no one group is in the ascendancy, as in a pluralist society, it becomes condescending or hypocritical for one group to claim that it tolerates the others. It is for this reason that toleration as a value has gone out of vogue, in contrast with the time of John Locke and Spinoza, when it was a value of crucial importance. Students have to be able to discuss and recognize differences of context, just as they have to be able to ask themselves when loyalty turns into blind fanaticism or when moderation is merely a label for indifference. It is hard to see how we can strengthen children's judgment without encouraging them to examine carefully the values upon which that judgment must rest.

Three orders of judgment

A very young child, having just observed a cat running through the room followed a moment later by a dog, might conceivably make such judgments as: (1) cats and dogs are quite different, (2) the dog's running caused the cat's running (or vice versa), and (3) dogs are not very nice to cats. In other words, any or all of these judgments might be made by a child, at say, the language-acquisition stage.

On the other hand, if we consider what is involved in attempting to strengthen judgment in an educational context, we might want to view these judgments as exemplifying three different orders whose differences are related to the roles they play in the teaching/learning process and in the subsequent life of the child. I want to emphasize that my aim is not to propose a general hierarchy of judgments but simply to suggest some functional distinctions that can be found operative in the pedagogical process.

Take the illustration I have just used, the child observing the cat and the dog. The first is a judgment of difference, the second a causal judgment, and the third an ethical judgment. These judgment types in turn express a still broader set of distinctions. Judgments of difference belong to an order that also comprises judgments of similarity and judgments of identity; causal judgments belong to an order that also comprises analogical judgments, hypothetical judgments, and numerous others; and ethical judgments belong to an order that encompasses social judgments, aesthetic judgments, professional and technological judgments, and many others. I shall call these the order of generic judgments, the order of mediating judgments, and the order of culminating judgments, not to suggest that some judgments are intrinsically more fundamental than others, but to suggest that for the purposes of strengthening judgment in a school setting all three types are needed.

In ordinary discourse, what people generally seem to mean when they speak of judgment are ethical, social, political, and aesthetic judgments and the like – in short, culminating judgments, judgments applied directly to life situations. People engaged in ordinary discourse are apt to view judgments of similarity, difference, and identity as highly abstract and remote from life situations. They are not likely to recognize the pertinence that considerations of comparison and contrast have for every effort we make to reach a determination or settlement. Nor are they likely to recognize the mediating role that still other judgments play in the making of decisions or the solving of problems.

What we see, then, is that practice in the making of culminating judgments can be strengthened by giving students practice in the making of generic and mediating judgments (in addition to giving them practice in making culminating judgments directly). It is thanks to generic judgments that we find it possible to connect and relate or to distinguish and differentiate, and these make it possible for us to generalize and individuate. Nevertheless, important as generic judgments may be, they are for the most part too formal to be of much use in making culminating judgments *directly.* Too many other considerations have to be taken into account in those exquisitely subtle and complex situations in which we have to make an ethical or aesthetic or professional judgment. We may, for example, be clear enough in our minds that all murders belong to the class of morally wrong and legally punishable actions, on the ground that murders are acts that have many things in common with those other acts. But "having things in common" is not the same as "belong to the class of," which is a judgment of membership. And even if we introduce this latter judgment, we are still a long way from being in a position to assert that what X did to Y was wrong. In addition to problems of membership, there will be problems of relevance, problems of instrumentality, problems of inference, and so on. Relevance surfaces when the question is asked "But was this murder or self-defense?" Instrumentality surfaces with the question "Was Y's death a consequence of what X did?" And inference is inescapable if the conclusion that what X did was wrong is to be drawn from the premises "All murder is wrong" and "What X did was murder."

What I am arguing, then, is that in the preparation of a curriculum aimed at strengthening children's reasoning and judgment, continual practice should be given in the making of generic and mediating judgments. This is not to say that very young children should be discouraged from making culminating judgments. However, their culminating judgments are likely to be more sagacious if they have been given practice in the making of generic and mediating judgments earlier on.

If I offer at this point characterization of the judgments in each of these orders, it is not because I think such brevity is what they deserve. Many volumes have been written about each of them, and much more needs to be said. As for the domain of culminating judgments, it is so vast and far-reaching that I shall make no effort at all at characterizing its contents.

Generic judgments

Judgments of identity. As similarities increase, they approach the condition of identity. Identity is therefore the limiting condition of increasing similarity. In natural language, identity is expressed by such phrases as "is equal to" or "is the same as." All mathematical equations take the principle of identity for granted. We do the same when we express ourselves in tautologies, definitions, and even synonyms. Whether two things can nevertheless be said to be identical with one another and whether one thing can be said to be identical with itself are matters of philosophical dispute.

Judgments of difference. This is one of the few types of judgment that have their own name ("distinctions"). Subsumed under it are discriminations of every possible sort: perceptual (to observe is to distinguish), conceptual, and logical. Distinctions are judgments of elementary unlikeness, of mere difference. When combined with judgments of membership (i.e., of inclusion or exclusion), they gravitate toward such categorical propositions as "No *S* are *P*" or "Some *S* are not *P*." When they are expressed relationally, they issue in such phrases as "is unlike," "is different from," and "is not the same as," but they can also express more explicit comparatives, such as "is happier than," "is longer than," or "is less safe than."

Judgments of similarity. These are judgments of simple, primitive likeness or resemblance. When working in tandem with judgments of membership, they facilitate the making of such categorical propositions as "All *S* are *P*" and "Some *S* are *P*." An act of comparison that leads to a determination of similarity is generally expressed by such phrases as "is like," "resembles," and "is similar to."

Mediating judgments

Judgments of composition. These are simply pronouncements that something is (or is not) a part of something else. They may use such phrases as "is a part of," "belongs to," "is a component of," and so on. When combined with an invalid inference, these part–whole judgments give rise to the so-called Fallacy of Composition, as in "Since his individual features are handsome, *it follows that* he has a handsome face." What is in question is not that his face comprises its individual features but that its quality can be logically inferred from theirs.

Judgments of inference. When we reason, we attempt to coordinate our knowledge, defend it, or extend it. Inference is counted on very heavily when it comes to *extending* knowledge. When we are certain that no loss of truth will occur in moving from what we know to what we don't know, the inferential judgment is considered a *deduction*. When we cannot be sure that the truth is being preserved, the inferential judgment is considered an *induction*. Moreover, deductive inference is governed by rules, whereas inductive inference is, at best, merely guided by rules. Judgments of inference are often expressed in such locutions as "It follows that" and "It means that." The fact that these phrases are not synonymous has been a source of vexation to a number of logicians.

Judgments of relevance. Relevance is a fairly fuzzy notion but an extremely useful one for all that. This is so because much thinking is wasted upon what later turn out to have been irrelevant considerations. No wonder, then, that many "informal fallacies" of reasoning turn out to be "fallacies of relevance." (This is true even with formal fallacies, such as the "assertion of the antecedent." Let it be true that "If my cat is sick, it meows." But if it is now asserted that my cat is *not* sick, nothing follows, because what the cat does when sick tells us nothing about what it does when well.) Judgments of relevance evidently involve the number of connections between the entities in question and the importance of those connections.

Causal judgments. These range from simple statements of cause–effect relationships, such as "The stone broke the window," to full-blown explanations. The judgment that a causal process has taken place may be conveyed by any of a vast number of verbs, such as "produced," "created," "generated," "affected," "effected," and the like.

Judgments of membership. These are classificatory judgments and are expressed in statements to the effect that a given thing or class of things is a member of some other class. (It is obvious that judgments of membership are not easily distinguished from judgments of composition.) Judgments of membership are guided by distinguishing criteria, and such criteria in turn make up generic definitions. Thus, whenever we cite an instance or example of a family or class, we are making a judgment of membership. Both "Mary is a girl" and "Mary is a Watson" are judgments of membership.

Analogical judgments. This family of judgments is both vast and important. There are exact analogies, like ratios ("Three is to five as six is to ten"), and there are inexact analogies, such as "Thumbs are to hands as big toes are to feet." Examples like these lead us to think of analogies as based on judgments of identity (3/5 = 3/5) or on judgments of similarity. In any event, analogical judgments form a category of utmost importance in every field of inquiry. Analogical judgments are central to inductive inference, since we are reasoning by analogy when we infer that, a number of similar cases having been observed to possess a certain characteristic, it is likely that a forthcoming case, also similar in other respects, will likewise possess this particular characteristic. And when it comes to sheer invention, whether artistic, scientific, or technological, it is unlikely that there is any mode of judgment that has greater utility than analogical judgment.

Judgments of appropriateness. Judgments of appropriateness range from determinations of what is *fit* to determinations of what is *equitable*. What guides us in the making of such judgments is not a particular rule or criterion but the whole context of the inquiry in which we are engaged, as revealed by our tact, taste, or sensibility. We make judgments of appropriateness when we shape, fashion, or proportion the act to fit the context. When people are accused of "lack of judgment" it is often the failure of this kind of judgment that the accusers have in mind.

Judgments of value. When things or matters are contrasted with one another with respect to value (e.g., "is better than," "is nicer than," "is more lovely than," "is more noble than," "is better made than"), using such criteria as originality, authenticity, perfection, coherence, and the like, the resulting expressions are judgments of value. When one judges the same things or matters by other criteria, the resulting expressions may be judgments of fact, of membership, and so on. The study of the making of judgments of value, as well as of the criteria to be employed in arriving at such determinations, is what is known as *criticism*.

Hypothetical judgments. These are not judgments of mere possibility but judgments of the consequences of possible happenings. Thus "It may rain tomorrow" is not a hypothetical judgment, but "If it rains tomorrow, the farmers will be happy" is. Hypothetical judgments, which take the form "If . . . , then . . . ," are therefore assertions subject to explicit conditions. They may alternatively be called conditional judgments.

Counterfactual judgments. If hypothetical judgments tell us what consequences will ensue if certain conditions do prevail, counterfactual judgments purport to enlighten us about what would have happened had matters been otherwise. Thus someone who asserts, "If the Nazis had won World War II, they would have dominated the world for a thousand years" is making a counterfactual judgment. Counterfactual judgments are especially relevant in the formulation of scientific laws, since they demonstrate that such laws would prevail even if certain circumstances now existing were not the case. If there were inhabitants of Mercury, the gravitational force they would experience could be calculated as the force we experience on Earth.

Practical judgments. Judgments of practice are made in accordance with received understandings as to what constitutes standard operating procedure in a given activity, field, or discipline. Farmers make judgments of practice when they decide when to harvest, as do district attorneys when they decide to prosecute alleged wrongdoers or as clergymen do when they decide on a particular sermon for a particular day. Judgments of practice are not mechanical but are guided by routines, precedents, customs, and traditions that allow for discretion but circumscribe it narrowly. There are times when judgments of practice and judgments of appropriateness complement each other and work, as it were, hand in hand; on other occasions, however, we may substitute the one for the other. We may turn our backs on established practice and try to deal with the case before us on its own merits, or we may deny that the case before us is unique and proceed to deal with it as others it resembles have been dealt with.

Judgments of fact. Judgments of fact are judgments that there is or is not sufficient evidence to warrant the assertion that something is the case. This is intricate, because it involves, among other things, being sure what counts for *evidence* (as opposed, for example, to mere testimony), and it involves being able to judge just when that evidence is *sufficient*. Anyone claiming something to be a fact must be concerned about just how much evidence is needed in order to justify making that claim.

Judgments of reference. Many judgments of identity or similarity are the result of acts of comparison, in which the conclusion has been reached that the entities under consideration *correspond* to one another. Other acts of comparison disclose that some things (e.g., signs) refer to or stand for other things. There are overlaps: A map of Japan stands for Japan and corresponds to it, whereas the word "Japan" merely stands for it. And two congruent geometrical constructions will correspond with one another without standing for one another.

Judgments of measure. Very often we make distinctions based on readily observable differences. Thus, we distinguish between hot and cold or night and day. But we may want a more precise way of differentiating degrees or gradation in sharply contrasting differences, so we construct a range of temperatures or we divide a night–day period into hours, minutes, and seconds. Now we can treat the degrees or gradations as units and superimpose a quantitative template over the qualitative texture of things. It is quantification of the world that makes judgments of measure and proportion possible.

Judgments of translation. As judgments of inference preserve, in the conclusion of an argument, the *truth* of its premises, so judgments of translation preserve, in a shift of contexts, a particular burden of *meaning.* We may write an expository paragraph and then conclude that our meaning could be conveyed at least as well by a cartoon or a graph. "The cat is on the table" (in English) preserves the meaning of "Le chat est sur le table" (in French). Some judgments of translation are scrupulously rule-governed, as is the case with the standardization of natural-language sentences into the canonical forms of statements in classical logic. And so meaning, like capital, is an exchange value, and judgments of translation are judgments of the soundness of such exchanges in the overall economy of meaning.

Instrumental judgments. These judgments govern the adjustment of means to ends and of ends to means. Such adjustment is sometimes assigned a very lofty status, and it is seen as an essential component of rationality. Be that as it may, it may nevertheless be contended that instrumental judgments are settlements or determinations that play some role in the heightening of the consummatory or culminating aspects of experience.

Judgments of division. My glimpse of the order of mediating judgments began with mention of judgments of composition and concludes with mention of their counterpart – judgments of division. In making judgments of division, we pronounce whether or not a property of a given whole is also a property of the parts of that whole. (The fallacy of division is committed by those who assume that what is a property of the whole *must* be a property of its parts. Chicago may be a windy city, but it does not follow that its inhabitants are therefore windy. Blood is red, but it does not follow that the particles that compose it are red. Water is wet, but this does not imply that it is constituted of wet hydrogen and wet oxygen.)

THE WHEEL OF JUDGMENT

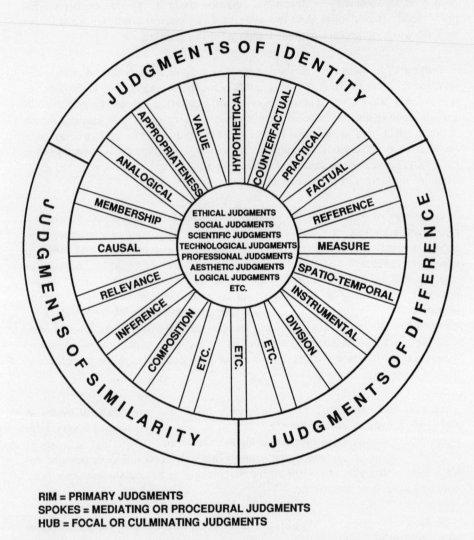

RIM = PRIMARY JUDGMENTS
SPOKES = MEDIATING OR PROCEDURAL JUDGMENTS
HUB = FOCAL OR CULMINATING JUDGMENTS

Figure 8

Absurd as the reasoning may be of those who commit fallacies of composition and division, it is not more absurd than the reasoning of those who assume that whatever has aesthetic quality must be composed of nonaesthetic ingredients and that whatever is moral must be constructed out of nonmoral elements. The domain of unsound judgments of composition and division is a very large one indeed.

I have no idea how many other categories there may be in the order of mediating judgments. I am not concerned to spell them out. I want merely to suggest that they have enormous preparatory value if we are looking ahead to the strengthening of student judgment in the various walks of life in which students are likely to tread. It seems to me we are bound to be foiled if we think that a given form of culminating judgment, such as the ethical, can be strengthened either by (1) consideration of ethical principles alone with no excursions into practice or (2) giving practice only in the making of ethical judgments without providing practice in the making of generic or mediating judgments.

It seems to me worth mentioning in addition that judgments, unlike skills, are minuscule versions of the persons who perform them. This is so in the sense that each and every judgment expresses the person who makes the judgment and at the same time appraises the situation or world about which the judgment is made. We are our judgments and they are us. This is why the strengthening of my judgment results in the growth and strengthening of myself as a person.

The balance wheel of judgment in educational settings

If history is sometimes characterized as a history of struggle, it can also be seen as a history of mediation. Often, indeed, the combatants themselves experience a fission in which half of them mediate while the other half continue the struggle. This balance of conflict and mediation will even be found internalized in individual participants so that, however many the directions in which they are pulled, it is judgment that works within them to redirect them toward wholeness and proportion and equity.

Judgment is called for whenever there are conflicting passions or conflicting goods or competing arguments. It is needed when the demands of the body must be weighed against the demands of the mind or when critical thinking is matched against creative thinking. As we wobble like tops through the vicissitudes of life, it is to judgment that we turn for equilibrium. Like the balance wheel of a gyroscope, it helps maintain our stability despite the crazy angles at which we sometimes find ourselves. A life with little judgment can be a glorious thing, but it is likely to be short; with a little more judgment, we might yet be able to prevail.

Still, I would not have it thought that the only role of judgment is in restoring stability, however important a role this may be. For there are other times when we come to see the central direction of our lives as bleak and unprofitable, when our better judgment concludes that things must be otherwise, and the sooner the better. On such an occasion, judgment may play the role of *agent provocateur* – an unsettling, disturbing force tipping the balance one way or another so as to clear the way for a new equilibrium. In the intellectual life, it is philosophical judgment that has often played this role.

In our working lives, judgment is certainly of much importance, and in the professions it is vital. It is for this reason that the education of professionals so often centers on the honing of professional judgment. The preparation of future lawyers and doctors includes considerable simulation of practice: moot courts, internships, and the like. The professors who conduct such training are fully prepared to have their students use them as models, with the result that doctors emerge from the tutelage of doctors, lawyers from the tutelage of lawyers, and so on. Professionalism and judgment are so closely associated as to be almost synonymous.

The centrality of judgment is not so clearly visible in the preparation of future teachers – neither in the work of the instructors in the colleges of education nor in the day-to-day work of the teachers themselves nor in the lives of the end recipients of all this preparation, the children. All too often the work of the teacher is seen as a series of questions, answers, and commands, of rewardings and punishings, wheedlings and cajolings. Once it is admitted that the cultivation of judgment is the pivot upon which the whole education of the child must turn, an inescapable logic will compel schools of education to make such cultivation central to the preparation of teachers. This will help, in turn, to bring about that recognition of the professional status of teachers to which so much lip service is paid but which is still so far from becoming a reality.

I am not saying that the teaching of content is useless and that we are in danger of turning children into idiot savants. But I do contend that the stress on their acquisition of information has been exaggerated and should take second place to the sharpening of their thinking and judgment.

There is at present a widespread recognition that something is amiss, but efforts at improvement often turn out to be merely cosmetic. There is nothing wrong with attempting to remodel lesson plans so as to make them more likely to encourage critical reflection and to strengthen judgment within and among the disciplines. But these efforts at "infusion" are bound to be fumbling, haphazard, and unavailing as long as students are not permitted to examine directly and for themselves the standards, criteria, concepts, and values that are needed to evaluate whatever it is they are talking and thinking about. Merely to encourage differences of opinion, open discussion, and debate will not provide a comfortable escalator to higher-order thinking. This will happen only if students are given access to the tools of inquiry, the methods and principles of reasoning, practice in concept analysis, experience in critical reading and writing, opportunities for creative description and narration as well as in the formulation of arguments and explanations, and a community setting in which ideas and intellectual contexts can be fluently and openly exchanged. These are educational conditions that provide an infrastructure upon which a sound superstructure of good judgment can be erected.

To withhold from children access to ideas and reasons and criteria for judgment and yet to expect them to judge well is about like withholding air from them and expecting them not to suffocate. But how else are we to make these intellectual tools available to them if not through a series of courses in philosophy, redesigned so as to be accessible to children? If they are afforded no opportunity to compare and contrast the reasons people have for calling things true and good, how can they be expected to know what they are talking about when they are asked to decide which statements are true and which are not or which things are good and which are not?

Philosophy is ready to be made a required part of the elementary and secondary school curriculum. This happens infrequently at present because the existing curriculum is so bloated as to exclude all "outsiders." But when the existing curriculum has been suitably slimmed down, philosophy will no longer have to masquerade, as it is often required to do nowadays, as a course in language arts or reading or social studies.

People sometimes remark that philosophy is too much for children, but this seems merely to be a euphemistic way of saying that teaching teachers to teach children philosophy is just too much trouble. Nevertheless, until schools of education recognize the central role of the strengthening of judgment in the education of children and the need to prepare teachers to perform this task, society will be reluctant to accord teachers the professional status which they now demand.

10 Dichotomies in the application of critical thinking

Anyone aware of the extensive research being carried on with regard to cognitive education, as well as of the innumerable theoreticians and practitioners who have at one time or another had cause to consider it or experiment with it, may be excused for being incredulous as to how limited the transition has actually been. Despite all the publicity, despite all the studies by school curriculum committees, despite all the proclamations by curriculum specialists, the fact remains that the schools have hardly gotten their feet wet in the area of bringing about a more reflective education. There is, to be sure, a great deal of genuine interest – as well as a great deal of genuine lack of interest. There are many sincere efforts at implementation. But the only interventions that remain in effect for more than a few years are those involving enthusiastic teachers, highly motivated administrators, and supportive parents, to say nothing of positive student participation.

The fact is that the conversion of the educational system – a system in which normal practice is so often explainable as sheer inertia – is a formidable task. It may not pose enormous difficulties in a country with a highly centralized system – a description that fits a great many countries. But it is incredibly difficult in a highly decentralized pluralistic society in which educational decisions are made in accordance with local home-rule traditions. Our own society is a curious combination. Politically, the order of the day at the national level is laissez-faire, in support of the home-rule ideology, but in fact when it comes to texts and testing programs, the power is in the hands of national publishing organizations, and when it comes to turf protection, the power is in the hands of national professional organizations. What stabilizes the schools and militates against meaningful change is, in brief, the market.

Education is many things, one of which is an enormous business. A great deal of advertising and merchandising takes place every year to give the impression that this year's product is significantly different from and better than last year's. The huge professional organizations may not openly endorse this stultifying sameness, but one has the impression that they perceive no viable alternative to it.

If the market is the major obstacle to educational progress toward a more reflective, more critical educational system, it is not the only obstacle. Schools are perplexed about the relative value of the various educational alternatives that are proposed by minuscule splinter organizations. Further, they are awed by the complexity of the process of change. For example, changeover requires administrative continuity, and as administrators leapfrog from one district hierarchy to another, the changes they initiate have a way of returning to square one when they leave.

Also, school districts generally do not have large reserves available for staff development. Their assumption seems to be that for most teachers professional preparation should have been completed by the time of certification. Yet districts recognize that teachers are serious professionals who want to continue their education, so a small amount of money and support are allocated for this purpose. However, there is virtually nothing for the kind of ongoing support and follow-up that are vital to the long-range success of any educational intervention.

In this chapter, I shall deal only with some of the obstacles to the introduction of thinking into the school curriculum. The emphasis is on critical thinking. The problems involved in implementing other aspects of higher-order, complex thinking will be taken up in later chapters.

Conceptual obstacles to the strengthening of thinking

I take up first the conceptual obstacles to the improvement of higher-order thinking in schools and colleges. Later I will deal with some of the more practical aspects of the problem.

Disagreements over the nature of thinking

We are not sure what thinking is, just as we are not sure what life is, or experience, or being human. When problems like the abortion issue come to the surface, the general public discovers that matters like these have to be confronted and deliberated upon by everyone. But we must first make provision in the schools for installing thinking as a fundamental aspect of education; and to do this, we need clues as to just what arguments we are dealing with. Following are some of the disagreements that emerge when we begin to consider what we must do to shift the focus of education from learning to thinking.

1. The conception of thinking as primarily *problem solving*
   versus
   The conception of thinking as primarily *problem seeking*

Comment. By and large, this difference exemplifies the radical difference between education in the sciences and education in the humanities. Science textbooks tend to treat scientific knowledge as *settled.* Students learn standard methods of problem solving and then are assigned problems that vary somewhat from the paradigm to see if they can extrapolate from the established approach. In the humanities, on the other hand, the subject matter is treated as intrinsically *problematic,* and students are encouraged to look for new problems of interpretation or conceptualization.

2. Seeing the objective of critical thinking as the attainment of better-founded beliefs

 versus

 Emphasizing the *process* of critical inquiry, so that beliefs are seen as merely psychological end states of no particular cognitive value

Comment. Inquiry commences when beliefs we had counted on are found to be unreliable, and it ceases with the acquisition of more reliable convictions. So belief is a state that precedes and also follows inquiry but is not a part of inquiry itself (unless one considers the fact that those who inquire believe in the process of inquiry). Obviously, we employ critical thinking to erode our biases and prejudices; that is, to straighten out our cockeyed beliefs. But belief as such is not part of critical thinking in the way that assuming, hypothesizing, deducing, explaining, and the like are parts of it. It is a psychological state that adds no further warrant to what is assertable.

3. Conceiving of critical and creative thinking as two sides of the same coin

 versus

 Conceiving of them as discontinuous, discrete, or even opposed to one another

Comment. There are many different conceptions of the creative/critical thinking dichotomy, ranging from those that see the two as mutually reinforcing to those that see them as merely compatible to those that envisage a fundamental opposition between them. A promising approach, I believe, is to consider both as forms of inquiry that merge in higher-order thinking.

4. Formulating the problem as one of getting students to think

 versus

 Conceding that students already think but need to learn to think better

Comment. We very often congratulate ourselves on having gotten students to think better when in fact all we have done is gotten them to think about the same things we are thinking about in the same way we think about them. This is a shift in the content of what is thought about, not an improvement in the quality of thinking. They may not be thinking either more or better, and they need to be doing both.

5. Ranking various thinking operations hierarchically

 versus

 Avoiding overall rankings and insisting that taxonomies be purely descriptive

Comment. The compromise that suggests itself here is that there are functional hierarchies within particular situations but no overall hierarchies. Thus, in a situation calling for justification, giving reasons may be a more important skill than defining terms, but in a different situation the reverse could be true.

6. Giving the concrete priority over the abstract in teaching for thinking
   versus
   Giving the abstract priority over the concrete

Comment. This debate has to be understood with regard to the presuppositions of current educational practice. Current assumptions are that the concrete should predominate in early childhood education (because young children "cannot handle abstractions," while the abstract should predominate in higher education (because college students need only to "have knowledge"; they don't need to "make judgments"). Both presuppositions are obviously unwarranted.

Disagreements over the proper psychological approach

Obviously, there are a great many disputes among psychologists, such as those over the nature of learning, the role of memory and concept formation, and the nature of intelligence and of affective factors, that have been followed keenly by educators because of the bearing these issues can be expected to have on education. Much hangs, therefore, upon the psychological approach that educators suppose to be correct when they begin the planning that will make their schools more reflective.

1. Attempting to understand children's cognitive development by studying what children *can't do without intervention*
   versus
   Attempting to understand such development by studying what children *can do with intervention*

Comment. This is, in part, the issue between Piaget and Vygotsky. Since virtually all educational situations involve adult mediation between the culture and the child, and since such mediation comes in a variety of styles, each with its own impact on children's learning, it is hazardous to accept the Piagetian approach as a norm for curriculum construction or for the devising of pedagogies. Piaget is so interested in determining what children cannot do unaided at a given stage that he is unable to explore how they can be helped to do it.

2. Stressing all the varieties of human intelligence (mathematical, musical, linguistic, etc.) so as to aim at the cultivation of all varieties
   versus
   Emphasizing only certain of those varieties

Comment. In the long run, Howard Gardner's emphasis on the variety of human intelligence is both correct and just, for it provides a fair and humane goal for the educational process. But it is of little consolation to those who are language-deficient and who discover that language and mathematics, rightly or wrongly, are the established currencies of the classroom. All of the child's potential modes of intelligence deserve to be developed, and the schools should develop literacy in each of these modes, but this will not begin to happen until the entire curriculum undergoes the agonizing reappraisal that is long overdue.

Disagreements over the role of philosophy

Among educators who favor allowing philosophy a role in education, there are disagreements that replicate some of the disagreements philosophers have among themselves. There may be few disputes among teachers and administrators as to whether children should be encouraged to learn philosophy or actually do it; the preference for the latter is near-unanimous. But it is still not clear to many whether *teachers* should be encouraged to do either or both. To me, the handwriting on the wall is legible enough: Until teachers have learned philosophy *and can do it,* prospects of thinking in education will not be very bright.

  1. Emphasizing *either* formal logic *or* informal logic *or* rhetoric
       versus
     Attempting to induce critical thinking in the classroom without recourse to any of these
  Comment. Insofar as critical thinking necessarily involves facility in the employment of criteria, and insofar as philosophy is the discipline that is, among other things, concerned with the establishment of criteria, it is difficult to see how we could responsibly engage in critical thinking without to some extent internalizing this aspect of philosophical practice. It is difficult to conceive of overcoming uncritical thinking without recourse to at least a moderate amount of logic.

  2. Conceiving of philosophy as having a special connection with good thinking
       versus
     Conceiving of philosophy as having no special connection with good thinking
  Comment. One tradition in philosophy (regarded by others as arrogant and imperialistic) sees philosophy as identical with excellent thinking. Another tradition, more moderate, holds that philosophical reflections on thinking have a directness and immediacy that psychological inquiry necessarily lacks. Insofar as philosophy claims to have an exclusive competence in thinking critically about thinking, the disagreement is probably incapable of resolution.

  3. Approaching thinking descriptively
       versus
     Approaching thinking normatively
  Comment. In one sense, this is a fallacious dichotomy. All norms presuppose descriptions, and all descriptions presuppose norms or criteria. Even in the case of formal logic, it is unclear whether its principles are to be taken as exclusively descriptive or exclusively normative. Nevertheless, to the extent that education involves the making of recommendations and not merely the retailing of descriptive information, it is unlikely that students can be encouraged to think more critically without becoming acquainted with the criteria by means of which critical and uncritical thinking are to be distinguished from one another. Both formal and empirical recommendations can be of value.

4. Contending that the only good model for good thinking is the scientific model

> versus

Contending that, just as literature is the discipline that is the appropriate aegis for instruction in writing, so philosophy is the appropriate aegis for instruction in thinking

Comment. Science, philosophy, and literature are all disciplines from which humanistic values can be extracted and formulated as recommendations for practice. But literature is too diffuse and diversified to serve as the primary aegis for thinking instruction, and science is too narrow and unified. Philosophy, with its tough insistence on logical rigor and its emphasis on flexibility, is a much more likely candidate.

Disagreements over preferred educational approaches

In addition to their disagreements over philosophical and psychological approaches, educators disagree among themselves with regard to matters that are purely educational or that connect educational quandaries with philosophical or psychological quandaries.

1. Claiming that all thinking is discipline-specific

> versus

Claiming that there are generic thinking skills that overarch the disciplines

Comment. Those who claim that all thinking is discipline-specific do so to bolster their case that critical thinking can be taught only in the context of each particular discipline; they contend that it cannot be taught per se. Their opponents contend that there are generic thinking skills (for example, some skills of formal logic, like *modus tollens*) that are not modified from one disciplinary context to the other, and that it would therefore be more efficient to teach such generic skills in an autonomous critical thinking course. I might add that the entire discipline of philosophy bears a unique relationship to the other disciplines, in that philosophy prepares students to think in those other disciplines. The reasoning, concept-formation, and judgment-shaping skills that philosophy strengthens in early elementary school are indispensable for the child's middle-school years. What philosophy provides throughout elementary school – a reservoir of fundamental humanistic ideas for classroom deliberation – is indispensable for secondary school, college, and citizenship, to say nothing of parenthood. The legend that philosophy is solely for the old is most unfortunate. It is essentially *preparatory,* and the sooner other disciplines acknowledge this the better it will be for thinking in education generally.

2. Attempting to make the separate disciplines more reflective by adding critical thinking exercises to each chapter of their curricula

> versus

Incorporating all cognitive exercises in an autonomous course in critical thinking

Comment. The first approach runs the danger of being superficial and the second of being irrelevant. There is, however, a middle path. We need both an independent course in critical thinking and infusion and reinforcement of critical thinking in the separate disciplines. The middle path is to direct the skills learned in the independent course to the "basic" skills of reading and writing. If reading and writing can be made more critical, students themselves will transfer this added reflectiveness to the particular disciplines.

    3. Attempting to teach critical thinking by teaching *about* it

          versus

       Attempting to teach it by stressing practice rather than theory

Comment. There is little or no evidence that teachers in preparation who have studied critical thinking research have thereby become better critical thinkers. The alternative, to stress the practice rather than the theory, is all right when dealing with teachers whose training is just beginning, but teachers whose training is well under way should be increasingly involved in inquiries that require that theory and practice be acquired together.

    4. Approaches that center the acquisition of cognitive skills on the teacher on the assumption that they will rub off on the students

          versus

       Approaches that use the teacher as a conduit to the students but in addition provide students with curricular models of thinking to supplement the teacher's modeling

Comment. The second alternative seems definitely preferable, especially if the "curricular model of thinking" is a children's story about a group of children forming their own community of cognitive inquiry. This is a powerful motivating device, and it is sad to say that most critical thinking approaches fail to provide anything of the kind to motivate students who feel no initial attraction to activities aimed at improving their reasoning and judgment.

    5. Approaches that utilize didactic methods of instruction, such as lecturing

          versus

       Approaches that seek to convert the classroom into a community of shared, cooperative cognitive inquiry

Comment. Only the second alternative recognizes the vital role of conversation and dialogue in the strengthening of reasoning and judgment. And only the second is consistent with the broader goal of a democratic and participatory society, even if the first need not be incompatible with such a goal. It is desirable, however, that we employ means that are consistent with the ends we are trying to attain.

Practical obstacles to the teaching of thinking

Anyone who points to the teacher as the sole source of the failure to encourage higher-order thinking in the schools is about as realistic as the infantry private in wartime who thinks that the cause of all his misery is the corporal who gives him orders. As we end another brutal century in human history, we should reflect on the universality of the refusal to be self-critical. It is found in virtually all forms of political association, from small towns to great and powerful nations. Everywhere the complacent indulgence of the fantasies of the military and of those who are economically powerful is the order of the day. Newspapers, radio, and television are accomplices in this, as are textbooks. In each nation there is the same fatuous self-indulgence, the same refusal to hold ourselves to the same rules and procedures as those to which others are held accountable. As nations slide reluctantly into regional "communities," it will be no great advance if, in these larger organizations, the same inability to be self-critical holds sway.

Little wonder, then, that the thinking in universities is not much different from the thinking in the societies to which they belong, or that the thinking in schools of education is not much different from the thinking in the universities to which they belong. It is simply unrealistic of us to expect that the beleagured faculties in schools of education are suddenly going to rise up against the system in which they have participated all these years and begin to turn out teachers who are adept at encouraging higher-order thinking. When anthropologists distinguish between societies that are flexible and "adaptable" and societies that are "adapted" and fixated, they would do well to include institutions of higher learning as falling into one or the other group.

Furthermore, schools of education are under great pressure to concentrate on instilling disciplinary knowledge into their prospective teachers so that these teachers will be able to dispense such knowledge when they arrive in their own classrooms. It is widely believed that if teachers knew their subjects better their students would be more knowledgeable and hence better educated. The fallacies in such thinking are obvious, but it is indeed grotesque when content is championed to the exclusion of skills, and all in the name of cultural literacy.

It may be that present moves to make nationally normed tests contain more questions of a reflective nature will accelerate and that this in turn will have repercussions on the curriculum and the way it is taught – if the adage that "the tests drive the system" is to be believed. Nevertheless, even if this were to take place, it would not put in question the way in which the existing disciplines have carved up and distributed the disciplines among themselves. There is little self-criticism in the educational establishment when it comes to reappraising the sovereignty of various turfs. Just how much time should be allotted to mathematics, history, English, reading, writing, and so on? If there are courses in reading and writing, shouldn't there be one in reasoning? And shouldn't philosophy be the aegis of such a course, as English is the aegis for courses in reading and writing? But these are questions that it is almost profitless to ask when the will to challenge the educational establishment is so manifestly lacking among those who make educational decisions.

And yet, in spite of all that has just been said, is it not possible that a new awareness may be emerging, one in which the fostering of higher-order thinking will be assigned a top priority and steps will be taken at all levels to implement that decision? Of course it is possible, but the magnitude of the task should not be underestimated. The retraining of existing teachers is a slow and arduous business, involving persistent follow-up visits and a determination on the part of administrators and teachers alike to persevere courageously until the new level of performance is reached. The reconstruction of schools of education is more difficult to envisage, and it may be that alternative certification routes may be a vehicle for some would-be teachers of philosophy for some time to come.

There are bright spots on the horizon as well, of course. That a critical thinking movement has emerged at all is an unexpected and heartening development, and that it should have garnered so much praise and acceptance is most encouraging. But the movement runs the danger of losing steam and simply evaporating if it fails to find a sense of direction, a guiding definition, and sets of practices that work. It also runs a danger if it identifies itself too closely with the devising of problem-solving recipes while ignoring the value-laden contexts in which problems occur. We are faced, for example, with ethical problems involving the environment and involving our relationship with nature at large. To say that the answers to these questions must be "humanistic" may be begging the question. The humanities can provide us with some guidance, of course, and it is foolish to turn our backs on what they have to offer. But even the wisdom of the past may not be enough to enable us to come to grips with the hard question of the relationships we humans are to have with the rest of nature as we emerge from the parochialism of our long history and begin at last to confront the question of how we are to live peaceably and productively in our cosmic environment as well as with one another.

11 Faulty assumptions concerning teaching for thinking

Faced with an epidemic of some unusual ailment, investigators will often begin by trying to establish the *criteria* by means of which they can distinguish cases of the specific illness from noncases. In effect, they begin with a working *definition* that is subject to modification.

Now, critical thinking is not a disease; it is, rather, a wholesome educational development. But it does have its perplexing aspects. As with the new form of illness, what is needed is a working definition of critical thinking that can guide teachers to encourage their students to think critically. This definition was provided in Chapters 6–8.

But a definition is not enough. Also needed is a careful examination of the *assumptions* we are likely to make about teaching, thinking, skills, content, and standards. This is because the most effective way to convert a working definition into a definition that does not work is to begin with assumptions that are incompatible with the definition. Let us consider some assumptions, keeping in mind that each may not be unsound by itself but that they may be ineffectual when taken collectively.

Misconception 1: Teaching for thinking is equivalent to teaching for critical thinking

If these two things were the same, then those who teach for thinking would be right when they reply, "Teach for critical thinking? Why, we're already doing it!" But are they? And if they are not, why not?

Let us invent the case of Mr. A. As a teacher, Mr. A is alert, forceful, and energetic. His mind is constantly on his subject and constantly awhirl with thoughts. He wants his pupils to think about the subject as he does, with the same interest and care and excitement he feels in himself. Consequently, he refrains from lecturing. Instead, he shoots questions, in rapid fire, at his students, because he knows that questions will make them think. Likewise, his homework assignments challenge the students to reflect. If asked about the intellectual behavior of his students, he will say that they tend to be thoughtless and indolent; they need to have their attention galvanized by a dramatic teacher who compels them to think more and more about the issues at hand rather than drift into aimless but pleasant reveries.

Comment

Perhaps Mr. A wants to increase the quantity of his students' thinking and assumes that he will thereby improve its quality. Perhaps he assumes that it is unrealistic to expect students to think *better*; one can only try to get them to think *more*. And to some extent, of course, he's right – more thinking in the classroom *is* better than less.

But is Mr. A correct in assuming that students, when not being taught, are simply thoughtless, mindless? Perhaps what he means is that their thoughts are unfocused and that he succeeds in focusing them. Or perhaps he believes that their thoughts are focused elsewhere and that he succeeds in focusing them on the topic at hand.

Mr. A is rightly suspicious of lecturing as a means of getting students to think critically, although it has its merits as a means of getting them to think. However, he monopolizes the questioning process instead of encouraging the students to think up the questions themselves. In so doing, he gets them thinking but not thinking for themselves – this being, in part, what the difference between answering questions and asking them comes down to. And even if he were to get them to ask questions, this would be no great advance if they were to believe that only he could provide the answers or if questioning were all they could do.

Misconception 2: Critical teaching will necessarily result in critical thinking

When genuine teaching occurs, both teachers and learners are involved in thinking, just as buyers and sellers are together involved in commercial transactions. But it does not follow that reflective teachers will necessarily produce reflective learners, just as it does not follow that rapid teachers will produce rapid learners.

Consider the case of Ms. B. Ms. B is justly proud of her reputation for knowing her subject and for demanding that her students acquire as much as possible of that knowledge for themselves before they depart from her course. Many students find her courses difficult; there seems to be so much material to cover, retain, and master. Some students feel that their previous courses have not prepared them with the skills needed for dealing with these complex and specialized topics. With this opinion the teacher will likely concur, adding that it is up to previous teachers to do their job better rather than that she herself should water down her course content by teaching skills.

Comment

There can be little doubt that Ms. B's knowledge of her subject is authoritative. Moreover, she has carefully examined the assumptions generally made by her colleagues (as well as her own), and it would be hard to deny that her grasp of her subject is the product of a great deal of critical thinking.

Now, thinking in general is the conscious processing of experience – or at least so I take it to be. And I assume that critical thinking begins with reflections on practical activity and eventuates in judgment. All of this is what Ms. B has done. She has processed the "raw, crude, macroscopic experience" (to use Dewey's terminology) of her professional life and converted it into the refined end products called knowledge. In the process, *she* has been compelled to think critically. It does not follow, however, that the students who learn those end products will be thereby empowered to think critically. For this to be possible, *they* must have access to at least some of the crude, raw, problematic material with which she herself began so that they can work their way through it as she did.

A further comment about Ms. B pertains to her attitude that students who enter her classroom must be prepared with the skills necessary for mastering the content she will provide and that she cannot be expected to take time out rehearsing them in such skills. But this is not the only way in which skill deficiencies can be made up. For example, if she were willing to conceive of her subject matter as problematic rather than as settled, as a starting point rather than as a terminus of inquiry, she might find that her students' cognitive proficiencies would improve concurrently with the progress of the inquiry.

While I have great respect for the importance of the teacher as a model of good thinking, I doubt there is much evidence to show that this alone is sufficient to bring about significant improvement in the way students think. There is a persistent conviction among those who educate teachers that if teachers think more critically, it will trickle down somehow to the students. I suspect that, short of a drastic overhaul of texts and tests and classroom methodologies, we may well see the phenomenon of teachers thinking more critically but students nowhere getting the benefit of it.

Misconception 3: Teaching about critical thinking is equivalent to teaching for critical thinking

Of all the faulty assumptions we might refer to in this matter, this is perhaps the most insidious and the most important, because it itself rests upon still deeper mistaken assumptions about the role of values in education. I cannot examine these underlying assumptions here in any detail; perhaps it will be sufficient to say that, in my opinion, *we will not be able to get students to engage in better thinking unless we teach them to employ criteria and standards by means of which they can assess their thinking for themselves.* I do not see this coming about through teaching *about* critical thinking as it is now understood and practiced.

For example, we can consider the case of Ms. C. Ms. C is quite fascinated by the question of how we think and is eager to make her students equally fascinated with it. Consequently, she is frequently to be found relating to other teachers, to students, and to parents the latest research findings with regard to the thinking process and its underlying conditions, or basing her teaching on these findings. She distinguishes among her students according to their cognitive styles or their right-brain/left-brain dominance or their stages of moral development or their sex or their body types – there are many ways of setting students apart. Having categorized and characterized students in accordance with the empirical differences noted by and reported by experimenters, her next job is to address each student as appropriately as possible, on the assumption that individual attention is needed in order to deal effectively with individual differences.

Comment

There can be no doubt that empirical research about teaching and learning can be useful to teachers, just as there can be no doubt that individual attention is often desirable because of the special characteristics of particular students. Nevertheless, these differences should not be construed as an excuse for fragmenting the class into a mere collection of isolated individuals. Teachers should pursue the creation of a classroom community of inquiry *in spite of* individual differences rather than settle for a rag-tag aggregation of individuals *because of* such differences. We can hardly hope to build an equitable pluralistic society if at the first sign of diversity we attempt to disband and segregate the classroom community.

Teaching students about critical thinking is about as unlikely to create a nation of critical thinkers as having students learn the results of research into bicycle riding is unlikely to create a nation of bicycle riders. (This is not to say that elementary school courses in psychology or in the psychology of cognition would be inappropriate in terms of the knowledge students would acquire from them. It is simply to say that critical thinking involves participating in *practical* reasoning, and teaching *about* critical thinking has little to contribute in this regard.)

In short, knowing more is not equivalent to thinking better. Critical thinking, like education generally, is a normative intervention whose aim is not simply to bring children's thinking into line with everyone else's thinking but to get them to be more reflective, more reasonable, and more judicious. Paradoxical as it may seem, teaching the facts about a subject cultivates a distanced, theoretical attitude toward that subject rather than a practical one.

Misconception 4: Teaching for critical thinking involves drill in thinking skills

As a child learns her first language in the midst of the life of the family, she is rarely drilled or rehearsed in grammar or usage. She finds herself immersed in a series of situations, each of which has its unique quality and in each of which there are utterances that have their unique meaning. Each context prescribes its meaning, and these meanings accrue to the speech acts and language utilized in those contexts. To divorce such acts from their contexts is to divorce them from their meaning, which is not salvaged by monotonous repetition. Now, where meaning is minimal (as for example in memorizing the multiplication table), drill may be justifiable, but where the meaning component is significant – and this is, one would hope, the desired state of affairs – drill is counterproductive because it involves a dissociation of the thinking process from the meanings we might otherwise have to think about. The intelligence produced by drills is likely to be an alienated intelligence.

Consider the arguments produced by Mr. D. He is an experienced teacher, quite aware of the powerful role that practice has in education. Very often, he reasons, we learn to do something by going out and doing it. This is the way we learn to swim, dance, and skate. Skills are matters of "knowing how"; contents are matters of "knowing that." Contents can be passed from one mind to another by teaching, but skills have to be acquired by practice. Consequently, Mr. D contends, since the quality of our thinking is a matter of skill, of knowing how to think, and since skills emerge out of practice, what better approach can there be to teaching for improved thinking than to give students lots of drill in performing specific thinking operations? Besides, according to Mr. D, if previous teachers have failed to provide the students with the skills necessary for coping with the contents of his course, then he has a responsibility for providing them himself.

Comment

Mr. D is making a number of assumptions that are frequently made by educators. The first is that, if students are lacking in the skills needed to master the content of a course, one can simply implant them or infuse them into the curriculum. Second, he assumes that the best way of teaching skills is by drill. And third, he assumes that skills are all that is needed.

With regard to the first question, one might inquire what the evidence is that the infusion approach works. And if it does work, is it because of its own merits or because it reinforces what has been acquired by the students in a separate course in critical thinking?

The response to the "building skills by thinking drills" approach is much the same. One can, first, ask if it works. And one can, second, ask how it compares with less artificial methods, such as logically disciplined dialogue in the classroom.

As for the third assumption, we may respond by pointing out that a good critical thinker is a good craftsperson and craft is never a mere aggregation of skills. We may be ever so skilled in drilling, filing, cutting, grinding metals, and so on, but if we lack such criteria as utility, serviceability, and beauty, or if we have such criteria but have low standards for satisfying them, we cannot be other than poor artisans, if artisans at all. So with critical thinking: It is essential that critical thinkers recognize, work with, and be prepared to appeal to the criteria that are relevant to the matters under investigation. It is also essential that they have high standards of performance, so that they do not permit themselves to engage in thinking that is shoddy: illogical or uncritical. And it is essential that they become adept at handling more than one skill at a time, for at any one moment numerous skills may be clustered together, while at the next moment they may have to be reorganized into a contrapuntal arrangement.

Mr. D needs to reflect much more thoroughly on his practice, so as to discover the kinds of situations in which drill is profitable and the kinds in which it is not. He also needs to ask himself how one can aim at going beyond mere skills to cultivation of the *art* of thinking well.

Misconception 5: Teaching for logical thinking is equivalent to teaching for critical thinking

If critical thinkers aim to avoid (among other things) being illogical, it is tempting to assume that critical thinking *is* being logical. If this were the case, it might follow that nothing more is needed than a good course in logic.

Ms. E, for example, has for a long time been fed up with the slovenly reasoning of her students. It is not enough, she argues, to teach them grammar and vocabulary or arithmetic and geometry; they have to learn how to reason logically. She therefore obtains permission to give a course in formal logic.

Comment

Ms. E is probably correct in her suspicion that the failure of the schools to insist upon elementary logical competence among students, while demanding an arithmetical competence perhaps even beyond what is needed for a balanced approach, represents a serious flaw in the educational process. But while Ms. E may be right that logical competence is necessary, it does not follow that logic, if added to the curriculum, would be sufficient to set matters right.

For one thing, teaching logic in isolation in no way shows students how to *apply* that logic to the subject matters of the various disciplines. Unless students are taught how to marry logical skills and course content, they will generally be helpless to do so on their own.

Our failure to integrate skills and content in the schools reflects our taking the model of the university too seriously in this regard. (There are ample other respects in which we do not take it seriously enough.) It is in the university that undergraduates are given, in each course, a paradigm of overspecialization. (The high schools eagerly ape the colleges on this point.) If I had my way, instead of giving undergraduates a course in logic or critical thinking and a course in biology or anthropology or philosophy, I would see to it that they got an introductory course in biological reasoning or anthropological reasoning or philosophical reasoning, so that the logical skills and the course content would be presented to the students as integrated with one another from the very start. (For majors, a senior course called "The study of _____ " would also be mandatory.)

Misconception 6: Teaching for learning is just as effective as teaching for critical thinking

Some educators would apparently like to defuse the demand for critical thinking by maintaining that teaching for learning is just as good and probably better.

This can be settled only by asking, "Good for what?" It depends on the goals of education. Are we trying to produce people who will grow up to be informed and knowledgeable citizens or people who will be reasonable and reflective citizens or both?

Ms. F's case is a case in point. Ms. F is, by the standards prevailing in her district, an exceptionally good teacher. But she is troubled and dissatisfied nevertheless. She knows her subject, and she teaches it the way she was taught to teach it. Why, then, when her students are tested, do they not seem to know all she expects them to know?

Comment

We may want students to grow up to be reasonable and reflective, but we test them on what they know – on what they have learned. There is a serious discrepancy here. Students and their parents expect that the education provided by schools will be relevant and applicable to life and the world in which we live. We cannot be expected to develop good judgment if we cannot see the applicability of what we are taught to our daily practice and daily experience.

The result is general dissatisfaction – among parents, among teachers, and among students – because the conception of education prevailing among those who make the tests in generally knowledge-based rather than judgment-based. And even when concessions are made by the test makers in the form of "reflective items," such concessions are likely to be grudging and inadequate. It is not that tests in pure abstract reasoning abilities are needed, but that we should be trying to find out if students *can make judgments based on what they know* and not merely whether or not they know it.

There are, I suspect, a great many teachers in Ms. F's situation. They can't figure out what's wrong. Some days they blame the students; some days they blame themselves. Until educators get their priorities straight – until, in other words, they agree upon a consistent and coherent set of criteria and standards applicable to the educational process – serious, well-intentioned teachers like the ones we have been considering here are going to continue to sense that something, somewhere, is wrong with the system while continuing to blame themselves for shortcomings.

Part III

Thinking: the forge of meaning

12   The concept of creative thinking

I have already offered a definition of *critical* thinking. I want to turn now to *creative* thinking. It is not so much, I have suggested, that creative thinking is made up of different components as that it contains components similar to those in critical thinking but differently organized. It therefore seems to me that creative thinking could best be defined as thinking conducive to judgment, guided by context, self-transcending, and sensitive to criteria. The comparison of the critical and the creative might be presented in this fashion:

Critical thinking	*Creative thinking*
Megacriterion: Truth (a kind of meaning)	Megacriterion: Meaning
Aims at judgment	Aims at judgment
Governed by singular criteria	Sensitive to contrasting criteria
Self-correcting	Self-transcending
Sensitive to context	Governed by context (holistic)

In contrasting the regulative ideas, or megacriteria, to which the two kinds of thinking appeal, I do not wish to suggest that creative thinking is uninterested in truth and critical thinking is uninterested in meaning. It is a matter of priorities. I am using the phrase "governed by" to suggest greater coercion than the phrase "sensitive to." Of course, creative thinking is sensitive to the criterion of truth, but it is *governed* by the context of the inquiry taking place. Of course critical thinking is *sensitive* to context, but criteria such as truth, rationality, and meaning are of paramount concern to it.

Because critical thinking has a primordial concern for truth, it has a genuine interest in avoiding error and falsehood. It therefore understands its self-monitoring as self-correcting, whereas creative thinking, more concerned with wholeness and invention, monitors itself with the aim of going beyond itself, transcending itself, as well as with the aim of achieving integrity.

By acknowledging that creative thinking is *sensitive* to criteria, I am trying to ward off giving the impression that such thinking is uncritical or irrational. As I said earlier, there is no creative thinking that is not shot through with critical judgments, just as there is no critical judgment that is not shot through with

193

creative judgments. We can, of course, construct abstract ideal types in which pure forms of thinking are delineated, but in actuality admixture is the rule. Creative thinking is not insensitive to analytical concerns, but it is not governed by such concerns.

My definition will no doubt be found objectionable on the ground that it makes no appeal to such traditional metacriteria as originality, innovation, uniqueness, sincerity, and the like. But I am dealing with creative *thinking* – the process, not the products. If there is uniqueness, it is not because the method of creative thinking differs from occasion to occasion but because the same method, when employed in highly diverse situations, produces highly diverse results.

My objective in this chapter is to consider not so much the implications that follow from this definition as the considerations that led up to it. I will therefore touch upon a number of points that can serve to connect the general notion of creativity as a form of inquiry with the specific formulation just provided.

To begin with, there is the traditional admonition to "follow the inquiry where it leads." Sound advice, no doubt, but a trifle vague. Both critical and creative thinking can be expected to be guided by the pervasive quality of the specific inquiry situation and to be sensitive to the configuration and contours of that situation. But critical thinking will do this by nosing out criteria and concepts by means of which the course of the inquiry can be governed. Creative thinking, on the other hand, will be sensitive to the way in which the pervasive quality embodies values and meanings and will find itself in the grip of powerful schemata that will seek to compel the thinking to move in this direction or that.

I have dealt elsewhere (in *What Happens in Art*) with the inquiry-guiding role of situational ("tertiary") qualities and with Dewey's reference to the fact that these qualities are not stable but are in "transition." In an effort to explain these transitions, I suggested four fundamental types of changes (or exchanges) that would today be classified as schemata. These four movements were presented as physiognomic projection (where human qualities are attributed to nature), introjection (where natural qualities are absorbed into the specifically human), dimensional exchange (where space is interpreted temporally and time spatially), and transensory exchange (where sense data are experienced or described in terms usually reserved for other sensory channels).[1] In that earlier work, I tried to show the foundational role of the body in metaphorical experience, and I was particularly reliant upon the ground-breaking work of Paul Schilder, especially with regard to his notion of the community of body imagery.[2]

Much of this, it seems to me, is corroborated by the recent work of Mark Johnson dealing with body experience, schemata, imagination, and meaning.[3] Johnson's understanding of schemata is particularly rich and detailed. Some of his examples are links, paths, scales, cycles, and center–periphery moves, all

---

[1] New York: Appleton-Century-Crofts, 1967, ch. 3, "Tertiary Qualities."

[2] *The Image and Appearance of the Human Body* (London: Routledge, 1935).

[3] *The Body in the Mind* (Chicago: University of Chicago Press, 1987).

of which act as constraints on our understanding of meaning, just as metaphorical systems guide and compel our reasoning.[4] In consequence, he is able to construct an exciting theory of imagination whose components are *categorization, schemata, metaphorical projections, metonymy (part–whole reversals),* and *narration.*[5]

In the present chapter, I will try to show that what Johnson considers schemata are often binary concepts whose opposition is dynamic and therefore develops a tension and propulsion of its own. For example, the intensely creative philosophical thought of the fifth century B.C. was to a considerable extent powered by the creative opposition of such pre-Socratic binary concepts as One–Many, Permanence–Change, and Appearance–Reality. Indeed, one of the ways in which creative thought is sensitive to criteria is manifested when such criteria appear in highly charged, dialectically linked combinations.

I also want to show that these conceptual pairs can be thought of as dimensions of creative thinking and can be portrayed as coordinates or axes that intersect with other coordinates. Higher-order thinking is itself such a dimension if it is thought of as occurring along the criterion-driven/context-driven axis. But other dimensions can be cited, such as assimilation/manipulation and discovery/invention.

While these coordinates may help us establish some sort of conceptual framework for creative thinking, there is still a need for consideration of some more dynamic, developmental factors that creativity involves. Some of these factors are generating, enlarging, breaking through, and thinking for oneself. I will also touch on these in the chapters that follow.

Two axes of creative thinking

When we work, our hands enter into dialogue with one another. Each does what it has to do: One holds while the other shapes or cuts. These behavioral differences are readily observable and describable but not so readily explainable. Similarly with instances of higher-order thinking: We can distinguish "analytic" from "intuitive" thinking (another pair of terms might do as well), but it would be much more difficult to explain how each functions, and for our present purposes it might not even be particularly profitable to attempt to do so. It may be enough to note for the present that some thinking is criterion-governed and some is governed by values that flood the entire context in which the thinking takes place. Some thinking moves smoothly and routinely, like a train on its tracks; some ranges at will, like a bird in flight, with the result that we see one kind of thinking as linear and explicative and the other as inventive and expansive. Some thinking seems to be purely computational; some seems conjectural, hypothetical, and imaginative. Some thinking is a mere collecting of thoughts that are pressed together mechanically, like a package of figs; in other cases, the thoughts are related to one another organically, each assuming a distinctive role but cooperating with the others

[4] Ibid., p. 137.   [5] Ibid., p. 171.

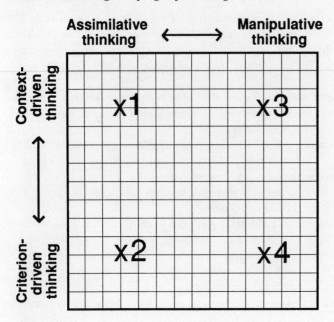

Figure 9

in the overall division of labor to give us a more complete picture. Some thinking is quantitative, some qualitative; some is expository, some narrative. The list goes on and on, but it will be enough if we recognize that higher-order thinking entails an interpenetration and interbreeding of two different forms of mental behavior, which we are free to conceptualize as rationality and creativity. Each form of behavior, the rational and the creative, is a form of inquiry; put together, the result is not merely additive but multiplicative.

In exploring the relationship between the rational and the creative, we can see these as a single axis and then look for an intersecting coordinate, such as the assimilation–manipulation axis. One way this axis is to be understood is in terms of the contrast between doing and undergoing or between being an agent and being a patient.

The resulting matrix enable us to plot a variety of combinations. For example, numbers 1 and 2 in Figure 9 are exemplified by aesthetic appreciation. The 1 represents the sort of thinking we do as we view or listen or read appreciatively, whereas 2 is the sort of thinking we do when we assimilate the world of art or the world of nature more critically. Numbers 3 and 4 represent more active, more constructive forms of thinking. We might see the relationship between 3 and 4 as exemplified by the relationship between artistic and technological thinking. Both are constructive, but one is driven by the context – by the quality of the situation – while the other is much more responsive to specifically identifiable criteria.

Take such mental acts as pondering and meditating. In one sense, they involve a working-over of the topic: kneading it, making it more supple and more manageable – in short, manipulating it. In another sense, they involve a dwelling upon the topic, immersing ourselves in what is thought about and allowing ourselves to be conditioned by it – in short, assimilating it. The same might be said of understanding and of judgment, although in each there are likely to be somewhat different proportions of the assimilative and the manipulative. Thus, all our mental acts can be placed on a continuum that ranges from the receptive and assimilative (like sensations) at one extreme to the active and manipulative (like inventions) at the other. (I discussed this earlier, in Chapter 4, in the section "Higher-Order Thinking in the Schools.")

The distinction between the assimilative and the manipulative dimensions can be especially helpful when it comes to describing and analyzing creative thinking, because it enables us to see that creativity is an *order* and that items can be arranged in that order according to their being more or less assimilative or more or less manipulative. At the same time, it is worth noting that rationality and creativity likewise partake of a single order, of which the extremes are, on the one hand, intensifying rationality and diminished creativity and, on the other hand, intensifying creativity and diminished rationality. In the center, of course, is the area of equilibrium, of creative rationality. So the differences within the order are mainly differences of degree. There is a germ of rationality in all creativity and a germ of creativity in all rationality, just as the cognitive always plays a role in what is predominantly affective, and the affective always plays a role in what is predominantly cognitive.

The discovery–invention axis

Discoveries and inventions seldom just happen. They are generally prepared in advance, although there are always the dangers of underpreparation and overpreparation. Thus, discoveries are very often made by those who are looking for something and have some general idea of what they are looking for but at the same time have an open mind about what might crop up. The more ingenious we are in making these advance preparations, the more the actual discovery, when it does occur, can be seen to have the attributes of an invention.

Likewise, inventions are frequently made by those who have just discovered something and whose surprise and exhilaration predispose them to envision some of the practical applications of that discovery. This is not to say that all of those who steep themselves in what is being discovered around the world are precisely those from whom inventions may be expected, for many of these people have not prepared themselves in other ways to engage in invention. But among those who do invent, it is very likely that they have been in touch with the discoveries taking place in their fields.

The interplay between discovery and invention can be found at any level of education. When children learn to read, for example, they are learning to discover the wealth of understanding and beauty that written language can contain. But they are also engaged in interpreting what they read and in forming opinions about or based upon what they read, and all of these are inventive activities. Even in the case of minuscule thinking skills, invention and discovery are frequently tied tightly together. For example, present an elementary school class with a somewhat unusual fact (e.g., "A bundle of hundred-dollar bills was found this morning on the volleyball court"). Ask for inferences. Then discuss what each inference presupposes. You will find that the inferences break new ground, for the students had not previously thought of finding hundred-dollar bills in their school-yard. On the other hand, each speculative possibility a child cites can be based upon a set of preexisting assumptions. The initial phase of the inquiry involves (1) imaginative *invention*; the subsequent phase involves (2) *disclosure of what was being assumed* or taken for granted and therefore involves (3) *discovery*.

Generativity

Jerome Kagan asserts, "Although a tree in a virgin forest exists even if no one is present, an idea we call creative requires the reaction of another, not just the judgment of the inventor or of history." He therefore restricts the word *creative* to description of "products that generate a specific cognitive and emotional response in an audience; hence, many valid ideas will not be judged creative while some invalid ones will be so judged."[6]

Kagan does not spell out just what this "specific cognitive and emotional response" should be, but I presume it could not be just any reaction. It would have to be a sympathetic and appreciative response or, even better, an analogously creative response. Or perhaps these consequences of creative thinking – sympathy, appreciation, and creativity – represent levels of intensity that correspond to the ascending value of the initially creative thinking that stimulated them.

We need not agree with Kagan's contention that ideas are creative *only* if they are generative in order to grant that generativity represents a significant dimension of creativity. Both the quantity and quality of such generativity would be relevant: quantity in terms of the size and scope of the audience affected; quality in terms of the degree of creativity generated in the audience.

It is obvious that generativity is particularly relevant with respect to teaching situations. The teacher who thinks creatively is a precious model for his or her students, provided that the teacher's aim is to inspire such thinking among the students rather than merely to display a breathtaking *tour de force*. It is not uncommon, however, for brilliant lecturers to provide their audiences with very few clues as to how this profusion of glittering ideas came into being or how those in the audience might go through a similar process. Of course, the more such lecturers conceal the origins of their thinking, the more spontaneous and uncanny such thinking seems to be. But if you are concerned with being an effective teacher,

[6] *Unstable Ideas: Temperament, Cognition, and Self* (Cambridge, Mass.: Harvard University Press, 1989), p. 206.

you have to forgo these dazzling, charismatic effects and seek instead to create the problem conditions that the students will have to think through themselves if they are to become independent and creative thinkers. Students have to learn to do their own thinking, and this means developing their own integrity as thinkers. Merely to imitate a brilliant teacher has the net effect of sacrificing their originality. This is often a hard lesson for students to learn, and they may have to find out by bitter experience that the more they imitate the more sparkling minds among their teachers, the less they will resemble them.

Amplification

C. S. Peirce distinguishes between explicative and ampliative reasoning.[7] The first, as exemplified by deduction, extends our thought without enlarging it. The second, as exemplified by induction and the use of analogy and metaphor, represents cognitive breakthroughs. It goes beyond the given and in the process compels our own thinking to go beyond the given. It stands for evolutionary growth rather than for stability or fixity. Ampliative reasoning not only expands our thinking but expands our capacity to think expansively.

Generalizations are enlargements or amplifications in the sense that they go beyond the information given, inferring from a group of instances that possess a similar character and that have in common a particular feature that all instances of that character have that particular feature in common. Generalizations, then, presume a certain *uniformity* in the evidence. Hypotheses are also representative of amplified thinking. Hypotheses may emerge in the presence of pieces of evidence that are highly *diversified*: here some apparently unrelated facts, here some inferences, here some generalizations, here some principles, and so on. Hypotheses also go beyond the information given, but they do so in order to explain or predict with regard to highly complex states of affairs rather than uniform phenomena.

Analogical reasoning presumes that things in nature may exhibit a certain *proportionality*, a proportionality that can best be expressed through similarities of relationships rather than through similarity of terms. Thus, we say that the relationship between A and B "is like" the relationship between C and D. Given this understanding, we can, if given A, B, and C, go beyond the information available to us and suppose D, which is to C as B is to A.

What must be kept in mind is that proportionalities (unless they are strict ratios) are based upon resemblances and hence are matters of judgment. It is for this reason that the strengthening of judgment in students generally involves extensive practice in the evaluation of analogies. This is why Plato thought music and mathematics so essential to education – because they embodied systems of proportion. This is also why Aristotle insisted that judgment rested not so much on strict equality (e.g., in equations) as on the approximation of equity.

---

[7] "The Probability of Induction," in Justus Buchler (ed.), *Philosophical Writings of Peirce* (New York: Dover, 1955), p. 180.

Metaphorical thinking – and indeed, figurative discourse generally – is ampliative rather than explicative. It represents a mixing of categories or schemata – a mixing that, from a literal or prosaic point of view, seems to be sheer impudence but from which issues a fresh and vigorous confluence of thought incomparably richer than more conventional ways of thinking. Metaphorical thinking is thus a synthesis of incompatibles that yields, like binocularity, a far greater depth of vision by the mere act of juxtaposition. It is thinking that, from the perspective of either of the categories it bridges over, is bound to seem false – a "category-mistake,"[8] just as thinking among the disciplines often seems false by the standards that exist within the disciplines.

Breaking through

According to Thomas Kuhn, scientists normally function within the paradigm of practice accepted by the scientific community. But in revolutionary periods, a paradigm of divergent practice may be asserted by dissident scientists, and in time this discrepant paradigm may come to dominate or even to replace the earlier system of practice-plus-theory until it becomes itself the normal paradigm. One thing Kuhn seems to be insisting on in all this is that there must always be a system; we cannot repudiate the existing system without being able to recommend a system with which to replace it.

It is just this point that is contested by Charles David Axelrod, in his examination of the sociological writings of Georg Simmel.[9] Simmel seems to have been regarded by the sociological community as an outsider who wrote only in "fragments," in contrast to the professionals who were insiders and whose systematic works were regarded as constructive contributions to the system of sociological understanding that existed in Simmel's day. The community found it difficult to accept or even take seriously Simmel's little essays on seemingly frivolous topics such as "the handle," "the face," and "the adventure." But Simmel made the point very explicitly that an adventure, like a dream or a work of art, might seem in one sense only remotely connected with a person's life and yet in another sense might speak to what was most central and most profound in that person's life. Likewise, the sociological fragment might seem, in one sense, hardly relevant to the sociological framework of the day and yet in another sense might provide insights that the normal paradigm systematically excluded. What Simmel represents, for Axelrod, is the creative individual refusing to give ground before the community, which rejects him as an outsider, an alien, a nonconformist, and a stranger because it cannot accommodate his profound perceptions and resents the foreign system implicit in them.

[8] Cf. Nelson Goodman, *Languages of Art* (Indianapolis, Ind.: Bobbs-Merrill, 1968), p. 73: "Indeed, a metaphor might be regarded as a calculated category-mistake – or rather as a happy and revitalizing, even if bigamous, second marriage."

[9] *Studies in Intellectual Breakthrough: Freud, Simmel, Buber* (Amherst: University of Massachusetts Press, 1979), pp. 35–50.

Axelrod sees breaking through as not quite the same as creativity; apparently he sees creativity as a departure from the past (hence its celebrated "originality") and breaking through a standing up to the community on behalf of one's individuality and uniqueness. Creativity does not intimate the sense of violent confrontation and struggle that is intimated by breakthrough.[10] Creativity is often achieved at the expense of inertia, slackness, habit; it is an overthrow of what is merely taken for granted. But a breakthrough is what follows from the clash between the community and a dissident individual who, as in Kierkegaard's "teleological suspension of the ethical," transcends conventional morality, then transcends universal ethics, and emerges at the still higher level of tragic ethical heroism. What is particularly perceptive in Axelrod's account of Simmel's sociology is his analysis of the dialogical relation between the individual and the community – that is, the community that regards the individual as a mere fragment versus the individual who appears to be fragmentary but nevertheless is part of a superior system, a superior paradigm that can be glimpsed by those with discernment. It is in the process of this confrontation that Simmel, with his sure grasp of such difficult concepts as meaning, individuality, art, and life, sheds more light on the nature of creativity by his oblique suggestions than do scholars who approach the problem head on.

I want, then, to consider Axelrod's notion of breakthrough as an aspect of creativity (just as Kagan sees generativity as an aspect of creativity) rather than as a contrasting concept. There is much here that recalls Freud's depiction of the struggle between the superego and the id,[11] as well as Mead's depiction of the struggle between the assimilated "me's" that go to make up the "generalized other" and the creative "I" that is the response to those me's.[12] But whether we see the dialogue as a struggle or not, it remains the case that at least one aspect of creativity is dialogical and involves a dialogue between the individual and the community.

Creativity and imagination

There are those, such as R. G. Collingwood, for whom the connection between creativity and imagination is so strong as to be virtually an identity relationship.[13] And there are those, such as Edward S. Casey, for whom imagination, while important, is not necessarily related to creativity. Imagining may be banal and repetitive, unspontaneous and unproductive.[14] Creativity on the other hand, may

[10] Ibid., pp. 1–14.
[11] Sigmund Freud, "The Ego and the Id," in John Rickman (ed.), *A General Selection from the Works of Sigmund Freud* (Garden City, N.Y.: Doubleday, 1957), pp. 210–35.
[12] George Herbert Mead, *Mind, Self and Society* (Chicago: University of Chicago Press, 1934), ch. xxii.
[13] *The Principles of Art* (Oxford: Clarendon Press, 1937), pp. 130–4.
[14] *Imagining: A Phenomenological Study* (Bloomington: Indiana University Press, 1976), p. 186. See also Francis Sparshott, "Imagination – The Very Idea," *Journal of Aesthetics and Art Criticism* 48:1 (Winter 1990), 1–8.

in some cases be much more strongly allied with conceiving than with imagining. Indeed, it is very difficult to distinguish between conceiving the possibilities inherent in a given situation or state of affairs and imagining them, or to specify which of the two mental acts is the more ingenious. Casey holds that the relationship between imagination and creativity is a nonnecessary one; the two often occur together, but either may occur without the other.

The notion of *play* can be very helpful as we attempt to understand the relationship between creativity and imagination. This is because imagining is so obviously playful thinking, and play, in turn, is so obviously imaginative action. Imagination is thus a kind of disembodied playfulness, whereas creativity is a kind of embodied imagination. Yet play need not be a free-wheeling release from all criteria, especially as it moves in the direction of the playing of games, which are rule-guided. And we must make room too for the concept of cognitive play, exemplars of which would be poetry and philosophy.

I think that, as time goes on, the most promising psychological approach to imagining will come from schema theory. Schemata, as dynamic cognitive structures, react sensitively to the addition or subtraction of an element, in that all the other elements readjust and realign themselves when the change is made. Moreover, they respond holistically to their own internal shifts and alterations. We can therefore conceive of an individual mind as containing countless such schemata, some moribund, some stirring sleepily, and some seething with activity – even though none of this is in the individual's field of awareness. For example, it may be that during sleep many of these schemata are as busy as factories, each churning out vast amounts of novel images and ideas, not for immediate use, perhaps, but to be retained for eventual use – in dreams or in art or in the formation of hypotheses or in any of an endless number of applications. Imagination can be conceived of, then, as a vast but semidissociated cognitive industry, in which autonomous schemata fabricate and stockpile a fund of imaginative material similar to our funded experience. Indeed, the contents of the two funds admix and coalesce and interpenetrate, so that it is not our funded experience alone that we bring to bear upon ever new perceptions or thoughts, but this superfund derived both from past experience and ongoing imaginative activity.

Creativity and thinking for ourselves

It is unprofitable to think of creativity as a process of emergence out of nowhere. It is rather a transformation of the given into something radically different – not a rabbit produced by magic out of a silk hat, but a silk purse produced by art out of a sow's ear.

Socrates and Kant are both severely critical of those who betray their own creativity by letting other people do their thinking for them. We should think for ourselves, and we should help other people think for themselves. Socrates conceives of himself as a teacher whose role, analogous to that of a midwife, is to help others bring to birth their own ideas. (We are free to speculate that this is the way he is able to get himself to think for himself.) It is not clear, however, to whom Socrates would assign the primary locus of creativity – to those who think for themselves or to those who promote such thinking in others.

This question is explored (along with countless others dealing with the nature of thinking) in the later work of Gilbert Ryle, but especially in his essay on how thinking might be taught.[15] Ryle first lists some of the things good teachers do, and it is a list worth summarizing:

1. They do not repeat themselves; when they must tell us the same things, they do so in different ways
2. They expect us to do things on our own with what they teach us, "applying it, re-phrasing it, accelerating it, drawing conclusions from it, marrying it with earlier lessons, etc. . . ."
3. They don't tell us, they *show* us what they want done and then get us to move or utter in similar ways
4. They tease us with questions and then question us about our answers
5. They make us practice and repractice our exercises, such as our conversions and syllogisms
6. "They lead us by the hand along a half-familiar track and leave us in the lurch to get ourselves over its final stretch"
7. They cite blatantly erroneous solutions, expecting us to pinpoint what is wrong in them or how to improve on them
8. "They draw our attention to partly analogous, but easier problems, and leave us to use these analogies as banisters"
9. They break up complex problems into simpler ingredients and then leave us to resolve the simpler problems and reunite the solutions
10. When we have hit upon a solution, they set us subsidiary or parallel problems

Having specified what good teachers in any subject do with their students, Ryle proceeds to argue that these are precisely the things we do with ourselves when we are trying to get ourselves to think. It is not exactly that we shuttle back and forth between the role of teacher and the role of learner when we are trying to think for ourselves. It is rather that we try to get ourselves to do what a good teacher would try to get us to do.

When we ponder, Ryle says, we are trying to make up for the fact that we are not being taught, and so we impose upon ourselves the sorts of tasks a teacher might impose on us. Ryle denies that he is affirming an identity here between being taught and thinking, but there is, he insists, an important connection between the two.

In thinking, the soul is not just conversing or debating with herself; she is experimentally conveying could-be lessons to herself. . . . In fact, the crude stuff of thinking has to consist of the perfectly ordinary vehicles of everyday interpersonal lesson-communication,

[15] "Thinking and Self-Teaching," in Konstantin Kolenda (ed.), *Symposium on Gilbert Ryle*, Rice University Studies 58:3 (Summer 1972), as reprinted in *Thinking: The Journal of Philosophy for Children* 1:3–4 (n.d.), 18–23.

though here employed not in its normal didactic task, but in the parasitic or higher-order task of query-tuition.[16]

Ryle concludes by restating the similarity between teaching, self-teaching, and thinking:

As A's well-charted teaching can occasionally dispel B's ignorance, so my uncharted thinking can occasionally dispel my own ignorance. Thinking is trying to better one's instructions; it is trying out promissory tracks which will exist, if they ever do exist, only after one has stumbled exploringly over ground where they are not.[17]

What I particularly want to emphasize about Ryle's analysis is that he begins by identifying the inquiry procedures or search operations that are characteristic of teacher–student dialogue. He then argues that, in our own private deliberations, we internalize the identical procedures. We institute, as it were, a dialogue with ourselves.

Thinking for ourselves is, then, dialogical. And if it is the case, as I suspect it is, that thinking for ourselves is the most appropriate paradigm of creative thought, then Ryle's suggestions would hold good in any workshop, studio, atelier, coaching session, or laboratory in which a teacher is trying to stimulate students to "be creative."

Indeed, it seems to me that this is precisely the hypothesis that needs to be verified, that an individual's creative thinking resembles the dialogical interchange between good teachers and their students as exemplified by the operations Ryle has specified. Is this how would-be artists can be encouraged to be creative? Would-be physicians and physicists? Would-be poets, lawyers, and biologists? For wherever we are taught a craft and somehow learn to transcend that craft, we find encouragement to think for ourselves. To learn a craft is to learn how others think and have thought – knowledge and expertise not to be scoffed at. To acquire an art, however, is to enter into dialogue with those others, parrying their thinking here, building on it there, rejecting it here, modifying it there, until we have discovered our own way of making, saying, or doing, which is to say we have discovered our own creativity.

The search techniques and inquiry procedures Ryle has mentioned are among those characteristic of the community of inquiry. These techniques and procedures are precisely those internalized by students, with the result that the methodical deliberations of the community are translated into the methodical deliberations and ponderings of the individual. We can say therefore that the community of inquiry is perhaps the most promising methodology for the encouragement of that fusion of critical and creative cognitive processing known as higher-order thinking.

Creativity and criteria

This heading encompasses two very different ways in which the concepts of creativity and criteria overlap. One way involves the use of criteria in the identifi-

[16] Ibid., p. 20.   [17] Ibid., p. 23.

cation and classification of instances of creativity. The other way deals with the employment of criteria by those engaged in creative thinking.

How do we identify instances of creativity?

Earlier, in discussing the ways in which criteria come to be accepted, I pointed out that the metacriteria often employed are *relevance, reliability,* and *strength* and that these correspond roughly to the way we select political candidates for office: first, by ascertaining if there is anything that would make them ineligible; second, by determining, on the basis of their records of achievements, their reliability; and third, by evaluating their potential, vis-à-vis those of other candidates, for bringing about the kinds of consequences we think desirable. It seems to me that those who wish to perform the classificatory task of identifying and categorizing instances of creativity are likely to have recourse to these same metacriteria for choosing the criteria that are to guide the work of classification.

In scouting about for criteria, we are likely to come up with half a dozen or a dozen or more that appear to be relevant and that brandish acceptable credentials. Those that come most immediately to mind are (in no particular order) originality, novelty, generativity, uniqueness, breakthrough capacity, surprisingness, inventiveness, liberating quality, productivity, freshness, imaginativeness, inspiredness, capacity to synthesize. These candidates would need to be analyzed to determine to what extent they are simply synonyms for creative thinking rather than criteria for it. We would also have to see if any are applicable more to the causes or effects of creative thinking than to such thinking itself. Surprisingness might be a case in point, although some psychologists, such as Jerome Bruner, think quite highly of it.[18]

Of those that remain after such screening and that therefore possess a prima facie plausibility, we might want to ask whether the classification of a particular episode of thinking as creative could be made of each candidate criterion when taken alone. For example, is uniqueness per se sufficient to justify calling a certain stretch of thinking creative? Now, we will probably be inclined to say no, and we will give as our reason that certain kinds of psychotic thinking can be highly rigid yet be unique. This in turn provides us with a clue to still another candidate criterion: flexibility. And indeed, as we pursue our inquiry, we will continue to find new criteria in the negatives of the criteria we employ for rejecting other candidates.

As a matter of fact, many psychologists do make use of *flexibility* as one of their standard criteria for creative thinking – along with *fluency* and *appropriateness.* By "fluency" they mean the richness and articulateness of thought in a

---

[18] See "The Conditions of Creativity," in Howard E. Gruber, Glenn Terrell, and Michael Wartheimer (eds.), *Contemporary Approaches to Creative Thinking* (New York: Atherton, 1962), pp. 1–30. See also R. J. Shapiro, "The Criterion Problem," in P. E. Vernon (ed.), *Creativity* (Baltimore: Penguin, 1970), pp. 257–69.

given context, frame of reference, language, or discipline.[19] By "flexibility" they mean the movement of thought from one frame of reference to the next, whereby greater generality and comprehensiveness are attained. And by "appropriateness" they mean the usefulness or applicability of thinking, its basis in actual evidence, or the likelihood of its dealing successfully with problematic situations.

This trinity of criteria suggests that perhaps no one criterion is sufficient and that more than one are needed. But how many? An answer that is often proposed is a quorum. Thus, for example, art historians will set up a number of criteria by means of which Baroque painting and sculpture may be identified as such. They might, for example, set up ten such criteria. And then they will identify a quorum number – say, four, so that any painting or sculpture that satisfies any four of the ten criteria will be considered Baroque. This does not rule out the possibility that there will be some pieces that we will insist on calling Baroque even though they satisfy only three or two or one but do so with such intensity that we have to use the classification.

Reference to *intensity* compels us to recall the importance of standards in the appeal to criteria. Standards represent, as I indicated earlier, the degree to which a criterion is satisfied. With reference to the identical criterion, some people may have a high standard of satisfaction and some a low one. This means that one criterion with a very high standard of satisfaction may be for some people equivalent to several criteria with a low standard of satisfaction. Often too we employ the metacriterion of intensity in order to compare criteria with one another.

How are criteria employed in creative thinking?

The question of whether criteria are *employed* in creative thinking is quite different from the question of the criteria by which creative thinking is *identified*. Since critical thinking and creative thinking are being considered here as ideal types rather than as empirical generalizations, we should be able to distinguish between them in clear-cut ways. Thus, if critical thinking is identified exclusively with criterion-guided thinking, then creative thinking must be guided – if it is guided at all – by something quite different.

Here I am compelled to acknowledge that, even as ideal types, critical and creative thinking may not be mutually exclusive. Take the questions of sensitivity to context. Both types of thinking manifest this feature; the only difference is that in creative thinking it is predominant, whereas in critical thinking it is, although still essential, of somewhat lesser importance. Is it not possible, then, that both critical and creative thinking may be criterion-guided but that this is a matter of greater importance in critical thinking than in creative thinking?

I think it may be necessary to make this concession, but with a proviso – that what counts as a criterion in critical thinking can function differently (although

---

[19] See, for example, the discussion of creativity in Raymond S. Nickerson, David N. Perkins, and Edward E. Smith, *The Teaching of Thinking* (Hillsdale, N.J.: Erlbaum, 1985), pp. 86–100.

still a member of the family of criteria) from what counts as a criterion in creative thinking. A criterion in critical thinking is a solitary concept that may be realized fully or partially or not at all. A given paragraph may be *true* fully, partially, or not at all. At the other extreme from the concept is not its opposite but its absence. On the other hand, in creative thinking, criteria tend to be composed of *dialectically related pairs* or sets where each concept is set over against its opposite and where the tension between these concepts helps to create the magical tension that holds together the various parts of the created work.

Thus, the author of a story may take her bearings from sets of contrasting categories whose various intersections give shape to the narrative as it unfolds. These may be pairs like Art–Life, Nature–Art, Life–Death, Permanence–Change, One–Many, Appearance–Reality, Part–Whole, or Cause–Effect. It is because the work of art is often the battleground of essentially conflicting concepts that it conveys that vastness of portent people find so mysterious in it and so aesthetically intriguing.

This does not mean that, of the two kinds of criteria (which might be called monological and dialogical), only creative thinking contains the dialogical kind. Take, for example, Monroe C. Beardsley's three canons, Unity, Complexity, and Intensity.[20] It would be an easy enough matter to see the first two as dialogically related but to see Intensity as monological. On the whole, however, I suspect that dialogically related concepts play a much greater role in creative thinking than do monological criteria. It is conceptual oppositions that suggest to the author not simply the direction in which to go but the sorts of episodes that are needed, which illustrations need to be amplified or clarified, and where the discourse needs to be sharpened.

To the question, then, of whether criteria are employed in creative thinking, I think the answer must be that they are – and primarily in the sense of paired and contrasting concepts that underpin the thematic choices or judgments. A secondary sense in which criteria are involved in creative thinking is that occasionally monological concepts like intensity (that is, the high-intensity/low-intensity range) play a directive role in the creative process. There is yet a third sense in which a criterion guides creativity, and that is the sense in which the tertiary quality, or whole-quality, of the creative situation guides the sequential moves that constitute the process of creative thinking. In such thinking, the pervasive quality of the process moves to expression in the created product. A detective, for example, discovers a problematic situation, and it is the overall structure of that situation that guides the successive moves the detective will make. In the case of the novelist, the problematic situation may be largely invented rather than discovered, but here again it is no less true that the way the situation shapes up – the way, for example, the plot emerges and takes over – is the controlling factor in the way the novelist will distribute clues, lures, blind alleys, and false scents.

---

[20] *Aesthetics: Problems in the Philosophy of Criticism* (New York: Harcourt Brace and World, 1958), pp. 464–6.

Tertiary qualities as contextual values

Now, creative thinking is a form of inquiry, and inquiry is always immersed or ensconced in a situation. Dewey tells us that each situation is unique in the sense that it has its own quality, a quality that cannot really be captured by words, although we select the best adjectives or adverbs we know in order to approximate it.[21] We may say that this situation is "distressing" or that one "cheerful," but these are *general* terms, while situations are uncompromisingly particular and individualized. If this situation is cheerful, it is cheerful in its own idiosyncratic way, which is identical with no other cheerfulness.

So Dewey is right that each situation is permeated with a tertiary quality, or whole-quality, and it is this quality that guides the inquiry into the situation. What needs to be added, however, is that the whole-quality is what it is by virtue of the network of relationships from which it emanates and upon which it rests.[22] Furthermore, because each relationship is a meaning, the composite of relationships is a composite meaning, and this composite meaning or meaning network is identical with the whole-quality of the situation.

The overall structure of the situation is a configuration of relationships. Each relationship has its own particular meaning and quality, and the configuration as a whole has its own unique meaning and quality. These qualitative meanings or meaningful qualities are what we mean by *values*, and this explains what we mean when we say that critical thinking is guided by criteria, whereas it is contextual values that guide creative thinking.[23]

There are, then, values exhibited by individual relationships, and there are values exhibited by the overall configuration of relationships in the creative situation. In between these microscopic and macroscopic values, there are those of intermediate magnitude that nevertheless have a special potency in controlling the direction of judgment. These powerful values are often the product of binary pairs of contrasting or confirming concepts.[24] For example, a writer in the process of composing a book may experience the conflict between unity and complexity very

21 *Logic: The Theory of Inquiry* (New York: Holt, 1938), p. 66. Dewey here calls a situation a "contextual whole" and on p. 68 asserts that "a situation is a whole in virtue of its immediately pervasive quality. . . . The pervasively qualitative is not only that which binds all constituents into a whole but it is also unique; it constitutes in each situation an *individual* situation, indivisible and unduplicable. . . . A universe of experience is the precondition of a universe of discourse. Without its controlling presence, there is no way to determine the relevancy, weight or coherence of any designated distinction or relation."

22 Ibid., p. 70.

23 See, for example, Gregor Sebba's insightful analyses in Helen Sebba and Hendrikus Boers (eds.), *Creativity: Lectures by Gregor Sebba* (Atlanta: Scholars Press, 1987). Gestaltists like Kurt Koffka and critical Gestaltists like Rudolf Arnheim have also done much fruitful work in this area. A balanced approach to critical and creative thinking is argued for by David Perkins, *The Mind's Best Work* (Cambridge, Mass.: Harvard University Press, 1981). Cf. also Robert J. Sternberg (ed.), *The Nature of Creativity* (Cambridge University Press, 1988).

24 In discussing the role of binary concepts as criteria, I have found very useful Kieran Egan's excellent *Teaching as Story Telling: An Alternative to Teaching and Curriculum in the Elementary School*

intensely. On the one hand, she feels compelled to be faithful to the highly differentiated and complicated subject matter with which she has to deal, and on the other hand, she wants to present her understanding of this in the most coherent way she can. So for her a controlling value is the unity–complexity conflict. And as she proceeds, it is evident that she is making definite progress in reducing incoherence to coherence, inconsistencies to consistency, and disunity to unity. These are binary pairs in which the relationships are not contrasting but confirming. Thus, binary concepts have a prepotent influence in terms of the way their special relationships guide the ongoing course of creative judgment making.

In stressing the role of binary criteria in creative thinking, I have not intended to assert that such thinking is insensitive to singular, monological criteria. An example of such a monological criterion in creative thinking would be *meaningfulness*. It should be understood, however, that in the case of binary criteria both criteria are live options (for example, both nature and art), whereas in the case of singular criteria, such as truth, meaning, or justice, the positive is live while the negative (falsehood, meaninglessness, injustice), being some version of emptiness or deprivation, is generally not.

Creativity and dialogue in the community of inquiry

A community of inquiry is a deliberative society engaged in higher-order thinking. This means that its deliberations are not merely chats or conversations; they are logically disciplined dialogues. The fact that they are logically structured, however, does not preclude their providing a stage for creative performance.

Take Joan. In the lecture courses she attends, she is normally a detached observer. The lecturers impress her with their erudition, and she is seldom so troubled by what any of them say as to think of asking a question, let alone making a comment or developing a thesis. But now she attends a seminar in which the instructor acts only as a facilitator of the dialogue, although at times she pauses to press individual students about what they may be taking for granted in their comments. And now the dialogue intensifies, and Joan comes to realize that there is another side to the issue that she had formerly understood from just a single point of view. And still the dialogue continues to intensify; soon Joan realizes there may be many sides, not just one or two. She leans forward, listening intently, and suddenly there bursts from her a comment that surprises her as much as it does the others. It does not settle the discussion, which sweeps on to the end of the period. Perhaps it made an important contribution; perhaps it made only a minor one. But as Joan goes home, what she takes with her and dwells upon is the comment she made, how she might have made it better, and how wonderful it was that she made it at all. She had been swept up in the dialogue, had overcome her normal reticence and self-consciousness, and had been brought to utterance. And it was she who spoke, she herself, in the first person; nor did it escape her,

(Chicago: University of Chicago Press, 1986). The book is a powerful argument for the use of stories to organize and present the content of all curricular disciplines.

as she spoke, that the others were listening raptly to her – an intoxicating experience for one who has never had it before. She told them her thoughts and she made them think – this is what goes through her mind as she walks along, still trying to figure out what happened to have so intensely moved her. Once again she rehearses what she said and savors it, even while reproaching herself for not having made the comment still more trenchantly. But as to how it happened, all she knows is that *it* – the situation – drew her utterance out of her. It did not teach her what to say, but it created an environment in which she found it important to say what she wanted to say. To do so, she had to teach herself how to speak, as it were for the first time.

The community of deliberative inquiry establishes conditions evocative of critical and creative thinking, and such thinking in turn furthers the objectives of both the community and its members. This is a very different set of conditions from the ones found in a classroom that stresses learning and knowledge – the acquisition of erudition. It is not that the lecture is an inferior or obsolete mode of pedagogy. It can be brilliant; it can be a work of art; it can often penetrate deeper into its subject matter from its single point of view than can a discussion from its multiple points of view. But to the extent that it is fascinating and charismatic, it turns its listeners into passive admirers rather than active inquirers. Too often it inhibits rather than encourages creativity, and the same is even true with regard to critical thinking. It appropriates the means of intellectual production instead of turning them over to the students so as to enable them to become productive themselves. This is no longer tolerable; we have to move toward a mixed academic economy.

I have been employing economic metaphors, alternating between creation and translation on the one hand and production and exchange on the other, because this seems to me a down-to-earth way of understanding the myriad ways of initiating new modes of expression or of modifying old ones. One mode of thinking takes from and lends to the other as we attempt to mold our thoughts into words and distill words into thoughts. If translation is thought of as symbolic exchange, and if an exemplar of symbolic exchange is dialogue, we can begin to understand why all thinking is dialogical, transactional, and translational. To translate what is thought into what is spoken or what is spoken into what is thought is not altogether unlike translating a text from one language into another or exchanging the currency of one language for the currency of another.

That we cannot separate creation from translation can readily be seen in the fact that the construction and enjoyment of metaphor – and metaphor, I take it, is an essential nugget of creativity – cannot be understood apart from translation. If one speaks, as Gwendolyn Brooks does, of love as "a golden hurt," we must be prepared to translate the language of pain into the language of colors and the language of colors into the language of metals. This cannot be done, we discover, without generating still other metaphors as we try to bridge over the abyss that separates each order of our experience from every other order. Nevertheless, as our experience with the learning of new natural languages teaches us, the time comes when we cease engaging in mechanical translations and begin to think in both languages simultaneously. It is much the same with creative thinking: The time comes when we stop trying to build bridges across the chasms that separate natural orders from one another and begin to think in those orders simultaneously.

Creative thinking and creativity

I do not pretend that creative thinking is the whole of creativity. It represents just one aspect of it, although again I am not sure what thinking and creativity are or where they leave off and other things begin. I would suggest, though, that thinking is some kind of *processing of experience,* and just as a data processor is not in touch with the sources of the data he or she processes, so we may not be in touch with the sources of our experience when we process it. The creative impulse evidently involves a constant reaching down to the sources of that experience and a constant reaching up to its fulfillment. The roots of human experience are in animal life and in nature generally. The more vehemently some people attack and seek to destroy those roots, the more vehemently those committed to creativity seek to revisit the roots again and again in order to bring their experience to fulfillment. The shuttling back and forth, the weaving and knitting together – these moves are thinking moves, but we should not confuse them with the richness and brilliance of human experience itself or with the enigma of what we call nature, in which human experience has its setting and its dwelling place.

13 Teachers and texts: the springs of inquiry

Educators must be wary on many scores, but two are outstanding. One is that it is very difficult to educate uninterested students. The other is that without the presence of certain favorable conditions it is very difficult to educate students well even if they are interested.

The favorable conditions to which I allude are (1) competent teaching, (2) an adequate curriculum, and (3) the formation of a community of inquiry. In this chapter, I shall touch briefly on the first two points, reserving the third for Chapter 14.

The three conditions in question are not altogether independent of one another. Teachers cannot be prepared in classrooms that are not communities of inquiry. Nor can it be the objective of such teachers to be able to work wholly without curriculum materials or without deliberative communities.

The increasing professionalization of the teacher may very well include a largely expanded knowledge base, but such knowledge should be thought of as a reservoir rather than as contents to be doled out to the students. Professionalization should entail the capacity to coordinate the three conditions just cited so as to foster the growth of students' reasoning and judgment. This is evidently what is meant when it is urged that teachers be effective "facilitators." What is characteristic of professionals, in addition to having a sound knowledge base, is their ability to coordinate highly complex and varied activities and the good sense – the reasonableness and judiciousness – they reveal as they go about their work. Teachers can no longer be thought of as schoolmasters, but they do need the organizational skills that will bring out the skills of others. Those who prepare future teachers cannot be allowed to overlook these requirements.

The voice of the text

In a far-ranging article on the decline of the philosophy of education, Suzanne de Castell has proposed as an explanation the failure of the philosophy of education "adequately to reflect upon the material basis of its production as written text." "Hence," she continues,

it has failed to recognize the ways in which the use of written language for speculative, as opposed to documentary purposes, has distinctive "shaping" effects upon the character of

212

speculation itself, which in turn both shapes and limits the range of its possible objects of study. This neglect becomes increasingly critical . . . the more philosophers of education attempt to derive educational theory from the actual practices of teachers.[1]

Drawing heavily on the work of Eric Havelock, she points out the powerful epistemological impact of the invention of the technology of writing. The transformation of mind from the Homeric to the Platonic world is a movement from the concrete work of particulars to the abstract realm of general ideas. The incidentals of place, time, and circumstance are replaced by what is absolute, enduring, universal, and necessary. Everything must be isolated from its setting in the great story and identified per se. Instead of "The just Agamemnon did so and so," we get "Justice is so and so." The depiction of conduct, which had been enmeshed in and structured by narrative, is replaced by abstract knowledge. Doings are replaced by knowings; theory replaces practice. De Castell argues that the attempt of philosophers of education "to conceptualize the multiple concrete activities of practitioners in terms of a unified, systematic corpus of general theoretical principles of practice"[2] cannot possibly succeed:

So long as our conception of practical theory remains limited to traditional forms, our writing of it restricted within canonical disciplinary discourses, and so long as the authority and privilege of such writing remains institutionally preserved only for "intellectuals" and not practitioners, we ensure for ourselves an endlessly recurrent discourse on the theoretical "problem" of theory and practice, a problem which would be readily dissolved "in practice," but whose preservation, it should be recognized, serves the interests of "scholarly productivity," however little this may do for the advancement of educational practice.[3]

The implications of the shift from the Homeric to the Platonic realm, from the spoken to the written, have been dealt with by many scholars other than de Castell and Havelock, but I am not aware of any who have tried to show, as de Castell has, the chilling implications for the philosophy of education. And yet I wonder if her strictures are not misplaced. It seems to me her barbs should be aimed not so much at the philosopher of education as at the developers of curricula. As long as textbooks are what they are, schools of education will prepare teachers in such a way that there are few alternatives to the use of such texts. Under these circumstances, I cannot see how it much matters that philosophers are obsessed with finding the theory of practice, for the first thing that needs to be done is to change the nature of the text.

Beginners (whether children or adults) do well to begin with "The just Agamemnon did so and so" rather than with "Justice *is* so and so." I think they would begin even better with first-person than with third-person narrative, whether first-person singular or first-person plural. We need not make any grandiose concessions to the thesis that a child's development recapitulates that of the species in order to accept the fact that, from an educational point of view, speaking precedes writing and the narrative form precedes the expository.

[1] "On Writing on Theory and Practice," *Journal of Philosophy of Education* 23:1 (1989), 39.
[2] Ibid., p. 40.   [3] Ibid., p. 48.

In the case of the voice of the text – whether it is to be third-person or first-person – the direction in which to move is not so readily apparent. The third-person voice, to the child, is the voice from on high, the voice from without rather than from within. It is the voice of the all-seeing, all-knowing, totally rational Other. It is the objective, authoritative, legitimate voice. What it says is what "*it*" or "*on*" or "*es*" says; what is said impersonally, by "one," by "them," by everyone. It possesses that God's-eye view of time that enables it to know the past as well as it knows the present, so that it is utterly to be trusted when it begins, "Once upon a time . . ." For this serene, imperturbable Apollonian voice, everything is ordered and everything is in its place. What it relates is what had to be, what was in the very nature of things, sometimes deified, never defiable.

The first-person voice, on the other hand, is the voice from within. If the voice of the Other is the first legitimate voice, then the voice from within seems at first to be illegitimate. If the voice of the Other is at first the establishment voice, then the voice from within is the voice of the dissenting individual.

If we are going to compose the text in the narrative form, we have a choice between Dick and Jane or I and We, between third person and first person. It seems to me that we would do well to begin with the first person and shift to the third person sometime before we shift from the narrative form to the expository form. The beginning of what Piaget terms the "formal stage" is about the time to move from the first- to the third-person narrative.

Since the usual text is an organized sequence of premasticated material that has been simplified conceptually and stylistically in order to make it acceptable to beginning readers, it drains readers of their interest instead of energizing them. A story, on the other hand, can make the subject come alive.[4]

Stories: gateways to understanding

Begin, then, with romance and adventure, as Whitehead counsels us. Begin with narrative, Gadamer Ricoeur and the hermeneutical circle advise us. Begin with story, Kieran Egan tells us.[5] But we hesitate. Not that we have anything against stories; we love them. But there is a time for stories, we say, and there is a time for other things, like serious learning, serious study, serious inquiry. When it is time for stories, we have literature, and literature, as we know, is full of wonderful things like values and meanings and ideals, and it causes us to have wonderful reactions, like feelings and emotions and all those good things. It is only that literature contains no really hard information – it is nothing but someone's fancy.

---

[4] See Kieran Egan, "The Other Half of the Child," *Thinking: The Journal of Philosophy for Children* 7:1 (n.d.), 2–5.

[5] Cf. Kieran Egan, *Teaching as Story Telling* (Chicago: University of Chicago Press, 1985), as well as Jerome Bruner, "Narrative and Paradigmatic Modes of Thought," in Elliot Eisner (ed.), *Learning and Teaching the Ways of Knowing* (Chicago: University of Chicago Press, 1985), pp. 97–115.

It contains no facts, and facts are what constitute knowledge, and knowledge is what we send our children to school to acquire.

So we continue to construct texts that we believe will reveal factual reality to the student. That is why we think we need the expository style; it will expose what there is to the mind of the reader. The picture of reality we want children to acquire does not really take much thinking, but it does take study. It is the studious child, not the inquisitive one, who will be rewarded with the vision of things as they really are. As a result, is it any wonder that children sit paralyzed before television, studying it intently as if to drain it of every possible meaning? Clearly children are trapped between the unpalatable information of the text and the uninformative entertainment of television.

We would like it to be thought that our reasons for preferring exposition to narrative are purely epistemological ones. Children must be taught the truth about the world, and exposition is the most reliable means. They must be taught the truth because they have to be prepared to face the world as it really is, not some writer's fanciful version of it.

And so what comes out, little by little, is that we have moral reasons, rather than epistemological ones, for preferring exposition. Exposition is sobering; narrative is intoxicating. Exposition is aloof and objective; narrative is enticing and seductive. Exposition exercises the mind; narrative exercises merely the senses and the imagination.

To the watchful puritan in us, literature does more than provide us with other worlds to dwell in. It suggests to us other ways of living in and thinking about the world we inhabit – ways that might be at odds with propriety and common sense. Literature provides us with models of thinking, feeling, and acting, models that we fear may be seductive to the innocent mind of the child. Freud was on target in calling this the conflict between the Reality Principle and the Pleasure Principle.

Could I be mistaken in my claim that curriculum developers are indifferent or resistant to the textual use of narrative, where the goal is the strengthening of thinking? I offer as evidence the 1989 yearbook of the Association for Supervision and Curriculum Development, *Toward the Thinking Curriculum: Current Cognitive Research.*[6] Here we find some of the most advanced practioners in the field of cognitive science dealing with the topic of the fostering of thinking in educational contexts. Much of what is said is exciting, if only because it finally substantiates what maverick curriculum developers have been saying (for example, about the role of the community and about cognitive apprenticeship) for years. But there is also what the book does *not* talk about. With regard to the role texts play in the promotion (or nonpromotion) of thinking, the authors are silent. Why? Because of their underlying assumption, presumably, that exposition and narration are two wholly different genres and serve two wholly different purposes.

---

[6] Edited by Lauren B. Resnick and Leopold E. Klopfer (Association for Supervision and Curriculum Development, 1989).

For didactic purposes, we use expository prose; for entertainment, we use narratives, such as stories. A story that could serve as a text is inconceivable. And if the authors were to be asked how they know this, they would undoubtedly point to existing narrative or dramatic literature and ask to be shown anything that could successfully serve as an elementary school text in a given discipline. What they do not see is that the story-as-text genre is already being created. And to the extent that it has already been created, it is what can serve as a model for the construction of the remainder. Serviceable examples of what has been created are the novels that are the readers in the Philosophy for Children program. That they may not be sterling literature is beside the point, for literature per se is not the genre to which they belong.

For higher-order thinking, we need texts that embody, and therefore model, both rationality and creativity. I have already identified rationality as making itself known in the third-person voice, while what makes itself evident in the first-person voice is creativity. And I have argued that creativity tends to be responsive to what already exists. (This is true even when creativity is pervasive and when we long for the refreshing voice of rationality. In those cases, rationality is what is responsive and creative.) Higher-order thinking involves constant shuttling back and forth, a constant dialogue, between rationality and creativity.

Nevertheless, in the typical situations in which thinking occurs, rationality seeks to enclose itself in monologue, and creativity exposes itself in dialogue. Rationality invokes criteria from on high, and creativity invokes intuitions from below. Yet each movement of thought can be seen as cooperative with and complementary to the other. Monologue and dialogue, rationality and creativity are simply warp and woof of the texture of thinking.

Narrative as a portrait of the thinking process

The text that starts the thinking process must itself be a model of the process. Somehow or other, educators have gotten the notion that modeling, which they agree is important, is restricted to the teacher's modeling for the students or the coach's modeling for the teacher. The idea of the text as model or portrait strikes many educators as impertinent and bizarre. But how could there be anything more to the point? If we want children – or students of any age – to form a community of inquiry, surely it would help to show them a community of inquiry and let them examine how it works. I shall call this model the fictional community of inquiry, in contrast to the actual community of inquiry that emerges in the classroom.

What characteristics would it be desirable for the fictional community of inquiry to possess? I shall list some of these here without attempting to distinguish at this point between those that I consider essential and those I consider merely auxiliary:

(1) *Literary acceptability.* The literary quality of the text should be passable; the text should be a satisfying work of craft if not of art. This is not to say that it

would be unreasonable to look forward to a time when major writers would consider it a challenge to write textbooks for children. But first we may have to create the market that will motivate them to do so.

(2) *Psychological acceptability.* In terms of social development, texts must be suitable to the age of the child to whom they are addressed while not being condescending in terms of intellectual level. We know from the success of Philosophy for Children that young children find complex ideas such as true, fair, good, right, and person attractive.

(3) *Intellectual acceptability.* It is perhaps unfair to compare philosophy with other disciplines. Philosophy has a very distinct advantage: Its key terms (like those just cited) are also terms familiar to children and part of their everyday speech. But familiar concepts are not essential. What is more important is being able to present aspects of the discipline in ways that children will find problematic and intriguing. The notion that children's texts have to be clear and unproblematic has been one of the most mischievous and misleading notions in all of education. Few children like brain-twisters, for motivation is generally lacking. But most children like stories, for these are mysteries into which they want to enter, secrets they want to be able to share. The problematicity of the text, then, can be in the overall story line and in the very nature of the narrative. A dialogical text, for example, can contain ambiguity, innuendo, irony, and many other qualities that expository prose of the textbook variety uniformly lacks but that children will pore over in an effort to squeeze out the meaning.

Needless to say, these three conditions are fairly minimal, but even they need to be spelled out very carefully. For example, fictional characters need to be sufficiently delineated for students to want to identify with them, and yet they must be sufficiently abstract and general so that students in vastly different settings will nevertheless feel akin to them.

When the text takes the form of a novel, it is possible to portray dialogues in which the contextual elements of time, place, and circumstance are largely omitted and contending arguments can be seen in their idealized purity or universality, just as *Peanuts* cartoons, by avoiding depictions of environments (or of adults), focus attention upon the children's dialogue. Cultural and historical contrasts then drop way, and we are left with vignettes that move us in the direction of a philosophy of childhood. Among contemporary writers, no one has seen more clearly than Michael Walzer the importance of what he calls "constructed or designed conversations" for the guidance of real deliberations among the citizenry, although he is still thinking more of the involvement of philosophers in an ongoing "conversation of mankind" than of the replacement of existing secondary texts with original narratives, such as in the Philosophy for Children curriculum.[7]

---

[7] See Michael Walzer, "A Critique of Philosophical Conversation," *Philosophical Forum* 21:1–2 (Fall–Winter 1989–90), 182–96. Cf. also Bruce Ackerman, *Social Justice in the Liberal State* (New Haven, Conn.: Yale University Press, 1980), p. 24. Ackerman seeks to show the internal restraints that should govern the conversation liberals have with one another, in contrast to the approach of

One of the most noteworthy advantages of the dialogical text is that readers do not have to grapple, as they do in the case of the secondary text, with the truth claims of the author. Dialogue thus eliminates cognitive advantage; it cancels out cognitive privilege and insists upon equality of cognitive opportunity. Claims must be supported by arguments; otherwise they are rejected. The godlike power of the author is neutralized, and reasonings can be judged purely on their merits.

Yet another characteristic of the dialogical text contributes to its superiority as a didactic instrument: what the Batesons call its capacity to deal with "some aspect of mental process in which ideally the interaction exemplifies the subject-matter."[8] Such a conversation the Batesons call a metalogue. For example, the parties to a discussion might be talking about the psychology of the double bind, which they define as "communication in the context of an emotionally important relationship in which there is unacknowledged contradiction between messages at different logical levels,"[9] and at the same time as they are talking about the double bind, they exhibit it. Other examples can be found in the Philosophy for Children novels, where concepts or relationships under discussion by the fictional characters are illustrated when the characters exhibit just those relationships or apply just those concepts to their own practice. Perhaps the best-known example is Plato's *Apology*, in which Socrates defends his method and principles before the Athenian jury and then is condemned to death by the jury, which rejects his arguments. In contrast, the later Platonic dialogues lack not only some kind of action or plot but precisely the kind of plot that would mirror the dialectic and move toward a resolution in the realm of action that would be a counterpoint to the resolution taking place in the realm of discussion.

In the ideal dialogical novel, a philosophical discussion of, say, fidelity would be engaged in by characters who also exhibit in their behavior faithfulness or betrayal; a discussion of reciprocity would be balanced by a plot in which the unilateral and the reciprocal would be clearly portrayed in the characters' conduct. Such a treatment provides the maximum impact upon the learner, for it achieves a perfect cognitive–affective equilibrium.

Three models of modeling

When we observe children engaged in higher-order thinking, we may try to account for it by postulating that children would normally or naturally engage in such thinking if they were not discouraged by adverse circumstances. Children are, some people have gone so far as to claim, "natural philosophers." Establish a free and benign environment, and children will naturally engage in higher-order

Habermas, which, as Walzer remarks, aims at a communicative harmony in which universalization of interests is preordained so as to rule out all bargaining and compromise.

[8] Gregory Bateson and Mary Catherine Bateson, *Angels Fear: Towards an Epistemology of the Sacred* (New York: Dutton, 1987), p. 210.

[9] Ibid., p. 207.

thinking. Models of such thinking are not required. I doubt that there is much evidence to support this claim.

We are led, then, to consider the alternative thesis, which is that modeling is needed in order to elicit higher-order thinking from children, 1 think this claim has more merit, but it is necessary to recognize a number of different kinds of modeling:

(1) *Other students as models.* In a community of inquiry, children will use other children's behavior as models for their own. Each child's conduct is seen as exemplary. If one child is silent, the others may be likewise. If one child asks a question, the others may again do likewise. These behaviors gradually become normal practice within the community. The practice of asking one another for reasons or of offering counterexamples develops when one student's initiative serves as the reason for other students to behave similarly.

(2) *The text as model.* As noted earlier in this chapter, the text may portray students engaged in higher-order thinking and may make explicit the logical or conceptual moves of the fictional characters in the text, with the result that the live students in the classroom take the behavior of these fictional characters as models of how to behave.

(3) *The teacher as model.* We should be wary of ascribing all the modeling for higher-order thinking to the teacher, as if the student were some kind of Clever Hans, the horse who could pick up subliminal cues from its trainer. True, the teacher does serve as a model, but not as a model of reasoning procedures. Nor is it that the teacher provides a model of a thinker liberated from the tyranny of right and wrong answers. I think rather that the teacher provides the model of someone who transcends rather than rejects right–wrong answers in the sense of caring more for the process of inquiry itself than for the answer that might be right or wrong at a given time. It is the behavior of such a teacher, it seems to me, that is especially cherished and relished by students, for it has an integrity they are quick to appreciate.

It is foolhardy to deprive children of models in an effort to assure that their thinking is wholly their own. They need as many models as they can get. What is most helpful to them is to be surrounded by models who value the process of inquiry above any particular dialogical exchange. What we then find is that the students themselves yield up their egocentrism and give themselves over to higher-order thinking, as athletes lose their preoccupation with their particular roles in a game and give themselves over to the game itself.

The text as system of concepts and as schema

When it comes to understanding how we organize information efficiently two devices stand out: the concept and the schema. In a sense, these exemplify the ancient distinction between the mechanical and the organic, and they may also illustrate the recent suggestion that all of nature is built either like a jigsaw puzzle or like a wave. The concept, that is, may be understood as an idea we have of a *class* of things that share one or more common features or as an idea we have of a *family* of things in which some features are shared by some members but no feature need be shared by all members. By means of the organizing principles embodied in the class and the family, we are able to construct concepts by means of which we cluster the information in a given cognitive domain and make it manageable. Without organizing principles, a domain is a mere aggregation of data. It looks like a conference table after a busy work session, strewn with cups, books, papers, ashtrays, and magic markers: in short, a mess, but a mess we can conceptualize by breaking it down into clusters.

A schema, on the other hand, is not a static aggregate or mechanical agglomeration. It is organic and dynamic; it moves, glides, unfolds, soars, swoops, settles down, and rests. Examples are an ocean wave, a bird in flight, a book, a movie, the career of a nation, or the history of a person's life. In a sense, a description and exposition appeal to our power to grasp what is described in terms of concepts, while narration appeals to our power to understand movement and growth. A narrative that employs schemata is propulsive, forward-moving. It is inquiry by indirection, moving ahead as a sailboat does, by tacking into the wind.

The traditional secondary text is a paradigm of conceptual organization. Its table of contents reveals a domain that has been logically organized and categorized, so that the constituent classes are mutually exclusive and jointly exhaustive. It represents the refined end product of the author's inquiries. It presents the reader with little more to do than ingest that end product and proceed slowly to digest it. But to do this requires enormous concentration on the reader's part, and the typical student response is to struggle through a few pages and then put the book down. The secondary text works by demanding a great investment of energy from the reader, with the result that many readers find themselves drained soon after they begin.

A schema, on the other hand, has its own dynamism. It does not have to have data fed into it the way a concept does; it attracts data the way a magnet attracts iron filings. It therefore not only contains energy but exudes it and energizes the reader at the same time as it provides a logical organization to the domain. The source of the schema's energy lies in the fact that every new detail that it incorporates has an impact and effect upon every other element. Whatever happens anywhere affects what happens everywhere, in contrast to a mechanical organization of inert particles, such as a bucket of sawdust, where the addition of a particle has virtually no effect on the rest. In a story, which is in many ways the ideal form of schema, every detail counts and adds to the quality of the whole. This is why the average unscholarly reader feels refreshed by reading short stories and novels but drained and exhausted by attempting to read technical or highly abstract expositions.

And this is why, if we are to make a Great Leap Forward in education, we must resort to the schematically organized text rather than to the traditional conceptually organized text, simply because the forces the one liberates in the student are so much greater. An analogy would be the spacecraft we send out into the solar system to survey the planets. If we had to pack into them all the energy they would need for their voyage, they would have to be enormously large and powerful. Instead, we equip them with just enough energy to get to the moon and let them be whipped around by the moon's gravitational pull and thrown out into some other body's orbit. In this fashion they make their way from one part of the solar system to the other, relying almost wholly on forces other than their own. If we are ever to move education into "warp speed," it will have to be by some such mobilization of the student's powers that we are not now able to tap.

At the same time as we sing the praises of schemata, we should be fully aware of their dangers. Like skills, they are ways of mobilizing energies so as to multiply their effectiveness, and this can be done for unethical purposes as well as ethical ones. Schemata can be employed to inculcate prejudices just as they can be employed to enhance student thinking and creativity. Thus, a problem of working with schemata is that they represent instruments that we cannot teach others to use effectively and humanely until we ourselves learn to use them in the same way.

Second, there is the problem of control. The human being comprises many subordinate and semiautonomous processes – processes that are active within but not actually controlled by the individual. Dreaming is an example. We know that dreams can be profoundly significant and revelatory, but though we may examine and analyze them, we do not control them. If we were to entrust ourselves to them, we would be abdicating our own autonomy and delegating at least a portion of it to forces moving in unknown directions. We must recognize the same thing with the cultivation of schemata: To the extent that they can be used to fascinate, captivate, or hypnotize, they can be dangerous. Indeed, those who represent the forces of inhumanity already know far better how to capitalize on the power of schemata than do those who advocate a just world and a just coming to terms with nature. Virtually every advertisement is schematic in form and manipulative in function, because it sets up a requiredness that our reason finds it difficult to cope with or resist.

Just as the text of the future should be a balance of the narrative and the expository, so it should be a balance of the conceptual and the schematic. No less should it balance the critical and the creative. And in each case what has to occur is not mere equilibrium but lively interpenetration and interfusion. The critical must always call upon the creative to rescue it from the prison of rigorous emptiness, and the creative must always call upon the critical to rescue it from the quicksand of unwarranted speculation and formless expression.

What the text of the future must have in common with works of art is capacity to promote experience that we enjoy for its own sake. On the other hand, the text must specify and structure that experience, eliciting the critical here and the creative there, modeling the inquiry process, portraying mental acts and skills in ways that no work of art is required to do, although many do it anyhow. The text of the future must therefore be a new hybrid genre (although not so new as all that, when we recall Plato's earlier dialogues), a work of art that has a specific job to do – to be consummatory in providing the experience upon which reflection will take place, and to be instrumental in providing trails leading toward that reasonableness and judiciousness that are characteristic of the educated person.

The rational curriculum

Those who make curricula aim them at the level where the children who will be using those curricula supposedly are – or at a level higher than the level at which those students are judged to be. The conception of levels held by the curriculum developers is established by data collections that tell them what these empirically certifiable levels are. Since the connections between the children at any one year and the same children the following year are causal connections and not logical ones, the curriculum that mirrors those levels will display no cumulative rational development from year to year. It will record, let us say, a more retentive memory or a larger vocabulary. And even if it does show a growth in logical proficiency from year to year, it will not be because increasing rationality is in any way thought to be the product of the study of the curriculum in previous years. Instead, it will be attributed to psychobiological developments that occur universally among growing children. Curriculum manufacturers, it appears, inhabit a universe in which there are stages of maturation rather than a building of rationality. That being the case, there is no need to rock the boat by a superfluous introduction of sequenced logical operations.

On the other hand, suppose we were to take seriously that students try to live up to (or down to) the level at which they are treated. Treat them as intelligent and reasonable, and they behave, or try to behave, intelligently and reasonably; treat them as stupid, and they provide us with ample evidence to prove that we are right. This being so, we should bend every effort to make curricula logical and rational in their sequencing rather than episodically and arbitrarily developmental.

We must thus ask ourselves which cognitive skills presuppose which and then endeavor to foster practice in the more primitive ones first so that these will be in place when the next group of skills is to be practiced. For example, we want students to be able to discover similarities among things that are very different and dissimilarities among things that are very much the same in other respects. To do this, we must first strengthen their ability to discern similarities and differences in general. This in turn means engaging them in the making of comparisons, as a result of which they discern respects in which things are the same and respects in which they are not. They also learn to use the foundational criteria of identity and difference. And yet, in point of fact, cognitive curricula have a way of emphasizing the affirmative or positive and deemphasizing the negative. They stress grouping and classification and categorization while soft-pedaling distinction making, questioning, and the providing of counterinstances. Now, this tendency is directly contrary to the cultivation of the critical spirit, which so much involves capacity for independent thinking, readiness to explore alternatives, and the courage to dissent. This is why, in the Philosophy for Children curriculum, distinction making is featured among the very first skills to be practiced (in grades K–2).

It is true that there are countries in the world where one is guilty until proven innocent rather than innocent until proven guilty, and it should not be surprising that in the same countries people are considered incapable of reason until they establish their reasonableness beyond reasonable doubt. But this cannot be acceptable in a fully democratic society, where we are innocent until proven guilty and deserve to be treated as reasonable until proven otherwise. On the other hand, the child's reasonableness is not merely an article of faith, because it can be seen also as the child's response to the rationality of the curriculum as well as to the respect accorded the child by the teacher and the other children. And the curriculum is part of the broader institution of the school, which needs likewise to be a rational institution if those moving through it are to be permanently touched by reason.

For elementary school students, the pedagogy of the community of inquiry is indispensable if the aim is to move quickly into higher-order thinking and remain there. To be sure, students in early elementary school are still in the process of acquiring the social skills that the community of inquiry presupposes; this is an important transitional period for them. On the other hand, students later on in secondary school and early in college are involved in very different kinds of transition, and the community of inquiry approach may have to be used more selectively for them. Alternatives such as cooperative learning, reciprocal teaching, and cognitive apprenticeship should be carefully explored in order to deal with the variety of circumstances in which education at these levels takes place.

Cognitive apprenticeship

Cognitive apprenticeship can be taken as a prototype of these alternative approaches. As proposed by Allan Collins, John Seely Brown, and Susan E. Newman,[10] cognitive apprenticeship involves:

(1) *Bringing tacit skills to consciousness.* Observation, problem solving, and metacognitive skills that are habitual or subliminal may have to be brought to the students' awareness so that they can be more deliberately practiced.

(2) *Comparison of expert and novice performances.* The instructor may, for example, paraphrase a paragraph, have a student do the same, and discuss and highlight the similarities and differences. Collins, Brown, and Newman call this process abstracted replay.

The reciprocal teaching of reading is an example of this abstracted replay. It involves four activities that the instructor first forms and then gets the learners to perform: formulating questions, summarizing, clarifying, and predicting. What the students learn to reflect on are the differences between the expert and novice performances and how these differences can be reduced. In the process, students become producers of questions and summaries and critics of them as well.

(3) *Modeling.* The instructor shows – not merely tells – how the desired performance is to be carried out.

[10] "Cognitive Apprenticeship: Teaching the Craft of Reading, Writing and Mathematics," *Thinking: The Journal of Philosophy for Children* 8:1 (n.d.), 2–10.

(4) *Coaching*. This involves review of the student's performance with the student and includes feedback, hints as to how performance might be improved, discussion of previously unnoticed aspects of the task, and so on.

(5) *Scaffolding*. This entails the teacher's carrying out parts of the overall task that the students cannot yet manage. Scaffolding includes the instructor's providing the students with explicit suggestions or supports. *Fading* is the gradual removal of those supports until the students are on their own.

(6) *Articulation, reflection, and exploration*. These are getting students to express and analyze their reasoning or inquiry procedures, getting them to compare these procedures with the procedures of experts, and getting them to find problems on their own and explore them without instructional support or scaffolding.

Collins, Brown, and Newman envisage cognitive apprenticeship as being useful in very elementary as well as in highly advanced domains. They see it called for in graduate school, where expert practice is indispensable, and they find it appropriate in the learning of reading, writing, and mathematics. But not all advocates of cognitive apprenticeship are in agreement about this, and many elementary school teachers who appreciate the approach are resistant to its application at their level. For secondary school and undergraduate education, on the other hand, it may be invaluable.

The devising of instructional manuals

To provide teachers with instructional manuals is to provide them with one of the most valuable forms of scaffolding. However, this may be a kind of scaffolding that should not be removed even when teachers think they are ready to dispense with it. This is because the manual may embody skills or procedures that lie outside the scope of most classroom teachers.

Curricula aimed at prompting higher-order thinking in a particular subject will contain, among other things, exercises and discussion plans. The discussion plans are primarily for the purpose of concept formation and clarification; the exercises have skill building as their objective. The basic unit of both is the question. The function of a question is to put in question a certain portion of the world as well as a certain portion of the powers of the respondent. Among the latter are the powers of the respondent to question the question's propriety: whether, for example, it assumes something not legitimate to assume or whether it is too vague. Equally important is the power of the question. A question is like a lens or laser beam that picks up diffuse light from a discipline and focuses it so that it penetrates.

This means, on the one hand, that the question is a way of engaging the student in directed practice dealing with a specific area of the problem at hand. The course of higher-order thinking may at appropriate moments be punctuated with pauses for such directed practice, or there may be a more general alternation from a period of dialogue to a period of skill building to a new period of dialogue to a new period of concept formation, all in the course of a single session.

On the other hand, the focusing power of the question means that questions can be constructed that represent the points of view of major figures in the discipline. One might even employ the occasion to enlist hypothetical questions from figures in other disciplines. If the question of color perception is being taken up, the curriculum constructor could invent questions that might have been asked by Goethe and Kandinsky and Newton as well as by Helmholz. If it is a question of relationships, questions that might have been raised by Leibniz, Diderot, Hegel, and James could be invented. In other words, each question focuses one beam of light from out of the culture, with the result that the set of questions making up the entire exercise is a still more comprehensive probing into what students do not understand or into what they take for granted.

As teachers work with manuals, they tend to internalize and appropriate their favorite exercises and discussion plans for use over and over, with the result that they do not have to use the manual as a crutch. It is like learning a language, where after a while you stop having to look up words in the dictionary because you have translated the language into a way in which you can think; you begin to think in the language. Yet much of the language – or the manual – still remains to be internalized on future occasions.

For the teaching of higher-order thinking, the instructional manual is as invaluable as the narrative text.[11] Each exercise in the manual functions as a probe that penetrates deep into the thinking process – far deeper, generally, than the teacher can get by casual conversation or discussion. The manual does not perform the modeling functions that the text performs, but it provides an elaborate scaffolding that is gradually absorbed into the building itself rather than ultimately being dismantled. Curricula aimed at helping students think about thinking do not necessarily get discarded after use like used paper cartons. Instead, because the dividing line between thinking and thinking about thinking is so fuzzy, curricula may become incorporated into their subject matter. Indeed, a case could be made that many of the writings that form the literature of philosophy consist of curriculum-like efforts to think about thinking and to help others do so as well.[12] Perhaps this is why Wittgenstein speculated about the possibility of a philosophy consisting of nothing but questions.

[11] For a definition of "text," see I. Bellert, "On a Condition of the Coherence of Texts," in *Semiotica* 2 (1970), as amplified in Paul Weingartner, "Normative Principles of Rational Communication," *Erkenntnis* 19 (1983), 405–16. Thus, according to Bellert, "If a sequence of sentences (at least 2) forms a text, then each sentence (except the first) has at least one common consequence together with at least one of its preceding sentences."

[12] Cf. M. M. Bakhtin, "The Problem of the Text in Linguistics, Philology and the Human Sciences: An Experiment in Philosophical Analysis," in Caryl Emerson and Michael Holquist (eds.), *Speech Genres and Other Late Essays*, trans. Vern W. McGee (Austin: University of Texas Press, 1989), pp. 103–31. At his best, Bakhtin can be as aphoristic as Wittgenstein and no less insightful.

Part IV

The nature and uses of the community of inquiry

14   Thinking in community

All inquiry is self-critical practice, and all of it is exploratory and inquisitive. Some aspects of inquiry are more experimental than others. And inquiry is generally social or communal in nature because it rests on a foundation of language, of scientific operations, of symbolic systems, of measurements and so on, all of which are uncompromisingly social.

But while all inquiry may be predicated upon community, it does not follow that all community is predicated upon inquiry. There is nothing self-contradictory in the notion of a fixated, tradition-bound community. The glue that holds a community together is practice, but it does not have to be self-critical practice.

Thus, there is something paradoxical, something faintly startling, about the notion of a community of inquiry; it unites two concepts that are not ordinarily found together or juxtaposed. This makes it all the more surprising that so unconventional a notion should be proposed as a master educational paradigm.

Since the features of the community of inquiry have been sketched in several of the preceding chapters, I do not wish to recapitulate here. There are, however, some points that do need elaboration.

First, I think we need to see that the community of inquiry is not aimless. It is a process that aims at producing a *product* – at some kind of settlement or judgment, however partial and tentative this may be. Second, the process has a sense of direction; it moves where the argument takes it. Third, the process is not merely conversation or discussion; it is dialogical. This means it has a structure. Just as a parliamentary debate is governed by parliamentary rules of order, so inquiry has its procedural rules, which are largely logical in nature. Fourth, we need to consider a bit more closely how rationality and creativity apply to the community of inquiry. Finally, there is the matter of using the community of inquiry to operationalize and implement the definitions of critical and creative thinking. We will look at these four points in this chapter.

Following the argument where it leads

It is often assumed that children are born as little savages and that they must learn to become civilized. Education is thought to have a decent influence upon them. As a result of its benign influence, they become social beings. It was this doctrine that George Herbert Mead stood on its head when he wrote that "the child does not become social by learning. He must be social in order to learn."[1] It was Mead, therefore, who first grasped the profound educational implications of fusing together, as Peirce had, the two independently powerful notions of *inquiry* and *community* into the single transformative concept of the *community of inquiry*. Dewey had already seen, Mead acknowledges, that the role of the teacher is to mediate rather than dominate: "To use Professor Dewey's phrase, instruction should be an interchange of experience in which the child brings his experience to be interpreted by the parent or teacher. This recognizes that education is interchange of ideas, is conversation – belongs to a universe of discourse."[2] Mead then addresses the question of what the topic of such conversation should be, and he gives us the unequivocal answer that it must be the subject matter of instruction:

Just insofar as the subject-matter of instruction can be brought into the form of problems arising in the experience of the child – just so far will the relation of the child to the instructor become a part of the natural solution of the problem – actual success of a teacher depends in large measure upon this capacity to state the subject-matter of instruction in terms of the experience of the children.[3]

Nor does Mead flinch when it comes to stating how a lesson or a textbook should be organized – they should be conducive to inquiry by being modeled on the way we think when we inquire. Thus, the ideal textbook "is so organized that the development of the subject-matter is in reality the action and reaction of one mind upon another mind. The dictum of the Platonic Socrates, that one must follow the argument where it leads in the dialogue, should be the motto of the writer of textbooks."[4] Mead all but says outright that the ideal textbook should be direct and fresh in its impact rather than something warmed over and secondhand; it should be brimful of the child's experience rather than being a desiccated version of the adult's experience; it should resound to the clash of ideas and the clash of minds; it should dramatically depict the encounter of the minds of the children with the subject matter of instruction; and it should follow the argument where it leads.

Now, the notion of following an argument where it leads has been a perplexing one ever since Socrates announced it as the guiding maxim of his own philsophical practice. If we think of the matter in more general terms, how *is* inquiry guided? If nature were everywhere equally enigmatic, we would not know where first to turn. But we do seem to know where first to turn; something establishes our priorities and gives us a sense of direction. What is it?

I find Dewey's answer a compelling one. Inquiry takes place in situations – in contextual wholes or fields. A situation is a whole by virtue of its "immediately pervasive quality."[5] This quality is not only what binds all constituents in the sit-

---

[1] "The Psychology of Social Consciousness Implied in Instruction," *Science* 31 (1910), 688–93, reprinted under the title "Language as Thinking" in *Thinking: The Journal of Philosophy for Children* 1:2 (n.d.), 23–6. The quotation is from the latter version, p. 26.

[2] Ibid., p. 25.   [3] Ibid.   [4] Ibid.

[5] *Logic: The Theory of Inquiry* (New York: Holt, 1938), p. 68.

uation into a whole but is also unique and indivisible. No two situations have the same permeating quality. The distinctions and relations we institute within them are recurrent and repeatable, but not their unique qualities. These qualities are not be be confused with what is "red" or "hard" or "sweet," for these are what we distinguish *within* a situation. Rather, they are akin to what we designate by such terms as "perplexing," "cheerful," and "disconsolate." These are the tertiary qualities that guide the artist and that are precipitated in created works of art. What George Yoos calls the primary aspects[6] are precisely these qualities. All inquiries are guided by such qualities, including Socratic inquiry. Every community of inquiry has about it a requiredness or *Prägnanz* that lends it a sense of direction, and every participant in such a community partakes of that qualitative presence, which is the tertiary quality of which Dewey speaks. It is a quality more readily possessed than described, but were it not present and acknowledged, the participants would lack any standard of *relevance* or *irrelevance*.

We learn from Dewey, then, that the progress of a community of inquiry is guided by the Gestalt quality of the unique, immediately experienced inquiry situation, and we learn from Mead that the educational community of inquiry actively discusses the subject matter under investigation. We need to know more, however, about the nature of this discussion. For example, must every discussion come to closure? Justus Buchler warns us not to confuse the product that discussions produce with the conclusions or closures that some people expect them to produce:

Where we can speak of a conclusion at all, it may be developed only after many hours, and then with qualifications befitting the circumstances. But, regardless of this, a product is inevitably established in any given hour of discussion. For the product need not take the form of an assertive conclusion. It may be an enumeration of possible views, or a fuller definition of a problem, or a growth of appreciative awareness. It may be more of an exhibiting than of an affirming. . . . Students may have no right to demand final answers, but they certainly have a right to expect some sense of intellectual motion or some feeling of discernment.[7]

Some feeling of discernment – right. Seldom have I seen children dissatisfied with the product they took from a philosophical discussion, even if it is only some modest philosophical distinction, for they recognize how before that acquisition they had even less. Children, unlike adults, do not look insistently for answers or conclusions. They look rather for the kind of transformation that philosophy provides – not giving a new answer to an old question, but transforming all the questions.[8]

For example, when Socrates poses Euthyphro the powerful question whether something is right because the gods command it or whether the gods command it because it is right, it is clear that nothing thereafter can be the same. To ask the question is to compel people to think differently about the world.

[6] "A Work of Art as a Standard of Itself," *Journal of Aesthetics and Art Criticism* 26 (Fall 1967), 81–9.
[7] "What Is a Discussion?" *Journal of General Education* 7:1 (October 1954), 7–17.
[8] This is a paraphrase of a remark by Gilbert Ryle in his essay "Hume," *Collected Papers*, vol. 1 (New York: Barnes and Noble, 1971), p. 160.

The logic of conversational discourse

When we speak of a community of inquiry, we cannot help noticing the contrast between the emphasis on the personal in the concept of community and the emphasis in inquiry on a logic that transcends the personal. So in contrasting conversation and dialogue we cannot help seeing in conversation a process in which the personal note is strong but the logical thread is weak, whereas in dialogue just the reverse is the case.

In contrasting conversation with dialogue, one of the things that are striking is the way in which conversation aims at equilibrium while dialogue aims at disequilibrium. In conversation, first one person has the ascendancy and then the other. There is reciprocity, but with the understanding that nothing is to move. A conversation seesaws between the protagonists, but the conversation itself does not move.

In a dialogue, on the other hand, disequilibrium is enforced in order to enforce forward movement. One cannot help thinking of the analogy with walking, where you move forward by constantly throwing yourself off balance. When you walk, you never have both feet solidly on the ground at the same time. Each step forward makes a further step forward possible; in a dialogue, each argument evokes a counterargument that pushes itself beyond the other and pushes the other beyond itself.

A conversation is an exchange: of feelings, of thoughts, of information, of understandings. A dialogue is an exploration, an investigation, an inquiry. Those who converse with one another do so cooperatively, like tennis players volleying as they practice genially and interminably. Those who engage in dialogue do so collaboratively, like law enforcement officers working together on the same case. The aim of those who volley is to extend the rally for as long as possible. The aim of the officers is to resolve the case in as short a time as possible.

The logic of dialogue has its roots in the logic of conversation. If we briefly consider here the discussions of conversation by Paul Grice and Ruth Saw, we will be able to discern the outlines of a logic that becomes progressively more pronounced as it moves from conversation to dialogue.

Grice proposes to examine "the conditions governing conversation"[9] and thus to be able to formulate the maxims we take for granted and endeavor to conform to whenever we engage in conversational discourse. He recognizes that our conversing resembles our thinking in that both are characterized by what William James called flights and perchings. Conversations are not smoothly continuous; there are gaps and seams everywhere. We blurt something out and then we back off. We allude and intimate; our partners gather and surmise. The work of conversation, of putting together what is meant from the bits and pieces that have

[9] "Logic and Conversation," *Studies in the Way of Words* (Cambridge, Mass.: Harvard University Press, 1989), p. 26.

merely been said, involves what Grice calls *implicature*. And implicature is made possible because conversation is a shared experience with shared values and shared meanings. Our conversational collaboration conforms to certain shared expectations. When we converse, our comments are elliptical, but we fill in the gaps voluntarily so as to achieve a single seamless skein of meaning that we each grasp at one end. In so doing, the maxim we conform to is what Grice calls the Co-operative Principle:

Make your conversational contribution such as is required, at the stage at which it occurs, by the accepted purpose or direction of the talk exchange in which you are engaged.

In other words, Grice advises us to allow the requiredness that we sense in the conversation to dictate to us just how and when we are to make our contribution. He sums up his strictures on conversational appropriateness by means of nine submaxims:

Quantity

1. Don't tell me less than I need to know. Make your contribution as informative as is required (for the current purposes of the exchange)
2. Don't tell me too much. Don't make your contribution more informative than is required

Quality

3. Contribute only the truth, not what you believe to be false
4. Don't say that for which you lack adequate evidence. I expect your contributions to be genuine and not spurious

Relation

5. Be relevant. There are different kinds and focuses of relevance, and these shift in the course of a talk exchange. What is contributed must be relevant to these shifting contextual changes

Manner

6. Be clear (avoid obscurity of expression)
7. Avoid ambiguity
8. Be brief (don't ramble on)
9. Be orderly[10]

I have compressed these maxims somewhat but without, I think, distorting them. Grice claims that these maxims can be gleaned from actual conversations – from intimations the conversations reveal regarding circumstances by which they are governed. And yet, like the principles of formal logic, these maxims are normative and stipulate what *ought* to be done in order that a genuine conversation take place.

[10] Ibid., pp. 26–8.

The art of conversation

Ruth L. Saw offers us an interpretation of the conditions that make for conversation.[11] She begins with some questions. What is a conversation? Could we properly describe a tenant and a landlord as having a conversation with regard to overdue rent? Does the judge call lawyers from both sides into his chambers for a conversation? Do we have a conversation with our children when we find they have not shown up in school for several days? How do conversations differ (if they do) from discussions? From dialogues? From arguments? What is the connection between conversation and communication?

The essence of conversation, Saw contends, is its innocence of any ulterior purpose. A conversation cannot be guided or directed, nor can we in any way attempt to manipulate the persons with whom we converse. Conversations are carried on for their own sake, very much as if they were pure art forms. "Whenever people speak in order to impress, to exhibit their wit, their wealth, their learning, or to bring about some advantage to themselves, they are failing to treat their hearer as a person, as an end in himself, and conversation with him as carried on for its own sake."[12]

Saw says it does not matter if the purpose of our manipulations is a commendable one; the end result still cannot be a conversation. If we are engaged in drawing out a child so that she may better display her intelligence, conversation cannot be said to take place. Or if we are devious in disclosing our attitudes, the interaction cannot be a conversational one.

Conversation is predicated upon there being a rational partnership of those who converse, a partnership of free and equal individuals. The direction the conversation takes will be determined not so much by the laws of consistency as by the developing needs of the conversation itself, much as a writer, halfway through a book, begins to find it dictating what must be written. The author may still introduce some surprises, just as those who engage in conversation may introduce revelations by which they surprise and delight one another. Indeed, so guileless is a conversation that in the course of it you listen to yourself in ways you previously had been unable to do. You listen to yourself talk and remark, "I must be jealous," thereby witnessing a disclosure about yourself no less objective than it would have been if you had inferred from the other person's remarks, "He must be jealous." For in a conversation you are capable of stepping back and listening to what you say, just as an artist can in the act of painting step back and take stock of what he or she has been doing.

For Saw, conversation is a symmetrical relationship. "A cannot converse with B if B does not converse with A."[13] It is a mutual exploration of one another's individualities. You cannot exact disclosures from the other without being prepared to make similar disclosures about yourself. Perhaps this stipulation can be

[11] "Conversation and Communication," inaugural lecture at Birkbeck College, 1962, as reprinted in *Thinking: The Journal of Philosophy for Children* 2:1 (n.d.), 55–64.
[12] Ibid., p. 64.   [13] Ibid., p. 60.

better understood if we go back to Saw's earlier distinction between "communicating something to someone" and "being in communication with someone." The first suggests conveying a content of some kind from one person to another. The second suggests that sort of interpersonal experience in which each participant causes the other to think; it is when we are truly in communication with others, Saw insists, that we are provoked to think independently.

The structure of dialogue

Unfortunately, Saw's treatment of dialogue is something of a caricature, since she lumps engaging in dialogue together with other forms of asymmetrical behavior such as giving orders to, taking instructions from, making suggestions to, vetoing the suggestions of, and countless other manipulative moves characteristic of hierarchical organizations. Her illustrations of dialogue are mostly of the edifying kind, such as can be found in Victorian children's books:

Harry: Papa, you promised to tell us something of the habits of bees on our next walk in the country.
Father: I am glad you reminded me, my boy, for we can all learn from these busy little creatures . . .

While discourse such as this may be considered dialogical, it is not of such ludicrous dialogues that communities of inquiry are constituted.

If Saw is correct, that the essence of conversation lies in its being nonpurposive, nonmanipulative discourse, then the other end of the discourse spectrum would be occupied by the persuasive arts that are the subject matter of rhetoric. Dialogue evidently lies somewhere between the two, for it is not wholly free from purpose, and it may well involve arguments whose purpose is to persuade. Dialogue, unlike conversation, is a form of inquiry, and since we follow inquiry wherever it leads, our dialogical behavior cannot be said to be nonpurposive. Nor do the participants in dialogue necessarily refrain from fashioning arguments to persuade other participants of the rightness of their convictions. Even here, however, there is room for disagreement. J. M. Bochenski, for example, maintains that persuasion of others is alien to all philosophical dialogue:

If a philosopher engages in a discussion, as he often does, this will not be in order to convince his adversary. The only thing he desires to achieve is *his own* conviction. He hopes either that he might learn from his opponent that his views are wrong and so gain a new and better grasp of reality, or that the arguments of his adversary may help him to formulate better, improve and strengthen his views.[14]

Bochenski seems to be ruling out only persuasion of others, not of oneself. Whether or not this interpretation is compatible with the community of inquiry concept will continue to be a topic for discussion, as it has been since the time of Socrates.

[14] "On Philosophical Dialogue," *Boston College Studies in Philosophy* 3 (1974), 56–85.

Dialogue and community

Martin Buber's espousal of dialogue is well known. He conceives of it as discourse in which "each of the participants really has in mind the other or others in their present and particular being, and turns to them with the intention of establishing a living mutual relation between himself and them." He contrasts such dialogue with monologue, which is self-serving; debates, in which each treats the other as a position rather than as a person; conversations, in which one is primarily concerned to make an impression on the other; friendly chats, in which each considers himself absolute and legitimate and the other relativized and questionable; and lovers' talk, in which each is concerned with enjoying his or her own private, precious experience. Buber proceeds to show the connection of dialogue with thinking on the one hand and community on the other.[15]

No doubt there are similarities between the ethical requirements Ruth Saw lays down for conversation and those Buber sets forth for dialogue. These normative considerations are useful for helping to distinguish between what is and what merely purports to be a community of inquiry. But while they are relevant, and perhaps even necessary, they are not sufficient. For one thing, communities of inquiry are characterized by dialogue that is disciplined by logic. One must reason in order to follow what is going on in them. For example, how could anyone lacking in logical understanding appreciate this story by Thackeray:

An old abbé, talking among a party of intimate friends, happened to say, "A priest has strange experiences; why, ladies, my first penitent was a murderer." Upon this, the principal nobleman of the neighborhood enters the room. "Ah, Abbé, here you are; do you know, ladies, I was the Abbé's first penitent, and I promise you my confession astonished him."[16]

When the classroom has been converted into a community of inquiry, the moves that are made in order to follow the argument where it leads are logical moves, and it is for this reason that Dewey correctly identifies logic with the methodology of inquiry.[17] As a community of inquiry proceeds with its deliberations, every move engenders some new requiredness. The discovery of a piece of evidence throws light on the nature of the further evidence that is now needed. The disclosure of a claim makes it necessary to discover the reasons for that claim. The making of an inference compels the participants to explore what was being assumed or taken for granted that led to the selection of that particular inference. A contention that several things are different demands that the question be raised of how they are to be distinguished. Each move sets up a train of countering or supporting moves. As subsidiary issues are settled, the community's sense of direction is confirmed and clarified, and the inquiry proceeds with renewed vigor.

[15] *Between Man and Man* (London: Kegan Paul, 1947), sect. II.
[16] The story is related by Morris R. Cohen and Ernest Nagel in *An Introduction to Logic and Scientific Method* (New York: Harcourt Brace, 1934), p. 174.
[17] *Logic*, p. 5.

Of course we should not delude ourselves with regard to these occasional settlements. They are perches or resting places, without finality. As Dewey puts it:

The "settlement" of a particular situation by a particular inquiry is no guarantee that *that* settled conclusion will always remain settled. The attainment of settled beliefs is a progressive matter; there is no belief so settled as not to be exposed to further inquiry. . . . In scientific inquiry, the criterion of what is taken to be settled, or to be knowledge, is being *so* settled that it is available as a resource in further inquiry; not being settled in such a way as not to be subject to revision in further inquiry.[18]

Settlements provide us with grounds for assuming, warrants for asserting. They represent *provisional judgments* rather than firm bases for absolute convictions.[19]

Thinking moves and mental acts

In a genuine community of inquiry, the dialogue enters into the subject matter through these logical (or critical thinking) moves. Thinking in a discipline means penetrating through the outward rind or crust of the discipline and actively engaging in cognitive processing of its subject matter. This is not what is going on when a teacher interrogates a class, after reading them a story, with such questions as "And what did Suzy say?" and "What did her grandfather do then?" and "Why do you think Suzy liked ice cream?" There is little meshing in such instances of the intellectual processes of the students with the contours and textures of the subject matter. In the sense of cognitive processing, thinking is work. It is not the leisurely strolling about of a tourist's visit but an active entry into the life of a

[18] Ibid., pp. 8–9.
[19] Kant is very helpful with regard to provisional judgments, and it is worth quoting him here at some length:

As concerns, however, *suspension* or *reservation* of our judgment, it consists in the resolve not to let a merely *provisional* judgment become a *determinate* one. A provisional judgment is one by which I suppose that there are more grounds *for* the truth of something than against it, that these grounds, however, do not suffice for a *determinate* or *definitive* judgment by which I decide straightway for the truth. Provisional judging is therefore a consciously problematic judging.

Reservation of judgment can take place with a twofold intent: *Either* to seek the grounds for a determinate judgment, *or never* to judge. In the first case the reservation of judgment is called critical (*suspensio judicii indagatoria*), in the latter, skeptical (*suspensio judicii sceptica*). For the skeptic renounces all judging, whereas the true philosopher, when he has not yet sufficient reasons for holding something to be true, merely suspends his judgment. . . .

We note here further that to leave one's judgment *in dubio* is something different from leaving it *in suspenso*. In the latter case I am always interested in the matter; in the former, however, to decide whether the thing is true or not does not always conform with my purpose or interests. . . .

Provisional judgments may therefore be regarded as *maxims* for the investigation of a matter. One could call them also *anticipations*, because one anticipates the judgment on a matter before one has the determinate judgment. Such [anticipatory] judgments thus have their good use, and it would be possible even to give rules on how to judge an object provisionally.

(Kant's *Logic,* trans. Robert S. Hartman and Wolfgang Schwartz [Indianapolis, Ind.: Bobbs-Merrill, 1974], pp. 82–3)

society. We immerse ourselves in a discipline as we might immerse ourselves in a culture, for in a sense every discipline is a culture, a language (or manner of using language), a form of life.[20] To learn to think in a discipline such as history is to learn how historians think and to think like them.

It is one of the great merits of literature that the mental acts of the characters in a story must be emulated by mental acts on the part of the reader. We identify with the characters in turn, so that when we read, "She reflected, 'What a beast he is!' " we reflect, "What a beast he is!" and when we read, "From the look on his face, she surmised that he was ready to apologize," we surmise that his apology will soon be forthcoming. The emulation of mental activities depicted in literature stimulates us to a more active and diversified mental life. Through literature we learn to identify mental acts by name; we would otherwise perform them without recognizing their differences.

To read a product of Jane Austen's thought or of Ernst Mach's thought is therefore to think, to some extent, what they thought in creating those products. Some aspects of the creative process remain hidden from us, of course, and we wonder about those aspects. Likewise, we wonder how nature works, and we try imaginatively to sink ourselves into its procedures in order to think how it might work. "Nature works like an artist," Aristotle tells us, but Paul Valéry is not sure and concludes that we really do not understand how nature, as a determined system, yet manages to invent its individuals and species in all their astonishing variety.[21]

The jury as an example of deliberative dialogue

If you have ever served on a jury, there are probably many aspects of that experience that are deeply etched in your memory: the plaintiff and the defendant, the judge, the lawyers, your fellow jurors, and the emotional drama you saw being enacted before your eyes and in which you played a role. But something else was memorable too: the deliberations with your fellow jurors as you struggled to arrive at a verdict.

Consider these deliberations. You were compelled by your jury duty to attend and participate in them. As a jury, you and the others were charged with arriving at a judgment (i.e., a verdict). It was expected that you would deliberate by reasoning together and in the process expose one another's errors in thinking. The process was, in other words, self-corrective. And it was further expected that you would fully take into account whatever special circumstances prevailed in this case.

---

[20] An argument for the view of a discipline as a language, culture, and form of life is to be found in Gregory Colomb, "Disciplinary 'Secrets' and the Apprentice Writer: The Lessons for Critical Thinking," *Resource Publication*, Institute for Critical Thinking, Montclair State College, ser. 1, no. 6 (1988), pp. 1–26.

[21] Paul Valéry, "Man and the Sea Shell," *The Collected Works of Paul Valéry*, ed. Jackson Matthews, vol. 13: *Aesthetics*, trans. Ralph Manheim, Bollingen Series XLV (Princeton, N.J.: Princeton University Press, 1964), pp. 80–2.

Keep in mind that you had listened carefully to the lawyers for each side. They presented arguments on behalf of their clients and in opposition to their counterparts across the way. These arguments were carefully constructed and often ingenious, but they were always one-sided. It was left to the jury to examine these differing versions of what happened and to arrive, through deliberation, at a single understanding of the evidence and the testimony that would enable you and the other members of the jury to reach a verdict.

Throughout the jury's deliberations, you as a member of the jury had to keep in mind the judge's briefing with regard to the fine points of the law, and the judge may have had to make additional explanations as your discussions continued. The matter seems quite simple; the jury has to find the rule that fits the case. But there are many murky intangibles: questions of motive or intent that may be unresolved or a certain vagueness in the formulation of the very law that appears to be most applicable. Yet a judgment must be arrived at, and the judge, in explaining the law, is in effect clarifying to you the criteria you must employ in reaching that judgment. Of course, the criteria do not consist of legal principles only; obviously, there are logical principles involved as well. If the case fits under the law precisely, then logic can be employed to reach the necessary conclusion. But matters are seldom so simple. The law may clearly state that thefts of property are punishable, but was this person the thief? The law may condemn a damaging breach of promise, but was this a breach of promise and was it damaging? So it is obvious that inferences must be drawn, and every act of inferring will be controlled by underlying assumptions of which you and the other jurors may or may not be conscious.

In their early sessions, the jurors on a case are tentative and cautious, although some may try to bring matters to a rapid conclusion through persuasive language reminiscent of the approaches used by the lawyers. Gradually, however, the jurors become more accustomed to one another and to the situation. Rules of decorum emerge: They recognize the need to back up their opinions with reasons, to listen carefully to one another's arguments, to support each other's ideas when these seem plausible. Rules of inquiry procedure emerge: When disputes arise over recollections of testimony, transcripts are called for. A visit to the crime site may be found necessary. Evidence is reexamined. New hypotheses are framed. The jurors, finding themselves isolated yet bound together in this strange voyage, begin to accept each other as persons. A face-to-face community emerges – a community of inquiry.

Inquiry? These jurors are not theoreticians, practitioners, or researchers with long experience in dealing with cases in court. Chances are this is their first such encounter. But the jury system is predicated on the assumption that they have, as citizens, sufficient reasonableness and judiciousness to discuss these matters intelligently, to pool their various talents and skills, and to come to a verdict that will be appropriate under the circumstances. The mandates of the law must be observed, but so must the claims of the litigants. The jurors have acquired, as the case has worn on, a certain circumspection, a way of looking at things in a more unified perspective, a tendency to assign weight to the evidence with an overall sense of proportion. It is out of such a context that their judgment will emerge, and the more astute and insightful they are in their deliberations, the more fair their ultimate decision is likely to be.

It is not my purpose here to examine the merits or limitations of the jury system. What interests me about it is that it is a model of a social insitution in which lay persons are brought together to deliberate about a matter of common interest and to arrive at a judgment that is as reasonable as possible.

There is something breathtakingly audacious about the democratic process, in that, in the case of the jury system, it entrusts inquiry to ordinary citizens, even in cases of the utmost gravity. The faith of the democratic system in the competence of lay persons to arrive at reasonable judgments in matters of great legal complexity, if only such persons are given sufficient time to deliberate, is utterly remarkable. (It should be noted that jurors are not given tests of reasoning proficiency before being allowed to serve, but they *are* excused if they have a personal interest in the case at issue. In other words, we trust their reasoning provided we do not have evidence of their partiality.) Michael Walzer offers this corroboration:

> We support the jury system, because we believe that disinterested jurors are more likely to get at the truth than anyone else. So why not make this a model for all truth-seeking and even for all right-seeking inquiries? The replacement of political debate with an idealized version of judicial deliberation is in fact the goal of a number of contemporary philosophers.[22]

Would that the faith that animates us in entrusting the jury with its deliberations might likewise animate us to entrust the normative aspects of education to the deliberations of classroom communities of inquiry where such communities are guided by skilled teachers, just as juries are guided by skilled magistrates. If the problems we face in our lives were well defined, we could entrust them to specialists or computers for resolution, but because they are ill defined, they require judgment, and the production of judgment requires deliberation. How better to prepare students for life than by enabling them to participate in deliberative communities that deal with matters that the students themselves consider important?

Learning from the experience of others

The community of inquiry is in one sense a learning together, and it is therefore an example of the value of shared experience. But in another sense it represents a magnification of the efficiency of the learning process, since students who thought that all learning had to be learning by oneself come to discover that they can also use and profit from the experience of others.

This seems so obvious as to be hardly worth noting, except that actual classroom experience reveals how little it is understood. It is not unusual to find college students who stop listening when one of their classmates begins to speak.

---

[22] "A Critique of Philosophical Conversation," *Philosophical Forum* 21:1–2 (Fall–Winter 1989–90), 195n.

They cannot conceive that their peers might have experience that complements their own (in which case they have much to gain by hearing it out), corroborates their own (in which case they might be prepared to hold their own convictions more firmly), or disagrees with their own (in which case they might have to re-examine their own positions).

Often the degree to which students think they can learn from each other's experience is inversely proportional to what they think they can learn from the instructor's experience. Nor are students mistaken in thinking they can benefit from adults who can mediate between children and the world. The adult often serves to translate the society's experience, its culture, to the student, and to translate the student's experience to the society. The community of inquiry embeds that translation in everyday school practice.

Toward the formation of classroom communities of inquiry

To bring this chapter to a close, I want to suggest what might be brought out if we were to unpack the notion of the community of inquiry by examining it stage by stage. In what follows, I have identified five relatively discrete stages, but I make no attempt to provide a further analysis of the series of steps that might be taken within each stage. My aim is, instead, to indicate what is going on, psychologically as well as pedagogically, at each stage.

I have chosen to use as an illustration a *philosophical* community of inquiry, not only because that is the kind I am most familiar with, but also because I think it provides a valuable prototype. It remains to be seen whether communities of inquiry in other disciplines will be successful only to the extent that this prototype is approximated.

I. The offering of the text

1. The text as a model, in story form, of a community of inquiry
2. The text as reflecting the values and achievements of past generations
3. The text as mediator between the culture and the individual
4. The text as a highly peculiar object of perception that carries mental reflection already within itself
5. The text portraying human relationships as possibly analyzable into logical relations
6. Taking turns reading aloud
   a. The ethical implications of alternating reading and listening
   b. The oral reproduction of the written text
   c. Turn taking as a division of labor: the beginnings of classroom community
7. Gradual internalization of the thinking behaviors of the fictional characters (e.g., to read how a fictional character asks a question may lead a real child to ask such a question in class)

8. Discovery by the class that the text is meaningful and relevant; the appropriation by the members of the class of those meanings

II. The construction of the agenda

1. The offering of questions: the initial response of the class to the text
2. Recognition by the teacher of the names of the contributing individuals
3. The construction of the agenda as a collaborative work of the community
4. The agenda as a map of areas of student interest
5. The agenda as an index of what students consider important in the text and as an expression of the group's cognitive needs
6. Cooperation of teacher and students in deciding where to begin the discussion

III. Solidifying the community

1. Group solidarity through dialogical inquiry
2. The primacy of activity over reflection
3. The articulation of disagreements and the quest for understanding
4. Fostering cognitive skills (e.g., assumption finding, generalization, exemplification) through dialogical practice
5. Learning to employ cognitive tools (e.g., reasons, criteria, concepts, algorithms, rules, principles)
6. Joining together in cooperative reasoning (e.g., building on each other's ideas, offering counterexamples or alternative hypotheses, etc.)
7. Internalization of the overt cognitive behavior of the community (e.g., introjecting the ways in which classmates correct one another until each becomes systematically self-corrective) – "intrapsychical reproduction of the interpsychical" (Vygotsky)
8. Becoming increasingly sensitive to meaningful nuances of contextual differences
9. Group collectively groping its way along, following the argument where it leads

IV. Using exercises and discussion plans

1. Employing questions from the academic tradition: recourse to professional guidance
2. Appropriation by the students of the methodology of the discipline
3. Opening students to other philosophical alternatives
4. Focusing on specific problems so as to compel the making of practical judgments
5. Compelling the inquiry to examine overarching regulative ideas such as truth, community, personhood, beauty, justice, and goodness

V. Encouraging further responses

1. Eliciting further responses (in the form of the telling or writing of stories, poetry, painting, drawing, and other forms of cognitive expression)[23]
2. Recognizing the synthesis of the critical and the creative with the individual and the communal
3. Celebrating the deepened sense of meaning that comes with strengthened judgment

---

[23] V. V. Davydov provides a helpful prescription for the employment of dialogue in art education, in "The Mental Development of Younger Schoolchildren in the Process of Learning Activity," *Soviet Education* 30:10 (1988), 3–16. This is a selection from his book *Problems of Developmental Teaching*, trans. Liv Tudge (Armonk, N.Y.: M. E. Sharpe, 1986). For more on the value of discussion in instruction, see Roland G. Tharp and Ronald Gallimore, *Rousing Minds to Life* (Cambridge University Press, 1988); W. Wilen (ed.), *Teaching and Learning through Discussion* (Springfield, Ill.: Charles C. Thomas, 1990); and Luis C. Moll (ed.), *Vygotsky and Education* (Cambridge University Press, 1990).

15 The political significance of the inquiring community

The community of inquiry approach is today a tiny but growing component of contemporary elementary education. It preceded the popular demand for critical thinking in the schools, and is arguably the best example of what that kind of educational reform can be. But has it any implications for political reform? This is what we must now consider: To what political ends can it be a means?

The political implications of teaching for inquiry

We are familiar enough with the notion of the means–end continuum: Every means may itself be the end of some previous means, and every end may itself be the means to some still further end.[1] We also know how hard it is to establish these connections. Experience compels us to acknowledge that we generally deal only with ends-*in-view* and means-*in-view* – slippery, shifting categories that resist our attempts to bring about some sort of mutual adjustment and that must be continually reformulated and defined in order to get them to link up efficiently. To wrestle with any adaptation of means to ends is to discover how schematic, oversimplified, and ideological our reasonings are in comparison with the brute, stubborn intransigence of the ways of the world.

The question of critical thinking is a case in point. To inquire as to its value is to provoke this sort of reply: Critical thinking improves resonableness, and democracy requires reasonable citizens, so critical thinking is a necessary means if our goal is a democratic society.[2] But once the flywheel of inquiry begins to turn,

---

[1] The term "means–end continuum" is of course John Dewey's; see *Theory of Valuation*, vol. 2, no. 4, of *International Encyclopedia of Unified Science* (Chicago: University of Chicago Press, 1939), pp. 40–50. One of the things Dewey is insistent upon here is that there are no "ends in themselves," in the sense of ends that issue as the sole consequences of particular means and that have themselves no other consequences. This is what is wrong with the claim that the end justifies the means: It implies that the means employed provide one desirable consequence and no others. So Dewey argues for "ends-in-view" – provisional, alterable ends – rather than the fixity and rigidity of "ends-in-themselves," and for deliberation about alternative ends-in-view as well as means by which these might be achieved.

[2] The connection between critical thinking and democracy has been forged by a great many thinkers, not least of whom is John Locke. Locke, especially in *Some Thoughts on Education*, insisted on the need for reasoned reflection by the citizens on the issues that confronted them, and he was categor-

it has trouble stopping, and we proceed to ask, "Why do we want a democratic society?" "Because," the answer comes back quickly enough, "it is that form of social arrangement that can best promote the quality of life for all its members." Here the going begins to get a bit sticky: for all its members and *only* it members? What about animals? They are not members of a democratic society – are they entitled to an enhanced quality of life? With our utility-centered approach, we shudder at the very idea that the happiness of animals has intrinsic value, we are inclined to think rather that their existence is to be counted only because it makes *us* happy. And then there are those inanimate parts of nature whose protection can be based on grounds that have little or nothing to do with anyone's happiness, such as that nature deserves our respect.

I mention these things only to show how ends that look simple, precise, and stable as we aim at them from a distance begin to blur and shift as we approach them more closely. This entails our making complementary adjustments in our means, and the entire means–end continuum is forced to writhe snakelike as we revise our specifications and review our priorities.

Thus, when we invoke a means–end relationship between reflective education and democracy, we must be prepared to make appropriate modifications in the one whenever we revise our specifications of the other. Any alteration in our concept of democracy will carry with it a requirement that the means-in-view be modified, and any alteration of our concept of reflective education will require that the ends-in-view be modified.

For example, suppose that education, upon refocusing, is characterized as "education *as* inquiry and education *for* inquiry."[3] This change in the means immediately calls for a change in the end that those means subtend. To the extent that the society is the product of the schools, the quality of its democracy will reflect the quality of its educational processes. When education becomes education *as* inquiry and education *for* inquiry, the social product of that institutional change will be democracy as inquiry and not merely democracy.

How significant is this alteration? Is it substantial or merely verbal? Some will say that democracy and inquiry are quite dissimilar, perhaps incompatible.[4]

---

ically clear about the relationship between reason and conduct: "The use and end of right Reasoning, (is) to have right Notions, and a right Judgment of things; to distinguish betwixt Truth and Falsehood, Right and Wrong; and to act accordingly" (para. 189). For a helpful analysis, see Nathan Tarcov, *Locke's Education for Liberty* (Chicago: University of Chicago Press, 1984).

[3] By "inquiry" I mean any form of self-critical practice whose aim is more comprehensive understanding or more expert judgment. In this sense, scientific inquiry is only one among many forms of inquiry that are to be found in the crafts and arts, in the humanities and professions, and indeed wherever human beings are engaged in making, saying, or doing. In view of the means–end relationship just discussed, it seems to me evident that if inquiry is to become an important characteristic of our society, we must have *education for inquiry,* and we cannot educate for inquiry unless we have education *as* inquiry – unless, that is, the qualitative character we desire to have in the end is loaded into the means.

[4] The conflict between the democratic process and scientific inquiry is a conflict between two methods, the first consensual and the second experimental. At present there is no jurisdictional dispute

Others will remark that as approaches to social problem-solving both are utilized but generally in different contexts. There are rare exceptions, of course, like trials involving both judge and jury. On the whole, though, our society is not one that seeks strenuously to merge the democratic and the inquiry processes. Consequently, we have seen little need to demand a school system that prepares students for such a society. At the most, we have talked about the need for having individual citizens be thoughtful. We have not taken seriously the notion that ours be an inquiring society.

It seems to me that the notion of democracy as inquiry merges rationality and consensus and that this merger is superior to being guided by either criterion alone. Legal reasoning may not be a perfect model for other institutions, but it does involve a sensible division of labor in which judges cognizant of the law are balanced by commonsensical juries, and both are balanced again by lawyers skilled in making rhetorical appeals on behalf of plaintiffs and defendants. Yet all are engaged in the inquiry process and aim at the achievement of reasonable results.

The democratic society we currently inhabit only reluctantly turns matters over to inquiry for decisions or recommendations, with the result that our problems – particularly the economic ones – are almost unmanageable. The rule of thumb we seem to be guided by, with the assent of both political parties, is that everything will be better for everybody if only more and more advantages can be thrust upon those who are already advantaged or superadvantaged. Such maxims, however, resolve nothing. The cynical slogans of the tobacco industry have only gradually given way to public acceptance of the results of inquiry to the effect that there is a clear causal connection between smoking and cancer. In countless other cases, however, raw economic power is capable of obtaining political cover for its operations regardless of the ascertainable negative impact of such operations on the environment or human beings.

If education is to prepare students to live as inquring members of an inquiring society, then that education must be education *as* inquiry as well as education *for* inquiry. This entails the conversion of each classroom into a deliberative and inquisitive community. It does not require the outlay of huge sums of money.

The mediating role of the classroom community

The social structure of the community of inquiry makes it a necessary bridge between the institutional character of the family and the democracy-as-inquiry character that must be realized in the society at large. No matter how genial the quality of relationships within the family may be, the hard fact of the dependency of the very young generally results in a certain degree of authoritarianism. The role of schools has been to provide a transitional institution: in part a surrogate for the family from which the child is emerging and in part a surrogate for the

between the two; there are various projects – in space, in medicine – in which inquiries are commissioned subject to political control.

larger society which the student will in time enter.[5] But because the roles of the child in the family and of the adult individual in the society are both seen as only partially participatory, the school as a transitional process or link between the two has adopted the same character.

What the community of inquiry provides is a nucleus that both represents and anticipates a society composed of participatory communities – a society that is a community of such communities. In recent years, such writers as Benjamin Barber have urged us to move from "liberal democracy" to "strong democracy." In the former, the participation of the individual is limited to the secrecy and isolation of the polling booth, whereas in the latter it is to be found in countless public communities that go to make up the democratic community as a whole.[6] But these writers seem to be unaware that the instances they cite are significantly noneducational in character and that the transition they seek cannot be achieved without an educational component.[7]

If we consider three contemporary movements – or should we say banners? – in education – critical thinking, philosophy in elementary school, and feminism – we note that they are differentially related to the community of inquiry pedagogy. To grade-school philosophy and feminism, I would say, such a pedagogy is essential, for they must necessarily deal with the failure of the existing social structure to take the educational rights of children and women seriously. The community of inquiry alone offers the equity of opportunity that has been traditionally denied to these groups. Thus, students in early elementary school are conceptually impoverished and undernourished because certain psychological theories reinforce certain social prejudices with regard to young children's capacities to deal with ideas. What elementary school philosophy does is give children access to the cultural reservoir of ideas from the very beginning of their schooling, kindergarten. In this way, philosophy for the young prevents that cognitive emaciation that so often sets in by the third or fourth grade and often results in students dropping out

---

[5] See George Herbert Mead, "The Psychology of Social Consciousness Implied in Instruction," *Science* 31 (1910), 688–93, and Joseph J. Schwab, interviewed in *Center Magazine* 9:6 (1976).

[6] Benjamin Barber, *Strong Democracy* (Berkeley and Los Angeles: University of California Press, 1984). See also Michael Walzer, *Radical Principles* (New York: Basic, 1980); Franz Neumann, *The Democratic and the Authoritarian State* (Glencoe, Ill.: Free Press, 1957); and Stanley Hoffman, "Some Notes on Democratic Theory and Practice," *Tocqueville Review* 2:1 (Winter 1980).

[7] The conservative appeal to community in recent writings is typified by Robert A. Nisbet, *The Quest for Community* (Oxford: Oxford University Press, 1953). A somewhat more positive role is assigned to community in Glenn Tinder, *Community: Reflections on a Tragic Ideal* (Baton Rouge: Louisiana State University Press, 1980). See in particular pp. 24–33, where he discusses "community as inquiry." Another attempt to connect community and inquiry is Julius Moravcsik's "Communal Ties," supplement to 62:1 of *Proceedings and Addresses of the American Philosophical Association* (September 1988), 211–25. I think Moravcsik perceives the special bond that exists between philosophic inquiry and the philosophic community. But he does not draw out the educational or political implications of his "normative communitarianism." For an analysis of Peirce's conception of the "community of inquiry," see John E. Smith, "Community and Reality," in Eugene Freeman (ed.), *The Relevance of Peirce* (La Salle, Ill.: Hegeler Institute, 1983), pp. 59–77, as well as Susan Haack, "Descartes, Peirce and the Cognitive Community," ibid., pp. 238–63.

of school altogether. Moreover, the conceptually stimulating setting provides an appropriate environment for the development of intellectual skills and craft, for the students can recognize their roles as cognitive apprentices and can appreciate their growing mastery of the skills needed to tap into the humanistic concepts and methodologies at the heart of their culture and its traditions.

Every child who has experienced an injustice is as ready as the participants in the *Republic* to discuss the nature of justice. Every child who arrives at an understanding through the making of comparisons can appreciate the excitement of Socrates, Plato, and Aristotle at discovering the colossal power of the twin criteria identity and difference. For children to find these matters out for themselves in a community of inquiry setting is for them to experience afresh the robust exuberance exhibited by Socrates and his companions in their conversations about the nature of the True, the Beautiful, and the Good. Indeed, children may be even more moved by ideas than adults are, and to discuss children's play as if it had to be physical/affective but could not be cognitive/affective is to reveal only a limited grasp of the intellectual potentialities of the child.

The notion that the democratic process needs further specification as an inquiry process is consistent with the Deweyan call for the intelligent guidance of shared experience and for active participation by all in varieties of association. But it will take a grass-roots movement to prepare for this change of direction, and the grass roots in this case are to be found in the classroom.

The classroom community can play a mediating role between the family and the society at large or between the particular cultural or ethnic background of each individual and the society at large. But it can also mediate between pressures to resolve social problems by democratic consensus, by scientific inquiry, or, for that matter, by brute social or economic power. In its deliberations, it can sort out issues into groups, distinguishing those that are immediately decidable from those that are deeply contestable. In this way, the classroom community of inquiry can serve as a valuable buffer zone, prohibiting a mad rush to judgment in cases that require prolonged study while demanding prompt action in cases where a definitive judgment is feasible and prompt action obligatory.

The political implications of teaching for judgment

The problem of legitimate authority has traditionally aroused logicians (as in the so-called fallacy of illegitimate authority) to a modest extent and political philosophers a great deal. To Plato, what conferred legitimacy on professionals was their knowledge, and since governance was a professional matter, there should be no breach between knowledge and power. It was deplorable, he felt, that those with knowledge should lack power and those with power should lack knowledge. Why should it always be one or the other but seldom both together?

Plato's complaint is understandable, but it does not go to the root of the problem we are having in putting democracy into practice. We find individuals today – in industry, in the military, in politics, and in countless other spheres of human activity – in whom knowledge and power coexist but who are virtually sealed off from one another. We are scandalized when we discover how incapable such individuals are of applying what they know to what they do, and when we try to account for their inadequacies we generally come back to the matter of their education.

As an elitist, Plato could prescribe prolonged and powerful training for those destined to be rulers. In our own era, with its inclinations toward mass democracy and its ideology that the people are sovereign, reflective, and intelligent, pressure on the institution of education is enormous. We despair of the ability of the schools to equip masses of citizens with knowledge that is anywhere near sufficient for the global problems with which we are faced, let alone to equip such citizens with the judgment needed to employ such knowledge wisely.

Always our answer to the complaint that the students turned out by the schools are unable to translate what they know into what they do is to prescribe still more knowledge. If teachers are ineffectual, it is because they do not know their subjects well enough. If elementary, secondary, or college students cannot do the work assigned to them, it is because the teachers have failed to teach them the content of the existing disciplines. Rarely do we hear it said that it is not the amount of content that is at fault but the emphasis on the acquisition of knowledge rather than on the strengthening of judgment. It is even more rare to hear someone say that perhaps the existing curriculum needs to be reappraised, on the possibility that it gives too much attention to some disciplines and too little – or none at all – to others.

If we have exaggerated the importance of the knowledge-acquisition aspect of education, we have slighted another phase: the transition from deliberation to judgment, and we have almost completely steered clear of the phase involving the transition from judgment to action. Nevertheless, in the society at large and in the classroom that is the seedbed of the society at large, the place to begin is with deliberation. How is deliberation to be encouraged, and how can it be structured so that it facilitates the acquisition of such components of judgment as sound reasoning; the ability to note differences among things that are fairly similar and similarities among things that are fairly different; a sense of perspective and a sense of proportion; dispositions to wonder, to inquire, and to be critical; the capacity to form and analyze concepts and arguments; and sensitivity to contextual uniformities and differences? No doubt this is a tall order. In practice the course we should follow is to set our sights on the improvement of reasonableness and judgment as the goals of education and then allow the transmission of knowledge to be adjusted accordingly. This course seems more likely to be successful than if we set our sights on acquisition of knowledge as a goal, with consequent adjustment of the degree to which judgment and reasonableness are to be cultivated.

As to how such deliberations are to be encouraged, I have already urged that we see the community of inquiry as the embryonic intersection of democracy and education. The community of inquiry represents the social dimension of democratic practice, for it both paves the way for the extended implementation of such practice and is emblematic of what such practice has the potentials to become. On the other hand, the cognitive dimension of democratic practice is best represented by that strand of the inquiry process that has been identified as the transition from deliberation to judgment.

Implications for the social studies curriculum

To the traditionalists in education, what will ensure that citizens will come to make the right judgments is that they be given the right knowledge – the right content. Consequently, according to these commentators, the fecklessness of the electorate at present is due to its ignorance of the essentials of history, economics, and the operations of government. As Lynne V. Cheyney puts it, "History text-books should present the events of the past so that their significance is clear."[8] We may presume that all contents are to be premasticated and "clarified." Nothing is to be presented as problematic for students to chew on. One can readily imagine Soviet historians of the Stalin era being instructed in quite similar fashion: The events of the Russian past must be presented in a way that will make their significance clear to the Soviet student – and future Soviet citizen.

The demand that our history books be clear and unambiguous seems to me to do away with the need for higher-order, complex thinking on the part of the students. It also makes us realize that some of those who join in the call for freedom of expression may have less enthusiasm for freedom of thought. For them, freedom of expression is tolerable only after the thoughts of students have been suitably sanitized. The emphasis on having students think for themselves – engage in deliberation and gain practice in judgment – is a way of answering the demand that social studies texts be "clarified" so that students will not have to think too much in order to understand them.

To nineteenth-century philosophers, the relationship between deliberation and judgment was couched in the language of thought and expression. Both Mill and Peirce pointed out with grave apprehension that without freedom of thought there could be no freedom of expression and without freedom of expression there could be no freedom of thought. Indeed, Peirce noted, we do not need others to persecute and oppress us; we can do a very good job of it on ourselves in a proper climate of intimidation.[9] But the pattern of mischief is clear enough: Deny any

[8] *American Memory: A Report on the Humanities in the Nation's Public Schools* (Washington, D.C.: National Endowment for the Humanities, n.d.), p. 28.

[9] See J. S. Mill, *On Liberty,* ch. 2; see also C. S. Peirce, in "The Fixation of Belief": "Wherever you are, let it be known that you seriously hold a tabooed belief, and you may be perfectly sure of being treated with a cruelty less brutal but more refined than hunting you like a wolf. Thus the greatest intellectual benefactors of mankind have never dared, and dare not now, to utter the whole of their thought; and thus a shade of *prima facie* doubt is cast upon every proposition which is considered essential to the security of society." He goes on to say, "Singularly enough, the persecution does not all come from without; but a man torments himself and is oftentimes distressed at finding himself believing propositions which he has been brought up to regard with aversion" (Justus Buchler [ed.], *Philosophical Writings of Peirce* [New York: Dover, 1955], p. 20).

connection between thought and expression (or deliberation and judgment) and then "clarify" the content to be learned. This will ensure that any subsequent judgments students might make will be "correct" ones.

Cheyney would like history books to be written more interestingly. and she is of the opinion that this can be done, first, by abandoning the "expanding environments" approach that begins with the home and school setting with which the child is familiar and moves outward and, second, by replacing the present texts with history the way it used to be: "myths, fables, stories from the distant past, and tales of heroes." Students in those days learned "about Daedalus and King Arthur, George Washington and Joan of Arc, exercising their imaginations and beginning to develop a sense of life in other times."[10] But it does not follow that introducing children to "the human ambitions and aspirations that are both the motivating force of history and its fascination" requires the abandonment of the "expanding environments" approach.

Discussions of truth, fairness, and friendship are as much a part of the child's cultural heritage as are Daedalus and King Arthur. There is nothing wrong with depicting real children in the ordinariness of their home or school environments thinking about and discussing what reality is or what a person is or whether everything must be either right or wrong. And if, to illustrate these discussions, teachers introduce their students to Daedalus and Joan of Arc, the students will have been thoroughly primed to give Daedalus and Joan a respectful, thoughtful, and imaginative reception.

Of course, the notion of "expanding environments" to which Cheyney objects is Dewey's, but it was the same John Dewey who once wrote that the very best in nature is not the ideal alone or the actual alone but the relationships between human ideals and those human activities attempting to realize such ideals.[11] Without an adequate understanding of ideals and the guiding role they play in human affairs – without, in other words, an understanding of the *relationships* between history and ourselves, science and ourselves, philosophy and ourselves – the subjects that students study will continue to be disembodied and alienated, and the judgments they make will often be warped, skewed, and superficial.

Soviet citizens are becoming more able to form astute political judgments as they gain access to documentary sources that have been critical of Stalinism and communism. It is not simply that they need to be informed about dissenting opinions. It is rather that they need to incorporate the tradition of critical thinking into their own political reflections. Likewise, our own citizens need access, while they are still in their formative years, to the intellectual sources that have been less than satisfied with democracy in its contemporary guise. But they have just as much to understand the paternalism that has deprived them of any opportunity to incorporate the tradition of critical thinking into their own political reflections.

[10] Cheyney, *American Memory*, p. 16.
[11] *A Common Faith* (New Haven, Conn.: Yale University Press, 1934).

Instead of scoffing at parents and students who claim that the elementary school curriculum is stodgy and irrelevant, we should subject it to a sober reappraisal that will (1) remove the bloatedness of some disciplines represented therein at the expense of others, (2) reduce the fragmentation endemic to the curriculum, and (3) introduce disciplines, such as philosophy and other humanities and arts, now absent but capable of supplying much that is needed to enliven the curriculum and make it relevant again. Certainly, if we rethink the goals of education and conclude that judgment is paramount among them, and if we recognize that the arts and humanities are essential to the cultivation of judgment, we will more readily acknowledge that they are essential to the kind of education we want and need. In the process, we might also demonstrate that philosophy, when taught in the dialogical fashion of the community of inquiry so that it is *done* rather than learned, is essential to education at every stage from kindergarten through graduate school.

Introducing children to political concepts

The idea of converting children's classrooms into communities brings up the notion of *community*, which for Ferdinand Tönnies[12] in the nineteenth century had strongly traditional implications, and which in the frequent references to it in contemporary literature often has conservative implications.[13] On the other hand, the notion of democracy as inquiry, when taken together with the classroom community as a seedbed of inquiry, is suggestive of the participatory democracy guided by intelligence espoused by Dewey.[14] Discussion of education for reasonableness and judgment often harks back to Locke's rather than to Rousseau's notions of liberal democracy.[15] What about more radical implications of philosophy for children?

Socialist literature has been singularly lacking in a comprehensive vision of the role of children in a post-capitalist society. Marx does not, to my knowledge, deal

[12] "*Gemeinschaft* and *Gesellschaft*," *Fundamental Concepts of Sociology*, trans. Charles P. Loomis (New York: American Book, 1940), pp. 3–29.

[13] The conservative interpretation has been spearheaded in recent years by the work of Robert A. Nisbet (see *The Quest for Community*). The Hegelian notion that communities emerge out of conflict-filled situations (as syntheses emerge out of opposed theses) was examined penetratingly by Georg Simmel in *Conflict and the Web of Affiliations*, trans. Kurt H. Wolff (New York: Free Press, 1955), as well as in more recent work by Lewis Coser in the spirit of Simmel's approach. Currently this is taking the form (in philosophy) of studies in the role of argument with regard to the formation of communities. At a conference in Venice (August 7–11, 1988) on this topic, the keynote address, by Else M. Barth and G. Thomas Goodnight, was "The Role of Argument in the Creation and Maintenance of Community."

[14] See *Liberalism and Social Action* (New York: Capricorn, 1963).

[15] E. H. Carr argues that modern democracy rests on three main propositions, all to be found in Locke: (1) the ultimate source of decisions about right and wrong is the *individual conscience*, (2) there exists among individuals in society a fundamental *harmony of interests*, and (3) the best method of reaching a decision in society is through *rational discussion* (*The New Society* [London: Macmillan, 1951], pp. 61–79).

with the fact that the child's state of primitive dependency cannot be as completely done away with as other types of class dependencies, such as serfdom, slavery, and the dependency of women. Nevertheless, Marx repeatedly makes the point that the intellectual tools constructed by the dominant class are acquired by the oppressed class and employed as weapons against their oppressors.[16]

Now, children do not have to overthrow adults in order to become adults themselves. They have only to wait a few years and it will happen to them automatically. Just the same, so long as they are children, their intellectual status is – or has been – different from that of adults in that they have not had access to the cognitive weapons that adults employ in their efforts to obtain a more just social order. It is not that, as children, they have no sense of injustice; on the contrary, as Piaget has shown, they feel injustices keenly.[17] But they have lacked a *concept* of justice to work with, along with such concepts as *freedom, rights, person, rationality,* and so on. Once they find out about such concepts and are able to make use of them in philosophical dialogues, what is to prevent them from making cases for themselves that adults find unanswerable because they share the same assumptions and appeal to the same criteria?

It may well be that the children of the future, together with the adults who represent their interests, will be able increasingly to avail themselves of forms of political leverage of which they are now unaware. Philosophy can help provide that awareness. But perhaps the major change will be the fact that children nurtured on philosophy in school will grow up to be parents who will nurture their own children on philosophy at home. There will be more intergenerational communication as a result, and it will be more cognitive in character. (To some extent it may help arrest the "red shift" according to which the generations, like galaxies, are moving farther and farther apart.)

No doubt it will be contended that philosophy did not make people conspicuously more reasonable when it was taught only to adults and will not make them conspicuously more reasonable when it is extended to children. But the difference may be more significant than it looks. Philosophy, in its traditional garb of the quest for wisdom, needs to be taught in the formative years; later is too late.

In making the practice of philosophy available to children, we have to be aware of the political implications of doing so. Consequently, we must be prepared to approach the matter with courage, discretion, and fair-mindedness. The courage will be required if ideas are introduced that have hitherto been kept out of children's range, even though children would have been willing and able to discuss them and interested in doing so. Discretion will be needed to ensure that children will instigate their inquiries on their own, piqued by the clues provided in the text, rather than being led by the hand into confronting the issues we as adults think is essential to confront – though the latter course may be necessary if the students, left to their own devices, manage to avoid it. Fair-mindedness will be

[16] Karl Marx, *Manifesto of the Communist Party,* Part One.
[17] Jean Piaget, *The Moral Judgment of the Child* (Glencoe, Ill.: Free Press, 1948), ch. 1.

necessary if we are not to try to compel children to think and act in accordance with our conception of justice. The danger is not so much that our conception may be wrong – although people ten generations from now will surely look back with astonishment at the barbarisms we today accept as civilized. The danger is that we will not permit children to come to their own conception of justice because we do not trust them to come to a conception that resembles our own and because we feel that any deviation on their part must be for the worse. If we are to escape Veblen's taunt that we are a world still "in the later stages of barbarism," we will have to foster political thinking that goes well beyond our current conceptions of justice, open-mindedness, tolerance, and other such intellectual and moral virtues.[18]

The community of inquiry is the necessary seedbed for the cultivation of philosophy in the elementary school, because it intermixes the critical concern with justice and the creative impulse toward caring. It produces respect for both principles and persons and thereby provides a model of democracy as inquiry.

Using the community of inquiry to combat prejudice

I have said that children can acquire from adults various ideas that can be turned against those very adults in the interest of achieving a more equitable society. Some of these ideas are truth, justice, person, and rights. They can also learn from adults that just as reasoning is truth preserving and translation is meaning preserving, so community is care preserving. It is a way of holding on, in society, to the healthy impulse toward interpersonal care and concern that often used to be present in the family.

From being uncaring, it is little more than a step to being prejudiced. It is customary to distinguish three forms of prejudice: prejudiced beliefs, prejudiced attitudes, and prejudiced behavior. The rigid inflexible beliefs that prejudicial attitudes and behavior have at their core are stereotypes. A stereotype is a set of characteristics that all members of a social category are thought to hold in common, regardless of whether or not they do. When we think stereotypically, we

---

[18] In this connection, I have profited from – although I have not always agreed with – Jane Roland Martin's "Moral Autonomy and Political Education," in Matthew Lipman and Ann Margaret Sharp (eds.), *Growing Up with Philosophy* (Philadelphia: Temple University Press, 1978), pp. 174–94. Cf., in the same volume, Louis I. Katzner's "Social Philosophy and Children," pp. 194–206. There are also some relevant comments in my review of two books by Robert Coles, *The Moral Lives of Children* and *The Political Lives of Children*. The review, entitled "On Morality as 'Life put to the test,' " appeared in *Journal of Education* 168:3 (1986), 104–9, and reaches this conclusion:

> The presuppositions of the clinical approach and of the educational approach are therefore at odds, in that one seeks to treat a patient by identifying the *causes* of his or her behavior, while the other attempts to help people think for themselves by identifying their *reasons* for thinking as they do. The two approaches are not incompatible, but each is in dire need of greater self-understanding. (p. 109)

In addition, one may wish to consult my review of William Hare's *In Defense of Open-Mindedness* (Kingston and Montreal: McGill and Queen's University Presses, 1985), pp. 287–90.

allow ourselves to ignore any facts that might be inconsistent with the stereotypes we hold. Stereotypical thinking generally is expressed in the form of unfair, biased, or intolerant attitudes; it may or may not be carried out into action. If we can devise ways of counteracting stereotypical thinking, we can reduce the likelihood that prejudiced attitudes and behavior will develop.

We must be prepared to face the fact that stereotypes, and prejudices in general, are such tangles of fallacious reasoning and nonrational attitudes that an attack on the reasoning strands alone is hardly likely to be effective. We must also be ready to realize that the ineffectiveness of our own approaches may be due to faulty assumptions we ourselves are making – or perhaps even to prejudices we ourselves hold – with regard to the nature of the problem.

For many people, prejudiced beliefs and attitudes are close to the core of their selves; the idea of relinquishing these unreasonable beliefs and attitudes causes them to become very defensive. Their ample self-esteem is based on extremely shaky foundations. They reject efforts to correct their prejudices, for this would result in a serious loss of self-esteem unless some other source of self-esteem could be provided at the same time. (It should be noted, in passing, that reduced self-esteem is itself a form of prejudice: prejudice against oneself.)

The community of inquiry is a highly promising process by means of which stereotypical thinking can be replaced by thinking that is more fair toward others and more accepting of others without destroying the positive self-images of the participants. As judgment is improved and strengthened, we replace with less prejudiced beliefs and attitudes the distorted views and dispositions about which we were hitherto so defensive.

In saying earlier that we must be prepared to deal with our own faulty assumptions when dealing with a problem as tricky as the nature of prejudice, I have in mind the readiness of many observers to conclude that, based on an overwhelming amount of evidence, white students outperform black students academically. But perhaps there is a hidden assumption here, one that compels us to rethink or even to reject these findings. Consider the discussion of the situation by the sociologist Robert Dreeben: "Again and again," Dreeben observes, "research has documented that on the average, the academic performance of white students exceeds that of blacks."[19] These racial differences in learning are often explained by socioeconomic and cultural differences in the family backgrounds. But Dreeben's research shows that when black and white first graders of similar aptitude received reading instruction *of similar quality*, they attained nearly equal levels of reading achievement. This means that when black students are provided with as much instructional time as white students and are given challenging rather than dull reading material, neither race nor socioeconomic background is a significant factor. Black and white students learn equivalently when the manner of teaching is equivalent and when black students receive "conceptual instruction that fosters . . . the interpretation of ideas so that students will be prepared for the

[19] "Closing the Divide," *American Educator* 11:4 (Winter 1987), 28.

intellectual demand of the upper-grade curriculum."[20] Dreeben shows that the case for ethnic inferiority of black students made by biologists and geneticists who fail to take the differences in instructional contexts into account is baseless.

Dreeben's experiment also suggests that the stereotype, like the schema, is self-fulfilling; it accepts only the evidence that confirms it and rejects or ignores whatever evidence might tend to disconfirm it. But where other schemata are functionally useful in helping to concentrate attention in a given field, stereotypes are dysfunctional and distorting and are persistent obstacles to arriving at equitable solutions to social problems. A number of researchers have given extensive attention to the factors conducive to stereotyping. Among them, Myron Rothbart has been concerned with the way in which an in-group is perceived as heterogeneous and differentiated while an out-group is perceived as homogeneous and undifferentiated.[21] Janet Ward Schofield has expressed doubts about the cultivation of color-blindness as an antidote to stereotyping, recommending instead a pluralistic approach to the structuring of contact situations.[22] And David L. Hamilton has attempted to show that stereotyping, to the extent that it has a cognitive basis, may yield to cognitive experiences, such as the disconfirmation that integration will lead to unfavorable consequences.[23]

Sociocultural antidotes

A variety of antidotes to stereotyping have been suggested. Many aim to bring about change by means of sociocultural or motivational changes. Three or four decades ago, the emphasis was on integration, but merely putting students from different backgrounds side by side accomplished little. The next move was to have students work together on common projects – the sort of collaboration that occurs in sports teams. The foremost exponent of this approach has been Robert E. Slavin.[24] Slavin has reported that when students work in ethnically mixed cooperative-learning groups, they gain in cross-ethnic friendships, and there are also gains in academic achievement.[25]

[20] Ibid., p. 35.
[21] "Memory Processes and Social Beliefs," in David L. Hamilton (ed.), *Cognitive Processes in Stereotyping and Intergroup Behavior* (Hillsdale, N.J.: Erlbaum, 1981), p. 178.
[22] "Black–White Contact in Desegregated Schools," in M. Hewstone and R. Brown (eds.), *Contact and Conflict in Intergroup Encounters* (Oxford: Blackwell Publisher, 1986), p. 91. See also her "Causes and Consequences of the Colorblind Perspective," *Prejudice, Discrimination and Racism* (New York: Academic Press, 1986), p. 250.
[23] "Stereotyping and Intergroup Behavior: Some Thoughts on the Cognitive Approach," in Hamilton (ed.), *Cognitive Processes in Stereotyping and Intergroup Behavior*, pp. 333–53. See also David L. Hamilton and George D. Bishop, "Attitudinal and Behavioral Effects of Initial Integration of White Suburban Neighborhoods," *Journal of Social Issues* 32:2 (1976), 66.
[24] "Cooperative Learning," *Review of Educational Research* 50:2 (Summer 1980), 315–42.
[25] "Cooperative Learning: Applying Contact Theory in Desegregated Schools," *Journal of Social Issues* 41:3 (1985), 45–62.

Cognitive antidotes

Direct cognitive interventions have also been proposed as a means of countering stereotypical thinking. It is doubtful, however, whether adult exhortations to young people asking or ordering them to give up their prejudices have much effect. They may even make matters worse. What Charles Glock and his associates recommend, in *Adolescent Prejudice*, is that we teach children to be critical so that they begin to think for themselves and come to reject social stereotypes voluntarily. We must instruct students in the logic of inference, the notion of causality, and the rules of evidence. We must teach them how group differences come about. And we must make clear to them that group differences are merely matters of degree.[26]

Richard Paul has argued that prejudice, bias, and irrationality can be overcome only by cultivating the art of thinking dialogically. According to his model of dialogical (multi-logical, as he calls it, in that it crosses domains) thinking, students learn to role-play and reason within opposing points of view, with respect to both disciplinary issues and those that go beyond disciplinary boundaries. Students learn not how to score points or how to defeat other perspectives but rather how to gain a clearer grasp of the strengths and weaknesses of opposing viewpoints.[27]

Another approach that may be considered cognitive can be derived from the feminists who argue that existing modes of instruction are rife with bias. Janice Moulton, for example, contends that the adversary method of argumentation equates aggression with success. Its aim is not to follow the inquiry where it leads but to prove the opponent's position to be false. Moulton advocates that dialogue replace argument, that cooperation be given precedence over competition, and that questions of meaning take priority over questions of truth.[28]

The community of inquiry as a cognitive/affective strategy

To many writers, the rise of prejudice is part of the fallout from the decline of community. The problem of the disintegrating community has been a favorite study of sociologists for the past two centuries as they seek to map the movement "from community to association"[29] or "from status to contract."[30] C. S. Peirce argued that we are bound to the idea of community by logic; logic requires that

[26] Charles Y. Glock et al., *Adolescent Prejudice* (New York: Harper and Row, 1975), pp. 155–63, 166–80.

[27] Debbie Walsh and Richard Paul, *The Goal of Critical Thinking: From Educational Ideal to Educational Reality* (Washington, D.C.: American Federation of Teachers, n.d.).

[28] "A Paradigm of Philosophy: The Adversary Method," in Sandra Harding and Merrill B. Hintikka (eds.), *Discovering Reality* (Boston: Reidel, 1983), pp. 149–64.

[29] Ferdinand Tönnies, *Fundamental Concepts of Sociology*, pp. 3–29.

[30] Henry Sumner Maine, *Ancient Law* (London: Oxford University Press, 1931), pp. 99–141.

we see how our interests are tied together and embrace the whole community – all individuals, all races, the people of all times.[31] And within this broad community, Peirce went on to argue, there is the community of inquirers.

Dewey drew the necessary inferences from Peirce; the fully democratic society will be the Great Community, the two outstanding features of which will be unimpeded inquiry and free communication.[32] To equip students for citizenship in such a society, the schools will themselves have to become democratic. This entails a restructuring of the social constitution of the schools, and of each individual classroom, for we cannot prepare children for the goal of participatory democratic citizenship unless we employ means that are consistent with that goal.

But Dewey saw what many advocates of cooperation in the classroom do not yet see: Community in the classroom is not enough. The classroom must be converted into a community *of inquiry*. It is to be an inquiring community, an interactive, collaborative, exploratory community. Should grievances and misperceptions arise within the community, they are to be treated as problematic and dealt with experimentally and rationally as would any other problematic subject matter. In brief, for Dewey the classroom is to be a microcosm of the Great Community, and if we are ever to get that Great Community, we must first have those microcosms in place. The schools of the present will breed the society of the future.[33]

Among the most insightful of Dewey's followers in education is Joseph Schwab. Schwab perceives that the classroom community alone is able to serve as the source of the dispositions needed for the community's preservation and for the further prosecution of inquiry. These propensities include not only the propensity to inquire, to communicate, to collaborate, and so on but also propensities for friendship and drawing together with neighboring communities.[34] While Schwab's own bent is toward science education, he evidently sees the limitations of Dewey's stress upon science as the model of all inquiry, for he takes pains to underline the importance of classroom dialogue.

We can summarize here by saying that some accounts of prejudice explain it as symptomatic of social disorganization; the more just and harmonious the society, the less frequently will prejudice in the cultural superstructure be encountered. But cooperation and collaboration are necessary, not merely ethnic coexistence or sex détente. Not *any* collaboration, but collaboration in inquiry. And not *only* scientific investigation, but other forms such as classroom dialogue.

It should be noted that the classroom community is the successor to the social environment of the family. Insofar as linguistic and logical acquisition within the family have been deficient, the classroom community provides a context in which

---

[31] "Some Consequences of Four Incapacities," in Buchler (ed.), *Philosophical Writings of Peirce*, p. 247. See also his article "On the Doctrine of Chances, with Later Reflections," ibid., p. 162.

[32] *The Public and Its Problems* (Denver: Alan Swallow, 1954), p. 184.

[33] *Experience and Education* (New York: Collier, 1963), pp. 86–112.

[34] Joseph J. Schwab, "On Building a Community of Inquiry," *The Great Ideas Today* (Chicago: Encyclopedia Britannica, 1976), and in *The Center Magazine* 9:6 (1976).

these deficiencies can be corrected. But it is doubtful if such strengthening can occur without some conducive social context analogous to the family.

In brief, the distortions of perception and reasoning that go by the name of stereotyping and are productive of prejudicial attitudes and behavior have both a cognitive and an affective basis. The affective factors are sociocultural and motivational. Disturbances of this kind require, for alleviation, that the prejudiced individuals participate in communities of inquiry where they can begin to internalize the attitudes of their peers toward themselves and begin to view themselves more critically.

The cognitive factors represent clusters of biased assumptions that are in turn derived from faulty reasonings. Correction of the reasoning processes can lead to the modification of assumptions in the direction of greater impartiality and objectivity. Practice in critical thinking can be helpful here, but just how much and under what circumstances are not yet clear. When we begin to realize how deeply structural the social causes of stereotyping are, we can begin to understand how puny are our efforts to correct matters through the formation of small communities of inquiry and through courses in critical thinking. Yet we may have no alternative but to persevere in these efforts.

As new winds of freedom sweep the world, brushing away long-established patterns of repression and intimidation, it becomes apparent that voices of prejudice are reveling in their freedom and are being heard more and more distinctly. As states become less repressive, advocates of prejudice become less intimidated in their efforts to intimidate the thinking of others. The decline of political authoritarianism and coercion creates a vacuum. Education must step into that vacuum with nonauthoritarian strategies for combating bias and bigotry. Otherwise we could be faced with the familiar predicament of winning a few battles but losing the war.

Conclusion

If there is a theory of education in Socrates, it is not one he works very hard to spell out; it is, rather, implicit in his practice. But Plato takes Socrates' practice very seriously indeed, and his response to it moves in the direction of theory. (This is not to deny that Plato is a great innovator in terms of educational practice as well.) It may not be unreasonable to speculate that Socrates' reflections on practice began with the practice of his contemporaries and moved to his own, while Plato's reflections began with the practice of Socrates and moved on to theoretical considerations.

Thus, Meno asks Socrates, "Is virtue something that can be taught? Or does it come by practice?" and Socrates replies, "Far from knowing whether it can be taught, I have no idea what virtue itself is." The discussion moves on to deal with what virtue is and returns to make its capacity to be taught contingent upon whether or not it is knowledge. But it is clear that Plato has more than a passing interest in the question "What is and is not teachable?"

This question continues to haunt us, and well it should. There are few today who would want to argue that "knowing that" is teachable while "knowing how" is not, for "knowing how" embraces craft as well as art, and matters of craft appear to be decidedly teachable. Indeed, the distinction between craft and art may hang on this single criterion, that craft deals with teachable knowings-how and art deals with unteachable ones. Even here, however, the footing is a bit unsteady, for we have to keep in mind Ryle's contention, referred to in Chapter 11, that you cannot teach me to think for myself but you can create an environment in which I can figure out how to teach myself to think for myself.

What this means is that rationality and creativity are not simply regulative ideas. They are ideal values that shape our lives. It is important not simply that we be rational and creative but that we live in such a way that rationality and creativity are urgently important matters to us. The domain over which these two values preside is the domain of matters worth teaching. (Irrationality and sterility can probably be taught, but it is worth no one's while to learn them. This is not to say it does not happen.) Matters that fall under the rubric of rationality are worth teaching and are teachable. Those that fall under the rubric of creativity are worth teaching but are not teachable; they can, nevertheless, be "encouraged," and so ways must be found to provide inventive and innovative courage to students so that they dare to be creative. What is not teachable may nevertheless be realizable.

The turn to thinking

The present book represents a series of reflections on the practice with which I have been most familiar for the past twenty years – that embodied in elementary school philosophy. That practice, in turn, has been guided to a considerable extent by *Harry Stottlemeier's Discovery*, a fictional portrait that I drew in 1969 of education as I hoped it could be. Although the fictional children were the products of my own fancy, I learned a great deal from the writing of that book that carried over into the world of real children in real classrooms. The implicit claim of the book was that when children are encouraged to discover what is rational and teachable, instead of having it drilled into them, they respond with enthusiasm and inventiveness. In other words, in a community of inquiry (that being the setting I attempted to portray in the novel) the dialogue develops naturally between the teachable and the unteachable, between craft and art, between rationality and creativity, between the expository and the narrative, between the group and the individual, between the third person and the first person, between logic and imagination, between the cognitive and the affective – in brief, between the halves of all those dualisms that so grievously afflict education. I have seen little in this period to lead me to think that these schisms cannot be healed, but I have seen much that has been instructive about just how difficult a process this can be.

In an article written in 1970, a year after *Harry Stottlemeier's Discovery*, but not published until six years later, I tried to make a case for the teaching of thinking in the schools and for the use of philosophy as the vehicle. At the time, a number of others, such as Hilda Taba, Louis Raths, and B. Othanel Smith, were deploring the lack of thinking in education, and some of them, like R. Bruce Raup, were deploring the lack of attention given to student judgment. However, the linking of this concern to the teaching of philosophy was virtually unheard of. (Over the years, the advocates of philosophy for children have been remarkably few. Socrates was apparently permissive in this respect, but Plutarch and Montaigne were much more forthright and articulate about it. And Derrida may be right when he claims that philosophy was always an important part of the education of the children of the aristocracy and that it was only when the bourgeoisie took over control of the schools and the curriculum that philosophy was expelled.) Nor did Dewey recognize the educational value of philosophy in the elementary school, so convinced was he that inquiry had to mean scientific inquiry.

To be sure, when I advocated philosophy in the schools, I was not talking about the traditional academic philosophy taught in the graduate schools of the universities. What I was talking about was a philosophy redesigned and reconstructed so as to make it available and acceptable and enticing to children. Moreover, the pedagogy by which this subject was to be presented would have to be just as drastically redesigned as the subject itself. I had that pedagogy in mind when writing the 1969 novel; the reader will discover it readily enough after perusing the first few pages. But it was not until later that Peirce's phrase came to mind as the best characterization of the new pedagogy: the community of inquiry. I saw this methodology as intrinsically bound up with grade-school philosophy – as utterly essential if we are to *do* philosophy and not merely learn a collection of names and dates, which is somewhat like trying to memorize the inscriptions in a graveyard.

Since that time, thinking has come into prominence among educators worldwide, and the form this has generally taken is the demand for *critical* thinking. Few educators, however, seem prepared to go on record as acknowledging a special connection between philosophy and the teaching of thinking or even between philosophy and the teaching of critical thinking. If pressed, some will recount their own dreadful experience with philosophy or will relate anecdotes revealing the irrelevance of philosophy instructors they have known. But when these explanations are offered, I suspect that they are merely pretexts.

The real reason is virtually unmentionable. It has to do with the fact that the omission of philosophy from the curriculum has been a colossal gaffe, but now that it is an accomplished fact there is, or so it seems to most educators, no way of making up for it. Our curricular deficits are like our incredible federal budget deficit – real avalanches that we try to make go away by not thinking about them. When all groups are party to the budget deficit, none are likely to come forth and offer to make the sacrifices that are necessary in order to set matters right, nor is there likely to be an accounting to show what brought the disaster about so it will not happen again. Similarly with the curricular deficit: It is likely to remain and get worse, because every profession that is ''in'' sees a reappraisal of the curriculum as utterly perilous to itself.

The case for philosophy

In each and every discipline, higher-order, complex thinking needs to be cultivated. This means that ultimately each course in a discipline must devote some time to consideration of the methodology of that discipline: its assumptions, its criteria, its procedures, and its modes of reasoning and judgment. After all, if it is an academic discipline, it is fully self-critical. Unless it practices self-criticism, it is not the discipline it tells itself it is. If it is not critical linguistics, it is not linguistics, and if it is not critical chemistry, it is not chemistry. Self-criticism is the aspect of itself each discipline must necessarily present to students, and not least of all to the beginning students in introductory courses in that discipline.

There is an authentic sense in which each discipline is a culture unto itself, with its own language and mores. Nevertheless, it is likely that their methodologies differ much less than do the disciplines themselves. If this is the case, and I think it is, then the student moving from course to course is likely to be inundated with duplications. To a considerable extent, logic and scientific method are generic rather than discipline-specific. If redundancy is to be prevented, therefore, there need to be courses for all students in generic methodology. (This is a very different thing from making a subject of study of the interdisciplinary. It seems to me that the auspices under which such courses could be offered should be those of philosophy.)

Philosophy encourages thinking *in* the disciplines because it assumes the burden of teaching the generic aspects of the thinking that goes on in any discipline and because it is a model of what it means for a discipline to reflect on and be critical of its own methodology. Philosophy has always taken it to be axiomatic that the unexamined course is not worth giving, although as often as not it has failed to live up to its own axioms.

Philosophy encourages thinking *about* the disciplines, inasmuch as one of its prime modes of operation is the "philosophy of" course: philosophy of mathematics, philosophy of the social sciences, philosophy of language, and so on. Indeed, the "philosophy of" course often discloses indigenous aspects of a discipline's methodology of which the practitioners of that discipline are not fully conscious.

Philosophy encourages thinking *among* the disciplines in order to forestall the provincialism that often accompanies professional specialization. The overspecialized mind is the bane of the academic life, and we need the persistently interdisciplinary reminder that philosophy represents to make us realize that what goes on at the seams and creases among the disciplines is at least as important as what goes on within them.

Finally, we need philosophy's insistence that when we speak of inquiry, we do not mean just scientific inquiry, and when we speak of methodology, we do not mean just scientific methodology. There are also artistic inquiry, humanistic inquiry, philosophical inquiry, professional inquiry – each has its own methodological dimension. Students need to become acquainted with this entire dimension or order of things and not with some one component of it.

The universities and the schools

In speaking of the need for more acute reflection on practice within and among the disciplines, I seem to be limiting my attention to higher education, just as, at earlier points, I was speaking only about elementary education. No doubt this oscillation from one perspective to another can be disturbing. The problem of education, however, is one that cannot be dealt with by focusing on either level. It is necessary to look at both, because the problem is precisely in the relationship between them and in their joint relationship to secondary education.

It is one of the peculiarities of discourse about education that elementary education is ritually deplored while higher education is ritually celebrated. Politicians point to our private colleges and universities and sigh, "If only our schools could be like them!" They stalwartly refuse to take the contextual differences into account and consider that if the colleges had to operate under the conditions customary in the schools, they would probably not operate any better than the schools now do.

Despite their archaic graduate programs, their bemused bureaucracies, and their instructors indifferent to matters of pedagogy, the universities are generally exempted from blame. Criticisms made by people outside the university are promptly rejected: "What do *they* know about what we do?" This is particularly true of criticisms emerging from the lower depths of the educational establishment; even their right to question is made to seem questionable. This is quite inexcusable.

We have got to confront the cyclical relationship that obtains between these educational levels. The teachers and administrators in the schools are the products of the university, and the products of the schools eventually make up the university's student body, instructional staff, and administrative corps. This means that the university's values form and shape the minds of those who run the schools, who form and shape the minds of the children, and these children, when grown up, flock (if fortunate) to the universities for one last reexposure to the university's values – for a final tune-up, as it were, before moving on to the responsibilities of citizenship. It is only when we admit that this cycle is a fact that we begin to fathom the irresponsibility of university spokespeople who gravely intimate that the sad shape of the freshman mind is something they had no hand in forming, although they will do the best they can to correct it.

The fact is that without the help of the university, the schools are virtually incapable of reforming themselves. And unless the schools are reformed, the university cannot look forward to a thoughtful student body and faculty. Each is dependent upon the other for constructive change instead of the bobbing up and down or the drifting here and there that have generally characterized their movements. Collaboration between colleges and schools is indispensable.

And yet not all partnerships are constructive. There can be sterile partnerships, as there can be partnerships in collusion. The partnership between the university and the school has to have projects, plans, and agendas to implement. This means there has to be an overall reappraisal of what is being done to discover what is not being done well. As usual, the things that may need to be looked at first are the discrepancies. And among these, the most glaring are the curricular discrepancies.

We know from Margaret Mead and other anthropologists that cultural gaps and inconsistencies are characteristic of cultures that build in the crises that plague them. Other cultures insist upon cultural continuities so that crises may be averted. In one culture, weaning is a crisis; in another, it is not. In one culture, adolescence is a crisis; in another, it is not. Everything depends on preparing members of the society for the stage of development that is to come.

In our own society, which is of course a very complex one, we have some areas of continuity and some of discontinuity. In education, for example, we may fail to prepare young people for a new and different subject – say, algebra – whereupon they virtually go into shock when they encounter it. Or we fail to prepare them to think for themselves, whereupon they fall flat on their faces when they get to a college that demands some thinking from them.

If we take seriously Bruner's dictum that anything that can be taught can be taught with integrity at any level, we can rule out the curricular discontinuities (such as the jump from arithmetic to algebra) that have been retained because it is traditional to have them around. The continuity from level to level could be a seamless one. (I am not denying that some subjects might be better taught – or better learned – at earlier rather than at later levels.) For every level, we have to ask ourselves, "What skills should students have acquired and what should they have learned prior to coming to the classroom this year in order to have the maximum chance of success?" After all, everything we learn presupposes a variety of things that we learned previously, whose presence makes this new learning relatively simple. A rational curriculum is one in which the skills and concepts needed for later learning are taught before they are needed. An irrational curriculum (of which science education might serve as an example) waits until the new concepts are to be learned to try to instill the skills and concepts that are preconditional to new learning.

Now, a flagrant example of a curricular discrepancy that flouts Bruner's dictum is the case of philosophy, which is an accepted component of university education but a rarity in the elementary school. One consequence, entirely predictable on the basis of what has just been said, is that students are not being prepared in the earlier grades to engage in philosophical studies at the university level. For those educators for whom philosophy is of negligible importance anyway, such a consequence is not exactly the greatest tragedy in the world. Even on the college campus, there is some ambivalence about philosophy. On the one hand, higher education without philosophy is admittedly almost unthinkable; on the other hand, philosophy appears to some on the campus to be parasitical upon the other disciplines and not to be a genuine discipline at all. Suspicion of philosophy is rooted in the fact that philosophy is generally perceived as an outside discipline that claims to have inside knowledge of the other disciplines. Furthermore, philosophers are perceived as outsiders who have a knack of making others feel like outsiders, for it is said to be problematic whether they are ignoramuses who pretend to know or savants who pretend not to. But if philosophy is something more than it is generally thought to be, if it is in fact the discipline that prepares us to think in the other disciplines, then its loss is indeed a matter of some seriousness.

What I am trying to understand in all this is the reason the universities have for complicity in the exclusion of philosophy from the elementary school curriculum. They deny, to be sure, that they exercise any influence whatsoever over the elementary schools' choice of subjects for students to study. But the fact is that the curriculum is established by the schools of education and that these schools take their cue, in turn, from the universities to which they belong. We cannot expect the schools of education to take an initiative on their own; they need to be prompted by the "higher values" of the universities.

Earlier, I suggested that not much change could be expected in education, because text publishers, test developers, state departments of education, local school boards, business interests, and school of education instructors are all locked together incestuously (much as there no longer appear to be sharp boundary lines between executives in the military, in industry, or in the government), so that no one group feels free to initiate change. But the university is a prestigious member of that group. It has the freedom and the power to propose college–school educational collaborations. And it has the initiative and the influence to enable it to persuade schools of education to move in the direction of a more rational curriculum, not merely by relabeling courses in homage to thinking but also by a profound reappraisal of what needs to be removed from a bloated curriculum in order to provide space for things that have previously and unjustifiably been excluded.

Much as we want to – or pretend we want to – we are not going to get higher-order thinking into elementary education until philosophy becomes a required grade-school course and other subjects are taught critically and reflectively. But this will not happen until the university itself reflects more deeply on its own values and its own practices. It must recognize its irresponsibility with regard to the students now moving up the educational ladder toward it and begin to bring pressure on those within its gates who claim to be powerless but in fact do have the power to make these changes. The university can also exert pressure on government officials who insist that they are powerless to act to bring about necessary changes but who do not seem to be powerless when it comes to blocking such changes as might be threatening to happen. Without such interventions, we have to be fairly pessimistic about the chances of the schools making meaningful progress toward higher-order thinking in the classroom.

Academic freedom

Finally, a word about academic freedom. One of the reasons we associate higher-order, complex thinking with the university and not with the elementary school is that academic freedom is an accepted prerogative in the one case and is more simulated than real in the other. The atmosphere of intellectual freedom in the university elicits intellectual creativity, just as the atmosphere of intellectual constraint in the elementary school elicits intellectual conformity. It is the difference in context that makes for the difference in the quality of thinking that takes place, not a difference in individual minds. Children are not less creative thinkers than are university students.

But, it will be said, academic freedom is possible only at the undergraduate and graduate levels; it is out of the question to permit it in the elementary schools. This, however, is a wall that has now been breached, and it has been breached by elementary school philosophy. Philosophy does not bring just itself into the elementary school classroom; it brings academic freedom along with it because it demonstrates that children can exercise such freedom responsibly.

Nevertheless, philosophy has shown only that academic freedom in the elementary school is *possible*. For it to become a fact, two further conditions are necessary: higher-order, complex thinking encouraged in all disciplines and advanced professionalization of teachers.

Fortunately, we are beginning to move toward all three of these goals. Fortunately too, it is now too late to turn back.

Select bibliography

Adams, Marilyn Jager. "Thinking Skills Curricula: Their Promise and Their Progress." *Educational Psychologist* 24:1 (1989), 25–77.

Aristotle. *The Basic Works of Aristotle,* edited by Richard McKeon. New York: Random House, 1941.

Austin, J. L. *How to Do Things with Words.* Cambridge, Mass.: Harvard University Press, 1962.

    Philosophical Papers. Oxford: Clarendon Press, 1961.

Barber, Benjamin. *Strong Democracy.* Berkeley and Los Angeles: University of California Press, 1984.

Baron, Joan Boykoff, and Robert J. Sternberg. *Teaching Thinking Skills: Theory and Practice.* New York: Freeman, 1987.

Baron, Jonathan. *Rationality and Intelligence.* Cambridge University Press, 1985.

Beardsley, Monroe. *Thinking Straight.* Englewood Cliffs, N.J.: Prentice-Hall, 1975.

Bloom, Benjamin S., Max D. Engelhart, Edward J. Furst, Walker H. Hill, and David R. Krathwohl (eds.). *Taxonomy of Educational Objectives,* vol. 1: *Cognitive Domain.* New York: McKay, 1956.

Brown, Harold I. *Rationality.* New York: Routledge, 1988.

Brown, John Seely, Allan Collins, and Paul Duguid. "Situated Cognition and the Culture of Learning." *Educational Researcher,* January–February 1989, pp. 32–42.

Bruner, J. S. *Processes of Cognitive Growth.* Worcester, Mass.: Clark University with Barre, 1968.

Bruner, J. S., and K. Connolly (eds.). *The Growth of Competence.* London: Academic Press, 1974.

Buchler, Justus. *Towards a General Theory of Human Judgment.* New York: Columbia University Press, 1951.

Buchler, Justus (ed.). *The Philosophy of Peirce: Selected Writings.* New York: Harcourt Brace, 1940.

Carey, Susan. "Semantic Development: The State of the Art." In Eric Wanner and Lila R. Gleitman (eds.), *Language Acquisition: The State of the Art.* Cambridge University Press, 1982, pp. 347–89.

Crawshay-Williams, Rupert. *Methods and Criteria of Reasoning.* London: Routledge and Kegan Paul, 1957.

Dewey, John. *The Child and the Curriculum.* Chicago: University of Chicago Press, 1902.

    Democracy and Education (1916). New York: Macmillan, 1944.

    Experience and Education (1938). New York: Collier, 1963.

    Logic: The Theory of Inquiry. New York: Holt, 1938.

Dickie, George. *Evaluating Art.* Philadelphia: Temple University Press, 1988.

Dreeben, Robert. "Closing the Divide." *American Educator* 11:4 (Winter 1987), 28–35.

Emmet, Dorothy. *Rules, Roles and Relations.* Boston: Beacon, 1975.

269

Faust, David. *The Limits of Scientific Reasoning.* Minneapolis: University of Minnesota Press, 1984.

Fischer, W. R. "Toward a Logic of Good Reasons." *Quarterly Journal of Speech,* 1978, p. 376.

Fisher, Alec (ed.). *Critical Thinking.* Norwich: University of East Anglia, 1988.

Freese, Hans-Ludwig. *Kinder sind Philosophen.* Berlin: Quadriga, 1989.

Gadamer, Hans-Georg. "Hermeneutics as Practical Philosophy," *Reason in the Age of Science.* Cambridge, Mass.: MIT Press, 1983, pp. 91–115.

   Philosophical Apprenticeships. Cambridge, Mass.: MIT Press, 1985.

Geach, P. T. "Comparatives." *Philosophia* 13:3–4 (October 1983), 235–46.

Geach, P. T., and M. Black (eds.). *Translations from the Philosophical Writings of Gottlob Frege.* Oxford: Blackwell Publisher, 1966.

Gewirth, Alan. "The Rationality of Reasonableness." *Synthèse* 57 (1983), 225–47.

Hamlyn, D. W. "Epistemology and Conceptual Development." In T. Mischel (ed.), *Cognitive Development and Epistemology.* London: Academic Press, 1971.

   Experience and the Growth of Understanding. London: Routledge and Kegan Paul, 1978.

Hirst, Paul H. (ed.). *Knowledge and the Curriculum.* London: Routledge and Kegan Paul, 1974.

Husserl, Edmund. *Experience and Judgment: Investigations in a Genealogy of Logic.* Evanston, Ill.: Northwestern University Press, 1973.

Inhelder, Barbel, and Jean Piaget. *The Early Growth of Logic in the Child.* New York: Norton, 1964.

Kapp, Ernst. *Greek Foundations of Traditional Logic.* New York: AMS Press, 1967.

Kuhn, Thomas S. *The Essential Tension.* Chicago: University of Chicago Press, 1977.

La Charité, Raymond C. *The Concept of Judgment in Montaigne.* The Hague: Martinus Nijhoff, 1968.

Lewis, C. I. *An Analysis of Knowledge and Valuation.* La Salle, Ill.: Open Court, 1971.

Link, Frances R. (ed.). *Essays on the Intellect.* Alexandria, Va.: ASCD, 1985.

Linn, M. C. "Theoretical and Practical Significance of Formal Reasoning." *Journal of Research in Science Teaching* 19 (1982), 727–42.

Lipman, Matthew. "Critical Thinking: What Can It Be?" *Educational Leadership,* April 1988, pp. 38–43.

   "Philosophy for Children." *Metaphilosophy* 7:1 (1976).

   Philosophy Goes to School. Philadelphia: Temple University Press, 1988.

Lipman, Matthew, and Ann Margaret Sharp. *Growing Up with Philosophy.* Philadelphia: Temple University Press, 1978.

Lipman, Matthew, Ann Margaret Sharp, and Frederick S. Oscanyan. *Philosophy in the Classsroom.* 2d ed. Philadelphia: Temple University Press, 1980.

Lloyd, G. E. R. *Polarity and Analogy: Two Types of Argumentation in Early Greek Thought.* Cambridge University Press, 1971.

Lyotard, Jean-François. *The Post-Modern Condition: A Report on Knowledge.* Minneapolis: University of Minnesota Press, 1984.

McPeck, John E. *Critical Thinking and Education.* New York: St. Martin's, 1981.

Margolis, Howard. *Patterns, Thinking and Cognition: A Theory of Judgment.* Chicago: University of Chicago Press, 1987.

Margolis, Joseph, Peter T. Manicas, Rom Harré, and Paul F. Secord. *Psychology: Designing the Discipline.* New York: Blackwell Publisher, 1987.

Mead, G. H. *Mind, Self and Society.* Chicago: University of Chicago Press, 1934.

Montaigne, Michel de. *Essays.* New York: Grolier, n.d.

Nickerson, Raymond S., David N. Perkins, and Edward E. Smith. *The Teaching of Thinking.* Hillsdale, N.J.: Erlbaum, 1985.

Nisbet, Richard E., et al. "Teaching Reasoning." *Science,* October 30, 1987, pp. 625–31.

Peel, E. A. *The Nature of Adolescent Judgment*. New York: Wiley Interscience, 1971.

Peirce, Charles Sanders. *Collected Papers*, edited by Charles Hartshorne and Paul Weiss. 8 vols. Cambridge, Mass.: Belknap Press of Harvard University Press, 1965–6.

"Some Consequences of Four Incapacities." In Justus Buchler (ed.), *Philosophical Writings of Peirce*. New York: Dover, 1955, pp. 228–50.

Perkins, David N. *The Mind's Best Work*. Cambridge, Mass.: Harvard University Press, 1981.

Perkins, David N., and Gavriel Salomon. "Are Cognitive Skills Context-Bound?" *Educational Researcher*, January–February 1989, pp. 16–25.

Peters, R. S. (ed.). *The Concept of Education*. London: Routledge and Kegan Paul, 1967.

Piaget, Jean. *Judgment and Reasoning in the Child*. London: Routledge, 1924.

Logic and Psychology. New York: Basic, 1957.

Pines, A. Leon. "Toward a Taxonomy of Conceptual Relations and the Implications for the Evaluation of Cognitive Structures." In Leo H. T. West and A. Leon Pines (eds.), *Cognitive Structure and Conceptual Change*. New York: Academic Press, 1985, pp. 101–29.

Prawat, Richard S. "Promoting Access to Knowledge, Strategy and Disposition in Students: A Research Synthesis." *Review of Educational Research* 59:1 (Spring 1989), 1–41.

Raup, R. Bruce, G. E. Axtelle, Kenneth D. Benne, and B. Othanel Smith. *The Improvement of Practical Intelligence*. New York: Harper and Row, 1950.

Raz, Joseph. *Practical Reasoning*. New York: Oxford University Press, 1978.

Resnick, Lauren B., and Leopold E. Klopfer. *Toward the Thinking Curriculum: Current Cognitive Research*. Alexandria, Va.: ASCD, 1989.

Rice, Eugene F., Jr. *The Renaissance Idea of Wisdom*. Westport, Conn.: Greenwood, 1958.

Russell, James. *The Acquisition of Knowledge*. New York: St. Martin's, 1978.

Ryle, Gilbert. *Collected Papers*. 2 vols. New York: Barnes and Noble, 1971.

Scheffler, Israel. *Conditions of Knowledge: An Introduction to Epistemology and Education*. Chicago: Scott, Foresman, 1965.

Smith, Barbara Herrnstein. *Contingencies of Value: Alternative Perspectives for Critical Theory*. Cambridge, Mass.: Harvard University Press, 1988.

Smith, Barry (ed.). *Practical Knowledge: Outlines of a Theory of Traditions and Skills*. London: Croom Helm, 1988.

Sokolowski, Robert. "Making Distinctions." *Journal of Metaphysics* 32:4 (June 1979), 639–76.

Sommers, Fred. "Predicability." In Max Black (ed.), *Philosophy in America*. Ithaca, N.Y.: Cornell University Press, 1965, pp. 262–81.

Vygotskii, Lev. *Thought and Language*, edited and translated by Eugenia Hanfman and Gertrude Vakar. Cambridge, Mass.: MIT Press, 1962.

Walsh, Debbie, and Richard Paul. *The Goal of Critical Thinking: From Educational Ideal to Educational Reality*. American Federation of Teachers, n.d.

Wittgenstein, Ludwig. *Philosophical Investigations*. Oxford: Blackwell Publisher, 1953.

Remarks on the Foundations of Mathematics, edited by C. H. von Wright, R. Rees, and G. E. Anscombe. Cambridge, Mass.: MIT Press, 1983.

Wright, Ian, and Carol La Bar. *Critical Thinking and Social Studies*. Canada: Grolier, 1987.

Index

absolutism, 55–7
abstract, the, 2, 109, 177
academic practice: normal vs. critical, 11–13,
  143–4
academic success, 27–8, 29
accountability, 118, 125
action, 145, 163
  from judgment, 249
  and reasons, 147–8
Adams, Marilyn J., 89–90
agenda in discussion of a text, 242
aggression, 257
algorithms, 22, 58, 61, 69–70, 106, 133, 149,
  161
  cognitive, 149
  and good thinking, 155
amoralism, 59
amplification, 199–200
analogical reasoning, 38, 64, 153, 199
applied-philosophy approach, 112
apprenticeship, 18–19, 76, 111, 215, 223
  model of education, 91–2
  traits of, 223–4
Aristotelian logic, 153
Aristotle, 9, 62, 75, 78, 80, 106, 111, 129,
  136, 156n, 199, 238, 248
Arons, Arnold B., 140–1
assimilation, 196–7
Auden, W. H., 154
Austen, Jane, 238
Austin, J. L., 42, 110
authority, 132, 147
autonomy, 19, 52–3, 72
Axelrod, Charles D., 200–1
Ayer, A. J., 112

Bacon, Francis, 146
Barber, Benjamin, 247
Baron, Jonathan, 103
Bartlett, Frederick C., 88
basic skills, 33, 110
Bateson, Gregory, 218
Bayles, Ernest, 107

Beardsley, Monroe C., 93–4, 104, 108, 207
belief, 3, 11, 144–5, 176, 237
believing, 143–4
Bell, David, 83
Bennett, William, 101
Bereiter, Carl, 103
Beyer, Barry, 112
Black, Max, 103–4, 108
Blair, J. Anthony, 110
Bloom, Benjamin S., 49, 51, 108
Blumenberg, Hans, 111
Bochenski, J. M., 235
Bono, Edward de, 58, 103
Brandt, Ron, 103, 112
Bransford, John, 103
bridging, 152–3
Brooks, Gwendolyn, 210
Brown, John S., 223–4
Bruner, Jerome, 30, 102, 103, 266
Buber, Martin, 18–19, 236
Buchler, Justus, 92–3, 231
Butts, Freeman, 112

Carey, Susan, 103
Casey, Edward S., 201–2
Castell, Suzanne de, 212–13
categorical imperative, 78
category mistake, 15, 73, 128, 200
  as metaphor, 128
Cavell, Stanley, 137–8
Cheyney, Lynne, 250–1
Chipman, Susan, 102
circumstances (see also context), 74, 85, 121,
  151
citizenship, 258
Clabby, John F., 149–50
classification, 63
coaching, 91, 224
cognitive psychology, 94–5n
Collingwood, Robin G., 201
Collins, Allan, 103, 111, 223–4
communication, 95, 235
community, 106, 215

community (*cont.*)
    and care, 254
    and inquiry, 229–30, 247n, 258
    and judgment, 138
community of inquiry, 3, 15–16, 92, 162, 186,
        204, 263
    advantages of, 121
    agenda of, 242
    and art, 138
    behaviors of, 52
    characteristics of, 15–16, 216–17, 229
    and children, 248
    and community, 258
    as democratic practice, 249
    and dialogue, 209–10, 236
    experience of, 209–10
    family and society, 246–7
    and feminism, 247
    fictional, 216
    and a jury, 239
    and lecturing, 210
    and modeling, 219
    models of, 216
    stages of, 241–3
    and stereotyping, 255
    and text, 241–2
"compare and contrast," 17
comparisons, 130, 133, 151
competency, 137
complexity, 70, 94
complex thinking, 23–4, 140–1
concept, 41–2
    binary, 155, 195, 208–9
    formation, 45, 224
    and information, 219–20, 221
concrete, the, 2, 109, 177
conformity, 143
connections, 130
consequences, 106, 146, 151
    sensitization to, 64
content, 92, 145, 181, 187–8
    and inquiry, 237
    and method, 92
    right, 250
context, 49–51, 121, 145, 186
    and relationships, 208
    sensitivity to, 64, 116, 121–2, 145, 150–1, 206
context-specific approach, 49–51
contingencies, 121
contrast, *see* "compare and contrast"
convention, 132, 151
conversation, 18, 217, 233
    appropriateness of, 233
    asymmetry of, 234
    and communication, 235
    conditions for, 234
    and dialogue, 232, 236
    essence of, 234

    at home, 31
    logic of, 232
    and metalogue, 218
cooperative learning, 91, 223
    and stereotyping, 256
Costa, Arthur, 112
Covington, Martin, 103
craft, 76–7, 187
    and art, 261
Crawshay-Williams, Rupert, 110
creative thinking
    as context-governed, 154
    and criteria, 207–8
    definition of, 193
    and experience, 211
    and judgment, 138
creativity, 66, 161
    axes of, 195–8
    criteria for, 205–6
    definition of, 198
    and imagination, 201–2
    and transformation, 202
    and translation, 210–11
credentials, 136
criteria, 3, 23, 64, 123, 130
    aesthetic, 93
    application to, 136–7
    definition of, 117, 126–7, 158
    definitions as, 127
    and disciplines, 119
    dominant, 87
    examples of, 132–6, 151–2
    and experience, 158
    formal, 119
    function of, 119
    informal, 119–20
    and judgment, 116, 124–5
    and a jury, 239
    kinds of, 117
    logic of, 131–2
    megacriteria, 71, 118–19
    and mental acts, 146
    metacriteria, 71, 118–19
    metaphysical, 93
    monological, 209
    multiple, 71
    phenomenological, 92–3
    and reliability, 129
    and strength, 129
    suppression of, 82
    and thinking, 207–8
    and values, 158
critic, 84
    characteristics of, 84
critical thinking, 56–8, 65, 103–4, 139
    and criteria, 124–5, 207–8
    definitions of, 115–16, 144, 150, 153–4,
        183, 193

and democracy, 244–5n
history of, 102–13
misconceptions about, 183–9
need for, 144
programs, 146
purpose of, 146
and schooling, 124
social interpretations of, 53–5
criticism, 3, 12, 168
of art, 93
of education, 101–2
and philosophy, 108
culture and crises, 265
curriculum, 222
rational, 266
reappraisal of, 252

Darwin, Charles, 105
Dearden, R. F., 108
decision-making approach, 111
definitions, 127, 134–5, 151, 183
as criteria, 127
deliberation, 62–3, 70, 249
democracy, 4, 64, 106–7
and citizenship, 258
and critical thinking, 244n
as inquiry, 252
liberal, 247
mass, 249
participatory, 252
in practice, 248
propositions of, 252n
and reflective education, 245
and scientific inquiry, 245–6n
strong, 247
democratic society, 245–6, 258
Derrida, Jacques, 111, 262
description, 41, 44
developmental psychologists, 2
developmental stages, 109
Dewey, John, 9, 17, 89, 104, 109, 148, 155,
194, 244n, 251, 262
on the classroom, 230, 258
on scientific inquiry, 15, 86, 105–8, 236–7
on thinking, 10–11, 208, 231
dialogue, 19, 41, 69, 154, 201, 236–7
asymmetry of, 235
and community of inquiry, 209–10
and conversation, 18, 209, 232, 236
as discourse, 236
essence of, 235
logical, 236
logic of, 232
and monologue, 236
philosophical, 235
and privilege, 218
didactic teaching, 180
and community of inquiry, 210

Diderot, Denis, 84–5
disciplines, 2
as cultures, 263
normative, 112
and self-criticism, 263
specificity, 179
and thinking, 2, 112
discourse, 139, 208
and education, 230
discoveries, 197–8
discursiveness, 154
distinctions, 130, 165
doing, 143–4, 148
Dreeben, Robert, 255–6
drill, 186–7

education, 29
American, 3
applicability of, 189
contemporary movements, 247
as discourse, 230
early childhood, 2
formal, 18
general, 18
goal of, 92, 189
as and for inquiry, 15, 245–6
and a jury, 240
liberal, 18
models of, 19
necessary conditions, 212
progressive, 107
reflective, 107, 174
and schooling, 145
educational fundamentalism, 101–2
educational practice, 13–14
educational reformers, 152
educational research, 12
Egan, Kieran, 208, 214
Elias, Maurice J., 149–50
empiricism, 84
ends and means, *see* means and ends
Ennis, Robert H., 49, 53, 107, 110, 112, 143–
5, 152
Euthyphro, 231
evaluation, 63
evidence, 123, 145, 168, 236
experience, 40, 63, 82, 88, 129, 155, 159
and creativity, 211
and discourse, 208n
mental, 93
prelinguistic, 30
shared, 240
and texts, 221
and theory-ladenness, 96
and thinking, 211
expert and novice performance, 223
explanation, 148
expression, freedom of, 250

facts, 135, 151, 168
  and narratives, 215
family, 7
feminism and community of inquiry, 247
Feuerstein, Reuven, 103
Fisher, Alec, 108
Flaubert, Gustave, 79
Fodor, Jerry, 42
Fogelin, Robert, 110
formal logic, 127
Frege, Gottlob, 104
Freud, Sigmund, 57, 201, 215
Frost, Robert, 137

Gadamer, Hans-Georg, 111, 214
Gardner, Howard, 177
Garver, Eugene, 59–60
generalizations, 199
generativity, 198–9, 201
Gestalt theory, 88–9
Glaser, Robert, 102
Glock, Charles, 257
Gombrich, Ernst, 87
Goodman, Nelson, 109
Gouldner, Alvin W., 139
Greene, Thomas, 112
Greeno, James, 103
Grice, Paul, 110, 232–3

Hamblin, C. L., 110
Hamilton, David L., 256
Hamlyn, D. W., 108
happiness, 2
Hare, Richard, 112
Harré, Rom, 42
Hart, H. L. A., 78–80
Havelock, Eric, 213
Head, *Sir* Henry, 88
Hegel, Georg W. F., 105
Hemingway, Ernest, 42
heuristics, 23, 161
  and good thinking, 155
higher-order thinking, 3, 19–23, 49, 65, 92
  characteristics of, 94
  and children, 218
  and community of inquiry, 68–9
  and creativity, 196
  critical and creative, 20–1
  definition of, 69–73
  as a dimension, 195
  and discursiveness, 154
  evaluation of, 96–7
  and intervention, 91
  and lower-order thinking, 34–5, 93–4
  and mental acts, 95–6
  and philosophy, 20
  and rationality, 196
  and teaching manuals, 225

teaching of, 20
  and texts, 216
Hirsch, E. D., 62, 101
Hirst, Paul H., 17–18, 108
history: approaches to, 251
Holmes, Oliver W., 82
Homer, 163
Hullfish, H. Gordon, 107
Hume, David, 83–4
hypothetical imperative, 78

ideals, 251
identity, 165
imagination, 195, 201
implication, 75
implicature, 233
individuality, 86–7
indoctrination, 143
inference, 75
  and truth, 38
informal logic, 75, 110–11, 127
information, 219–20, 221
  organizing of, 41
infusion, 172, 179–80, 187
inquiry, 40, 45, 86, 105, 154, 157, 162, 194,
    208, 229
  and academic practice, 144–5
  appropriateness of, 118
  and community, 229–30
  and content, 237
  direction of, 230
  ethical, 147–8
  and evidence, 236
  and judgment, 17
  and paradigms, 14
  into practice, 13
  processes of, 140–1
  scientific, *see* scientific inquiry
  as self-correcting, 121
  and thinking, 194
institutions: models of, 7
intellect, 2
intellectual virtues, 129
intelligence and the curriculum, 177
intervention, 177
  types of, 90–1
inventions, 197–8

James, Henry, 95
James, William, 74, 89, 232
Johnson, Mark, 194–5
Johnson, Ralph, 110
Johnson-Laird, Philip, 103
Jones, Beau Fly, 103
judgment, 16–17, 19, 62–3, 65, 71
  to action, 249
  aesthetic, 84–5, 138
  and community, 138

and context, 60
and creative thinking, 138
and criteria, 130–1
critical/creative, 80–1, 83, 85, 86–7, 160–1
definitions of, 115–16
and disciplines, 145
and educational responsibility, 159–60
examples of, 152
good, 115–16, 124, 145
inventive, 84
logic of, 130
normative, 83–4
of practice, 159
principled, 159
provisional, 237
and reasoning, 160
and relationships, 60–1, 74, 84–5
right, 250
role of, 171
and the self, 171
and sentences, 42
teaching procedures, 63–4
types of, 116, 164–70
typology of, 130–1
value-guided, 132
and values, 160
and way of life, 137
jury, 238–40, 246
and community of inquiry, 239
and criteria, 239
and education, 240
and self-correction, 238

Kagan, Jerome, 198, 201
Kahane, Howard, 110
Kant, Immanuel, 9, 78, 80, 81, 82–5, 87, 202,
    237n
Kierkegaard, Søren, 201
knowledge, 62, 114–15
declarative, 140–1
knowing how, 187, 261
knowing more, 186
knowing that, 187, 261
operative, 140–1
and power, 248–9
right, 250
and texts, 215
Kuhn, Thomas S., 157n, 200

language acquisition, 27–8, 30–1
and academic success, 28
rules of, 31
Lawrence, D. H., 79
lecturing, *see* didactic teaching
Leibniz, Gottfried W., 84, 96, 105
Lewis, David, 132
literacy, 65
literary skills, 36

literature and mental acts, 238
Lochhead, Jack, 103
Locke, John, 9, 163, 244–5n, 252n
logic, 188
necessity of, 178

Mach, Ernst, 238
McPeck, John, 3, 112
Mannheim, Karl, 55–8
manuals, 224–5
Marx, Karl, 56, 252–3
Mead, George H., 51, 105, 201, 230–1, 247n
Mead, Margaret, 265
meaning, 36–9, 62, 72–3, 77, 88, 95, 106,
    123, 151, 169, 186
acquisition of, 36
means and ends, 64, 81, 136, 155, 157, 244–5
in view, 244
measurement, 132
megacriteria (*see also* criteria): examples of,
    119, 193
Meichenbaum, Donald, 103
Meno, 261
mental acts, 95–6
and criteria, 146
and judgment, 96
and literature, 238
and states, 95–6
Merleau-Ponty, Maurice, 88
metacognition, 121
metacriteria (*see also* criteria), 128–30, 131,
    205
examples of, 119, 194
meta-, 129
metaphors, 128, 133
Metcalf, Lawrence, 107
method (*see also* content), 92
Michalos, Alex, 110
Mill, John S., 250
mind, 2
Missimer, Connie, 53
modeling, 180, 223
and community of inquiry, 219
types of, 219
models, 11
and teachers, 219
and texts, 216, 219
monologue and dialogue, 236
Montaigne, Michel de, 262
Moravcsik, Julius, 247
Moulton, Janice, 257
moves, 75–7
multiple solutions, 70–1

Naess, Arne, 111
narration, 41, 44
narratives, 43, 68, 162, 214–18, 241
and facts, 215

narratives (*cont.*)
  as textbooks, 11, 216
nature, 158, 238
Newman, Susan E., 223–4
Newmann, Fred M., 54–5
Nickerson, Ray, 49, 111
Nietzsche, Friedrich W., 42
norms, 106, 134, 143

Oakeshott, Michael, 18–19, 108
objectives
  behavioral, 109
  cognitive, 109
operations, 75–6
"ought to be," *see* norms
overspecialization, 188

paradigms, 200
  of educational practice, 13–14
parents, 2, 7
particular, the, 162–3
parts and wholes, 64, 89, 155
Passmore, John, 108
Paul, Richard, 51, 56–8, 112, 257
Peirce, Charles Sanders, 15, 92–3, 105, 121,
    138, 199, 230, 250, 257–8, 263
Perelman, Chaim, 111
performances, 136
  criterion-based, 148
Perkins, David, 103, 153
perspectives, 133, 151
persuasion, 235
Peters, R. S., 108
Phenix, Philip, 112
philosophy, 3, 30, 82, 107, 108, 110, 112, 125,
    150, 252, 262
  and academic freedom, 267–8
  applied, 112
  as criticism, 108
  departments of, 2
  in education, 262–3, 266
  and formative years, 253
  and persuasion, 235
  and politics, 253
  in schools, 24–5, 60, 142, 163, 172–3, 217,
    253–4
  and teachers, 179
  and thinking, 178–9
  as thinking about, 264
  as thinking among, 264
  as thinking in, 264
  and transformation of thought, 231
Philosophy for Children program, 38, 90, 112,
    123, 147, 217, 218, 222
philosophy of education, 212–13
  analytic, 108
Piaget, Jean, 17, 109–10, 177, 214, 253
Plato, 41, 105, 107, 120, 199, 221, 248–9, 261

play, 202
Plutarch, 262
Popper, Karl, 54
practice, 11, 117, 143, 146, 159, 168, 172
  cognitive, 130
  guided, 148–50
  normal, 134
  reflection on, 12–13
  and theory, 213
precedent, 132
prejudice, 44, 89, 254–5
  cognitive and affective, 259
  and community, 257–8
  forms of, 254
  reduction of, 63
  and self-esteem, 255
  and thinking, 257
principle(s), 133–4, 151, 159
  Cooperative, 233
  Pleasure, 215
  normative, 134
  Reality, 215
problem, 73
problem seeking, 175
problem solving, 175, 182
problem-solving approach, 111, 148–50
process, 73, 145
  democratic, 240
  and product, 73, 80, 89
proportionality, 199
psychological assumptions, 177
purposes, 136, 151

Quellmalz, Edys S., 49
questions: function of, 224–5

racial differences, 255–6
Raths, Louis, 107, 262
rationalism, 84
rationality, 66
  types of, 8
Raup, R. Bruce, 262
readers, 90
readiness, 30
reading comprehension, 37–8
  and reasoning, 47
reasonableness, 8, 16, 64–5, 66
  and schooling, 8–9
reasoning, 27, 45, 65
  and academic success, 27, 29
  analogical, 38
  deficiencies, 31–2
  and judgment, 160
  and literary skills, 36
  misconceptions about, 33–4
reasons
  and acts, 147–8
  appropriate, 128

and explanation, 148
good, 118
reform
  educational, 244
  political, 244
relationism, 55–6
relationships, 16–17
  cause–effect, 167
  in education, 251
  existential, 133
  and judgment, 60–2
  kinds of, 17, 61–2
relativism, 55–7
relevance, 127, 128–9, 140, 166, 231
reliability, 127, 128–9
requirements, 133, 151
Resnick, Lauren B., 49, 69, 103
responsibility, 118
  moral, 147
Rhees, Rush, 79
Richards, I. A., 111
Ricoeur, Paul, 111, 214
Rorty, Richard, 82
Rothbart, Myron, 256
Royce, Josiah, 103–5
rules, 84, 134, 151
Rumelhart, David E., 88
Ryle, Gilbert, 26, 108, 110, 203–4, 261

Salomon, Gavriel, 153
Santayana, George, 83, 160
Sarason, Seymour, 55
Sartre, Jean-Paul, 83
Saw, Ruth, 232, 234–6
Scheffler, Israel, 107, 108
schema(ta), 41–4, 87–8, 194–5, 202, 256
  dangers of, 221
  and Gestalt, 89
  and information, 219–20, 221
  and Philosophy for Children, 90
  theory, 87–9
  and thinking skills, 89
Schilder, Paul, 88, 194
Schofield, Janet W., 256
school, 7–8
  defense of, 101–2
  evaluation of, 96–7
  as a transition, 247
  and universities, 264–5
school administrators, 3
schooling, 1, 77, 79–80
  aspects of, 9
  and believing, 143–4
  and doing, 143–4
  and education, 145
  effects of, 9–10
  and reasonableness, 8–9
schools of education, 2, 7–8, 181, 182

Schrag, Francis, 73–4
Schwab, Joseph, 258
scientific inquiry, 15, 105–6, 107, 236–7, 245n
  and democracy, 245–6n
scientific knowledge, 18
Scriven, Michael, 110
Sebba, Gregor, 208n
Segal, Judith, 102
self-correction, 12, 64, 72, 116, 121, 124, 145, 150, 238
  examples of, 150
  and a jury, 238
self-criticism, 12, 181, 263
self-regulation, 72
sentences, 41–2
settlement, 237
Shakespeare, William, 146
Shaver, James, 112
Shure, Myrna, 150
Siegel, Harvey, 53, 128
Siegler, Robert, 103
Simmel, Georg, 200–1
skepticism, 145
skills, 76, 125, 137, 187–8
  and action, 80
  cognitive, 34–5, 40–6
  development of, 29–30
  generic, 112
  hierarchy of, 49–51
  information-organizing, 41–5
  inquiry, 40
  kinds of, 34–5
  limits of, 78–80
  literary, 36
  nesting of, 35
  reasoning, 40
  sequencing of, 50
  translation, 45–6
Slavin, Robert E., 256
Smith, B. Othanel, 107, 262
Smith, Frank, 81n
social communication, 51–2
Socrates, 9, 41, 59, 111, 202–3, 230–1, 235, 248, 261–2
Sophists, 111
Spearman, Charles, 92
speech, *see* discourse
Spinoza, Benedict de, 3, 163
Spivak, George, 150
spontaneity, 10, 82–3
standardization, 132
standards, 120, 125, 134, 136, 143, 151, 206
state, the, 7
Stebbing, Susan, 104
stereotyping, 254–6
  antidotes for, 256–7
  and cooperative learning, 256
Sternberg, Robert, 103

Stoics, 114
story, *see* narrative
strength, 127, 129–30
Suppes, Patrick, 85n
surprise, 161

Taba, Hilda, 112, 262
talking, 32
Taylor, Charles, 156n
teachers, 10, 230
  accountability, 249
  defense of, 101–2
  good, 203
  as models, 219
  and moral authority, 147–8
  and philosophy, 178
  preparation of, 172, 213
  and reasoning, 31–2
  retraining of, 182
  and teaching thinking, 39, 183–9
teaching (*see also* didactic teaching), 184, 204
  about, 185–6
  for, 185–6
  for learning, 188–9
  reciprocal, 91, 223
testing, 2, 46–7
test results, 135
tests, 12, 135, 151, 189
  criterion-referenced, 133
  reflective, 181
texts, 1, 8, 12, 213
  children's, 217
  and community of inquiry, 241–2
  dialogical, 217–18
  as experience, 221
  and higher-order thinking, 216
  ideal, 230
  and knowledge, 215
  as models, 216, 219
  and narratives, 216
  as problematic, 250
  problems of, 217
  secondary, 218, 220
  and thinking, 216
  voice of, 214
theory and practice, 213
thinker, 73
thinking (*see also* higher-order thinking), 92
  algorithmic, 58–60
  as an art, 74
  complex, 23–4, 140–1
  critical/creative, 51, 80, 86–7, 92, 138, 154
  dialogical, 56, 257
  excellent, 23–4, 49
  and experience, 211
  good, 2, 179
  grading of, 73–4

heuristic, 58–60
hierarchies, 176
ideological, 57–8
lateral, 58
logical, 58
as means–ends, 155
metaphorical, 200
monological, 56
multilogical, 56
for oneself, 185–6, 202–4, 250, 257, 261
reflective, 106
and science, 179
scientific, 85n
and texts, 216
thinking better, 176
thinking more, 184
types of, 195
uncritical, 117
vertical, 58
Thomas Aquinas, Saint, 132
Tinder, Glenn, 247n
Tönnies, Ferdinand, 252
Toulmin, Stephen, 110
transfer, 89–90, 153
transitions, 32–3, 156n, 194
  family to classroom, 32
  in language, 32
translation, 32–3, 38, 45, 151, 153
  and creation, 210
  and logic, 46
truth and meaning, 37–8

uncertainty, 71–2
unity, 94
universal, the, 162–3

Valéry, Paul, 238
validity, 133, 140
values, 23, 132, 151, 155, 157, 167, 185, 208
  and binary concepts, 208
  classification, 107
  and criteria, 156
  ideal, 261
  and judgment, 160
Veblen, Thorstein, 12, 254
Vygotsky, Lev, 17, 102, 110, 177, 242

Walzer, Michael, 240
Weber, Max, 83
Whitehead, Alfred N., 214
wholes and parts, 64, 89, 155
wisdom, 114–15
Wittgenstein, Ludwig, 79–80, 104, 110, 137, 138, 225
writing, 81n

Yoos, George, 87, 231